THE THEORY OF MONEY
AND CREDIT

LUDWIG VON MISES

THE THEORY OF MONEY AND CREDIT

by LUDWIG VON MISES

Translated from the German by H. E. Batson

Liberty Fund

Indianapolis
1981

This book is published by Liberty Fund, Inc., a foundation established to encourage study of the ideal of a society of free and responsible individuals.

The cuneiform inscription that serves as the design motif for our endpapers is the earliest-known written appearance of the word "freedom" (*amagi*), or "liberty." It is taken from a clay document written about 2300 B.C. in the Sumerian city-state of Lagash.

This edition of *The Theory of Money and Credit* follows the text, with stylistic changes and footnote corrections, of the translation from the German by H. E. Batson, published in 1934 by Jonathan Cape Ltd., of London, and in 1953 by Yale University Press. The foreword by Murray N. Rothbard was written for this edition, published in 1981 by Liberty Fund, Inc.

Library of Congress Cataloging in Publication Data

Von Mises, Ludwig, 1881–1973.
  The theory of money and credit.

  Translation of Theorie des Geldes und der Umlaufsmittel.
  Includes bibliographical references.
  1. Money. I. Title.
HG221.V652 1980 332.4'01 79-25752
ISBN 0-913966-70-3 (hardcover edition)
ISBN 0-913966-71-1 (softcover edition)

92	91	90	89	88	C	6	5	4	3	2
01	00	99	98	97	P	9	8	7	6	5

CONTENTS

Foreword, by Murray N. Rothbard (1981) 13
Preface to the New Edition (1952) 17
Introduction, by Lionel Robbins (1934) 19
Preface to the English Edition (1934) 23
Preface to the Second German Edition (1924) 33

PART ONE
THE NATURE OF MONEY

Chapter 1 The Function of Money

1 The General Economic Conditions for the Use of Money 41
2 The Origin of Money 42
3 The "Secondary" Functions of Money 46

Chapter 2 On the Measurement of Value

1 The Immeasurability of Subjective Use-Values 51
2 Total Value 58
3 Money as a Price Index 61

Chapter 3 The Various Kinds of Money

1 Money and Money Substitutes 63
2 The Peculiarities of Money Substitutes 67
3 Commodity Money, Credit Money, and Fiat Money 73
4 The Commodity Money of the Past and of the Present 76

Chapter 4 Money and the State

1 The Position of the State in the Market 83
2 The Legal Concept of Money 84
3 The Influence of the State on the Monetary System 87

Chapter 5 Money as an Economic Good
  1 Money Neither a Production Good nor a Consumption Good .. 95
  2 Money as Part of Private Capital 103
  3 Money Not a Part of Social Capital 107

Chapter 6 The Enemies of Money
  1 Money in the Socialist Community 109
  2 Money Cranks 111

PART TWO
THE VALUE OF MONEY

Chapter 7 The Concept of the Value of Money
  1 Subjective and Objective Factors in the Theory of the
    Value of Money 117
  2 The Objective Exchange Value of Money 120
  3 The Problems Involved in the Theory of the Value of Money ... 122

Chapter 8 The Determinants of the Objective Exchange Value, or
Purchasing Power, of Money
  (I) *The Element of Continuity in the Objective Exchange Value of Money*
  1 The Dependence of the Subjective Valuation of Money on the
    Existence of Objective Exchange Value 129
  2 The Necessity for a Value Independent of the Monetary
    Function Before an Object Can Serve as Money 131
  3 The Significance of Preexisting Prices in the Determination of
    Market Exchange Ratios 133
  4 The Applicability of the Marginal-Utility Theory to Money 136
  5 "Monetary" and "Nonmonetary" Influences Affecting the
    Objective Exchange Value of Money 145

  (II) *Fluctuations in the Objective Exchange Value of Money Evoked by
    Changes in the Ratio Between the Supply of Money and the Demand
    for It*
  6 The Quantity Theory 146
  7 The Stock of Money and the Demand for Money 153
  8 The Consequences of an Increase in the Quantity of Money
    While the Demand for Money Remains Unchanged or Does
    Not Increase to the Same Extent 160
  9 Criticism of Some Arguments Against the Quantity Theory 168
  10 Further Applications of the Quantity Theory 174

  (III) *A Special Cause of Variations in the Objective Exchange Value of
    Money Arising from the Peculiarities of Indirect Exchange*
  11 "Dearness of Living" 177
  12 Wagner's Theory: The Influence of the Permanent
    Predominance of the Supply Side over the Demand Side on
    the Determination of Prices 178

13 Wieser's Theory: The Influence on the Value of Money Exerted
by a Change in the Relations Between Natural Economy and
Money Economy 180
14 The Mechanism of the Market as a Force Affecting the
Objective Exchange Value of Money 185

(IV) *Excursuses*
15 The Influence of the Size of the Monetary Unit and Its
Subdivisions on the Objective Exchange Value of Money 189
16 A Methodological Comment 191

Chapter 9 The Problem of the Existence of Local Differences in the
Objective Exchange Value of Money
1 Interlocal Price Relations 195
2 Alleged Local Differences in the Purchasing Power of Money .. 197
3 Alleged Local Differences in the Cost of Living 200

Chapter 10 The Exchange Ratio Between Money of Different Kinds
1 The Twofold Possibility of the Coexistence of Different Kinds of
Money 205
2 The Static or Natural Exchange Ratio Between Different Kinds
of Money 207

Chapter 11 The Problem of Measuring the Objective Exchange Value of
Money and Variations in It
1 The History of the Problem 215
2 The Nature of the Problem 216
3 Methods of Calculating Index Numbers 217
4 Wieser's Refinement of the Methods of Calculating Index
Numbers 219
5 The Practical Utility of Index Numbers 222

Chapter 12 The Social Consequences of Variations in the Objective
Exchange Value of Money
1 The Exchange of Present Goods for Future Goods 225
2 Economic Calculation and Accountancy 234
3 Social Consequences of Variations in the Value of Money When
Only One Kind of Money Is Employed 237
4 The Consequences of Variations in the Exchange Ratio
Between Two Kinds of Money 243

Chapter 13 Monetary Policy
1 Monetary Policy Defined 247
2 The Instruments of Monetary Policy 250
3 Inflationism 251
4 Restrictionism or Deflationism .... : 262
5 Invariability of the Objective Exchange Value of Money as the
Aim of Monetary Policy 268
6 The Limits of Monetary Policy 270
7 Excursus: The Concepts Inflation and Deflation 271

Chapter 14 The Monetary Policy of Etatism
  1 The Monetary Theory of Etatism 275
  2 National Prestige and the Rate of Exchange 277
  3 The Regulation of Prices by Authoritative Decree 279
  4 The Balance-of-Payments Theory as a Basis of Currency Policy 282
  5 The Suppression of Speculation 286

PART THREE
MONEY AND BANKING

Chapter 15 The Business of Banking
  1 Types of Banking Activity 293
  2 The Banks as Negotiators of Credit 294
  3 The Banks as Issuers of Fiduciary Media 296
  4 Deposits as the Origin of Circulation Credit 300
  5 The Granting of Circulation Credit 304
  6 Fiduciary Media and the Nature of Indirect Exchange 308

Chapter 16 The Evolution of Fiduciary Media
  1 The Two Ways of Issuing Fiduciary Media 311
  2 Fiduciary Media and the Clearing System 314
  3 Fiduciary Media in Domestic Trade 320
  4 Fiduciary Media in International Trade 325

Chapter 17 Fiduciary Media and the Demand for Money
  1 The Influence of Fiduciary Media on the Demand for Money in
     the Narrower Sense 331
  2 The Fluctuations in the Demand for Money 334
  3 The Elasticity of the System of Reciprocal Cancellation 336
  4 The Elasticity of a Credit Circulation Based on Bills, Especially
     on Commodity Bills 339
  5 The Significance of the Exclusive Employment of Bills as Cover
     for Fiduciary Media 347
  6 The Periodical Rise and Fall in the Extent to Which Bank Credit
     Is Requisitioned 348
  7 The Influence of Fiduciary Media on Fluctuations in the
     Objective Exchange Value of Money 352

Chapter 18 The Redemption of Fiduciary Media
  1 The Necessity for Complete Equivalence Between Money and
     Money Substitutes 355
  2 The Return of Fiduciary Media to the Issuer on Account of
     Lack of Confidence on the Part of the Holders 357
  3 The Case Against the Issue of Fiduciary Media 359
  4 The Redemption Fund 361
  5 The So-called Banking Type of Cover for Fiduciary Media 368
  6 The Significance of Short-Term Cover 371
  7 The Security of the Investments of the Credit-issuing Banks ... 372

8 Foreign Bills of Exchange as a Component of the Redemption
Fund 374

Chapter 19 Money, Credit, and Interest
1 On the Nature of the Problem 377
2 The Connection Between Variations in the Ratio Between the
Stock of Money and the Demand for Money and Fluctuations
in the Rate of Interest 384
3 The Connection Between the Equilibrium Rate and the Money
Rate of Interest 388
4 The Influence of the Interest Policy of the Credit-issuing Banks
on Production 396
5 Credit and Economic Crises 403

Chapter 20 Problems of Credit Policy
(I) *Prefatory Remark*
1 The Conflict of Credit Policies 405

(II) *Problems of Credit Policy Before the War*
2 Peel's Act 406
3 The Nature of Discount Policy 412
4 The Gold-Premium Policy 416
5 Systems Similar to the Gold-Premium Policy 421
6 The Nonsatisfaction of the So-called Illegitimate Demand for
Money 423
7 Other Measures for Strengthening the Stock of Metal Held by
the Central Banks-of-Issue 425
8 The Promotion of Check and Clearing Transactions as a Means
of Reducing the Rate of Discount 426

(III) *Problems of Credit Policy in the Period Immediately After the War*
9 The Gold-Exchange Standard 429
10 A Return to a Gold Currency 432
11 The Problem of the Freedom of the Banks 434
12 Fisher's Proposal for a Commodity Standard 438
13 The Basic Questions of Future Currency Policy 445

PART FOUR
MONETARY RECONSTRUCTION

(This part was written in 1952 and first appeared in the
1953 American edition by Yale University Press)

Chapter 21 The Principle of Sound Money
1 The Classical Idea of Sound Money 453
2 The Virtues and Alleged Shortcomings of the Gold Standard . . . 456
3 The Full-Employment Doctrine 463
4 The Emergency Argument in Favor of Inflation 466

Chapter 22 Contemporary Currency Systems
　1 The Inflexible Gold Standard 471
　2 The Flexible Standard 472
　3 The Freely Vacillating Currency 473
　4 The Illusive Standard 474

Chapter 23 The Return to Sound Money
　1 Monetary Policy and the Present Trend Toward All-round
　　Planning... 477
　2 The Integral Gold Standard............................... 480
　3 Currency Reform in Ruritania 485
　4 The United States' Return to a Sound Currency 490
　5 The Controversy Concerning the Choice of the New Gold
　　Parity 495
　6 Concluding Remarks 499

Appendix A　On the Classification of Monetary Theories
(*This Appendix was first published as a journal article in 1917–1918, it
was later used as a chapter in the 2nd German edition of 1924, but was
then relegated to the Appendix in the Batson translation of 1934*)
　1 Catallactic and Acatallactic Monetary Doctrine 503
　2 The "State" Theory of Money 506
　3 Schumpeter's Attempt to Formulate a Catallactic
　　Claim Theory 512
　4 "Metallism" 515
　5 The Concept of "Metallism" in Wieser and Philippovich 518
　6 Note: The Relation of the Controversy About Nominalism to
　　the Problems of the Two English Schools of Banking Theory ... 524

Appendix B　Translator's Note on the Translation of Certain
　Technical Terms 525

Index 527

Biographical Note 539

Note on Silver Demereteia 541

FOREWORD
By Murray N. Rothbard

L udwig von Mises' *The Theory of Money and Credit* is, quite simply, one of the outstanding contributions to economic thought in the twentieth century. It came as the culmination and fulfillment of the "Austrian School" of economics, and yet, in so doing, founded a new school of thought of its own.

The Austrian School came as a burst of light in the world of economics in the 1870s and 1880s, serving to overthrow the classical, or Ricardian, system which had arrived at a dead end. This overthrow has often been termed the "marginal revolution," but this is a highly inadequate label for the new mode of economic thinking. The essence of the new Austrian paradigm was analyzing *the individual* and his actions and choices as the fundamental building block of the economy. Classical economics thought in terms of broad classes, and hence could not provide satisfactory explanations for value, price, or earnings in the market economy. The Austrians began with the actions of the individual. Economic value, for example, consisted of the *valuations* made by choosing individuals, and prices resulted from market interactions based on these valuations.

The Austrian School was launched by Carl Menger, professor of economics at the University of Vienna, with the publication of his

Principles of Economics (Grundsätze der Volkswirtschaftslehre) in 1871.[1]
It was further developed and systematized by Menger's student
and successor at Vienna, Eugen von Böhm-Bawerk, in writings from
the 1880s on, especially in various editions of his multivolume *Capital and interest.*[2] Between them, and building on their fundamental
analysis of individual valuation, action, and choice, Menger and
Böhm-Bawerk explained all the aspects of what is today called
"micro-economics": utility, price, exchange, production, wages, interest, and capital.

Ludwig von Mises was a "third-generation" Austrian, a brilliant
student in Böhm-Bawerk's famous graduate seminar at the University of Vienna in the first decade of the twentieth century. Mises'
great achievement in *The Theory of Money and Credit* (published in
1912) was to take the Austrian method and apply it to the one glaring
and vital *lacuna* in Austrian theory: the broad "macro" area of money
and general prices.

For monetary theory was still languishing in the Ricardian mold.
Whereas general "micro" theory was founded in analysis of individual action, and constructed market phenomena from these
building blocks of individual choice, monetary theory was still "holistic," dealing in aggregates far removed from real choice. Hence,
the total separation of the micro and macro spheres. While all other
economic phenomena were explained as emerging from individual
action, the supply of money was taken as a given external to the
market, and supply was thought to impinge mechanistically on an
abstraction called "the price level." Gone was the analysis of individual choice that illuminated the "micro" area. The two spheres
were analyzed totally separately, and on very different foundations.
This book performed the mighty feat of integrating monetary with
micro theory, of building monetary theory upon the individualistic
foundations of general economic analysis.

Eugen von Böhm-Bawerk died soon after the publication of *The
Theory of Money and Credit*, and the orthodox Böhm-Bawerkians,

---

[1] The English translation of Menger's *Grundsätze* only first appeared in 1950. See Carl
Menger, *Principles of Economics* (New York: New York University Press, 1981).

[2] The first complete English translation of the third/fourth German edition, by
George D. Hunke and Hans F. Sennholz, was published by Libertarian Press,
South Holland, Ill., in 1959; it includes: Volume I, *History and Critique of Interest
Theories*; Volume II, *Positive Theory of Capital*; and Volume III, *Further Essays on
Capital and Interest.*

locked in their old paradigm, refused to accept Mises' new break-
through in the theory of money and business cycles. Mises therefore
had to set about the arduous task of founding his own neo-Austrian,
or Misesian, school of thought. He was handicapped by the fact
that his post at the University of Vienna was not salaried; yet, all
during the 1920s, many brilliant students flocked to his *Privat-
seminar*.

In the English-speaking world, acceptance of Misesian ideas was
gravely hampered by the simple but significant fact that few economists read any language other than English. Mises' *The Theory of
Money and Credit* was not translated into English until 1934, and the
result was two decades of neglect of the Misesian insights. Cash
balance analysis was developed in the late 1920s in England by Sir
Dennis H. Robertson, but his approach was holistic and aggrega-
tive, and not built out of individual action. The purchasing power
parity theory came to England and the United States only through
the flawed and diluted form propounded by the Swedish economist
Gustav Cassel. And neglect of the Čuhel-Mises theory of ordinal
marginal utility allowed Western economists, led by Hicks and Allen
in the mid-1930s, to throw out marginal utility altogether in favor
of the fallacious "indifference curve" approach, now familiar in
micro textbooks.

Mises' integration of micro and macro theory, his developed theory of money and the regression theorem, as well as his sophisti-
cated analysis of inflation, were all totally neglected by later
economists. The idea of integrating macro theory on micro foundations is further away from current economic practice than ever
before.

Only Mises' business cycle theory penetrated the English-speaking world, and this feat was accomplished by personal rather than
literary means. Mises' outstanding follower, Friedrich A. von
Hayek, immigrated to London in 1931 to assume a teaching post at
the London School of Economics. Hayek, who had concentrated on
developing Mises' insights into a systematic business cycle theory,
managed quickly to convert the best of the younger generation of
English economists, and one of the brightest of the group, Lionel
Robbins, was responsible for the English translation of *The Theory
of Money and Credit*. For a few glorious years in the early 1930s, such
youthful luminaries of English economics as Robbins, Nicholas Kal-

dor, John R. Hicks, Abba P. Lerner, and Frederic Benham fell under the strong influence of Hayek. In the meanwhile, Austrian followers of Mises' business cycle theory—notably Fritz Machlup and Gottfried von Haberler—began to be translated or published in the United States. Also in the United States, young Alvin H. Hansen was becoming the leading proponent of the Mises-Hayek cycle theory.

Mises' business cycle theory was being adopted precisely as a cogent explanation of the Great Depression, a depression which Mises anticipated in the late 1920s. But just as it was being spread through England and the United States, the Keynesian revolution swept the economic world, converting even those who knew better. The conversion process won, not by patiently rebutting Misesian or other views, but simply by ignoring them, and leading the economic world into old and unsound inflationist views dressed up in superficially impressive new jargon. By the end of the 1930s only Hayek, and none of the other students of himself or Mises, had remained true to the Misesian view of business cycles. Mises' *The Theory of Money and Credit*, in its English version, barely had time to be read before the Keynesian revolution of 1936 rendered pre-Keynesian thought, particularly on business cycles, psychologically inaccessible to the next generation of economists.

Mises added part four to the 1953 English-language edition of *The Theory of Money and Credit*. But Keynesian economics was riding high, and the world of economics was scarcely ready to resume attention to the Misesian insights. Now, however, and particularly since his death in 1973, Misesian economics has experienced a remarkable resurgence, especially in the United States. There are conferences, symposia, books, articles, and dissertations abounding in Austrian and Misesian economics. With the Keynesian system in total disarray, reeling from chronic and accelerating inflation punctuated by periods of inflationary recession, economists are more receptive to Misesian cycle theory than they have been in four decades. Let us hope that this new edition will stimulate economists to reexamine the other sparkling insights in this grievously neglected masterpiece, and that Mises' integration of money and banking with micro theory will serve as the basis for future advances in monetary thought.

PREFACE TO THE NEW EDITION

Forty years have passed since the first German-language edition of this volume was published. In the course of these four decades the world has gone through many disasters and catastrophes. The policies that brought about these unfortunate events have also affected the nations' currency systems. Sound money gave way to progressively depreciating fiat money. All countries are today vexed by inflation and threatened by the gloomy prospect of a complete breakdown of their currencies.

There is need to realize the fact that the present state of the world and especially the present state of monetary affairs are the necessary consequences of the application of the doctrines that have got hold of the minds of our contemporaries. The great inflations of our age are not acts of God. They are man-made or, to say it bluntly, government-made. They are the offshoots of doctrines that ascribe to governments the magic power of creating wealth out of nothing and of making people happy by raising the "national income."

One of the main tasks of economics is to explode the basic inflationary fallacy that confused the thinking of authors and statesmen from the days of John Law down to those of Lord Keynes. There cannot be any question of monetary reconstruction and economic recovery as long as such fables as that of the blessing of "expansionism" form an integral part of official doctrine and guide the economic policies of the nations.

None of the arguments that economics advances against the inflationist and expansionist doctrine is likely to impress demagogues. For the demagogue does not bother about the remoter consequences of his policies. He chooses inflation and credit expansion although he knows that the boom they create is short-lived and must inevitably end in a slump. He may even boast of his neglect of the long-run effects. In the long run, he repeats, we are all dead; it is only the short run that counts.

But the question is, how long will the short run last? It seems that statesmen and politicians have considerably overrated the duration of the short run. The correct diagnosis of the present state of affairs is this: We have outlived the short run and have now to face the long-run consequences that political parties have refused to take into account. Events turned out precisely as sound economics, decried as orthodox by the neo-inflationist school, had prognosticated.

In this situation an optimist may hope that the nations will be prepared to learn what they blithely disregarded only a short time ago. It is this optimistic expectation that prompted the publishers to republish this book and the author to add to it as an epilogue an essay on monetary reconstruction (part four).

LUDWIG VON MISES

New York
June 1952

INTRODUCTION

O f all branches of economic science, that part which relates to
money and credit has probably the longest history and the
most extensive literature. The elementary truths of the Quantity
Theory were established at a time when speculation on other types
of economic problems had hardly yet begun. By the middle of the
nineteenth century when, in the general theory of value, a satisfactory statical system had not yet been established, the pamphlet
literature of money and banking was tackling, often with marked
success, many of the subtler problems of economic dynamics. At
the present day, with all our differences, there is no part of economic
theory which we feel to be more efficient to lend practical aid to the
statesman and to the man of affairs, than the theory of money and
credit.

Yet for all this there is no part of the subject where the established
results of analysis and experience have been so little systematized
and brought into relation with the main categories of theoretical
economics. Special monographs exist by the hundred. The pamphlet literature is so extensive as to surpass the power of any one
man completely to assimilate it. Yet in English, at any rate,
there has been so little attempt at synthesis of this kind that,
when Keynes came to write his *Treatise on Money*, he was compelled to lament the absence, not only of an established tradition of

arrangement, but even of a single example of a systematic treatment of the subject on a scale and of a quality comparable with that of the standard discussions of the central problems of pure equilibrium theory.

In these circumstances it is hoped that the present publication will meet a very real need among English-speaking students. For the work of which it is a translation, the *Theorie des Geldes und der Umlaufsmittel* of Professor von Mises of Vienna, does meet just this deficiency. It deals systematically with the chief propositions of the theory of money and credit, and it brings them into relation both with the main body of analytical economics and with the chief problems of contemporary policy to which they are relevant. Commencing with a rigid analysis of the nature and function of money, it leads by a highly ingenious series of approximations, from a discussion of the value of money under simple conditions in which there is only one kind of money and no banking system, through an analysis of the phenomena of parallel currency and foreign exchanges, to an extensive treatment of the problems of modern banking and the effects of credit creation on the capital structure and the stability of business. In continental circles it has long been regarded as the standard textbook on the subject. It is hoped that it will fill a similar role in English-speaking countries. I know few works which convey a more profound impression of the logical unity and the power of modern economic analysis.

It would be a great mistake, however, to suppose that systematization of the subject constituted the only, or indeed the chief, merit of this work. So many of the propositions which it first introduced have now found their way into the common currency of modern monetary theory that the English reader, coming to it for the first time more than twenty years after its first publication, may be inclined to overlook its merits as an original contribution to knowledge—a contribution from which much of what is most important and vital in contemporary discussions takes its rise. Who in 1912 had heard of forced saving, of disparities between the equilibrium and the money rates of interest and of the cycle of fluctuations in the relations between the prices of producers' goods and consumers' goods which is the result of the instability of credit? They are all here, not as *obiter dicta* on what are essentially side issues, as is occasionally the case in the earlier literature, but as central parts of a fully articulated theoretical system—a system which the author has had the somewhat melancholy satisfaction of seeing abundantly verified by the march of subsequent events, first in the great inflations of the immediately postwar period and later in the events which gave rise to the depression from which the world is now suffering. Nor should we overlook its contributions to the more abstract parts of the theory of the value of money. Professor von Mises shares with Marshall and one or two others the merit of having assimilated the treatment of this theory to the general categories of the pure theory of value: and his emphasis in the course of this assimilation on the relation between uncertainty and the size of the cash holding and the dependence of certain monetary phenomena on the absence of foresight, anticipates much that has proved most fruitful in more recent speculation in these matters. In spite of a tendency observable in some quarters to revert to more mechanical forms of the quantity theory, in particular to proceed by way of a multiplication of purely tautological formulae, it seems fairly clear that further progress in the explanation of the more elusive monetary phenomena is likely to take place along this path.

The present translation is based upon the text of the second German edition, published in 1924. Certain passages of no great interest to English readers have been omitted and a chapter dealing with more or less purely German controversies has been placed in an appendix. The comments on policy, however, in part three, chapter twenty, have been left as they appeared in 1924.[1] But the author, who has most generously lent asistance at every stage of the translation, has written a special introduction in which he outlines his views on the problems which have emerged since that date. A note in the appendix gives the German equivalents to the technical terms

---

[1] Except for one minor change of tense. In the second edition, the author prefaced the first major division of the last chapter of part three with a note to the effect that this section was to be read as referring to the time about 1912, when it was originally written. In the present edition, in order to prevent certain misunderstandings that seemed possible even if this note had been reprinted in its proper place on p. 406, certain practices and circumstances (especially in sections 4 to 8) have been described in the *past* tense. (Cf. pp. 406 n. z, 416 n., and also 429 n.)

which have been employed to designate the different kinds of money, and discusses in detail the translation of one term for which no exact English equivalent existed.

LIONEL ROBBINS

London School of Economics
September 1934

PREFACE TO THE ENGLISH EDITION

The outward guise assumed by the questions with which banking and currency policy is concerned changes from month to
month and from year to year. Amid this flux, the theoretical apparatus which enables us to deal with these questions remains unaltered. In fact, the value of economics lies in its enabling us to
recognize the true significance of problems, divested of their accidental trimmings. No very deep knowledge of economics is usually
needed for grasping the immediate effects of a measure; but the
task of economics is to foretell the remoter effects, and so to allow
us to avoid such acts as attempt to remedy a present ill by sowing
the seeds of a much greater ill for the future.

Ten years have elapsed since the second German edition of the
present book was published. During this period the external appearance of the currency and banking problems of the world has
completely altered. But closer examination reveals that the same
fundamental issues are being contested now as then. Then, England
was on the way to raising the gold value of the pound once more
to its prewar level. It was overlooked that prices and wages had
adapted themselves to the lower value and that the reestablishment
of the pound at the prewar parity was bound to lead to a fall in
prices which would make the position of the entrepreneur more
difficult and so increase the disproportion between actual wages

and the wages that would have been paid in a free market. Of course, there were some reasons for attempting to reestablish the old parity, even despite the indubitable drawbacks of such a proceeding. The decision should have been made after due consideration of the pros and cons of such a policy. The fact that the step was taken without the public having been sufficiently informed beforehand of its inevitable drawbacks, extraordinarily strengthened the opposition to the gold standard. And yet the evils that were complained of were not due to the resumption of the gold standard, as such, but solely to the gold value of the pound having been stabilized at a higher level than corresponded to the level of prices and wages in the United Kingdom.

From 1926 to 1929 the attention of the world was chiefly focused upon the question of American prosperity. As in all previous booms brought about by expansion of credit, it was then believed that the prosperity would last forever, and the warnings of the economists were disregarded. The turn of the tide in 1929 and the subsequent severe economic crisis were not a surprise for economists; they had foreseen them, even if they had not been able to predict the exact date of their occurrence.

The remarkable thing in the present situation is not the fact that we have just passed through a period of credit expansion that has been followed by a period of depression, but the way in which governments have been and are reacting to these circumstances. The universal endeavor has been made, in the midst of the general fall of prices, to ward off the fall in money wages, and to employ public resources on the one hand to bolster up undertakings that would otherwise have succumbed to the crisis, and on the other hand to give an artificial stimulus to economic life by public works schemes. This has had the consequence of eliminating just those forces which in previous times of depression have eventually effected the adjustment of prices and wages to the existing circumstances and so paved the way for recovery. The unwelcome truth has been ignored that stabilization of wages must mean increasing unemployment and the perpetuation of the disproportion between prices and costs and between outputs and sales which is the symptom of a crisis.

This attitude was dictated by purely political considerations. Governments did not want to cause unrest among the masses of their wage-earning subjects. They did not dare to oppose the doctrine that regards high wages as the most important economic ideal and believes that trade-union policy and government intervention can maintain the level of wages during a period of falling prices. And governments have therefore done everything to lessen or remove entirely the pressure exerted by circumstances upon the level of wages. In order to prevent the underbidding of trade-union wages, they have given unemployment benefits to the growing masses of those out of work and they have prevented the central banks from raising the rate of interest and restricting credit and so giving free play to the purging process of the crisis.

When governments do not feel strong enough to procure by taxation or borrowing the resources to meet what they regard as irreducible expenditure, or, alternatively, so to restrict their expenditure that they are able to make do with the revenue that they have, recourse on their part to the issue of inconvertible notes and a consequent fall in the value of money are something that has occurred more than once in European and American history. But the motive for recent experiments in depreciation has been by no means fiscal. The gold content of the monetary unit has been reduced in order to maintain the domestic wage level and price level, and in order to secure advantages for home industry against its competitors in international trade. Demands for such action are no new thing either in Europe or in America. But in all previous cases, with a few significant exceptions, those who have made these demands have not had the power to secure their fulfillment. In this case, however, Great Britain began by abandoning the old gold content of the pound. Instead of preserving its gold value by employing the customary and never-failing remedy of raising the bank rate, the government and parliament of the United Kingdom, with bank rate at four and one-half percent, preferred to stop the redemption of notes at the old legal parity and so to cause a considerable fall in the value of sterling. The object was to prevent a further fall of prices in England and above all, apparently, to avoid a situation in which reductions of wages would be necessary.

The example of Great Britain was followed by other countries, notably by the United States. President Roosevelt reduced the gold content of the dollar because he wished to prevent a fall in wages and to restore the price level of the prosperous period between 1926 and 1929.

In central Europe, the first country to follow Great Britain's example was the Republic of Czechoslovakia. In the years immediately after the war, Czechoslovakia, for reasons of prestige, had heedlessly followed a policy which aimed at raising the value of the krone, and she did not come to a halt until she was forced to recognize that increasing the value of her currency meant hindering the exportation of her products, facilitating the importation of foreign products, and seriously imperiling the solvency of all those enterprises that had procured a more or less considerable portion of their working capital by way of bank credit. During the first few weeks of the present year, however, the gold parity of the krone was reduced in order to lighten the burden of the debtor enterprises, and in order to prevent a fall of wages and prices and so to encourage exportation and restrict importation. Today, in every country in the world, no question is so eagerly debated as that of whether the purchasing power of the monetary unit shall be maintained or reduced.

It is true that the universal assertion is that all that is wanted is the reduction of purchasing power to its previous level, or even the prevention of a rise above its present level. But if this is all that is wanted, it is very difficult to see why the 1926–29 level should always be aimed at, and not, say, that of 1913.

If it should be thought that index numbers offer us an instrument for providing currency policy with a solid foundation and making it independent of the changing economic programs of governments and political parties, perhaps I may be permitted to refer to what I have said in the present work on the impossibility of singling out any particular method of calculating index numbers as the sole scientifically correct one and calling all the others scientifically wrong. There are many ways of calculating purchasing power by means of index numbers, and every single one of them is right, from certain tenable points of view; but every single one of them is also wrong, from just as many equally tenable points of view. Since each method of calculation will yield results that are different from those of every other method, and since each result, if it is made the basis of practical measures, will further certain interests and injure others, it is obvious that each group of persons will declare for those methods that will best serve its own interests. At the very moment when the manipulation of purchasing power is declared to be a legitimate concern of currency policy, the question of the level at which this purchasing power is to be fixed will attain the highest political significance. Under the gold standard, the determination of the value of money is dependent upon the profitability of gold production. To some, this may appear a disadvantage; and it is certain that it introduces an incalculable factor into economic activity. Nevertheless, it does not lay the prices of commodities open to violent and sudden changes from the monetary side. The biggest variations in the value of money that we have experienced during the last century have originated not in the circumstances of gold production, but in the policies of governments and banks-of-issue. Dependence of the value of money on the production of gold does at least mean its independence of the politics of the hour. The dissociation of the currencies from a definitive and unchangeable gold parity has made the value of money a plaything of politics. Today we see considerations of the value of money driving all other considerations into the background in both domestic and international economic policy. We are not very far now from a state of affairs in which "economic policy" is primarily understood to mean the question of influencing the purchasing power of money. Are we to maintain the present gold content of the currency unit, or are we to go over to a lower gold content? That is the question that forms the principal issue nowadays in the economic policies of all European and American countries. Perhaps we are already in the midst of a race to reduce the gold content of the currency unit with the object of obtaining transitory advantages (which, moreover, are based on self-deception) in the commercial war which the nations of the civilized world have been waging for decades with increasing acrimony, and with disastrous effects upon the welfare of their subjects.

It is an unsatisfactory designation of this state of affairs to call it an emancipation from gold. None of the countries that have "abandoned the gold standard" during the last few years has been able to affect the significance of gold as a medium of exchange either at home or in the world at large. What has occurred has not been a departure from gold, but a departure from the old legal gold parity of the currency unit and, above all, a reduction of the burden of the debtor at the cost of the creditor, even though the principal aim of the measures may have been to secure the greatest possible stability of nominal wages, and sometimes of prices also.

Besides the countries that have debased the gold value of their currencies for the reasons described, there is another group of countries that refuse to acknowledge the depreciation of their money in terms of gold that has followed upon an excessive expansion of the domestic note circulation, and maintain the fiction that their currency units still possess their legal gold value, or at least a gold value in excess of its real level. In order to support this fiction they have issued foreign-exchange regulations which usually require exporters to sell foreign exchange at its legal gold value, that is, at a considerable loss. The fact that the amount of foreign money that is sold to the central banks in such circumstances is greatly diminished can hardly require further elucidation. In this way a "shortage of foreign exchange" (*Devisennot*) arises in these countries. Foreign exchange is in fact unobtainable at the prescribed price, and the central bank is debarred from recourse to the illicit market in which foreign exchange is dealt in at its proper price because it refuses to pay this price. This "shortage" is then made the excuse for talk about transfer difficulties and for prohibitions of interest and amortization payments to foreign countries. And this has practically brought international credit to a standstill. Interest and amortization are paid on old debts either very unsatisfactorily or not at all, and, as might be expected, new international credit transactions hardly continue to be a subject of serious consideration. We are no longer far removed from a situation in which it will be impossible to lend money abroad because the principle has gradually become accepted that any government is justified in forbidding debt payments to foreign countries at any time on grounds of "foreign-exchange policy." The real meaning of this foreign-exchange policy is exhaustively discussed in the present book. Here let it merely be pointed out that this policy has much more seriously injured international economic relations during the last three years than protectionism did during the whole of the preceding fifty or sixty years, the measures that were taken during the world war included. This throttling of international credit can hardly be remedied otherwise than by setting aside the principle that it lies within the discretion of every government, by invoking the shortage of foreign exchange that has been caused by its own actions, to stop paying interest to foreign countries and also to prohibit interest and amortization payments on the part of its subjects. The only way in which this can be achieved will be by removing international credit transactions from the influence of national legislatures and creating a special international code for it, guaranteed and really enforced by the League of Nations. Unless these conditions are created, the granting of new international credit will hardly be possible. Since all nations have an equal interest in the restoration of international credit, it may probably be expected that attempts will be made in this direction during the next few years, provided that Europe does not sink any lower through war and revolution. But the monetary system that will constitute the foundation of such future agreements must necessarily be one that is based upon gold. Gold is not an ideal basis for a monetary system. Like all human creations, the gold standard is not free from shortcomings; but in the existing circumstances there is no other way of emancipating the monetary system from the changing influences of party politics and government interference, either in the present or, so far as can be foreseen, in the future. And no monetary system that is not free from these influences will be able to form the basis of credit transactions. Those who blame the gold standard should not forget that it was the gold standard that enabled the civilization of the nineteenth century to spread beyond the old capitalistic countries of Western Europe, and made the wealth of these countries available for the development of the rest of the world. The savings of the few advanced capitalistic countries of a small part of Europe have called into being the modern productive equipment of the whole world. If the debtor countries refuse to pay their existing debts, they certainly ameliorate their immediate situation. But it is very questionable whether they do not at the same time greatly damage their future prospects. It consequently seems misleading in discussions of the currency question to talk of an opposition between the interests of creditor and debtor nations, of those which are well supplied with capital and those which are ill supplied. It is the interests of the *poorer* countries, who are dependent upon the importation of foreign capital for developing their productive resources, that make the throttling of international credit seem so extremely dangerous.

The dislocation of the monetary and credit system that is nowadays going on everywhere is *not* due—the fact cannot be repeated too often—to any inadequacy of the gold standard. The thing for which the monetary system of our time is chiefly blamed, the fall in prices during the last five years, is not the fault of the gold standard, but the inevitable and ineluctable consequence of the expansion of credit, which was bound to lead eventually to a collapse. And the thing which is chiefly advocated as a remedy is nothing but another expansion of credit, such as certainly might lead to a transitory boom, but would be bound to end in a correspondingly severer crisis.

The difficulties of the monetary and credit system are only a part of the great economic difficulties under which the world is at present suffering. It is not only the monetary and credit system that is out of gear, but the whole economic system. For years past, the economic policy of all countries has been in conflict with the principles on which the nineteenth century built up the welfare of the nations. International division of labor is now regarded as an evil, and there is a demand for a return to the autarky of remote antiquity. Every importation of foreign goods is heralded as a misfortune, to be averted at all costs. With prodigious ardour, mighty political parties proclaim the gospel that peace on earth is undesirable and that war alone means progress. They do not content themselves with describing war as a reasonable form of international intercourse, but recommend the employment of force of arms for the suppression of opponents even in the solution of questions of domestic politics. Whereas liberal economic policy took pains to avoid putting obstacles in the way of developments that allotted every branch of production to the locality in which it secured the greatest productivity to labor, nowadays the endeavor to establish enterprises in places where the conditions of production are unfavorable is regarded as a patriotic action that deserves government support. To demand of the monetary and credit system that it should do away with the consequences of such perverse economic policy, is to demand something that is a little unfair.

All proposals that aim to do away with the consequences of perverse economic and financial policy, merely by reforming the monetary and banking system, are fundamentally misconceived. Money is nothing but a medium of exchange and it completely fulfills its function when the exchange of goods and services is carried on more easily with its help than would be possible by means of barter. Attempts to carry out economic reforms from the monetary side can never amount to anything but an artificial stimulation of economic activity by an expansion of the circulation, and this, as must constantly be emphasized, must necessarily lead to crisis and depression. Recurring economic crises are nothing but the consequence of attempts, despite all the teachings of experience and all the warnings of the economists, to stimulate economic activity by means of additional credit.

This point of view is sometimes called the "orthodox" because it is related to the doctrines of the Classical economists who are Great Britain's imperishable glory; and it is contrasted with the "modern" point of view which is expressed in doctrines that correspond to the ideas of the Mercantilists of the sixteenth and seventeenth centuries. I cannot believe that there is really anything to be ashamed of in orthodoxy. The important thing is not whether a doctrine is orthodox or the latest fashion, but whether it is true or false. And although the conclusion to which my investigations lead, that expansion of credit cannot form a substitute for capital, may well be a conclusion that some may find uncomfortable, yet I do not believe that any logical disproof of it can be brought forward.

LUDWIG VON MISES

Vienna
June 1934

PREFACE TO THE
SECOND GERMAN EDITION

When the first edition of this book was published twelve years ago, the nations and their governments were just preparing for the tragic enterprise of the Great War. They were preparing, not merely by piling up arms and munitions in their arsenals, but much more by the proclamation and zealous propagation of the ideology of war. The most important economic element in this war ideology was inflationism.

My book also dealt with the problem of inflationism and attempted to demonstrate the inadequacy of its doctrines; and it referred to the changes that threatened our monetary system in the immediate future. This drew upon it passionate attacks from those who were preparing the way for the monetary catastrophe to come. Some of those who attacked it soon attained great political influence; they were able to put their doctrines into practice and to experiment with inflationism upon their own countries.

Nothing is more perverse than the common assertion that economics broke down when faced with the problems of the war and postwar periods. To make such an assertion is to be ignorant of the literature of economic theory and to mistake for economics the doctrines based on excerpts from archives that are to be found in the writings of the adherents of the historico-empirico-realistic school. Nobody is more conscious of the shortcomings of economics than economists themselves, and nobody regrets its gaps and failings more. But all the theoretical guidance that the politician of the last ten years needed could have been learned from existing doctrine. Those who have derided and carelessly rejected as "bloodless abstraction" the assured and accepted results of scientific labor should blame themselves, not economics.

It is equally hard to understand how the assertion could have been made that the experience of recent years has necessitated a revision of economics. The tremendous and sudden changes in the value of money that we have experienced have been nothing new to anybody acquainted with currency history; neither the variations in the value of money, nor their social consequences, nor the way in which the politicians reacted to either, were new to economists. It is true that these experiences were new to many etatists, and this is perhaps the best proof that the profound knowledge of history professed by these gentlemen was not genuine but only a cloak for their mercantilistic propaganda.

The fact that the present work, although unaltered in essentials, is now published in a rather different form from that of the first edition is not due to any such reason as the impossibility of explaining new facts by old doctrines. It is true that, during the twelve years that have passed since the first edition was published, economics has made strides that it would be impossible to ignore. And my own occupation with the problems of catallactics has led me in many respects to conclusions that differ from those of the first edition. My attitude toward the theory of interest is different today from what it was in 1911; and although, in preparing this as in preparing the first edition, I have been obliged to postpone any treatment of the problem of interest (which lies outside the theory of indirect exchange), in certain parts of the book it has nevertheless been necessary to refer to the problem. Again, on the question of crises my opinions have altered in one respect: I have come to the conclusion that the theory which I put forward as an elaboration and continuation of the doctrines of the Currency School is in itself a sufficient explanation of crises and not merely a supplement to an explanation in terms of the theory of direct exchange, as I supposed in the first edition.

Further I have become convinced that the distinction between statics and dynamics cannot be dispensed with even in expounding the theory of money. In writing the first edition, I imagined that I should have to do without it, in order not to give rise to any mis-understandings on the part of the German reader. For in an article that had appeared shortly before in a widely read symposium, Alt-mann had used the concepts "static" and "dynamic," applying them to monetary theory in a sense that diverged from the terminology of the modern American school.[1] Meanwhile, however, the significance of the distinction between statics and dynamics in modern theory has probably become familiar to everybody who, even if not very closely, has followed the development of economics. It is safe to employ the terms nowadays without fear of their being confused with Altmann's terminology. I have in part revised the chapter on the social consequences of variations in the value of money in order to clarify the argument. In the first edition the chapter on monetary policy contains long historical discussions; the experiences of recent years afford sufficient illustrations of the fundamental argument to allow these discussions now to be dispensed with.

A section on problems of banking policy of today has been added, and one in which the monetary theory and policy of the etatists are briefly examined. In compliance with a desire of several colleagues I have also included a revised and expanded version of a short essay on the classification of theories of money, which was published some years ago in volume 44 of the *Archiv für Sozialwissenschaft und Sozialpolitik.*

For the rest, it has been far from my intention to deal critically with the flood of new publications devoted to the problems of money and credit. In science, as Spinoza says, "the truth bears witness both to its own nature and to that of error." My book contains critical arguments only where they are necessary to establish my own views and to explain or prepare the ground for them. This omission can be the more easily justified in that this task of criticism is skillfully performed in two admirable works that have recently appeared.[2]

---

[1] See Altmann, "Zur deutschen Geldlehre des 19. Jahrhunderts," in *Die Entwicklung der deutschen Volkswirtschaftslehre im 19. Jahrhundert, Schmoller Festschrift* (Leipzig, 1908).

[2] See Döring, *Die Geldtheorien seit Knapp*, 1st ed. (Greifswald, 1921; 2d ed. Greifswald,

The concluding chapter of part three, which deals with problems of credit policy, is reprinted as it stood in the first edition. Its arguments refer to the position of banking in 1911, but the significance of its theoretical conclusions does not appear to have altered. They are supplemented by the above-mentioned discussion of the problems of present-day banking policy that concludes the present edition. But even in this additional discussion, proposals with any claim to absolute validity should not be sought for. Its intention is merely to show the nature of the problem at issue. The choice among all the possible solutions in any individual case depends upon the evaluation of pros and cons; decision between them is the function not of economics but of politics.

LUDWIG VON MISES

Vienna
March 1924

1922); Palyi, *Der Streit um die Staatliche Theorie des Geldes* (Munich and Leipzig, 1922) (also in *Schmoller's Jahrbuch,* 45. Jahrgang). Also see the acute investigations of G. M. Verrijn Stuart, *Inleiding tot de Leer der Waardevastheid van het Geld* ('s Gravenhage, 1919).

THE THEORY OF MONEY
AND CREDIT

PART ONE

THE NATURE OF MONEY

CHAPTER 1

The Function of Money

1

The General Economic Conditions for the Use of Money

Where the free exchange of goods and services is unknown, money is not wanted. In a state of society in which the division of labor was a purely domestic matter and production and consumption were consummated within the single household it would be just as useless as it would be for an isolated man. But even in an economic order based on division of labor, money would still be unnecessary if the means of production were socialized, the control of production and the distribution of the finished product were in the hands of a central body, and individuals were not allowed to exchange the consumption goods allotted to them for the consumption goods allotted to others.

The phenomenon of money presupposes an economic order in which production is based on division of labor and in which private property consists not only in goods of the first order (consumption goods), but also in goods of higher orders (production goods). In such a society, there is no systematic centralized control of production, for this is inconceivable without centralized disposal over the means of production. Production is "anarchistic." What is to be produced, and how it is to be produced, is decided in the first place by the owners of the means of production, who produce, however, not only for their own needs, but also for the needs of others, and in their valuations take into account, not only the use-value that they themselves attach to their products, but also the use-value that these possess in the estimation of the other members of the community. The balancing of production and consumption takes place in the market, where the different producers meet to exchange goods and services by bargaining together. The function of money is to facilitate the business of the market by acting as a common medium of exchange.

2

The Origin of Money

Indirect exchange is distinguished from direct exchange according as a medium is involved or not.

Suppose that A and B exchange with each other a number of units of the commodities m and n. A acquires the commodity n because of the use-value that it has for him. He intends to consume it. The same is true of B, who acquires the commodity m for his immediate use. This is a case of direct exchange.

If there are more than two individuals and more than two kinds of commodity in the market, indirect exchange also is possible. A may then acquire a commodity p, not because he desires to consume it, but in order to exchange it for a second commodity q which he does desire to consume. Let us suppose that A brings to the market two units of the commodity m, B two units of the commodity n, and C two units of the commodity o, and that A wishes to acquire one unit of each of the commodities n and o, B one unit of each of the commodities o and m, and C one unit of each of the commodities m and n. Even in this case a direct exchange is possible if the subjective valuations of the three commodities permit the exchange of each unit of m, n, and o for a unit of one of the others. But if this or a similar hypothesis does not hold good, and in by far the greater number of all exchange transactions it does not hold good, then indirect exchange becomes necessary, and the demand for goods for immediate wants is supplemented by a demand for goods to be exchanged for others.[1]

Let us take, for example, the simple case in which the commodity p is desired only by the holders of the commodity q, while the commodity q is not desired by the holders of the commodity p but by those, say, of a third commodity r, which in its turn is desired only by the possessors of p. No direct exchange between these persons can possibly take place. If exchanges occur at all, they must be indirect; as, for instance, if the possessors of the commodity p exchange it for the commodity q and then exchange this for the commodity r which is the one they desire for their own consumption. The case is not essentially different when supply and demand do not coincide quantitatively; for example, when one indivisible good has to be exchanged for various goods in the possession of several persons.

Indirect exchange becomes more necessary as division of labor increases and wants become more refined. In the present stage of economic development, the occasions when direct exchange is both possible and actually effected have already become very exceptional. Nevertheless, even nowadays, they sometimes arise. Take, for instance, the payment of wages in kind, which is a case of direct exchange so long on the one hand as the employer uses the labor for the immediate satisfaction of his own needs and does not have to procure through exchange the goods in which the wages are paid, and so long on the other hand as the employee consumes the goods he receives and does not sell them. Such payment of wages in kind is still widely prevalent in agriculture, although even in this sphere its importance is being continually diminished by the extension of capitalistic methods of management and the development of division of labor.[2]

---

[1] See Wicksell, *Über Wert, Kapital und Rente* (Jena, 1893; London, 1933), pp. 50 f.

[2] The conclusion that indirect exchange is necessary in the majority of cases is extremely obvious. As we should expect, it is among the earliest discoveries of economics. We find it clearly expressed in the famous fragment of the Pandects of Paulus: "Quia non semper nec facile concurrebat, ut, cum tu haberas, quod ego desiderarem, invicem haberem, quod tu accipere velles" (Paulus, lib. 33 ad edictum 1.1 pr. D. de contr. empt. 18, 1).

Schumpeter is surely mistaken in thinking that the necessity for money can be proved solely from the assumption of indirect exchange (see his *Wesen und Hauptinhalt der theoretischen Nationalökonomie* [Leipzig, 1908], pp. 273 ff.). On this point, cf. Weiss,

Thus along with the demand in a market for goods for direct consumption there is a demand for goods that the purchaser does not wish to consume but to dispose of by further exchange. It is clear that not all goods are subject to this sort of demand. An individual obviously has no motive for an indirect exchange if he does not expect that it will bring him nearer to his ultimate objective, the acquisition of goods for his own use. The mere fact that there would be no exchanging unless it was indirect could not induce individuals to engage in indirect exchange if they secured no immediate personal advantage from it. Direct exchange being impossible, and indirect exchange being purposeless from the individual point of view, no exchange would take place at all. Individuals have recourse to indirect exchange only when they profit by it; that is, only when the goods they acquire are more marketable than those which they surrender.

Now all goods are not equally marketable. While there is only a limited and occasional demand for certain goods, that for others is more general and constant. Consequently, those who bring goods of the first kind to market in order to exchange them for goods that they need themselves have as a rule a smaller prospect of success than those who offer goods of the second kind. If, however, they exchange their relatively unmarketable goods for such as are more marketable, they will get a step nearer to their goal and may hope to reach it more surely and economically than if they had restricted themselves to direct exchange.

It was in this way that those goods that were originally the most marketable became common media of exchange; that is, goods into which all sellers of other goods first converted their wares and which it paid every would-be buyer of any other commodity to acquire first. And as soon as those commodities that were relatively most marketable had become common media of exchange, there was an increase in the difference between their marketability and that of all other commodities, and this in its turn further strengthened and broadened their position as media of exchange.[3]

Die moderne Tendenz in der Lehre vom Geldwert, Zeitschrift für Volkswirtschaft, Sozialpolitik und Verwaltung, vol. 19, pp. 518 ff.
[3] See Menger, *Untersuchungen über die Methode der Sozialwissenschaften und der politischen Okonomie insbesondere* (Leipzig, 1883), pp. 172 ff.; *Grundsätze der Volkswirtschaftslehre,* 2d ed. (Vienna, 1923), pp. 247 ff.

Thus the requirements of the market have gradually led to the selection of certain commodities as common media of exchange. The group of commodities from which these were drawn was originally large, and differed from country to country; but it has more and more contracted. Whenever a direct exchange seemed out of the question, each of the parties to a transaction would naturally endeavor to exchange his superfluous commodities, not merely for more marketable commodities in general, but for the *most* marketable commodities; and among these again he would naturally prefer whichever particular commodity was the most marketable of all. The greater the marketability of the goods first acquired in indirect exchange, the greater would be the prospect of being able to reach the ultimate objective without further maneuvering. Thus there would be an inevitable tendency for the less marketable of the series of goods used as media of exchange to be one by one rejected until at last only a single commodity remained, which was universally employed as a medium of exchange; in a word, money.

This stage of development in the use of media of exchange, the exclusive employment of a single economic good, is not yet completely attained. In quite early times, sooner in some places than in others, the extension of indirect exchange led to the employment of the two precious metals gold and silver as common media of exchange. But then there was a long interruption in the steady contraction of the group of goods employed for that purpose. For hundreds, even thousands, of years the choice of mankind has wavered undecided between gold and silver. The chief cause of this remarkable phenomenon is to be found in the natural qualities of the two metals. Being physically and chemically very similar, they are almost equally serviceable for the satisfaction of human wants. For the manufacture of ornaments and jewelry of all kinds the one has proved as good as the other. (It is only in recent times that technological discoveries have been made which have considerably extended the range of uses of the precious metals and may have differentiated their utility more sharply.) In isolated communities, the employment of one or the other metal as sole common medium of exchange has occasionally been achieved, but this short-lived unity has always been lost again as soon as the isolation of the community has succumbed to participation in international trade.

Economic history is the story of the gradual extension of the economic community beyond its original limits of the single household to embrace the nation and then the world. But every increase in its size has led to a fresh duality of the medium of exchange whenever the two amalgamating communities have not had the same sort of money. It would not be possible for the final verdict to be pronounced until all the chief parts of the inhabited earth formed a single commercial area, for not until then would it be impossible for other nations with different monetary systems to join in and modify the international organization.

Of course, if two or more economic goods had exactly the same marketability, so that none of them was superior to the others as a medium of exchange, this would limit the development toward a unified monetary system. We shall not attempt to decide whether this assumption holds good of the two precious metals gold and silver. The question, about which a bitter controversy has raged for decades, has no very important bearings upon the theory of the nature of money. For it is quite certain that even if a motive had not been provided by the unequal marketability of the goods used as media of exchange, unification would still have seemed a desirable aim for monetary policy. The simultaneous use of several kinds of money involves so many disadvantages and so complicates the technique of exchange that the endeavor to unify the monetary system would certainly have been made in any case.

The theory of money must take into consideration all that is implied in the functioning of several kinds of money side by side. Only where its conclusions are unlikely to be affected one way or the other, may it proceed from the assumption that a single good is employed as common medium of exchange. Elsewhere, it must take account of the simultaneous use of several media of exchange. To neglect this would be to shirk one of its most difficult tasks.

3

The "Secondary" Functions of Money

The simple statement, that money is a commodity whose economic function is to facilitate the interchange of goods and services, does not satisfy those writers who are interested rather in the accumulation of material than in the increase of knowledge. Many investigators imagine that insufficient attention is devoted to the remarkable part played by money in economic life if it is merely credited with the function of being a medium of exchange; they do not think that due regard has been paid to the significance of money until they have enumerated half a dozen further "functions"—as if, in an economic order founded on the exchange of goods, there could be a more important function than that of the common medium of exchange.

After Menger's review of the question, further discussion of the connection between the secondary functions of money and its basic function should be unnecessary.[4] Nevertheless, certain tendencies in recent literature on money make it appear advisable to examine briefly these secondary functions—some of them are coordinated with the basic function by many writers—and to show once more that all of them can be deduced from the function of money as a common medium of exchange.

This applies in the first place to the function fulfilled by money *in facilitating credit transactions*. It is simplest to regard this as part of its function as medium of exchange. Credit transactions are in fact nothing but the exchange of present goods against future goods. Frequent reference is made in English and American writings to a function of money as a standard of deferred payments.[5] But the original purpose of this expression was not to contrast a particular function of money with its ordinary economic function, but merely to simplify discussions about the influence of changes in the value of money upon the real amount of money debts. It serves this purpose admirably. But it should be pointed out that its use has led many writers to deal with the problems connected with the general economic consequences of changes in the value of money merely from the point of view of modifications in existing debt relations and to overlook their significance in all other connections.

The functions of money *as a transmitter of value through time and space* may also be directly traced back to its function as medium of

---

[4] See Menger, *Grundsätze*, pp. 278 ff.
[5] See Nicholson, *A Treatise on Money and Essays on Present Monetary Problems* (Edinburgh, 1888), pp. 21 ff.; Laughlin, *The Principles of Money* (London, 1903), pp. 22 f.

exchange. Menger has pointed out that the special suitability of goods for hoarding, and their consequent widespread employment for this purpose, has been one of the most important causes of their increased marketability and therefore of their qualification as media of exchange.[6] As soon as the practice of employing a certain economic good as a medium of exchange becomes general, people begin to store up this good in preference to others. In fact, hoarding as a form of investment plays no great part in our present stage of economic development, its place having been taken by the purchase of interest-bearing property.[7] On the other hand, money still functions today as a means for transporting value through space.[8] This function again is nothing but a matter of facilitating the exchange of goods. The European farmer who emigrates to America and wishes to exchange his property in Europe for a property in America, sells the former, goes to America with the money (or a bill payable in money), and there purchases his new homestead. Here we have an absolute textbook example of an exchange facilitated by money.

Particular attention has been devoted, especially in recent times, to the function of money *as a general medium of payment*. Indirect exchange divides a single transaction into two separate parts which are connected merely by the ultimate intention of the exchangers to acquire consumption goods. Sale and purchase thus apparently become independent of each other. Furthermore, if the two parties to a sale-and-purchase transaction perform their respective parts of the bargain at different times, that of the seller preceding that of the buyer (purchase on credit), then the settlement of the bargain, or the fulfillment of the seller's part of it (which need not be the same thing), has no obvious connection with the fulfillment of the buyer's part. The same is true of all other credit transactions, especially of the most important sort of credit transaction—lending. The apparent lack of a connection between the two parts of the single transaction has been taken as a reason for regarding them as independent

[6] Cf. Menger, *Grundsätze*, pp. 284 ff.
[7] That is, apart from the exceptional propensity to hoard gold, silver, and foreign bills, encouraged by inflation and the laws enacted to further it.
[8] Knies in particular (*Geld und Kredit*, 2d ed. [Berlin, 1885], vol. 1, pp. 233 ff.) has laid stress upon the function of money as interlocal transmitter of value.

proceedings, for speaking of the payment as an independent legal
act, and consequently for attributing to money the function of being
a common medium of *payment*. This is obviously incorrect. "If the
function of money as an object which facilitates dealings in commodities and capital is kept in mind, a function that includes the
payment of money prices and repayment of loans . . . there remains
neither necessity nor justification for further discussion of a special
employment, or even function of money, as a medium of payment."[9]

The root of this error (as of many other errors in economics) must
be sought in the uncritical acceptance of juristical conceptions and
habits of thought. From the point of view of the law, outstanding
debt is a subject which can and must be considered in isolation and
entirely (or at least to some extent) without reference to the origin
of the obligation to pay. Of course, in law as well as in economics,
money is only the common medium of exchange. But the principal,
although not exclusive, motive of the law for concerning itself with
money is the problem of payment. When it seeks to answer the
question, What is money? it is in order to determine how monetary
liabilities can be discharged. For the jurist, money is a medium of
payment. The economist, to whom the problem of money presents
a different aspect, may not adopt this point of view if he does not
wish at the very outset to prejudice his prospects of contributing to
the advancement of economic theory.

---

[9] Cf. Menger, *Grundsätze*, pp. 282 f.

CHAPTER 2

On the Measurement of Value

1

The Immeasurability of Subjective Use-Values

Although it is usual to speak of money as a measure of value and prices, the notion is entirely fallacious. So long as the subjective theory of value is accepted, this question of measurement cannot arise. In the older political economy, the search for a principle governing the measurement of value was to a certain extent justifiable. If, in accordance with an objective theory of value, the possibility of an objective concept of commodity values is accepted, and exchange is regarded as the reciprocal surrender of equivalent goods, then the conclusion necessarily follows that exchange transactions must be preceded by measurement of the quantity of value contained in each of the objects that are to be exchanged. And it is then an obvious step to regard money as the measure of value.

But modern value theory has a different starting point. It conceives of value as the significance attributed to individual commodity units by a human being who wishes to consume or otherwise dispose of various commodities to the best advantage. Every economic transaction presupposes a comparison of values. But the necessity for such a comparison, as well as the possibility of it, is due only to the circumstance that the person concerned has to choose between several commodities. It is quite irrelevant whether this choice is between a commodity in his own possession and one in somebody else's possession for which he might exchange it, or between the different uses to which he himself might put a given quantity of productive resources. In an isolated household, in which (as on Robinson Crusoe's desert island) there is neither buying nor selling, changes in the stocks of goods of higher and lower orders do nevertheless occur whenever anything is produced or consumed; and these changes must be based upon valuations if their returns are to exceed the outlay they involve. The process of valuation remains fundamentally the same whether the question is one of transforming labor and flour into bread in the domestic bakehouse, or of obtaining bread in exchange for clothes in the market. From the point of view of the person making the valuation, the calculation whether a certain act of production would justify a certain outlay of goods and labor is exactly the same as the comparison between the values of the commodities to be surrendered and the values of the commodities to be acquired that must precede an exchange transaction. For this reason it has been said that every economic act may be regarded as a kind of exchange.[1]

Acts of valuation are not susceptible of any kind of measurement. It is true that everybody is able to say whether a certain piece of bread seems more valuable to him than a certain piece of iron or less valuable than a certain piece of meat. And it is therefore true that everybody is in a position to draw up an immense list of comparative values; a list which will hold good only for a given point of time, since it must assume a given combination of wants and commodities. If the individual's circumstances change, then his scale of values changes also.

But subjective valuation, which is the pivot of all economic activity, only arranges commodities in order of their significance; it does not measure this significance. And economic activity has no other basis than the value scales thus constructed by individuals. An exchange will take place when two commodity units are placed in a different order on the value scales of two different persons. In a market, exchanges will continue until it is no longer possible for

[1] See Simmel, *Philosophie des Geldes*, 2d ed. (Leipzig, 1907), p. 35; Schumpeter, *Wesen und Hauptinhalt der theoretischen Nationalökonomie* (Leipzig, 1908), p. 50.

reciprocal surrender of commodities by any two individuals to result in their each acquiring commodities that stand higher on their value scales than those surrendered. If an individual wishes to make an exchange on an economic basis, he has merely to consider the comparative significance in his own judgment of the quantities of commodities in question. Such an estimate of relative values in no way involves the idea of measurement. An estimate is a direct psychological judgment that is not dependent on any kind of intermediate or auxiliary process.

(Such considerations also provide the answer to a series of objections to the subjective theory of value. It would be rash to conclude, because psychology has not succeeded and is not likely to succeed in measuring desires, that it is therefore impossible ultimately to attribute the quantitatively exact exchange ratios of the market to subjective factors. The exchange ratios of commodities are based upon the value scales of the individuals dealing in the market. Suppose that A possesses three pears and B two apples; and that A values the possession of two apples more than that of three pears, while B values the possession of three pears more than that of two apples. On the basis of these estimations an exchange may take place in which three pears are given for two apples. Yet it is clear that the determination of the numerically precise exchange ratio 2 : 3, taking a single fruit as a unit, in no way presupposes that A and B know exactly *by how much* the satisfaction promised by possession of the quantities to be acquired by exchange exceeds the satisfaction promised by possession of the quantities to be given up.)

General recognition of this fact, for which we are indebted to the authors of modern value theory, was hindered for a long time by a peculiar sort of obstacle. It is not altogether a rare thing that those very pioneers who have not hesitated to clear new paths for themselves and their followers by boldly rejecting outworn traditions and ways of thinking should yet shrink sometimes from all that is involved in the rigid application of their own principles. When this is so, it remains for those who come after to endeavor to put the matter right. The present is a case in point. On the subject of the measurement of value, as on a series of further subjects that are very closely bound up with it, the founders of the subjective theory of value refrained from the consistent development of their own doctrines. This is especially true of Böhm-Bawerk. At least it is especially striking in him; for the arguments of his which we are about to consider are embodied in a system that would have provided an alternative and, in the present writer's opinion, a better, solution of the problem, if their author had only drawn the decisive conclusion from them.

Böhm-Bawerk points out that when we have to choose in actual life between several satisfactions which cannot be had simultaneously because our means are limited, the situation is often such that the alternatives are on the one hand one big satisfaction and on the other hand a large number of homogeneous smaller satisfactions. Nobody will deny that it lies in our power to come to a rational decision in such cases. But it is equally clear that a judgment merely to the effect that a satisfaction of the one sort is greater than a satisfaction of the other sort is inadequate for such a decision; as would even be a judgment that a satisfaction of the first sort is *considerably* greater than one of the other sort. Böhm-Bawerk therefore concludes that the judgment must definitely affirm how many of the smaller satisfactions outweigh one of the first sort, or in other words how many times the one satisfaction exceeds one of the others in magnitude.[2]

The credit of having exposed the error contained in the identification of these two last propositions belongs to Čuhel. The judgment that so many small satisfactions are outweighed by a satisfaction of another kind is in fact *not* identical with the judgment that the one satisfaction is so many times greater than one of the others. The two would be identical only if the satisfaction afforded by a number of commodity units taken together were equal to the satisfaction afforded by a single unit on its own multiplied by the number of units. That this assumption cannot hold good follows from Gossen's law of the satisfaction of wants. The two judgments, "I would rather have eight plums than one apple" and "I would rather have one apple than seven plums," do not in the least justify the conclusion that Böhm-Bawerk draws from them when he states that therefore the satisfaction afforded by the consumption of an apple is more

---

[2] Cf. Böhm-Bawerk, "Grundzüge der Theorie des wirtschaftlichen Güterwertes," *Jahrbücher für Nationalökonomie und Statistik* (1886), New Series, vol. 13, p. 48.

than seven times but less than eight times as great as the satisfaction afforded by the consumption of a plum. The only legitimate conclusion is that the satisfaction from one apple is greater than the total satisfaction from seven plums but less than the total satisfaction from eight plums.[3]

This is the only interpretation that can be harmonized with the fundamental conception expounded by the marginal-utility theorists, and especially by Böhm-Bawerk himself, that the utility (and consequently the subjective use-value also) of units of a commodity decreases as the supply of them increases. But to accept this is to reject the whole idea of measuring the subjective use-value of commodities. Subjective use-value is not susceptible of any kind of measurement.

The American economist Irving Fisher has attempted to approach the problem of value measurement by way of mathematics.[4] His success with this method has been no greater than that of his predecessors with other methods. Like them, he has not been able to surmount the difficulties arising from the fact that marginal utility diminishes as supply increases, and the only use of the mathematics in which he clothes his arguments, and which is widely regarded as a particularly becoming dress for investigations in economics, is to conceal a little the defects of their clever but artificial construction.

Fisher begins by assuming that the utility of a particular good or service, though dependent on the supply of that good or service, is independent of the supply of all others. He realizes that it will not be possible to achieve his aim of discovering a unit for the measurement of utility unless he can first show how to determine the proportion between two given marginal utilities. If, for example, an individual has 100 loaves of bread at his disposal during one year, the marginal utility of a loaf to him will be greater than if he had 150

---

[3] See Čuhel, *Zur Lehre von den Bedürfnissen* (Innsbruck, 1906), pp. 186 ff.; Weiss, *Die moderne Tendenz in der Lehre vom Geldwert, Zeitschrift für Volkswirtschaft, Sozialpolitik und Verwaltung,* vol. 19, pp. 532 ff. In the last edition of his masterpiece *Capital and Interest,* revised by himself, Böhm-Bawerk endeavored to refute Čuhel's criticism, but did not succeed in putting forward any new considerations that could help toward a solution of the problem (see *Kapital und Kapitalzins,* 3d ed. [Innsbruck, 1909–12], pp. 331 ff. Exkurse, pp. 280 ff.).
[4] See Fisher, *Mathematical Investigations in the Theory of Value and Prices,* Transactions of the Connecticut Academy (New Haven, 1892), vol. 9, pp. 14 ff.

loaves. The problem is, to determine the arithmetical proportion between the two marginal utilities. Fisher attempts to do this by comparing them with a third utility. He therefore supposes the individual to have B gallons of oil annually as well, and calls β that increment of B whose utility is equal to that of the 100th loaf of bread. In the second case, when not 100 but 150 loaves are available, it is assumed that the supply of B remains unchanged. Then the utility of the 150th loaf may be equal, say, to the utility of $\beta/2$. Up to this point it is unnecessary to quarrel with Fisher's argument; but now follows a jump that neatly avoids all the difficulties of the problem. That is to say, Fisher simply continues, as if he were stating something quite self-evident: "Then the utility of the 150th loaf is said to be half the utility of the 100th." Without any further explanation he then calmly proceeds with his problem, the solution of which (if the above proposition is accepted as correct) involves no further difficulties, and so succeeds eventually in deducing a unit which he calls a "util." It does not seem to have occurred to him that in the particular sentence just quoted he has argued in defiance of the whole of marginal-utility theory and set himself in opposition to all the fundamental doctrines of modern economics. For obviously this conclusion of his is legitimate only if the utility of β is equal to twice the utility of $\beta/2$. But if this were really so, the problem of determining the proportion between two marginal utilities could have been solved in a quicker way, and his long process of deduction would not have been necessary. Just as justifiably as he assumes that the utility of β is equal to twice the utility of $\beta/2$, he might have assumed straightaway that the utility of the 150th loaf is two-thirds of that of the 100th.

Fisher imagines a supply of B gallons that is divisible into n small quantities β, or $2n$ small quantities $\beta/2$. He assumes that an individual who has this supply B at his disposal regards the value of commodity unit x as equal to that of β and the value of commodity unit y as equal to that of $\beta/2$. And he makes the further assumption that in both valuations, that is, both in equating the value of x with that of β and in equating the value of y with that of $\beta/2$, the individual has the same supply of B gallons at his disposal.

He evidently thinks it possible to conclude from this that the utility of β is twice as great as that of $\beta/2$. The error here is obvious.

The individual is in the one case faced with the choice between x (the value of the 100th loaf) and $\beta = 2\beta/2$. He finds it impossible to decide between the two, i.e., he values both equally. In the second case he has to choose between y (the value of the 150th loaf) and $\beta/2$. Here again he finds that both alternatives are of equal value. Now the question arises, what is the proportion between the marginal utility of β and that of $\beta/2$? We can determine this only by asking ourselves what the proportion is between the marginal utility of the nth part of a given supply and that of the $2n$th part of the same supply, between that of $\beta/_n$ and that of $\beta/_{2n}$. For this purpose let us imagine the supply B split up into $2n$ portions of $\beta/_{2n}$. Then the marginal utility of the $(2n-1)$th portion is greater than that of the $2n$th portion. If we now imagine the same supply B divided into n portions, then it clearly follows that the marginal utility of the nth portion is equal to that of the $(2n-1)$th portion plus that of the $2n$th portion in the previous case. It is not twice as great as that of the $2n$th portion, but more than twice as great. In fact, even with an unchanged supply, the marginal utility of several units taken together is not equal to the marginal utility of one unit multiplied by the number of units, but necessarily greater than this product. The value of two units is greater than, but not twice as great as, the value of one unit.[5]

Perhaps Fisher thinks that this consideration may be disposed of by supposing β and $\beta/2$ to be such small quantities that their utility may be reckoned infinitesimal. If this is really his opinion, then it must first of all be objected that the peculiarly mathematical conception of infinitesimal quantities is inapplicable to economic problems. The utility afforded by a given amount of commodities, is either great enough for valuation, or so small that it remains imperceptible to the valuer and cannot therefore affect his judgment. But even if the applicability of the conception of infinitesimal quantities were granted, the argument would still be invalid, for it is obviously impossible to find the proportion between two finite marginal utilities by equating them with two infinitesimal marginal utilities.

Finally, a few words must be devoted to Schumpeter's attempt

---

[5] See also Weiss, *op. cit.*, p. 538.

to set up as a unit the satisfaction resulting from the consumption of a given quantity of commodities and to express other satisfactions as multiples of this unit. Value judgments on this principle would have to be expressed as follows: "The satisfaction that I could get from the consumption of a certain quantity of commodities is a thousand times as great as that which I get from the consumption of an apple a day," or "For this quantity of goods I would give at the most *a thousand times this apple.*"[6] Is there really anybody on earth who is capable of adumbrating such mental images or pronouncing such judgments? Is there any sort of economic activity that is actually dependent on the making of such decisions? Obviously not.[7] Schumpeter makes the same mistake of starting with the assumption that we need a measure of value in order to be able to compare one "quantity of value" with another. But valuation in no way consists in a comparison of two "quantities of value." It consists solely in a comparison of the importance of different wants. The judgment "Commodity *a* is worth more to me than commodity *b*" no more presupposes a measure of economic value than the judgment "*A* is dearer to me—more highly esteemed—than *B*" presupposes a measure of friendship.

2

Total Value

If it is impossible to measure subjective use-value, it follows directly that it is impracticable to ascribe "quantity" to it. We may say, the value of this commodity is greater than the value of that; but it is not permissible for us to assert, this commodity is worth *so much.* Such a way of speaking necessarily implies a definite unit. It really amounts to stating how many times a given unit is contained in the quantity to be defined. But this kind of calculation is quite inapplicable to processes of valuation.

The consistent application of these principles implies a criticism also of Schumpeter's views on the total value of a stock of goods. According to Wieser, the total value of a stock of goods is given by

---

[6] Cf. Schumpeter, *op. cit.*, p. 290.
[7] Cf. further Weiss, *op. cit.*, pp. 534 ff.

multiplying the number of items or portions constituting the stock by their marginal utility at any given moment. The untenability of this argument is shown by the fact that it would prove that the total stock of a free good must always be worth nothing. Schumpeter therefore suggests a different formula in which each portion is multiplied by an index corresponding to its position on the value scale (which, by the way, is quite arbitrary) and these products are then added together or integrated. This attempt at a solution, like the preceding, has the defect of assuming that it is possible to measure marginal utility and "intensity" of value. The fact that such measurement is impossible renders both suggestions equally useless. Mastery of the problem must be sought in some other way.

Value is always the result of a process of valuation. The process of valuation compares the significance of two complexes of commodities from the point of view of the individual making the valuation. The individual making the valuation and the complexes of goods valued, that is, the subject and the objects of the valuation, must enter as indivisible elements into any given process of valuation. This does not mean that they are necessarily indivisible in other respects as well, whether physically or economically. The subject of an act of valuation may quite well be a group of persons, a state or society or family, so long as it acts in this particular case as a unit, through a representative. And the objects thus valued may be collections of distinct units of commodities so long as they have to be dealt with in this particular case as a whole. There is nothing to prevent either subject or object from being a single unit for the purposes of one valuation even though in another their component parts may be entirely independent of each other. The same people who, acting together through a representative as a single agent, such as a state, make a judgment as to the relative values of a battleship and a hospital, are the independent subjects of valuations of other commodities, such as cigars and newspapers. It is just the same with commodities. Modern value theory is based on the fact that it is not the abstract importance of different kinds of need that determines the scales of values, but the intensity of specific desires. Starting from this, the law of marginal utility was developed in a form that referred primarily to the usual sort of case in which the collections of commodities are divisible. But there are also cases in which the total supply must be valued as it stands.

Suppose that an economically isolated individual possesses two cows and three horses and that the relevant part of his scale of values (that item valued highest being placed first) is as follows: 1, a cow; 2, a horse; 3, a horse; 4, a horse; 5, a cow. If this individual has to choose between one cow and one horse he will rather be inclined to sacrifice the cow than the horse. If wild animals attack one of his cows and one of his horses, and it is impossible for him to save both, then he will try to save the horse. But if the whole of his stock of either animal is in danger, his decision will be different. Supposing that his stable and cowshed catch fire and that he can only rescue the occupants of one and must leave the others to their fate, then if he values three horses less than two cows he will attempt to save not the three horses but the two cows. The result of that process of valuation which involves a choice between one cow and one horse is a higher estimation of the horse. The result of the process of valuation which involves a choice between the whole available stock of cows and the whole available stock of horses is a higher estimation of the stock of cows.

Value can rightly be spoken of only with regard to specific acts of appraisal. It exists in such connections only; there is no value outside the process of valuation. There is no such thing as abstract value. Total value can be spoken of only with reference to a particular instance of an individual or other valuing "subject" having to choose between the total available quantities of certain economic goods. Like every other act of valuation, this is complete in itself. The person making the choice does not have to make use of notions about the value of units of the commodity. His process of valuation, like every other, is an immediate inference from considerations of the utilities at stake. When a stock is valued as a whole, its marginal utility, that is to say, the utility of the last available unit of it, coincides with its total utility, since the total supply is one indivisible quantity. This is also true of the total value of free goods, whose separate units are always valueless, that is, are always relegated to a sort of limbo at the very end of the value scale, promiscuously intermingled with the units of all the other free goods.[8]

---

[8] See also Clark, *Essentials of Economic Theory* (New York, 1907), p. 41. In the first German edition of the present work, the above argument contained two further

3

Money as a Price Index

What has been said should have made sufficiently plain the un-
scientific nature of the practice of attributing to money the function
of acting as a measure of price or even of value. Subjective value is
not measured, but graded. The problem of the measurement of
objective use-value is not an economic problem at all. (It may incidentally be remarked that a measurement of efficiency is not possible for every species of commodity and is at the best only available
within separate species, while every possibility, not only of measurement, but even of mere scaled comparison, vanishes as soon as
we seek to establish a relation between two or more kinds of efficiency. It may be possible to measure and compare the calorific value
of coal and of wood, but it is in no way possible to reduce to a
common objective denominator the objective efficiency of a table
and that of a book.)

Neither is objective exchange value measurable, for it too is the
result of the comparisons derived from the valuations of individuals. The objective exchange value of a given commodity unit may
be expressed in units of every other kind of commodity. Nowadays
exchange is usually carried on by means of money, and since every
commodity has therefore a price expressible in money, the exchange
value of every commodity can be expressed in terms of money. This
possibility enabled money to become a medium for expressing values when the growing elaboration of the scale of values which resulted from the development of exchange necessitated a revision of
the technique of valuation.

That is to say, opportunities for exchanging induce the individual
to rearrange his scales of values. A person in whose scale of values
the commodity "a cask of wine" comes after the commodity "a sack
of oats" will reverse their order if he can exchange a cask of wine
in the market for a commodity that he values more highly than a
sack of oats. The position of commodities in the value scales of

---

sentences that summarized in an inadequate fashion the results of investigation into
the problem of total value. In deference to certain criticisms of C. A. Verrijn Stuart
(*Die Grundlagen der Volkswirtschaft* [Jena, 1923], p. 115), they were omitted from the
second edition.

individuals is no longer determined solely by their own subjective use-value, but also by the subjective use-value of the commodities that can be obtained in exchange for them, whenever the latter stand higher than the former in the estimation of the individual. Therefore, if he is to obtain the maximum utility from his resources, the individual must familiarize himself with all the prices in the market.

For this, however, he needs some help in finding his way among the confusing multiplicity of the exchange ratios. Money, the common medium of exchange, which can be exchanged for every commodity and with which every commodity can be procured, is preeminently suitable for this. It would be absolutely impossible for the individual, even if he were a complete expert in commercial matters, to follow every change of market conditions and make the corresponding alterations in his scale of use-values and exchange values, unless he chose some common denominator to which he could reduce each exchange ratio. Because the market enables any commodity to be turned into money and money into any commodity, objective exchange value is expressed in terms of money. Thus money becomes a price index, in Menger's phrase. The whole structure of the calculations of the entrepreneur and the consumer rests on the process of valuing commodities in money. Money has thus become an aid that the human mind is no longer able to dispense with in making economic calculations.[9] If in this sense we wish to attribute to money the function of being a measure of prices, there is no reason why we should not do so. Nevertheless, it is better to avoid the use of a term which might so easily be misunderstood as this. In any case the usage certainly cannot be called correct—we do not usually describe the determination of latitude and longitude as a "function" of the stars.[10]

---

[9] On the indispensability of money for economic calculation, see my book *Die Gemeinwirtschaft: Untersuchungen über den Sozialismus* (Jena, 1922), pp. 100 ff.

[10] [This chapter deals with technical matters which may present difficulty to readers unacquainted with general economic theory. It may be omitted on a first reading, but it is essential to complete understanding of certain issues, such as the index-number problem, which are dealt with later.—Editor.]

CHAPTER 3

The Various Kinds of Money

1

Money and Money Substitutes

When an indirect exchange is transacted with the aid of money, it is not necessary for the money to change hands physically; a perfectly secure claim to an equivalent sum, payable on demand, may be transferred instead of the actual coins. In this by itself there is nothing remarkable or peculiar to money. What is peculiar, and only to be explained by reference to the special characteristics of money, is the extraordinary frequency of this way of completing monetary transactions.

In the first place, money is especially well adapted to constitute the substance of a generic obligation. Whereas the fungibility of nearly all other economic goods is more or less circumscribed and is often only a fiction based on an artificial commercial terminology, that of money is almost unlimited. Only that of shares and bonds can be compared with it. The sole factor that could possibly prevent any of these from being completely fungible is the difficulty of subdividing their separate units; and various expedients have been adopted, which, at least as far as money is concerned, have entirely robbed this difficulty of all practical significance.

A still more important circumstance is involved in the nature of the function that money performs. A claim to money may be transferred over and over again in an indefinite number of indirect exchanges without the person by whom it is payable ever being called upon to settle it. This is obviously not true as far as other economic goods are concerned, for these are always destined for ultimate consumption.

The special suitability for facilitating indirect exchanges possessed by absolutely secure and immediately payable claims to money, which we may briefly refer to as money substitutes, is further increased by their standing in law and commerce.

Technically, and in some countries legally as well, the transfer of a banknote scarcely differs from that of a coin. The similarity of outward appearance is such that those who are engaged in commercial dealings are usually unable to distinguish between those objects that actually perform the function of money and those that are merely employed as substitutes for them. The businessman does not worry about the economic problems involved in this; he is only concerned with the commercial and legal characteristics of coins, notes, checks, and the like. To him, the facts that banknotes are transferable without documentary evidence, that they circulate like coins in round denominations, that no right of recovery lies against their previous holders, that the law recognizes no difference between them and money as an instrument of debt settlement, seem good enough reason for including them within the definition of the term *money*, and for drawing a fundamental distinction between them and cash deposits, which can be transferred only by a procedure that is much more complex technically and is also regarded in law as of a different kind. This is the origin of the popular conception of money by which everyday life is governed. No doubt it serves the purposes of the bank official, and it may even be quite useful in the business world at large, but its introduction into the scientific terminology of economics is most undesirable.

The controversy about the concept of money is not exactly one of the most satisfactory chapters in the history of our science. It is chiefly remarkable for the smother of juristic and commercial technicalities in which it is enveloped and for the quite undeserved significance that has been attached to what is after all merely a question of terminology. The solution of the question has been regarded as an end in itself and it seems to have been completely forgotten that the real aim should have been simply to facilitate further investigation. Such a discussion could not fail to be fruitless.

In attempting to draw a line of division between money and those objects that outwardly resemble it, we only need to bear in mind the goal of our investigation. The present discussion aims at tracing the laws that determine the exchange ratio between money and other economic goods. This and nothing else is the task of the economic theory of money. Now our terminology must be suited to our problem. If a particular group of objects is to be singled out from among all those that fulfill a monetary function in commerce and, under the special name of money (which is to be reserved to this group alone), sharply contrasted with the rest (to which this name is denied), then this distinction must be made in a way that will facilitate the further progress of the investigation.

It is considerations such as these that have led the present writer to give the name of money substitutes and not that of money to those objects that are employed like money in commerce but consist in perfectly secure and immediately convertible claims to money.

Claims are not goods;[1] they are means of obtaining disposal over goods. This determines their whole nature and economic significance. They themselves are not valued directly, but indirectly; their value is derived from that of the economic goods to which they refer. Two elements are involved in the valuation of a claim: first, the value of the goods to whose possession it gives a right; and, second, the greater or less probability that possession of the goods in question will actually be obtained. Furthermore, if the claim is to come into force only after a period of time, then consideration of this circumstance will constitute a third factor in its valuation. The value on January 1 of a right to receive ten sacks of coal on December 31 of the same year will be based not directly on the value of ten sacks of coal, but on the value of ten sacks of coal to be delivered in a year's time. This sort of calculation is a matter of common experience, as also is the fact that in reckoning the value of claims their soundness or security is taken into account.

Claims to money are, of course, no exception. Those which are

---

[1] See Böhm-Bawerk, *Rechte und Verhältnisse* (Innsbruck, 1881), pp. 120 ff.

payable on demand, if there is no doubt about their soundness and no expense connected with their settlement, are valued just as highly as cash and tendered and accepted in the same way as money.[2] Only claims of this sort—that is, claims that are payable on demand, absolutely safe as far as human foresight goes, and perfectly liquid in the legal sense—are for business purposes exact substitutes for the money to which they refer. Other claims, of course, such as notes issued by banks of doubtful credit or bills that are not yet mature, also enter into financial transactions and may just as well be employed as general media of exchange. This, according to our terminology, means that they are money. But then they are valued independently; they are reckoned equivalent neither to the sums of money to which they refer nor even to the worth of the rights that they embody. What the further special factors are that help to determine their exchange value, we shall discover in the course of our argument.

Of course it would be in no way incorrect if we attempted to include in our concept of money those absolutely secure and immediately convertible claims to money that we have preferred to call money substitutes. But what must be entirely condemned is the widespread practice of giving the name of money to certain classes of money substitutes, usually banknotes, token money, and the like, and contrasting them sharply with the remaining kinds, such as cash deposits.[3] This is to make a distinction without any adequate difference; for banknotes, say, and cash deposits differ only in mere externals, important perhaps from the business and legal points of view, but quite insignificant from the point of view of economics.

On the other hand, arguments of considerable weight may be urged in favor of including all money substitutes without exception in the single concept of money. It may be pointed out, for instance, that the significance of perfectly secure and liquid claims to money is quite different from that of claims to other economic goods; that whereas a claim on a commodity must sooner or later be liquidated, this is not necessarily true of claims to money. Such claims may pass from hand to hand for indefinite periods and so take the place of

---

[2] Wagner, *Beiträge zur Lehre von den Banken* (Leipzig, 1857), pp. 34 ff.
[3] For instance, Helfferich, *Das Geld*, 6th ed. (Leipzig, 1923), pp. 267 ff.; English trans., *Money* (London, 1927), pp. 284 ff.

money without any attempt being made to liquidate them. It may be pointed out that those who require money will be quite satisfied with such claims as these, and that those who wish to spend money will find that these claims answer their purpose just as well; and that consequently the supply of money substitutes must be reckoned in with that of money, and the demand for them with the demand for money. It may further be pointed out that whereas it is impossible to satisfy an increase in the demand, say, for bread by issuing more breadtickets without adding to the actual supply of bread itself, it is perfectly possible to satisfy an increased demand for money by just such a process as this. It may be argued, in brief, that money substitutes have certain peculiarities of which account is best taken by including them in the concept of money.

Without wishing to question the weight of such arguments as these, we shall on grounds of convenience prefer to adopt the narrower formulation of the concept of money, supplementing it with a separate concept of money substitutes. Whether this is the most advisable course to pursue, whether perhaps some other procedure might not lead to a better understanding of our subject matter, must be left to the judgment of the reader. To the author it appears that the way chosen is the only way in which the difficult problems of the theory of money can be solved.

2

The Peculiarities of Money Substitutes

Economic discussion about money must be based solely on economic considerations and may take legal distinctions into account only insofar as they are significant from the economic point of view also. Such discussion consequently must proceed from a concept of money based, not on legal definitions and discriminations, but on the economic nature of things. It follows that our decision not to regard drafts and other claims to money as constituting money itself must not be interpreted merely in accordance with the narrow juristic concept of a claim to money. Besides strictly legal claims to money, we must also take into account such relationships as are not claims in the juristic sense, but are nevertheless treated as such in commercial practice because some concern or other deals with them as if they actually did constitute claims against itself.[4]

There can be no doubt that the German token coins minted in accordance with the Coinage Act of July 9, 1873, did not in law constitute claims to money. Perhaps there are some superficial critics who would be inclined to classify these coins actually as money because they consisted of stamped silver or nickel or copper discs that had every appearance of being money. But despite this, from the point of view of economics these token coins merely constituted drafts on the national Treasury. The second paragraph of section nine of the Coinage Act (in its form of June 1, 1909) obliged the Bundesrat to specify those centers that would pay out gold coins on demand in return for not less than 200 marks' worth of silver coins or fifty marks' worth of nickel and copper coins. Certain branches of the Reichsbank were entrusted with this function. Another section of the Coinage Act (sec. 8) provided that the Reich would always be in a position actually to maintain this convertibility. According to this section, the total value of the silver coins minted was never to exceed twenty marks per head of the population, nor that of the nickel and copper coins two and one-half marks per head. In the opinion of the legislature, these sums represented the demand for small coins, and there was consequently no danger that the total issue of token coinage would exceed the public demand for it. Admittedly, there was no statutory recognition of any right to conversion on the part of holders of token coins, and the limitation of legal tender (sec. 9, par. 1) was only an inadequate substitute for this. Nevertheless, it is a matter of general knowledge that the token coins were in fact cashed without any demur at the branches of the Reichsbank specified by the chancellor.

Exactly the same sort of significance was enjoyed by the Reich Treasury notes, of which not more than 120 million marks' worth were allowed to be in circulation. These also (sec. 5 of the act of April 30, 1874) were always cashed for gold by the Reichsbank on behalf of the Treasury. It is beside the point that the Treasury notes were not legal tender in private transactions while everybody was obliged to accept silver coins in amounts up to twenty marks and

---

[4] See Laughlin, *The Principles of Money* (London, 1903), pp. 516 ff.

nickel and copper coins in amounts up to one mark; for, although they were not legally bound to accept them in settlement of debts, people in fact accepted them readily.

Another example is afforded by the German thaler of the period from the introduction of the gold standard until the withdrawal of the thaler from circulation on October 1, 1907. During the whole of this period the thaler was undoubtedly legal tender. But if we seek to go behind this expression, whose juristic derivation makes it useless for our present purpose, and ask if the thaler was *money* during this period, the answer must be that it was not. It is true that it was employed in commerce as a medium of exchange; but it could be used in this way solely because it was a claim to something that really was money, that is, to the common medium of exchange. For although neither the Reichsbank nor the Reich nor its separate constituent kingdoms and duchies nor anybody else was obliged to cash them, the Reichsbank, acting on behalf of the government, always took pains to ensure that no more thalers were in circulation than were demanded by the public. It achieved this result by refusing to press thalers on its customers when paying out. This, together with the circumstance that thalers were legal tender both to the bank and to the Reich, was sufficient to turn them in effect into drafts that could always be converted into money, with the result that they circulated at home as perfectly satisfactory substitutes for money. It was repeatedly suggested to the directors of the Reichsbank that they should cash their own notes not in gold but in thalers (which would have been well within the letter of the law) and pay out gold only at a premium, with the object of hindering the export of it. But the bank steadily refused to adopt this or any proposal of a similar nature.

The exact nature of the token coinage in other countries has not always been so easy to understand as that of Germany, whose banking and currency system was fashioned under the influence of such men as Bamberger, Michaelis, and Soetbeer. In some legislation, the theoretical basis of modern token-coinage policy may not be so easy to discover or to demonstrate as in the examples already dealt with. Nevertheless, all such policy has ultimately the same intent. The universal legal peculiarity of token coinage is the limitation of its power of payment to a specified maximum sum; and as a rule this provision is supplemented by legislative restriction of the amount that may be minted.

There is no such thing as an economic concept of token coinage. All that economics can distinguish is a particular subgroup within the group of claims to money that are employed as substitutes for money, the members of this subgroup being intended for use in transactions where the amounts involved are small. The fact that the issue and circulation of token coins are subjected to special *legal* rules and regulations is to be explained by the special nature of the purpose that they serve. The general recognition of the right of the holder of a banknote to receive money in exchange for it while the conversion of token coins is in many countries left to administrative discretion is a result of the different lines of development that notes and token coinage have followed respectively. Token coins have arisen from the need for facilitating the exchange of small quantities of goods of little value. The historical details of their development have not yet been brought to light and, almost without exception, all that has been written on the subject is of purely numismatical or metrological importance.[5] Nevertheless, one thing can safely be asserted: token coinage is always the result of attempts to remedy deficiencies in the existing monetary system. It is those technical difficulties, that hinder the subdivision of the monetary unit into small coins, that have led, after all sorts of unsuccessful attempts, to the solution of the problem that we adopt nowadays. In many countries, while this development has been going on, a kind of fiat money[6] has sometimes been used in small transactions, with the very inconvenient consequence of having two independent kinds of money performing side by side the function of a common medium of exchange. To avoid the inconveniences of such a situation the small coins were brought into a fixed legal ratio with those used in larger transactions and the necessary precautions were taken to pre-

[5] See Kalkmann, *Englands Übergang zur Goldwährung im 18. Jahrhundert* (Strassburg, 1895), pp. 64 ff.; Schmoller, "Über die Ausbildung einer richtigen Scheidemünzpolitik vom 14. bis zum 19. Jahrhundert," *Jahrbuch für Gesetzgebung, Verwaltung und Volkswirtschaft im Deutschen Reich* 24 (1900): 1247–74; Helfferich, *Studien über Geld und Bankwessen* (Berlin, 1900), pp. 1–37.
[6] On the concepts of commodity money, credit money, and fiat money, see sec. 3 of this chap.

vent the quantity of small coins from exceeding the requirements of commerce. The most important means to this end has always been the restriction of the quantity minted to that which seems likely to be needed for making small payments, whether this is fixed by law or strictly adhered to without such compulsion. Along with this has gone the limitation of legal tender in private dealings to a certain relatively small amount. The danger that these regulations would prove inadequate has never seemed very great, and consequently legislative provision for conversion of the token coins has been either entirely neglected or left incomplete by omission of a clear statement of the holder's right to change them for money. But everywhere nowadays those token coins that are rejected from circulation are accepted without demur by the state, or some other body such as the central bank, and thus their nature as claims to money is established. Where this policy has been discontinued for a time and the attempt made by suspending effectual conversion of the token coins to force more of them into circulation than was required, they have become credit money, or even commodity money. Then they have no longer been regarded as claims to money, payable on demand, and therefore equivalent to money, but have been valued independently.

The banknote has followed quite a different line of development. It has always been regarded as a claim, even from the juristic point of view. The fact has never been lost sight of that if its value was to be kept equal to that of money, steps would have to be taken to ensure its permanent convertibility into money. That a cessation of cash payments would alter the economic character of banknotes could hardly escape notice; in the case of the quantitatively less important coins used in small transactions it could more easily be forgotten. Furthermore, the smaller quantitative importance of token coins means that it is possible to maintain their permanent convertibility without establishing special funds for the purpose. The absence of such special funds may also have helped to disguise the real nature of token coinage.[7]

---

[7] On the nature of token coinage, see Say, *Cours complet d'économie politique pratique,* 3d ed. (Paris, 1852), vol, 1, p. 408; and Wagner, *Theoretische Sozialökonomik* (Leipzig, 1909), Part II pp. 504 ff. Very instructive discussions are to be found in the memoranda and debates that preceded the Belgian Token Coinage Act of 1860. In the memoran-

Consideration of the monetary system of Austria-Hungary is particularly instructive. The currency reform that was inaugurated in 1892 was never formally completed, and until the disruption of the Hapsburg monarchy the standard remained legally what is usually called a paper standard, since the Austro-Hungarian Bank was not obliged to redeem its own notes, which were legal tender to any amount. Nevertheless, from 1900 to 1914 Austria-Hungary really possessed a gold standard or gold-exchange standard, for the bank did in fact readily provide gold for commercial requirements. Although according to the letter of the law it was not obliged to cash its notes, it offered bills of exchange and other claims payable abroad in gold (checks, notes, and the like), at a price below the upper theoretical gold point. Under such conditions, those who wanted gold for export naturally preferred to buy claims of this sort, which enabled them to achieve their purpose more cheaply than by the actual export of gold.

For internal commerce as well, in which the use of gold was exceptional since the population had many years before gone over to banknotes and token coins,[8] the bank cashed its notes for gold without being legally bound to do so. And this policy was pursued, not accidentally or occasionally or without full recognition of its significance, but deliberately and systematically, with the object of permitting Austria and Hungary to enjoy the economic advantages of the gold standard. Both the Austrian and the Hungarian governments, to whose initiative this policy of the bank was due, cooperated as far as they were able. But in the first place it was the bank itself which had to ensure, by following an appropriate discount policy, that it would always be in a position to carry out with promp-

dum of Pirmez, the nature of modern convertible token coins is characterized as follows: "With this property (of convertibility) the coins are no longer merely coins; they become claims, promises to pay. The holder no longer has a mere property right to the coin itself [*jus in re*]; he has a claim against the state to the amount of the nominal value of the coin [*jus ad rem*], a right which he can exercise at any moment by demanding its conversion. Token coins cease to be money and become a credit instrument [*une institution de crédit*], banknotes inscribed on pieces of metal . . ." (see *Loi décrétant la fabrication d'une monnaie d'appoint . . . précédée des notes sur la monnaie de billon en Belgique ainsi que la discussion de la loi à la Chambre des Représentants* [Brussels, 1860], p. 50).

[8] The silver gulden in Austria-Hungary held the same position as the silver thaler in Germany from 1873 to 1907. It was legal tender, but economically a claim to money, since the bank-of-issue in fact always cashed it on demand.

titude its voluntary undertaking to redeem its notes. The measures that it took with this purpose in view did not differ fundamentally in any way from those adopted by the banks-of-issue in other gold-standard countries.[9] Thus the notes of the Austro-Hungarian Bank were in fact nothing but money substitutes. The money of the country, as of other European countries, was gold.

3

Commodity Money, Credit Money, and Fiat Money

The economic theory of money is generally expressed in a terminology that is not economic but juristic. This terminology has been built up by writers, statesmen, merchants, judges, and others whose chief interests have been in the legal characteristics of the different kinds of money and their substitutes. It is useful for dealing with those aspects of the monetary system that are of importance from the legal point of view; but for purposes of economic investigation it is practically valueless. Sufficient attention has scarcely been devoted to this shortcoming, despite the fact that confusion of the respective provinces of the sciences of law and economics has nowhere been so frequent and so fraught with mischievous consequences as in this very sphere of monetary theory. It is a mistake to deal with economic problems according to legal criteria. The juristic phraseology, like the results of juristic research into monetary problems, must be regarded by economics as one of the objects of its investigations. It is not the task of economics to criticize it, although it is entitled to exploit it for its own purposes. There is nothing to be said against using juristic technical terms in economic argument where this leads to no undesirable consequences. But for its own special purposes, economics must construct its own special terminology.

---

[9] See my articles "Das Problem gesetzlicher Aufnahme der Barzahlungen in Öster-reich-Ungarn," *Jahrbuch für Gesetzgebung, Verwaltung und Volkswirtschaft im Deutschen Reich* 33 (1909): 985–1037; "Zum Problem gesetzlicher Aufnahme der Barzahlungen in Österreich-Ungarn," *ibid.* 34 (1910): 1877–84; "The Foreign Exchange Policy of the Austro-Hungarian Bank," *Economic Journal* 19 (1909): 201–11; "Das vierte Privilegium der Österreichisch-Ungarischen Bank," *Zeitschrift für Volkswirtschaft, Sozialpolitik und Verwaltung* 21 (1912): 611–24.

There are two sorts of thing that may be used as money: on the one hand, physical commodities as such, like the metal gold or the metal silver; and, on the other hand, objects that do not differ technologically from other objects that are not money, the factor that decides whether they are money being not a physical but a legal characteristic. A piece of paper that is specially characterized as money by the imprint of some authority is in no way different, technologically considered, from another piece of paper that has received a similar imprint from an unauthorized person, just as a genuine five-franc piece does not differ technologically from a "genuine replica." The only difference lies in the law that regulates the manufacture of such coins and makes it impossible without authority. (In order to avoid every possible misunderstanding, let it be expressly stated that all that the law can do is to regulate the issue of the coins and that it is beyond the power of the state to ensure in addition that they actually shall become money; that is, that they actually shall be employed as a common medium of exchange. All that the state can do by means of its official stamp is to single out certain pieces of metal or paper from all the other things of the same kind so that they can be subjected to a process of valuation independent of that of the rest. Thus it *permits* those objects possessing the special legal qualification to be used as a common medium of exchange while the other commodities of the same sort remain mere commodities. It can also take various steps with the object of encouraging the actual employment of the qualified commodities as common media of exchange. But these commodities can never become money just because the state commands it; money can be created only by the usage of those who take part in commercial transactions.)

We may give the name *commodity money* to that sort of money that is at the same time a commercial commodity; and the name *fiat money* to money that comprises things with a special legal qualification. A third category may be called *credit money,* this being that sort of money which constitutes a claim against any physical or legal person. But these claims must not be both payable on demand and absolutely secure; if they were, there could be no difference between their value and that of the sum of money to which they referred, and they could not be subjected to an independent process of valuation on the part of those who dealt with them. In some way or other the maturity of these claims must be postponed to some future time. It can hardly be contested that fiat money in the strict sense of the word is theoretically conceivable. The theory of value proves the possibility of its existence. Whether fiat money has ever actually existed is, of course, another question, and one that cannot offhand be answered affirmatively. It can hardly be doubted that most of those kinds of money that are not commodity money must be classified as credit money. But only detailed historical investigation could clear this matter up.

Our terminology should prove more useful than that which is generally employed. It should express more clearly the peculiarities of the processes by which the different types of money are valued. It is certainly more correct than the usual distinction between metallic money and paper money. Metallic money comprises not only standard money but also token coins and such coins as the German thaler of the period 1873–1907; and paper money, as a rule, comprises not merely such fiat money and credit money as happen to be made of paper, but also convertible notes issued by banks or the state. This terminology is derived from popular usage. Previously, when more often than nowadays "metallic" money really was money and not a money substitute, perhaps the nomenclature was a little less inappropriate than it is now. Furthermore, it corresponded—perhaps still corresponds—to the naive and confused popular conception of value that sees in the precious metals something "intrinsically" valuable and in paper credit money something necessarily anomalous. Scientifically, this terminology is perfectly useless and a source of endless misunderstanding and misrepresentation. The greatest mistake that can be made in economic investigation is to fix attention on mere appearances, and so to fail to perceive the fundamental difference between things whose externals alone are similar, or to discriminate between fundamentally similar things whose externals alone are different.

Admittedly, for the numismatist and the technologist and the historian of art there is very little difference between the five-franc piece before and after the cessation of free coinage of silver, while the Austrian silver gulden even of the period 1879 to 1892 appears to be fundamentally different from the paper gulden. But it is re-

grettable that such superficial distinctions as this should still play
a part in economic discussion.

Our threefold classification is not a matter of mere terminological
gymnastics; the theoretical discussion of the rest of this book should
demonstrate the utility of the concepts that it involves.

The decisive characteristic of commodity money is the employment for monetary purposes of a commodity in the technological
sense. For the present investigation, it is a matter of complete indifference what particular commodity this is; the important thing
is that it is the commodity in question that constitutes the money,
and that the money is merely this commodity. The case of fiat money
is quite different. Here the deciding factor is the stamp, and it is not
the material bearing the stamp that constitutes the money, but the
stamp itself. The nature of the material that bears the stamp is a
matter of quite minor importance. Credit money, finally, is a claim
falling due in the future that is used as a general medium of exchange.

4

The Commodity Money of the Past and of the Present

Even when the differentiation of commodity money, credit money,
and fiat money is accepted as correct in principle and only its utility
disputed, the statement that the freely mintable currency of the present day and the metallic money of previous centuries are examples
of commodity money is totally rejected by many authorities and by
still more of the public at large. It is true that as a rule nobody denies
that the older forms of money were commodity money. It is further
generally admitted that in earlier times coins circulated by weight
and not by tale. Nevertheless, it is asserted, money changed its
nature long ago. The money of Germany and England in 1914, it is
said, was not gold, but the mark and the pound. Money nowadays
consists of "specified units with a definite significance in terms of
value, that is assigned to them by law" (Knapp). "By 'the standard'
we mean the units of value (florins, francs, marks, etc.) that have
been adopted as measures of value, and by 'money' we mean the
tokens (coins and notes) that represent the units that function as a

measure of value. The controversy as to whether silver or gold or both together should function as a standard and as currency is an idle one, because neither silver nor gold ever has performed these functions or ever could have done so" (Hammer).[10]

Before we proceed to test the truth of these remarkable assertions, let us make one brief observation on their genesis—although it would really be more correct to say renascence than to say genesis, since the doctrines involved exhibit a very close relationship with the oldest and most primitive theories of money. Just as these were, so the nominalistic monetary theories of the present day are, characterized by their inability to contribute a single word toward the solution of the chief problem of monetary theory—one might in fact simply call it *the* problem of monetary theory—namely, that of explaining the exchange ratios between money and other economic goods. For their authors, the economic problem of value and prices simply does not exist. They have never thought it necessary to consider how market ratios are established or what they signify. Their attention is accidentally drawn to the fact that a German thaler (since 1873), or an Austrian silver florin (since 1879), is essentially different from a quantity of silver of the same weight and fineness that has not been stamped at the government mint. They notice a similar state of affairs with regard to "paper money." They do not understand this, and endeavor to find an answer to the riddle. But at this point, just because of their lack of acquaintance with the theory of value and prices, their inquiry takes a peculiarly unlucky turn. They do not inquire how the exchange ratios between money and other economic goods are established. This obviously seems to them quite a self-evident matter. They formulate their problem in another way: *How does it come about that three twenty-mark pieces are equivalent to twenty thalers despite the fact that the silver contained in the thalers has a lower market value than the gold contained in the marks?* And their answer runs: *Because the value of money is determined by the state, by statute, by the legal system.* Thus, ignoring the most important facts of monetary history, they weave an artificial network of falla-

---

[10] See esp. Hammer, *Die Hauptprinzipien des Geld-und Währungswesens und die Lösung der Valutafrage* (Vienna, 1891), pp. 7 ff.; Gesell, *Die Anpassung des Geldes und seiner Verwaltung an die Bedürfnisse des modernen Verkehres* (Buenos Aires, 1897), pp. 21 ff.; Knapp, *Staatliche Theorie des Geldes,* 3d ed. (Munich, 1921), pp. 20 ff.

cies; a theoretical construction that collapses immediately the question is put: *What exactly are we to understand by a unit of value?* But such impertinent questions can only occur to those who are acquainted with at least the elements of the theory of prices. Others are able to content themselves with references to the "nominality" of the unit of value. No wonder, then, that these theories should have achieved such popularity with the man in the street, especially since their kinship with inflationism was bound to commend them strongly to all "cheap-money" enthusiasts.

It may be stated as an assured result of investigation into monetary history that at all times and among all peoples the principal coins have been tendered and accepted, not by tale without consideration of their quantity and quality, but only as pieces of metal of specific degrees of weight and fineness. Where coins have been accepted by tale, this has always been in the definite belief that the stamp showed them to be of the usual fineness of their kind and of the correct weight. Where there were no grounds for this assumption, weighing and testing were resorted to again.

Fiscal considerations have led to the promulgation of a theory that attributes to the minting authority the right to regulate the purchasing power of the coinage as it thinks fit. For just as long as the minting of coins has been a government function, governments have tried to fix the weight and content of the coins as they wished. Philip VI of France expressly claimed the right "to mint such money and give it such currency and at such rate as we desire and seems good to us"[11] and all medieval rulers thought and did as he in this matter. Obliging jurists supported them by attempts to discover a philosophical basis for the divine right of kings to debase the coinage and to prove that the true value of the coins was that assigned to them by the ruler of the country.

Nevertheless, in defiance of all official regulations and prohibitions and fixing of prices and threats of punishment, commercial practice has always insisted that what has to be considered in valuing coins is not their face value but their value as metal. The value

---

[11] See Luschin, *Allgemeine Münzkunde und Geldgeschichte des Mittelalters und der neureren Zeit* (Munich, 1904), p. 215; Babelon, *La théorie féodale de la monnaie (Extrait des mémoires de l'Académie des Inscriptions et Belles-Lettres*, vol. 38, Part I [Paris, 1908], p. 35).

of a coin has always been determined, not by the image and su-
perscription it bears nor by the proclamation of the mint and market
authorities, but by its metal content. Not every kind of money has
been accepted at sight, but only those kinds with a good reputation
for weight and fineness. In loan contracts, repayment in specific
kinds of money has been stipulated for, and in the case of a change
in the coinage, fulfillment in terms of metal required.[12] In spite of
all fiscal influences, the opinion gradually gained general acceptance, even among the jurists, that it was the metal value—the *bonitas
intrinseca* as they called it—that was to be considered when repaying
money debts.[13]

Debasement of the coinage was unable to force commercial practice to attribute to the new and lighter coins the same purchasing
power as the old and heavier coins.[14] The value of the coinage fell
in proportion to the diminution of its weight and quality. Even price
regulations took into account the diminished purchasing power of
money due to its debasement. Thus the Schöffen or assessors of
Schweidnitz in Silesia used to have the newly minted pfennigs
submitted to them, assess their value, and then in consultation with
the city council and elders fix the prices of commodities accordingly.
There has been handed down to us from thirteenth-century Vienna
a *forma institutionis que fit per civium arbitrium annuatim tempore quo
denarii renovantur pro rerum venalium qualibet emptione* in which the
prices of commodities and services are regulated in connection with
the introduction of a new coinage in the years 1460 to 1474. Similar
measures were taken on similar occasions in other cities.[15]

Wherever disorganization of the coinage had advanced so far that
the presence of a stamp on a piece of metal was no longer any help
in determining its actual content, commerce ceased entirely to rely
on the official monetary system and created its own system of measuring the precious metals. In large transactions, ingots and trade

---

[12] For important references, see Babelon, *op. cit.*, p. 35.
[13] See Seidler, "Die Schwankungen des Geldwertes und die juristische Lehre von
dem Inhalt der Geldschulden," *Jahrbücher für Nationalökonomie und Statistik* (1894),
3d. Series, vol. 7, p. 688.
[14] For earlier conditions in Russia, see Gelesnoff, *Grundzüge der Volkswirtschaftslehre*,
trans. into German by Altschul (Leipzig, 1918), p. 357.
[15] See Luschin, *op. cit.*, pp. 221 f.

tokens were used. Thus, the German merchants visiting the fair at
Geneva took ingots of refined gold with them and made their purchases with these, employing the weights used at the Paris market,
instead of using money. This was the origin of the Markenskudo or
scutus marcharum, which was nothing but the merchants' usual
term for 3.765 grams of refined gold. At the beginning of the fif-
teenth century, when the Geneva trade was gradually being transferred to Lyons, the gold mark had become such a customary unit
of account among the merchants that bills of exchange expressed
in terms of it were carried to and from the market. The old Venetian
lire di grossi had a similar origin.[16] In the giro banks that sprang up
in all big commercial centers at the beginning of the modern era we
see a further attempt to free the monetary system from the authorities' abuse of the privilege of minting. The clearinghouse business
of these banks was based either on coins of a specific fineness or on
ingots. This bank money was commodity money in its most perfect
form.

The nominalists assert that the monetary unit, in modern countries at any rate, is not a concrete commodity unit that can be defined
in suitable technical terms, but a nominal quantity of value about
which nothing can be said except that it is created by law. Without
touching upon the vague and nebulous nature of this phraseology,
which will not sustain a moment's criticism from the point of view
of the theory of value, let us simply ask: What, then, were the mark,
the franc, and the pound before 1914? Obviously, they were nothing
but certain weights of gold. Is it not mere quibbling to assert that
Germany had not a gold standard but a mark standard? According
to the letter of the law, Germany was on a gold standard, and the
mark was simply the unit of account, the designation of 1/2790 kg.
of refined gold. This is in no way affected by the fact that nobody
was bound in private dealings to accept gold ingots or foreign gold
coins, for the whole aim and intent of state intervention in the monetary sphere is simply to release individuals from the necessity of
testing the weight and fineness of the gold they receive, a task which
can only be undertaken by experts and which involves very elaborate
precautionary measures. The narrowness of the limits within which

---

[16] *Ibid.,* p. 155; Endemann, *Studien in der romanisch-kanonistischen Wirtschafts-und
Rechtslehre bis gegen Ende des 17. Jahrhunderts* (Berlin, 1874), vol. 1, pp. 180 ff.

the weight and fineness of the coins are legally allowed to vary at the time of minting, and the establishment of a further limit to the permissible loss by wear of those in circulation, are much better means of securing the integrity of the coinage than the use of scales and nitric acid on the part of all who have commercial dealings. Again, the right of free coinage, one of the basic principles of modern monetary law, is a protection in the opposite direction against the emergence of a difference in value between the coined and uncoined metal. In large-scale international trade, where differences that are negligible as far as single coins are concerned have a cumulative importance, coins are valued, not according to their number, but according to their weight; that is, they are treated not as coins but as pieces of metal. It is easy to see why this does not occur in domestic trade. Large payments within a country never involve the actual transfer of the amounts of money concerned, but merely the assignment of claims, which ultimately refer to the stock of precious metal of the central bank.

The role played by ingots in the gold reserves of the banks is a proof that the monetary standard consists in the precious metal, and not in the proclamation of the authorities.

Even for present-day coins, so far as they are not money substitutes, credit money, or fiat money, the statement is true that they are nothing but ingots whose weight and fineness are officially guaranteed.[17] The money of those modern countries where metal coins with no mint restrictions are used is commodity money just as much as that of ancient and medieval nations.

---

[17] Chevalier, *Cours d'économie politique, III., La monnaie* (Paris, 1850), pp. 21 ff; Goldschmidt, *Handbuch des Handelsrechts* (Erlangen, 1868), vol. 1, Part II, pp. 1073 ff.

CHAPTER 4

Money and the State

1

The Position of the State in the Market

The position of the state in the market differs in no way from that of any other parties to commercial transactions. Like these others, the state exchanges commodities and money on terms which are governed by the laws of price. It exercises its sovereign rights over its subjects to levy compulsory contributions from them; but in all other respects it adapts itself like everybody else to the commercial organization of society. As a buyer or seller the state has to conform to the conditions of the market. If it wishes to alter any of the exchange ratios established in the market, it can only do this through the market's own mechanism. As a rule it will be able to act more effectively than anyone else, thanks to the resources at its command outside the market. It is responsible for the most pronounced disturbances of the market because it is able to exercise the strongest influence on demand and supply. But it is nonetheless subject to the rules of the market and cannot set aside the laws of the pricing process. In an economic system based on private ownership of the means of production, no government regulation can alter the terms of exchange except by altering the factors that determine them.

Kings and republics have repeatedly refused to recognize this. Diocletian's edict *de pretiis rerum venalium,* the price regulations of the Middle Ages, and the maximum prices of the French Revolution are the most well-known examples of the failure of authoritative interference with the market. These attempts at intervention were not frustrated by the fact that they were valid only within the state boundaries and ignored elsewhere. It is a mistake to imagine that similar regulations would have led to the desired result even in an isolated state. It was the functional, not the geographical, limitations of the government that rendered them abortive. They could have achieved their aim only in a socialistic state with a centralized organization of production and distribution. In a state that leaves production and distribution to individual enterprise, such measures must necessarily fail of their effect.

The concept of money as a creature of law and the state is clearly untenable. It is not justified by a single phenomenon of the market. To ascribe to the state the power of dictating the laws of exchange, is to ignore the fundamental principles of money-using society.

2

The Legal Concept of Money

When both parties to an exchange fulfill their obligations immediately and surrender a commodity for ready cash, there is usually no motive for the judicial intervention of the state. But when the exchange is one of present goods against future goods it may happen that one party fails to fulfill his obligations although the other has carried out his share of the contract. Then the judiciary may be invoked. If the case is one of lending or purchase on credit, to name only the most important examples, the court has to decide how a debt contracted in terms of money can be liquidated. Its task thus becomes that of determining, in accordance with the intent of the contracting parties, what is to be understood by *money* in commercial transactions. From the legal point of view, money is not the common medium of exchange, but the common medium of payment or debt settlement. But money only becomes a medium of payment by virtue of being a medium of exchange. And it is only because it is a medium of exchange that the law also makes it the medium for fulfilling obligations not contracted in terms of money, but whose literal fulfillment is for some reason or other impossible.

The fact that the law regards money only as a means of canceling outstanding obligations has important consequences for the legal definition of money. What the law understands by money is in fact not the common medium of exchange but the legal medium of payment. It does not come within the scope of the legislator or jurist to define the economic concept of money.

In determining how monetary debts may be effectively paid off there is no reason for being too exclusive. It is customary in business to tender and accept in payment certain money substitutes instead of money itself. If the law refused to recognize the validity of money substitutes that are sanctioned by commercial usage, it would only open the door to all sorts of fraud and deceit. This would offend against the principle *malitiis non est indulgendum*. Besides this, the payment of small sums would, for technical reasons, hardly be possible without the use of token money. Even ascribing the power of debt settlement to banknotes does not injure creditors or other recipients in any way, so long as the notes are regarded by the businessman as equivalent to money.

But the state may ascribe the power of debt settlement to other objects as well. The law may declare anything it likes to be a medium of payment, and this ruling will be binding on all courts and on all those who enforce the decisions of the courts. But bestowing the property of legal tender on a thing does not suffice to make it money in the economic sense. Goods can become common media of exchange only through the practice of those who take part in commercial transactions; and it is the valuations of these persons alone that determine the exchange ratios of the market. Quite possibly, commerce may take into use those things to which the state has ascribed the power of payment; but it *need* not do so. It may, if it likes, reject them.

Three situations are possible when the state has declared an object to be a legal means of fulfilling an outstanding obligation. First, the legal means of payment may be identical with the medium of exchange that the contracting parties had in mind when entering into their agreement; or, if not identical, it may yet be of equal value with this medium at the time of payment. For example, the state may proclaim gold as a legal medium for settling obligations contracted in terms of gold, or, at a time when the relative values of gold and silver are as 1 to 15½, it may declare that liabilities in terms of gold may be settled by payment of 15½ times the quantity of silver. Such an arrangement is merely the legal formulation of the presumable intent of the agreement. It damages the interests of neither party. It is economically neutral.

The case is otherwise when the state proclaims as medium of payment something that has a higher or lower value than the contractual medium. The first possibility may be disregarded; but the second, of which numerous historical examples could be cited, is important. From the legal point of view, in which the fundamental principle is the protection of vested rights, such a procedure on the part of the state can never be justified, although it might sometimes be vindicated on social or fiscal grounds. But it always means, not the fulfillment of obligations, but their complete or partial cancellation. When notes that are appraised commercially at only half their face value are proclaimed legal tender, this amounts fundamentally to the same thing as granting debtors legal relief from half of their liabilities.

State declarations of legal tender affect only those monetary obligations that have already been contracted. But commerce is free to choose between retaining its old medium of exchange or creating a new one for itself, and when it adopts a new medium, so far as the legal power of the contracting parties reaches, it will attempt to make it into a standard of deferred payments also, in order to deprive of its validity, at least for the future, the standard to which the state has ascribed complete powers of debt settlement. When, during the last decade of the nineteenth century, the bimetallist party in Germany gained so much power that the possibility of experiment with its inflationist proposals had to be reckoned with, gold clauses began to make their appearance in long-term contracts. The recent period of currency depreciation has had a similar effect. If the state does not wish to render all credit transactions impossible, it must recognize such devices as these and instruct the courts to acknowledge them. And, similarly, when the state itself enters into ordinary business dealings, when it buys or sells, guarantees loans or borrows, makes payments or receives them, it must recognize the common business medium of exchange as money. The legal standard, the particular group of things that are endued with the property of unlimited legal tender, is in fact valid only for the settlement of existing debts, unless business usage itself adopts it as a general medium of exchange.

3

The Influence of the State on the Monetary System

State activity in the monetary sphere was originally restricted to the manufacture of coins. To supply ingots of the greatest possible degree of similarity in appearance, weight, and fineness, and provide them with a stamp that was not too easy to imitate and that could be recognized by everybody as the sign of the state coinage, was and still is the premier task of state monetary activity. Beginning with this, the influence of the state in the monetary sphere has gradually extended.

Progress in monetary technique has been slow. At first, the impression on a coin was merely a proof of the genuineness of its material, including its degree of fineness, while the weight had to be separately checked at each payment. (In the present state of knowledge this cannot be stated dogmatically; and in any case the development is not likely to have followed the same lines everywhere.) Later, different kinds of coins were distinguished, all the separate coins of any particular kind being regarded as interchangeable. The next step after the innovation of classified money was the development of the parallel standard. This consisted in the juxtaposition of two monetary systems, one based on gold commodity money, and one on silver. The coins belonging to each separate system constituted a self-contained group. Their weights bore a definite relation to each other, and the state gave them a legal relation also, in the same proportion, by sanctioning the commercial practice which had gradually been established of regarding different coins of the same metal as interchangeable. This stage was reached without further state influence. All that the state had done till then in the monetary sphere was to provide the coins for commercial use. As controller of the mint, it supplied in handy form pieces of metal of specific weight and fineness, stamped in such a way that everybody could recognize without difficulty what their metallic content was and whence they originated. As legislator, the state attributed legal tender to these coins—the significance of this has just been expounded—and as judge it applied this legal provision. But the matter did not end at this stage. For about the last two hundred years the influence of the state on the monetary system has been greater than this. One thing, however, must be made clear; even now the state has not the power of directly making anything into money, that is to say into a common medium of exchange. Even nowadays, it is only the practice of the individuals who take part in business that can make a commodity into a medium of exchange. But the state's influence on commercial usage, both potential and actual, has increased. It has increased, first, because the state's own importance as an economic agent has increased; because it occupies a greater place as buyer and seller, as payer of wages and levier of taxes, than in past centuries. In this there is nothing that is remarkable or that needs special emphasis. It is obvious that the influence of an economic agent on the choice of a monetary commodity will be the greater in proportion to its share in the dealings of the market; and there is no reason to suppose that there should be any difference in the case of the one particular economic agent, the state.

But, besides this, the state exercises a special influence on the choice of the monetary commodity, which is due not to its commercial position nor to its authority as legislator and judge, but to its official standing as controller of the mint and to its power to change the character of the money substitutes in circulation.

The influence of the state on the monetary system is usually that ascribed to its legislative and judicial authority. It is assumed that the law, which can authoritatively alter the tenor of existing debt relations and force new contracts of indebtedness in a particular direction, enables the state to exercise a deciding influence in the choice of the commercial medium of exchange.

Nowadays the most extreme form of this argument is to be found in Knapp's *State Theory of Money;*[1] but very few German writers are

---

[1] Knapp, *Staatliche Theorie des Geldes* (3d. ed., 1921); trans. into English by H. M. Lucas and J. Bonar as *The State Theory of Money* (London, 1924).

completely free from it. Helfferich may be mentioned as an example. It is true that this writer declares, with regard to the origin of money, that it is perhaps doubtful whether it was not the function of common medium of exchange alone that sufficed to make a thing money and to make money the standard of deferred payments of every kind. Nevertheless, he constantly regards it as quite beyond any sort of doubt that for our present economic organization certain kinds of money in some countries, and the whole monetary system in other countries, are money, and function as a medium of exchange, only because compulsory payments and obligations contracted in terms of money must or may be fulfilled in terms of these particular objects.[2]

It would be difficult to agree with views of this nature. They fail to recognize the meaning of state intervention in the monetary sphere. By declaring an object to be fitted in the juristic sense for the liquidation of liabilities expressed in terms of money, the state cannot influence the choice of a medium of exchange, which belongs to those engaged in business. History shows that those states that have wanted their subjects to accept a new monetary system have regularly chosen other means than this of achieving their ends.

The establishment of a legal ratio for the discharge of obligations incurred under the regime of the superseded kind of money constitutes a merely secondary measure which is significant only in connection with the change of standard which is achieved by other means. The provision that taxes are in future to be paid in the new kind of money, and that other liabilities imposed in terms of money will be fulfilled only in the new money, is a *consequence* of the transition to the new standard. It proves effective only when the new kind of money has become a common medium of exchange in commerce generally. A monetary policy can never be carried out merely by legislative means, by an alteration in the legal definitions of the content of contracts of indebtedness and of the system of public expenditure; it must be based on the executive authority of the state as controller of the mint and as issuer of claims to money, payable on demand, that can take the place of money in commerce. The necessary measures must not merely be passively recorded in the

---

[2] See Helfferich, *Das Geld*, 6th ed. (Leipzig, 1923), p. 294; English trans., *Money* (London, 1927), p. 312.

protocols of legislative assemblies and official gazettes, but—often at great financial sacrifice—must be actually put into operation.

A country that wishes to persuade its subjects to go over from one precious-metal standard to another cannot rest content with expressing this aspiration in appropriate provisions of the civil and fiscal law. It must make the new money take the commercial place of the old. Exactly the same is true of the transition from a credit-money or fiat-money standard to commodity money. No statesman faced with the task of such a change has ever had even a momentary doubt about the matter. It is not the enactment of a legal ratio and the order that taxes are to be paid in the new money that are the decisive steps, but the provision of the necessary quantity of the new money and the withdrawal of the old.

This may be confirmed by a few historical examples. First, the impossibility of modifying the monetary system merely by the exercise of authority may be illustrated by the ill success of bimetallistic legislation. This was once thought to offer a simple solution of a big problem. For thousands of years, gold and silver had been employed side by side as commodity money; but the continuance of this practice had constantly grown more burdensome, for the parallel standard, or simultaneous employment as currency of two kinds of commodity, has many disadvantages. Since no spontaneous assistance was to be expected from the individuals engaged in business, the state decided to intervene in the hope of cutting the Gordian knot. Just as it had previously removed certain obvious difficulties by declaring that debts contracted in terms of thalers might be discharged by payment of twice as many half-thalers or four times as many quarter-thalers, so it now proceeded to establish a fixed ratio between the two different precious metals. Debts payable in silver, for instance, could be discharged by payment of $1:15\frac{1}{2}$ times the same weight of gold. It was thought that this had solved the problem, while in fact the difficulties that it involved had not even been suspected; as events were to prove. All the results followed that are attributed by Gresham's law to the legislative equating of coins of unequal value. In all debt settlements and similar payments, only that money was used which the law rated more highly than the market. When the law had happened to hit upon the existing market ratio as its par, then this effect was delayed a little until the next movement in the prices of the precious metals. But it was bound to occur as soon as a difference arose between the legislative and the market ratios of the two kinds of money. The parallel standard was thus turned, not into a double standard, as the legislators had intended, but into an alternative standard.

The primary result of this was a decision, for a little while at least, between the two precious metals. Not that this was what the state had intended. On the contrary, the state had no thought whatever of deciding in favor of the use of one or the other metal; it had hoped to secure the circulation of both. But the official regulation, which in declaring the reciprocal substitutability of gold and silver money overestimated the market ratio of the one in terms of the other, merely succeeded in differentiating the utility of the two for monetary purposes. The consequence was the increased employment of one of the metals and the disappearance of the other. The legislative and judicial intervention of the state had completely failed. It had been demonstrated, in striking fashion, that the state alone could not make a commodity into a common medium of exchange, that is, into money, but that this could be done only by the common action of all the individuals engaged in business.

But what the state fails to achieve through legislative means may be to a certain degree within its power as controller of the mint. It was in the latter capacity that the state intervened when the alternative standard was replaced by permanent monometallism. This happened in various ways. The transition was quite simple and easy when the action of the state consisted in preventing a return to the temporarily undervalued metal in one of the alternating monometallic periods by rescinding the right of free coinage. The matter was even simpler in those countries where one or the other metal had gained the upper hand before the state had reached the stage necessary for the modern type of regulation, so that all that remained for the law to do was to sanction a situation that was already established.

The problem was much more difficult when the state attempted to persuade businessmen to abandon the metal that was being used and adopt the other. In this case, the state had to manufacture the necessary quantity of the new metal, exchange it for the old currency, and either turn the metal thus withdrawn from circulation into token coinage or sell it for nonmonetary use or for recoinage abroad. The reform of the German monetary system after the foundation of the Reich in 1871 may be regarded as a perfect example of the transition from one metallic commodity standard to another. The difficulties that this involved, and that were overcome by the help of the French war indemnity, are well known. They were involved in the performance of two tasks—the provision of the gold and the disposal of the silver. This and nothing else was the essence of the problem that had to be solved when the decision was taken to change the standard. The Reich completed the transition to gold by giving gold and claims to gold in exchange for the silver money and claims to silver money held by its citizens. The corresponding alterations in the law were mere accompaniments of the change.[3]

The change of standard occurred in just the same way in Austria-Hungary, Russia, and the other countries that reformed their monetary systems in the succeeding years. Here also the problem was merely that of providing the requisite quantities of gold and setting them in circulation among those engaged in business in place of the media previously employed. This process was extraordinarily facilitated and, what was even more to the point, the amount of gold necessary for the changeover was considerably decreased, by the device of permitting the coins constituting the old fiat money or credit money to remain wholly or partly in circulation, while fundamentally changing their economic character by transforming them into claims that were always convertible into the new kind of money. This gave a different outward appearance to the transaction, but it remained in essence the same. It is scarcely open to question that the steps taken by those countries that adopted this kind of monetary policy consisted essentially in the provision of quantities of metal.

The exaggeration of the importance in monetary policy of the power at the disposal of the state in its legislative capacity can only

---

[3] See Helfferich, *Die Reform des deutschen Geldwesens nach der Gründung des Reiches* (Leipzig, 1898), vol. 1, pp. 307 ff; Lotz, *Geschichte und Kritik des deutschen Bankgesetzes vom 14. März 1875* (Leipzig, 1888), pp. 137 ff.

be attributed to superficial observation of the processes involved in the transition from commodity money to credit money. This transition has normally been achieved by means of a state declaration that inconvertible claims to money were as good means of payment as money itself. As a rule, it has not been the object of such a declaration to carry out a change of standard and substitute credit money for commodity money. In the great majority of cases, the state has taken such measures merely with certain fiscal ends in view. It has aimed to increase its own resources by the creation of credit money. In the pursuit of such a plan as this, the diminution of the money's purchasing power could hardly seem desirable. And yet it has always been this depreciation in value which, through the coming into play of Gresham's law, has caused the change of monetary standard. It would be quite out of harmony with the facts to assert that cash payments had ever been stopped; that is, that the permanent convertibility of the notes had been suspended, with the intention of effecting a transition to a credit standard. This result has always come to pass against the will of the state, not in accordance with it.

Business usage alone can transform a commodity into a common medium of exchange. It is not the state, but the common practice of all those who have dealings in the market, that creates money. It follows that state regulation attributing general power of debt liquidation to a commodity is unable of itself to make that commodity into money. If the state creates credit money—and this is naturally true in a still greater degree of fiat money—it can do so only by taking things that are already in circulation as money substitutes (that is, as perfectly secure and immediately convertible claims to money) and isolating them for purposes of valuation by depriving them of their essential characteristic of permanent convertibility. Commerce would always protect itself against any other method of introducing a government credit currency. The attempt to put credit money into circulation has never been successful, except when the coins or notes in question have already been in circulation as money substitutes.[4]

This is the limit of the constantly overestimated influence of the state on the monetary system. What the state can do in certain

---

[4] See Subercaseaux, *Essai sur la nature du papier monnaie* (Paris, 1909), pp. 5 ff.

circumstances, by means of its position as controller of the mint, by means of its power of altering the character of money substitutes and depriving them of their standing as claims to money that are payable on demand, and above all by means of those financial resources which permit it to bear the cost of a change of currency, is to persuade commerce to abandon one sort of money and adopt another. That is all.

CHAPTER 5

Money as an Economic Good

1

Money Neither a Production Good nor a Consumption Good

It is usual to divide economic goods into the two classes of those which satisfy human needs directly and those which only satisfy them indirectly: that is, consumption goods, or goods of the first order; and production goods, or goods of higher orders.[1] The attempt to include money in either of these groups meets with insuperable difficulties. It is unnecessary to demonstrate that money is not a consumption good. It seems equally incorrect to call it a production good.

Of course, if we regard the twofold division of economic goods as exhaustive we shall have to rest content with putting money in one group or the other. This has been the position of most economists; and since it has seemed altogether impossible to call money a consumption good, there has been no alternative but to call it a production good.

This apparently arbitrary procedure has usually been given only a very cursory vindication. Roscher, for example, thought it suffi-

---

[1] See Menger, *Grundsätze der Volkswirtschaftslehre*, 2d ed. (Vienna, 1923), pp. 20 ff.; Wieser, *Über den Ursprung und die Hauptgesetze des wirtschaftlichen Wertes* (Vienna, 1884), pp. 42 ff.

cient to mention that money is "the chief instrument of every transfer" (*vornehmstes Werkzeug jeden Verkehrs*).[2]

In opposition to Roscher, Knies made room for money in the classification of goods by replacing the twofold division into production
goods and consumption goods by a threefold division into means
of production, objects of consumption, and media of exchange.[3] His
arguments on this point, which are unfortunately scanty, have
hardly attracted any serious attention and have been often misunderstood. Thus Helfferich attempts to confute Knies's proposition,
that a sale-and-purchase transaction is not in itself an act of production but an act of (interpersonal) transfer, by asserting that the
same sort of objection might be made to the inclusion of means of
transport among instruments of production on the grounds that
transport is not in itself an act of production but an act of (interlocal)
transfer and that the nature of goods is no more altered by transport
than by a change of ownership.[4]

Obviously, it is the ambiguity of the German word *Verkehr* that
has obscured the deeper issues here involved. On the one hand,
Verkehr bears a meaning that may be roughly translated by the word
commerce; that is, the exchange of goods and services on the part
of individuals. But it also means the transfer through space of persons, goods, and information. These two groups of things denoted
by the German word *Verkehr* have nothing in common but their
name. It is therefore impossible to countenance the suggestion of
a relationship between the two meanings of the word that is
involved in the practice of speaking of "*Verkehr* in the broader
sense," by which is meant the transfer of goods from one person's possession to that of another, and "*Verkehr* in the narrower
sense," by which is meant the transfer of goods from one point
in space to another.[5] Even popular usage recognizes two distinct
meanings here, not a narrower and a broader version of the
same meaning.

---

[2] Roscher, *System der Volkswirtschaft,* ed. Pöhlmann, 24th ed. (Stuttgart, 1906), vol. 1, p. 123.
[3] See Knies, *Geld und Kredit,* 2d ed. (Berlin, 1885), vol. 1, pp. 20 ff.
[4] See Helfferich, *Das Geld,* 6th ed. (Leipzig, 1923), pp. 264 f.; *Money* (London, 1924), p. 280.
[5] E.g. Philippovich, *Grundriss der politischen Ökonomie* 1st–3d eds. (Tübingen, 1907), vol. 2; Wagner, *Theoretische Sozialökonomik* (Leipzig, 1909), vol. 1, Part 2 p. 1.

The common nomenclature of the two meanings, as also their incidental confusion, may well be attributable to the fact that exchange transactions often, but by no means always, go hand in hand with acts of transport, through space and vice versa.[6] But obviously this is no reason why science should impute an intrinsic similarity to these essentially different processes.

It should never have been called in question that the transportation of persons, goods, and information is to be reckoned part of production, so far as it does not constitute an act of consumption, as do pleasure trips for example. All the same, two things have hindered recognition of this fact. The first is the widespread misconception of the nature of production. There is a naive view of production that regards it as the bringing into being of matter that did not previously exist, as creation in the true sense of the word. From this it is easy to derive a contrast between the creative work of production and the mere transportation of goods. This way of regarding the matter is entirely inadequate. In fact, the role played by man in production always consists solely in combining his personal forces with the forces of Nature in such a way that the cooperation leads to some particular desired arrangement of material. No human act of production amounts to more than altering the position of things in space and leaving the rest to Nature.[7] This disposes of one of the objections to regarding transportation as a productive process.

The second objection arises from insufficient insight into the nature of goods. It is often overlooked that, among other natural qualities, the position of a thing in space has important bearings on its capacity for satisfying human wants. Things that are of perfectly identical technological composition must yet be regarded as specimens of different kinds of goods if they are not in the same place and in the same state of readiness for consumption or further production. Till now the position of a good

---

[6] The older meaning, at least the only earlier meaning in literature, appears to have been that relating to the sale of goods. It is remarkable that even Grimm's *Dictionary*, vol. 12, published in 1891, contains no mention of the meaning relating to transportation.

[7] See J. S. Mill, *Principles of Political Economy* (London, 1867), p. 16; Böhm-Bawerk, *Kapital und Kapitalzins*, pp. 10 ff.

in space has been recognized only as a factor determining its economic or noneconomic nature. It is hardly possible to ignore the fact that drinking water in the desert and drinking water in a well-watered mountain district, despite their chemical and physical similarity and their equal thirst-quenching properties, have nevertheless a totally different significance for the satisfaction of human wants. The only water that can quench the thirst of the traveler in the desert is the water that is on the spot, ready for consumption.

Within the group of economic goods itself, however, the factor of situation has been taken into consideration only for goods of certain kinds—those whose position has been fixed, whether by man or nature; and even among these, attention has seldom been given to any but the most outstanding example, land. As far as movable goods are concerned, the factor of situation has been treated as negligible.

This attitude is in consonance with commercial technology. The microscope fails to reveal any difference between two lots of beet sugar, of which one is warehoused in Prague and the other in London. But for the purposes of economics it is better to regard the two lots of sugar as goods of different kinds. Strictly speaking, only those goods should be called goods of the first order which are already where they can immediately be consumed. All other economic goods, even if they are ready for consumption in the technological sense, must be regarded as goods of higher orders which can be transmuted into goods of the first order only by combination with the complementary good, "means of transport." Regarded in this light, means of transport are obviously production goods. "Production," says Wieser, "is the utilization of the more advantageous among remote conditions of welfare."[8] There is nothing to prevent us from interpreting the word *remote* in its literal sense for once, and not just figuratively.

We have seen that transfer through space is one sort of production; and means of transport, therefore, so far as they are not consumption goods such as pleasure yachts and the like, must be included among production goods. Is this true of money as well?

[8] Wieser, *Über den Ursprung und die Hauptgesetze des wirtschaftlichen Wertes*, p. 47. See also Böhm-Bawerk, *op. cit.*, pp. 131 f.; Clark, *The Distribution of Wealth* (New York, 1908), p. 11.

Are the economic services that money renders comparable with those rendered by means of transport? Not in the least. Production is quite possible without money. There is no need for money either in the isolated household or in the socialized community. Nowhere can we discover a good of the first order of which we could say that the use of money was a necessary condition of its production.

It is true that the majority of economists reckon money among production goods. Nevertheless, arguments from authority are invalid; the proof of a theory is in its reasoning, not in its sponsorship; and with all due respect for the masters, it must be said that they have not justified their position very thoroughly in this matter. This is most remarkable in Böhm-Bawerk. As has been said, Knies recommends the substitution of a threefold classification of economic goods into objects of consumption, means of production, and media of exchange, for the customary twofold division into consumption goods and production goods. In general, Böhm-Bawerk treats Knies with the greatest respect and, whenever he feels obliged to differ from him, criticizes his arguments most carefully. But in the present case he simply disregards them. He unhesitatingly includes money in his concept of social capital, and incidentally specifies it as a product destined to assist further production. He refers briefly to the objection that money is an instrument, not of production, but of exchange; but instead of answering this objection, he embarks on an extended criticism of those doctrines that treat stocks of good in the hands of producers and middlemen as goods ready for consumption instead of as intermediate products.

Böhm-Bawerk's argument proves conclusively that production is not completed until the goods have been brought to the place where they are wanted, and that it is illegitimate to speak of goods being ready for consumption until the final process of transport is completed. But it contributes nothing to our present discussion; for the chain of reasoning gives way just at the critical link. After having proved that the horse and wagon with which the farmer brings home his corn and wood must be reckoned as means of production and as capital, Böhm-Bawerk adds that "logically all the objects and apparatus of 'bringing home' in the broader economic sense, the things that have to be transported, the roads, railways, and ships, and the commercial tool *money*, must be included in the concept of capital."[9]

This is the same jump that Roscher makes. It leaves out of consideration the difference between transport, which consists in an alteration of the utility of things, and exchange, which constitutes a separate economic category altogether. It is illegitimate to compare the part played by money in production with that played by ships and railways. Money is obviously not a "commercial tool" in the same sense as account books, exchange lists, the stock exchange, or the credit system.

Böhm-Bawerk's argument in its turn has not remained uncontradicted. Jacoby objects that while it treats money and the stocks of commodities in the hands of producers and middlemen as social capital, it nevertheless maintains the view that social capital is a pure economic category and independent of all legal definitions, although money and the "commodity" aspect of consumption goods are peculiar to a "commercial" type of economic organization.[10]

The invalidity of this criticism, so far as it is an objection to regarding commodities as production goods, is implied by what has been said above. There is no doubt that Böhm-Bawerk is in the right here, and not his critic. It is otherwise with the second point, the question of the inclusion of money. Admittedly, Jacoby's own discussion of the capital concept is not beyond criticism, and Böhm-Bawerk's refusal to accept it is probably justified.[11] But that does not concern us at present. We are only concerned with the problem of the concept of goods. On this point as well Böhm-Bawerk disagrees with Jacoby. In the third edition of volume two of his masterpiece, *Capital and Interest*, he argues that even a complex socialistic organization could hardly do without undifferentiated orders or certificates of some sort, "like money," which refer to the product awaiting distribution.[12] This particular argument of his was not directly aimed

---

[9] Böhm-Bawerk, *op. cit.*, Part II pp. 131 ff. See also, on the historical aspect, Jacoby, *Der Streit um den Kapitalsbegriff* (Jena, 1908), pp. 90 ff; Spiethoff, "Die Lehre vom Kapital," *Schmoller-Festschrift Die Entwicklung der deutschen Volkswirtschaftslehre im 19. Jahrhundert* (Leipzig, 1908), vol. 4, p. 26.

[10] See Jacoby, *op. cit.*, pp. 59 f.

[11] See Böhm-Bawerk, *op. cit.*, p. 125 n.

[12] *Ibid.*, p. 132 n.

at our present problem. Nevertheless, it is desirable to inquire whether the opinion expressed in it does not contain something that may be useful for our purpose as well.

Every sort of economic organization needs not only a mechanism for production but also a mechanism for distributing what is produced. It will scarcely be questioned that the distribution of goods among individual consumers constitutes a part of production, and that in consequence we should include among the means of production not only the physical instruments of commerce such as stock exchanges, account books, documents, and the like, but also everything that serves to maintain the legal system which is the foundation of commerce, as, for example, fences, railings, walls, locks, safes, the paraphernalia of the law courts, and the equipment of the organs of government entrusted with the protection of property. In a socialist state, this category might include among other things Böhm-Bawerk's "undifferentiated certificates" (to which, however, we cannot allow the description "like money"; for since money is not a certificate, it will not do to say of a certificate that it is like money. Money is always an economic good, and to say of a claim, which is what a certificate is, that it is like money, is only to drop back into the old practice of regarding rights and business connections as goods. Here we can invoke Böhm-Bawerk's own authority against himself).[13]

What prevents us nevertheless from reckoning money among these "distribution goods" and so among production goods (and incidentally the same objection applies to its inclusion among consumption goods) is the following consideration. The loss of a consumption good or production good results in a loss of human satisfaction; it makes mankind poorer. The gain of such a good results in an improvement of the human economic position; it makes mankind richer. The same cannot be said of the loss or gain of money. Both changes in the available quantity of production goods or consumption goods and changes in the available quantity of money involve changes in values; but whereas the changes in the value of the production goods and consumption goods do not mitigate the loss or reduce the gain of satisfaction resulting from the

---

[13] Böhm-Bawerk, *Rechte und Verhältnisse*, pp. 36 ff.

changes in their quantity, the changes in the value of money are accommodated in such a way to the demand for it that, despite increases or decreases in its quantity, the economic position of mankind remains the same. An increase in the quantity of money can no more increase the welfare of the members of a community, than a diminution of it can decrease their welfare. Regarded from this point of view, those goods that are employed as money are indeed what Adam Smith called them, "dead stock, which . . . produces nothing."[14]

We have shown that, under certain conditions, indirect exchange is a necessary phenomenon of the market. The circumstance that goods are desired and acquired in exchange not for their own sakes but only in order to be disposed of in further exchange can never disappear from our type of market dealing, because the conditions that make it inevitable are present in the overwhelming majority of all exchange transactions. Now the economic development of indirect exchange leads to the employment of a common medium of exchange, to the establishment and elaboration of the institution of money. Money, in fact, is indispensable in our economic order. But as an economic good it is not a physical component of the social distributive apparatus in the way that account books, prisons, or firearms are. No part of the total result of production is dependent on the collaboration of money, even though the use of money may be one of the fundamental principles on which the economic order is based.

Production goods derive their value from that of their products. Not so money; for no increase in the welfare of the members of a society can result from the availability of an additional quantity of money. The laws which govern the value of money are different from those which govern the value of production goods and from those which govern the value of consumption goods. All that these have in common is their general underlying principle, the fundamental economic law of value. This is a complete justification of the suggestion put forward by Knies that economic goods should be divided into means of production, objects of consumption, and media of exchange; for, after all, the primary object of economic terminology is to facilitate investigation into the theory of value.

---

[14] Smith, *The Wealth of Nations*, Cannan's ed. (London, 1930).

2

Money as Part of Private Capital

We have not undertaken this investigation into the relationship between money and production goods merely for its terminological interest. What is of importance for its own sake is not our ultimate conclusion, but the incidental light shed by our argument upon those peculiarities of money that distinguish it from other economic goods. These special characteristics of the common medium of exchange will receive closer attention when we turn to consider the laws that regulate the value of money and its variations.

But the result of our reasoning, too, the conclusion that money is not a production good, is not entirely without significance. It will help us to answer the question whether money is capital or not. This question in its turn is not an end in itself, but it provides a check upon the answer to a further problem concerning the relations between the equilibrium rate of interest and the money rate of interest, which will be dealt with in the third part of this book. If each conclusion confirms the other, then we may assume with a considerable degree of assurance that our arguments have not led us into error.

The first grave difficulty in the way of any investigation into the relation between money and capital arises from the difference of opinion that exists about the definition of the concept of capital. The views of scholars on the definition of capital are more divergent than their views on any other point of economics. None of the many definitions that have been suggested has secured general recognition; nowadays, in fact, the controversy about the theory of capital rages more fiercely than ever. If from among the large number of conflicting concepts we select that of Böhm-Bawerk to guide us in our investigation into the relation of money to capital, we could justify our procedure merely by reference to the fact that Böhm-Bawerk is the best guide for any serious attempt to study the problem of interest, even if such a study leads eventually (and by no means entirely without indebtedness to the labor that Böhm-Bawerk bestowed on this problem) to conclusions that differ widely from those which he himself arrived at. Furthermore, all those weighty arguments with which Böhm-Bawerk established his concept and defended it against his critics support such a choice. But quite apart from these, a reason that appears to be quite decisive is provided by the fact that no other concept of capital has been developed with equal clarity.[15] This last point is particularly important. It is not the object of the present discussion to arrive at any kind of conclusion respecting terminology or to provide any criticism of concepts, but merely to shed some light on one or two points that are of importance for the problem of the relations between the equilibrium and the money rates of interest. Hence it is less important for us to classify things correctly than to avoid vague ideas about their nature. Various opinions may be held as to whether money should be included in the concept of capital or not. The delimitation of concepts of this nature is merely a question of expediency, in connection with which it is quite easy for differences of opinion to arise. But the economic function of money is a matter about which it should be possible to arrive at perfect agreement.

Of the two concepts of capital that Böhm-Bawerk distinguishes, following the traditional economic terminology, that of what is called private or acquisitive capital is both the older and the wider. This was the original root idea from which the narrower concept of social or productive capital was afterward separated. It is therefore logical to begin our investigation by inquiring into the connection between private capital and money.

Böhm-Bawerk defines private capital as the aggregate of the products that serve as a means to the acquisition of goods.[16] It has never been questioned that money must be included in this category. In fact, the development of the scientific concept of capital starts from the notion of an interest-bearing sum of money. This concept of capital has been broadened little by little until at last it has taken the form which it bears in modern scientific discussion, on the whole in approximate coincidence with popular usage.

The gradual evolution of the concept of capital has meant at the

---

[15] This is true even bearing in mind the discussions of Menger and Clark. But in any case, an investigation, both of this matter and of the problems dealt with in part 3, chap. 19, which started from Menger's or Clark's capital concept would lead eventually to the same result as one based on Böhm-Bawerk's definition.

[16] See Böhm-Bawerk, *Kapital und Kapitalzins*, pp. 54 f.

same time an increasing understanding of the function of money as capital. Early in history the lay mind discovered an explanation of the fact that money on loan bears interest—that money, in fact, "works." But such an explanation as this could not long satisfy scientific requirements. Science therefore countered it with the fact that money itself is barren. Even in ancient times general recognition must have been accorded to the view which later in the shape of the maxim *pecunia pecunium parere non potest* was to be the basis of all discussion of the problem of interest for hundreds and even thousands of years, and Aristotle undoubtedly did not state it in the famous passage in his *Politics* as a new doctrine but as a generally accepted commonplace.[17] Despite its obviousness, this perception of the physical unfruitfulness of money was a necessary step on the way to full realization of the problem of capital and interest. If sums of money on loan do bear "fruit," and it is not possible to explain this phenomenon by the physical productivity of the money, then other explanations must be sought.

The next step toward an explanation was provided by the observation that after a loan is made the borrower as a rule exchanges the money for other economic goods, and that those owners of money who wish to obtain a profit from their money without lending it do the same. This was the starting point for the extension of the concept of capital referred to above, and for the development of the problem of the money rate of interest into the problem of the "natural" rate of interest.

It is true that centuries passed before these further steps were accomplished. At first there was a complete halt in the development of the theory of capital. Further progress was in fact not desired; what was already attained sufficed perfectly; for the aim of science then was not to explain reality but to vindicate ideals. And public opinion disapproved of the taking of interest. Even later, when the taking of interest was recognized in Greek and Roman law, it was still not considered respectable, and all the writers of classical times strove to outdo one another in condemning it. When the church adopted this proscription of interest, and attempted to support its

---

[17] I, 3, 23.

attitude by quotations from the Bible, it cut the ground away from beneath all unauthorized attempts to deal with the matter. Every theorist who turned his attention to the problem was already convinced that the taking of interest was harmful, unnatural, and uncharitable, and found his principal task in the search for new objections to it. It was not for him to explain how interest came to exist, but to sustain the thesis that it was reprehensible. In such circumstances it was easy for the doctrine of the sterility of money to be taken over uncritically by one writer from another as an extraordinarily powerful argument against the payment of interest, and thus, not for the sake of its content but for the sake of the conclusion it supported, to become an obstacle in the way of the development of interest theory. It became a help and no longer a hindrance to this development, when a move was made toward the construction of a new theory of capital after the downfall of the old canonist theory of interest. Its first effect, then, was to necessitate an extension of the concept of capital, and consequently of the problem of interest. In popular usage and in the terminology of scholars, capital was no longer "sums of money on loan" but "accumulated stocks of goods."[18]

The doctrine of the unfruitfulness of money has another significance for our problem. It sheds light on the position of money within the class of things constituting private capital. Why do we include money in capital? Why is interest paid for sums of money on loan? How is it possible to use sums of money, even without lending them, so that they yield an income? There can be no doubt about the answers to these questions. Money is an acquisitive instrument only when it is exchanged for some other economic good. In this respect money may be compared with those consumption goods that form part of private capital only because they are not consumed by their owners themselves but are used for the acquisition of other goods or services by means of exchange. Money is no more acquisitive capital than these consumption goods are; the real acquisitive capital consists in the goods for which the money or the consumption goods are exchanged. Money that is lying "idle," that is, money that is not exchanged for other goods, is not a part of capital; it

---

[18] See Böhm-Bawerk, *Kapital und Kapitalzins*, Part I, pp. 16 ff., Part II, pp. 23 ff.

produces no fruit. Money is part of the private capital of an individual only if and so far as it constitutes a means by which the individual in question can obtain other capital goods.

3

Money Not a Part of Social Capital

By social or productive capital Böhm-Bawerk means the aggregate of the products intended for employment in further production.[19] If we accept the views expounded above, according to which money cannot be included among productive goods, then neither can it be included in social capital. It is true that Böhm-Bawerk includes it in social capital, as the majority of the economists that preceded him had done. This attitude follows logically from regarding money as a productive good; this is its only justification, and in endeavoring to show that money is not a productive good we have implied how baseless a justification it is.

In any case, perhaps we may suggest that those writers who include money among productive goods and consequently among capital goods are not very consistent. They usually reckon money as a part of social capital in that division of their systems where they deal with the concepts of money and capital, but certain obvious further conclusions are not drawn from this. On the contrary, where the doctrine of the nature of money as capital should logically be applied it appears to have been suddenly forgotten. In reviewing the determinants of the rate of interest, writers emphasize over and over again that it is not the greater or smaller quantity of money that is of importance, but the greater or smaller quantity of other economic goods. To reconcile this assertion, which is indubitably a correct summary of the matter, with the other assertion that money is a productive good, is simply impossible.

---

[19] *Ibid.*, Part II pp. 54 f., 130 ff.

CHAPTER 6

The Enemies of Money

1

Money in the Socialist Community

It has been shown that under certain conditions, which occur the more frequently as division of labor and the differentiation of wants are extended, indirect exchange becomes inevitable; and that the evolution of indirect exchange gradually leads to the employment of a few particular commodities, or even one commodity only, as a common medium of exchange. When there is no exchange of any sort, and hence no indirect exchange, the use of media of exchange naturally remains unknown. This was the situation when the isolated household was the typical economic unit, and this, according to socialist aspirations, is what it will be again one day in that purely socialistic order where production and distribution are to be systematically regulated by a central body. This vision of the future socialistic system has not been described in detail by its prophets; and, in fact, it is not the same vision which they all see. There are some among them who allow a certain scope for exchange of economic goods and services, and so far as this is the case the continued use of money remains possible.

On the other hand, the certificates or orders that the organized society would distribute to its members cannot be regarded as money. Supposing that a receipt was given, say, to each laborer for each hour's labor, and that the social income, so far as it was not employed for the satisfaction of collective needs or the support of those not able to work, was distributed in proportion to the number of receipts in the possession of each individual, so that each receipt represented a claim to an aliquot part of the total amount of goods to be distributed. Then the significance of any particular receipt as a means of satisfying the wants of an individual, in other words its value, would vary in proportion to the size of the total dividend. If, with the same number of hours of labor, the income of the society in a given year was only half as big as in the previous year, then the value of each receipt would likewise be halved.

The case of money is different. A decrease of fifty percent in the real social income would certainly involve a reduction in the purchasing power of money. But this reduction in the value of money need not bear any direct relation to the decrease in the size of the income. It might accidentally happen that the purchasing power of money was exactly halved also; but it need not happen so. This difference is of fundamental importance.

In fact, the exchange value of money is determined in a totally different way from that of a certificate or warrant. Titles like these are not susceptible of an independent process of valuation at all. If it is certain that a warrant or order will always be honored on demand, then its value will be equal to that of the goods to which it refers. If this certainty is not absolute, the value of the warrant will be correspondingly less.

If we suppose that a system of exchange might be developed even in a socialist society—not merely the exchange of labor certificates but, say, the exchange of consumption goods between individuals—then we may conceive of a place for the function of money even within the framework of such a society. This money would not be so frequently and variously employed as in an economic order based on private ownership of the means of production, but its use would be governed by the same fundamental principles.

These considerations dictate the attitude toward money that must be assumed by any attempt to construct an imaginary social order, if self-contradiction is to be avoided. So long as such a scheme completely excludes the free exchange of goods and services, then it follows logically that it has no need for money; but so far as any sort of exchange at all is allowed, it seems that indirect exchange achieved by means of a common medium of exchange must be permitted also.

2

Money Cranks

Superficial critics of the capitalistic economic system are in the habit of directing their attacks principally against money. They are willing to permit the continuance of private ownership of the means of production and consequently, given the present stage of division of labor, of free exchange of goods also; and yet they want this exchange to be achieved without any medium, or at least without a *common* medium, or money. They obviously regard the use of money as harmful and hope to overcome all social evils by eliminating it. Their doctrine is derived from notions that have always been extraordinarily popular in lay circles during periods in which the use of money has been increasing.

All the processes of our economic life appear in a monetary guise; and those who do not see beneath the surface of things are only aware of monetary phenomena and remain unconscious of deeper relationships. Money is regarded as the cause of theft and murder, of deception and betrayal. Money is blamed when the prostitute sells her body and when the bribed judge perverts the law. It is money against which the moralist declaims when he wishes to oppose excessive materialism. Significantly enough avarice is called the love of money; and all evil is attributed to it.[1]

The confused and vague nature of such notions as these is obvious. It is not so clear whether it is thought that a return to direct exchange by itself will be able to overcome all the disadvantages of the use of money, or whether it is thought that other reforms will be necessary as well. The world makers and world improvers responsible for these notions feel no obligation to follow up their ideas

---

[1] On the history of such ideas, see Hildebrand, *Die Nationalökonomie der Gegenwart und Zunkunft* (Frankfurt, 1848), pp. 118 ff.; Roscher, *System der Volkswirtschaft*, ed. Pöhlmann, 24th ed. (Stuttgart, 1906), vol. 1, pp. 345 f.; Marx, *Das Kapital*, 7th ed. (Hamburg, 1914), vol. 1, pp. 95 f. n.

inexorably to their final consequences. They prefer to call a halt at the point where the difficulties of the problem are just beginning. And this, incidentally, accounts for the longevity of their doctrines; so long as they remain nebulous, they offer nothing for criticism to seize upon.

Even less worthy of serious attention are those schemes of social reform which, while not condemning the use of money in general, object to the use of gold and silver. In fact, such hostility to the precious metals has something very childish in it. When Thomas More, for example, endows the criminals in his utopia with golden chains and the ordinary citizens with gold and silver chamber pots,[2] it is in something of the spirit that leads primitive mankind to wreak vengeance on lifeless images and symbols.

It is hardly worthwhile to devote even a moment to such fantastic suggestions, which have never been taken seriously. All the criticism of them that was necessary has been completed long ago.[3] But one point, which usually escapes notice, must be emphasized.

Among the many confused enemies of money there is one group that fights with other theoretical weapons than those used by its usual associates. These enemies of money take their arguments from the prevailing theory of banking and propose to cure all human ills by means of an "elastic credit system, automatically adapted to the need for currency." It will surprise no one acquainted with the unsatisfactory state of banking theory to find that scientific criticism has not dealt with such proposals as it should have done, and that it has in fact been incapable of doing so. The rejection of schemes such as Ernest Solvay's "social comptabilism"[4] is to be attributed solely to the practical man's timidity and not to any strict proof of the weaknesses of the schemes, which has indeed not been forthcoming. All the banking theorists whose views are derived from the system of Tooke and Fullarton (and this includes nearly all present-day writers) are helpless with regard to Solvay's theory and others

---

[2] More, *Utopia*.

[3] See Marx, *Zur Kritik der politischen Ökonomie*, ed. Kautsky (Stuttgart, 1897), pp. 70 ff.; Knies, *Geld und Kredit*, 2d ed. (Berlin, 1885), vol. 1, pp. 239 ff.; Aucuy, *Les systèmes socialistes d'Éxchange* (Paris, 1908), pp. 114 ff.

[4] See the three memoranda published in 1889 in Brussels by Solvay under the title *La monnaie et le Compte*, and also his *Gesellschaftlicher Comptabilismus* (Brussels, 1897). Solvay's theories also contain various other fundamental errors.

of the same kind. They would like to condemn them, since their own feelings as well as the trustworthy judgments of practical men warn them against the airy speculations of reformers of this type; but they have no arguments against a system which, in the last analysis, involves nothing but the consistent application of their own theories.

The third part of this book is devoted exclusively to problems of the banking system. There the theory of the elasticity of credit is subjected to a detailed investigation, the results of which perhaps render any further discussion of this kind of doctrine unnecessary.

PART TWO

THE VALUE OF MONEY

CHAPTER 7

The Concept of the Value of Money

1

Subjective and Objective Factors in the Theory of the Value of Money

The central element in the economic problem of money is the objective exchange value of money, popularly called its purchasing power. This is the necessary starting point of all discussion; for it is only in connection with its objective exchange value that those peculiar properties of money that have differentiated it from commodities are conspicuous.

This must not be understood to imply that subjective value is of less importance in the theory of money than elsewhere. The subjective estimates of individuals are the basis of the economic valuation of money just as of that of other goods. And these subjective estimates are ultimately derived, in the case of money as in the case of other economic goods, from the significance attaching to a good or complex of goods as the recognized necessary condition for the existence of a utility, given certain ultimate aims on the part of some individual.[1] Nevertheless, while the utility of other goods depends on certain external facts (the objective use-value of the commodity) and certain internal facts (the hierarchy of human needs), that is, on conditions that do not belong to the category of the economic at

[1] See Böhm-Bawerk, *Kapital und Kapitalzins*, pp. 211 ff.

all but are partly of a technological and partly of a psychological nature, the subjective value of money is conditioned by its objective *exchange* value, that is, by a characteristic that falls within the scope of economics.

In the case of money, subjective use-value and subjective exchange value coincide.[2] Both are derived from objective exchange value, for money has no utility other than that arising from the possibility of obtaining other economic goods in exchange for it. It is impossible to conceive of any function of money, *qua* money, that can be separated from the fact of its objective exchange value. As far as the use-value of a commodity is concerned, it is immaterial whether the commodity also has exchange value or not; but for money to have use-value, the existence of exchange value is essential.

This peculiarity of the value of money can also be expressed by saying that, as far as the individual is concerned, money has no use-value at all, but only subjective exchange value. This, for example, is the practice of Rau[3] and Böhm-Bawerk.[4] Whether the one or the other phraseology is employed, scientific investigation of the characteristic will lead to the same conclusions. There is no reason to enter upon a discussion of this point, especially since the distinction between value in use and value in exchange no longer holds the important place in the theory of value that it used to have.[5] All that we are concerned with is to show that the task of economics in dealing with the value of money is a bigger one than its task in dealing with the value of commodities. When explaining the value of commodities, the economist can and must be content to take subjective use-value for granted and leave investigation of its origins to the psychologist; but the real problem of the value of money only begins where it leaves off in the case of commodity

---

[2] See Walsh, *The Fundamental Problem in Monetary Science* (New York, 1903), p. 11; and in like manner, Spiethoff, "Die Quantitätstheorie insbesondere in ihrer Verwertbarkeit als Haussetheorie," *Festgaben für Adolf Wagner* (Leipzig, 1905), p. 256.

[3] See Rau, *Grundsätze der Volkswirtschaftslehre*, 6th ed. (Leipzig, 1855), p. 80.

[4] See Böhm-Bawerk, *op. cit.*, Part II, p. 275. And similarly in Wieser, *Der natürliche Wert*, p. 45; "Der Geldwert und seine Veränderungen," *Schriften des Vereins für Sozialpolitik* 132: 507.

[5] See Böhm-Bawerk, *op. cit.*, Part II, pp. 273 ff.; Schumpeter, *Wesen und Hauptinhalt der theoretischen Nationalökonomie* (Leipzig, 1908), p. 108.

values, viz., at the point of tracing the objective determinants of its subjective value, for there is no subjective value of money without objective exchange value. It is not the task of the economist, but of the natural scientist, to explain why corn is useful to man and valued by him; but it is the task of the economist alone to explain the utility of money. Consideration of the subjective value of money without discussion of its objective exchange value is impossible. In contrast to commodities, money would never be used unless it had an objective exchange value or purchasing power. The subjective value of money always depends on the subjective value of the other economic goods that can be obtained in exchange for it. Its subjective value is in fact a derived concept. If we wish to estimate the significance that a given sum of money has, in view of the known dependence upon it of a certain satisfaction, we can do this only on the assumption that the money possesses a given objective exchange value. "The exchange value of money is the anticipated use-value of the things that can be obtained with it."[6] Whenever money is valued by anybody it is because he supposes it to have a certain purchasing power.

It might possibly be objected that the mere possession by money of an undefined amount of objective exchange value is not alone sufficient to guarantee the possibility of using it as a medium of exchange; that it is also necessary that this purchasing power should be present in *a certain degree,* neither too great nor too small, but such that the proportion between the value of the units of money and that of the units of commodity is a convenient one for carrying through the ordinary exchange transactions of daily life; that even if it were true that half of the money in a country could perform the same service as the whole stock if the value of the monetary unit were doubled, yet it is doubtful if a similar proposition could be asserted of the case in which its value was increased a millionfold, or diminished to one-millionth, in inverse correspondence with changes in the quantity of it, since such a currency would hardly be capable of fulfilling the functions of a common medium of exchange so well as the currencies in actual use; that we should try to imagine

---

[6] Wieser, *Der natürliche Wert*, p. 46.

a commodity money of which a whole ton, or one of which only a thousandth of a milligram was equivalent to a dollar, and think of the inconveniences, the insuperable obstacles in fact, which the employment of such a medium would inevitably place in the way of commerce.

However true this may be, the question of the actual dimensions of the exchange ratio between money and commodities and of the size of the monetary unit is not an economic problem. It is a question that belongs to discussion of the technical conditions that make any particular good suitable for use as money. The relative scarcity of the precious metals, great enough to give them a high objective exchange value but not so great as that of the precious stones or radium and therefore not great enough to make their exchange value *too* high, must indeed be reckoned, along with such of their other characteristics as their practically unlimited divisibility, their malleability, and their powers of resistance to destructive external influences, as among the factors that were once decisive in causing them to be recognized as the most marketable goods and consequently to be employed as money. But nowadays, as monetary systems have developed, the particular level of value of the precious metals no longer has any important bearing on their use as money. The modern organization of the clearing system and the institution of fiduciary media have made commerce independent of the volume and weight of the monetary material.

2

The Objective Exchange Value of Money

It follows from what has been said that there can be no discussion of the problem of the value of money without consideration of its objective exchange value. Under modern conditions, objective exchange value, which Wieser also calls *Verkehrswert* (or value in business transactions), is the most important kind of value, because it governs the social and not merely the individual aspect of economic life. Except in its explanation of the fundamentals of value theory, economics deals almost exclusively with objective exchange value.[7]

---

[7] *Ibid.*, p. 52.

And while this is true to some extent of all goods, including those which are useful apart from any exchange value which they possess, it is still truer of money.

"The objective exchange value of goods is their objective significance in exchange, or, in other words, their capacity in given circumstances to procure a specific quantity of other goods as an equivalent in exchange."[8] It should be observed that even objective exchange value is not really a property of the goods themselves, bestowed on them by nature, for in the last resort it also is derived from the human process of valuing individual goods. But the exchange ratios that are established between different goods in commercial transactions, and are determined by the collective influence of the subjective valuations of all the persons doing business in the market, present themselves to separate individuals, who usually have an infinitesimal influence on the determination of the ratios, as accomplished facts, which in most cases have to be accepted unconditionally. It has thus been easy for false abstraction from this state of affairs to give rise to the opinion that each good comes to the market endowed with a definite quantity of value independent of the valuations of individuals.[9] From this point of view, goods are not *exchanged* for one another, by human beings; they simply *exchange*.

Objective exchange value, as it appears in the subjective theory of value, has nothing except its name in common with the old idea developed by the Classical School of a value in exchange inherent in things themselves. In the value theory of Smith and Ricardo, and in that of their successors, value in exchange plays the leading part. These theories attempt to explain all the phenomena of value by starting from value in exchange, which they interpret as labor value or cost-of-production value. For modern value theory their terminology can claim only a historical importance, and a confusion of the two concepts of exchange value need no longer be feared. This removes the objections that have recently been made to the continued use of the expression "objective exchange value."[10]

If the objective exchange value of a good is its power to command

---

[8] Böhm-Bawerk, *op cit.*, Part II, pp. 214 f.
[9] See Helfferich, *Das Geld*, 6th ed. (Leipzig, 1923), pp. 301 f.
[10] Thus Schumpeter, *op. cit.*, p. 109.

a certain quantity of other goods in exchange, its *price* is this actual quantity of other goods. It follows that the concepts of price and objective exchange value are by no means identical. "But it is, nevertheless, true that both obey the same laws. For when the law of price declares that a good actually commands a particular price, and explains why it does so, it of course implies that the good is able to command this price, and explains why it is able to do so. The law of price comprehends the law of exchange value."[11]

By "the objective exchange value of money" we are accordingly to understand the possibility of obtaining a certain quantity of other economic goods in exchange for a given quantity of money; and by "the price of money" this actual quantity of other goods. It is possible to express the exchange value of a unit of money in units of any other commodity and speak of the commodity price of money; but in actual life this phraseology and the concept it expresses are unknown. For nowadays money is the sole indicator of prices.

3

The Problems Involved in the Theory of the Value of Money

The theory of money must take account of the fundamental difference between the principles which govern the value of money and those which govern the value of commodities. In the theory of the value of commodities it is not necessary at first to pay any attention to objective exchange value. In this theory, all phenomena of value and price determination can be explained with subjective use-value as the starting point. It is otherwise in the theory of the value of money; for since money, in contrast to other goods, can fulfill its economic function only if it possesses objective exchange value, an investigation into its subjective value demands an investigation first into this objective exchange value. In other words, the theory of the value of money leads us back through subjective exchange value to objective exchange value.

Under the present economic system, which is founded on the division of labor and the free exchange of products, producers as a rule do not work directly on their own behalf but with a view to

---

[11] See Böhm-Bawerk, *op. cit.*, Part II, p. 217.

supplying the market. Consequently their economic calculations are determined not by the subjective use-values of their products, but by their subjective exchange values. Valuations which ignore the subjective exchange value, and consequently the objective exchange value, of a product and take account only of its subjective use-value, are nowadays most exceptional. They are on the whole limited to those cases in which the object has a sentimental value. But if we disregard those things to which certain individuals attach a symbolical significance because they remind them of experiences or persons that they wish to remember, while in the eyes of others for which they have not this personal interest the things possess a very much lower value or even no value at all, it cannot be denied that human valuations of goods are based upon their exchange value. It is not use-value, but exchange value, that appears to govern the modern economic order. Nevertheless, if we trace to its deepest springs, first the subjective and then the objective exchange value of commodities, we find that in the last resort it is still the subjective use-value of things that determines the esteem in which they are held. For, quite apart from the fact that the commodities acquired in exchange for the products are always valued according to their subjective use-value, the only valuations that are of final importance in the determination of prices and objective exchange value are those based on the subjective use-value that the products have for those persons who are the last to acquire them through the channels of commerce and who acquire them for their own consumption.

The case of money is different. Its objective exchange value cannot be referred back to any sort of use-value independent of the existence of this objective exchange value. In the origins of monetary systems, money is still a commodity which eventually ceases to circulate on reaching the hands of a final buyer or consumer.[12] In the early stages of the history of money there were even monetary commodities whose natural qualities definitely precluded their employment as money for more than a short time. An ox or a sack of corn cannot remain in circulation for ever; it has sooner or later to be withdrawn for consumption if that part of its value which does

---

[12] See Wieser, "Der Geldwert und seine geschichtlichen Veränderungen," *Zeitschrift für Volkswirtschaft, Sozialpolitik und Verwaltung* 13 (1904): 45.

not depend on its employment as money is not to be diminished by a deterioration of its substance. In a developed monetary system, on the other hand, we find commodity money, of which large quantities remain constantly in circulation and are never consumed or used in industry; credit money, whose foundation, the claim to payment, is never made use of; and possibly even fiat money, which has no use at all except as money.

Many of the most eminent economists have taken it for granted that the value of money and of the material of which it is made depends solely on its industrial employment and that the purchasing power of our present-day metallic money, for instance, and consequently the possibility of its continued employment as money, would immediately disappear if the properties of the monetary material as a useful metal were done away with by some accident or other.[13] Nowadays this opinion is no longer tenable, not merely because there is a whole series of phenomena which it leaves unaccounted for, but chiefly because it is in any case opposed to the fundamental laws of the theory of economic value. To assert that the value of money is based on the nonmonetary employment of its material is to eliminate the real problem altogether.[14] Not only have we to explain the possibility of fiat money, the material of which has a far lower value without the official stamp than with it; we must also answer the question, whether the possibility of a monetary employment of the commodity money material affects its utility and consequently its value, and if so to what extent. The same problem arises in the case of credit money.

Part of the stock of gold at the command of mankind is used for monetary purposes, part for industrial. A change from one kind of use to the other is always possible. Ingots pass from the vaults of the banks to the workshops of the goldsmiths and gilders, who also directly withdraw current coins from circulation and melt them down. On the other hand, things made of gold, even with a high value as works of art, find their way to the mint when unfavorable market conditions render a sale at anything higher than the bullion price impossible. One and the same piece of metal can even fulfill

---

[13] Thus even as late as Menger, *Grundsätze der Volkswirtschaftslehre* (Vienna, 1871), p. 259 n; and also Knies, *Geld und Kredit* (Berlin, 1885), vol. 1, p. 323.
[14] See Simmel, *Philosophie des Geldes*, 2d ed. (Leipzig, 1907), p. 130.

both purposes simultaneously, as will be seen if we think of ornaments that are used as money or of a coin that is worn by its owner as jewelry until he parts with it again.[15]

Investigations into the foundations of the value of money must eliminate those determinants that arise from the properties of the monetary material as a commodity, since these present no peculiarity that could distinguish the value of money from that of other commodities. The value of commodity money is of importance for monetary theory only insofar as it depends on the peculiar economic position of the money, on its function as a common medium of exchange. Changes in the value of the monetary material that arise from its characteristics as a commodity are consequently to be considered only so far as they seem likely to make it more or less suitable for performing the function of money. Apart from this, monetary theory must take the value of the monetary material that arises from its industrial usefulness as given.

The material of which commodity money is made must have the same value whether it is used as money or otherwise. Whether a change in the value of gold originates in its employment as money or in its employment as a commodity, in either case the value of the whole stock changes uniformly.[16]

It is otherwise with credit money and fiat money. With these, the substance that bears the impression is essentially insignificant in the determination of the value of the money. In some circumstances it may have a relatively high exchange value comprising a considerable fraction of the total exchange value of the individual coin or note. But this value, which is not based on the monetary properties of the coin or note, only becomes of practical importance at the moment when the value based on the monetary property vanishes, that is, at the moment when the individuals participating in commerce cease to use the coin or note in question as a common medium of exchange. When this is not the case, the coins or notes bearing the monetary impression must have a higher exchange value than

---

[15] But, as a general rule, objects of art, jewelry and other things made of precious metal should not be regarded as constituting part of the stock of metal which performs the function of commodity money. They are goods of the first order, in relation to which the bullion or coined metal must be regarded as goods of superior orders.

[16] See Wieser, "Der Geldwert und seine geschichtlichen Veränderungen," p. 46.

other pieces of the same material so long as these are not marked out by any special characteristics.

Again, in the case of credit money the claims used as money have similarly a different exchange value from other claims of the same kind that are not used as money. The hundred-gulden notes which circulated as money in Austria-Hungary before the reform of the currency had a higher exchange value than, say, a government security with a nominal value of a hundred gulden, notwithstanding the fact that the latter bore interest and the former did not.

Until gold was used as money it was valued merely on account of the possibility of using it for ornamental purposes. If it had never been used as money, or if it had ceased to be so used, its present-day value would be determined solely by the extent to which it was known to be useful in industry. But additional opportunities of using it provided an addition to the original reasons for esteeming it; gold began to be valued partly because it could be used as a common medium of exchange. It is not surprising that its value consequently rose, or that at least a decrease in its value which possibly would have occurred for other reasons was counterbalanced. Nowadays the value of gold, our principal modern monetary material, is based on both possibilities of employment, on that for monetary purposes and on that for industrial purposes.[17]

---

[17] More than two hundred years ago, John Law, far ahead of his time and with an insight amounting to genius, had seized upon this truth: "Il est raisonnable de penser que l'argent s'échangeait sur le pied de ce qu'il était évalué pour les usages, comme métal, et q'on le donnait comme monnaie dans les échanges à raison de sa valeur. Le nouvel usage de la monnaie, auquel l'argent fut appliqué, dut ajouter à sa valeur, parce que, comme monnaie, obviait aux désavantages et aux inconvénients de l'échange; et conséquemment les demandes d'argent venant à s'augmenter, il reçut une valeur additionnelle, égale à l'accroissement de la demande occasionnée par son usage comme monnaie. Et cette valeur additionnelle n'est pas plus imaginaire que la valeur que l'argent avait dans les échanges comme métal, parce que telle ou telle valeur dérivait de son application à tels ou tels usages, et quelle était plus grande ou moindre, suivant les demandes d'argent comme métal, en proportion de sa quantité. Le valeur additionnelle que l'argent reçut de son usage comme monnaie provient de ses qualités, qui le rendaient propre a cet usage; et cette valeur fut en raison de la demande additionnelle occasionnée par son usage comme monnaie. Si l'une et l'autre de ces valeurs sont imaginaires, alors toutes les valeurs le sont; car aucune chose n'a de valeur que par l'usage auquel on l'applique, et à raison des demandes qu'on en fait, proportionellement à sa quantité" (*Considérations sur le numéraire et le commerce*, ed. Daire, Économistes financiers du XVIIIe siècle, 2nd. ed. [Paris, 1851]), pp. 447 f. See further Walras, *Théorie de la monnaie* (Lausanne, 1886), p. 40; Knies, *op. cit.*, vol. 1, p. 324. Objective theories of value are unable to comprehend this

It is impossible to say how far the present value of money depends on its monetary employment and how far on its industrial employment. When the institution of money was first established, the industrial basis of the value of the precious metals may have preponderated; but with progress in the monetary organization of economic life the monetary employment has become more and more important. It is certain that nowadays the value of gold is largely supported by its monetary employment, and that its demonetization would affect its price in an overwhelming fashion.[18] The sharp decline in the price of silver since 1873 is recognized as largely due to the demonetization of this metal in most countries. And when, between 1914 and 1918, many countries replaced gold by banknotes and Treasury notes so that gold flowed to those countries that had remained on a gold standard, the value of gold fell very considerably.

The value of the materials that are used for the manufacture of fiat money and credit money is also influenced by their use as money as well as by all their other uses. The production of token coins is nowadays one of the most important uses of silver, for example. Again, when the minting of coins from nickel was begun over fifty years ago, the price of nickel rose so sharply that the director of the English mint stated in 1873 that if minting from nickel were continued the cost of the metal alone would exceed the face value of the coins.[19] If we prefer to regard this sort of use as industrial and not monetary, however, it is because token coins are not money but money substitutes, and consequently the peculiar interactions between changes in the value of money and changes in the value of the monetary material are absent in these cases.

The task of the theory of the value of money is to expound the laws which regulate the determination of the objective exchange value of money. It is not its business to concern itself with the determination of the value of the material from which commodity

---

fundamental principle of the theory of the value of money. This is best shown by the lack of comprehension with which Marx confronts the arguments of Law cited above (see Marx, *Das Kapital*, 7th ed. (Hamburg, 1914) vol. 1, p. 56, n. 46; trans. E. and C. Paul into English).

[18] See Heyn, *Irrtümer auf dem Gebiete des Geldwesens* (Berlin, 1900), p. 3; Simmel, *op. cit.*, pp. 116 ff.

[19] Jevons, *Money and the Mechanism of Exchange*, 13th ed. (London, 1902), pp. 49 f.

money is made so far as this value does not depend on the monetary, but on the other, employment of this material. Neither is it its task to concern itself with the determination of the value of those materials that are used for making the concrete embodiments of fiat money. It discusses the objective exchange value of money only insofar as this depends on its monetary function.

The other forms of value present no special problems for the theory of the value of money. There is nothing to be said about the subjective value of money that differs in any way from what economics teaches of the subjective value of other economic goods. And all that it is important to know about the objective *use*-value of money may be summed up in the one statement—it depends on the objective exchange value of money.

CHAPTER 8

The Determinants of the Objective Exchange Value, or Purchasing Power, of Money

(I)
The Element of Continuity in the
Objective Exchange Value of Money

1

The Dependence of the Subjective Valuation of Money on the Existence of Objective Exchange Value

According to modern value theory, price is the resultant of the interaction in the market of subjective valuations of commodities and price goods. From beginning to end, it is the product of subjective valuations. Goods are valued by the individuals exchanging them, according to their subjective use-values, and their exchange ratios are determined within that range where both supply and demand are in exact quantitative equilibrium. The law of price stated by Menger and Böhm-Bawerk provides a complete and numerically precise explanation of these exchange ratios; it accounts exhaustively for all the phenomena of direct exchange. Under bilateral competition, market price is determined within a range whose upper limit is set by the valuations of the lowest bidder among the actual buyers and the highest offerer among the excluded would-be sellers, and whose lower limit is set by the valuations of the lowest offerer among the actual sellers and the highest bidder among the excluded would-be buyers.

This law of price is just as valid for indirect as for direct exchange. The price of money, like other prices, is determined in the last resort by the subjective valuations of buyers and sellers. But, as has been said already, the subjective use-value of money, which coincides with its subjective exchange value, is nothing but the anticipated use-value of the things that are to be bought with it. The subjective value of money must be measured by the marginal utility of the goods for which the money can be exchanged.[1]

It follows that a valuation of money is possible only on the assumption that the money has a certain objective exchange value. Such a *point d'appui* is necessary before the gap between satisfaction and "useless" money can be bridged. Since there is no direct connection between money as such and any human want, individuals can obtain an idea of its utility and consequently of its value only by assuming a definite purchasing power. But it is easy to see that this supposition cannot be anything but an expression of the exchange ratio ruling at the time in the market between the money and commodities.[2]

Once an exchange ratio between money and commodities has been established in the market, it continues to exercise an influence beyond the period during which it is maintained; it provides the basis for the further valuation of money. Thus the past objective exchange value of money has a certain significance for its present and future valuation. The money prices of today are linked with those of yesterday and before, and with those of tomorrow and after.

But this alone will not suffice to explain the problem of the element of continuity in the value of money; it only postpones the explanation. To trace back the value that money has today to that which it had yesterday, the value that it had yesterday to that which it had the day before, and so on, is to raise the question of what

---

[1] See pp. 121–22 above. Also Böhm-Bawerk, *Kapital und Kapitalzins*, Part II, p. 274; Wieser, *Der natürliche Wert*, p. 46. (Eng. trans. *The Theory of Natural Value*.)
[2] See Wieser, "Der Geldwert und seine Veränderungen," Schriften des Vereins für Sozialpolitik. 132:513 ff.

determined the value of money in the first place. Consideration of the origin of the use of money and of the particular components of its value that depend on its monetary function suggests an obvious answer to this question. The first value of money was clearly the value which the goods used as money possessed (thanks to their suitability for satisfying human wants in other ways) at the moment when they were first used as common media of exchange. When individuals began to acquire objects, not for consumption, but to be used as media of exchange, they valued them according to the objective exchange value with which the market already credited them by reason of their "industrial" usefulness, and only as an additional consideration on account of the possibility of using them as media of exchange. The earliest value of money links up with the commodity value of the monetary material. But the value of money since then has been influenced not merely by the factors dependent on its "industrial" uses, which determine the value of the material of which the commodity money is made, but also by those which result from its use as money. Not only its supply and demand for industrial purposes, but also its supply and demand for use as a medium of exchange, have influenced the value of gold from that point of time onward when it was first used as money.[3]

2

The Necessity for a Value Independent of the Monetary Function Before an Object Can Serve as Money

If the objective exchange value of money must always be linked with a preexisting market exchange ratio between money and other economic goods (since otherwise individuals would not be in a position to estimate the value of the money), it follows that an object cannot be used as money unless, at the moment when its use as money begins, it already possesses an objective exchange value based on some other use. This provides both a refutation of those theories which derive the origin of money from a general agreement

---

[3] See Knies, *Geld und Kredit* (Berlin, 1885), vol. 1, p. 324.

to impute fictitious value to things intrinsically valueless[4] and a confirmation of Menger's hypothesis concerning the origin of the use of money.

This link with a preexisting exchange value is necessary not only for commodity money, but equally for credit money and fiat money.[5] No fiat money could ever come into existence if it did not satisfy this condition. Let us suppose that, among those ancient and modern kinds of money about which it may be doubtful whether they should be reckoned as credit money or fiat money, there have actually been representatives of pure fiat money. Such money must have come into existence in one of two ways. It may have come into existence because money substitutes already in circulation, that is, claims payable in money on demand, were deprived of their character as claims, and yet still used in commerce as media of exchange. In this case, the starting point for their valuation lay in the objective exchange value that they had at the moment when they were deprived of their character as claims. The other possible case is that in which coins that once circulated as commodity money are transformed into fiat money by cessation of free coinage (either because there was no further minting at all or because minting was continued only on behalf of the Treasury), no obligation of conversion being *de jure* or *de facto* assumed by anybody, and nobody having any grounds for hoping that such an obligation ever would be assumed by anybody. Here the starting point for the valuation lies in the objective exchange value of the coins at the time of the cessation of free coinage.

Before an economic good begins to function as money it must already possess exchange value based on some other cause than its monetary function. But money that already functions as such may remain valuable even when the original source of its exchange value has ceased to exist. Its value then is based entirely on its function as common medium of exchange.[6]

---

[4] Thus Locke, *Some Considerations of the Consequences of the Lowering of Interest and Raising the Value of Money,* 2d ed. (London, 1696), p. 31.

[5] See Subercaseaux, *Essai sur la nature du papier monnaie (Paris,* 1909), pp. 17 f.

[6] See Simmel, *Philosophie des Geldes,* 2d ed. (Leipzig, 1907), pp. 115 f.; but, above all, Wieser, "Der Geldwert und seine Veränderungen," p. 513.

3

The Significance of Preexisting Prices in the Determination of Market Exchange Ratios

From what has just been said, the important conclusion follows that a historically continuous component is contained in the objective exchange value of money.

The past value of money is taken over by the present and transformed by it; the present value of money passes on into the future and is transformed in its turn. In this there is a contrast between the determination of the exchange value of money and that of the exchange value of other economic goods. All preexisting exchange ratios are quite irrelevant so far as the actual levels of the reciprocal exchange ratios of other economic goods are concerned. It is true that if we look beneath the concealing monetary veil to the real exchange ratios between goods we observe a certain continuity. Alterations in real prices occur slowly as a rule. But this stability of prices has its cause in the stability of the price determinants, not in the law of price determination itself. Prices change slowly because the subjective valuations of human beings change slowly. Human needs, and human opinions as to the suitability of goods for satisfying those needs, are no more liable to frequent and sudden changes than are the stocks of goods available for consumption, or the manner of their social distribution. The fact that today's market price is seldom very different from yesterday's is to be explained by the fact that the circumstances that determined yesterday's price have not greatly changed overnight, so that today's price is a resultant of nearly identical factors. If rapid and erratic variations in prices were usually encountered in the market, the conception of objective exchange value would not have attained the significance that it is actually accorded both by consumer and producer.

In this sense, reference to an inertia of prices is unobjectionable, although the errors of earlier economists should warn us of the real danger that the use of terms borrowed from mechanics may lead to a "mechanical" system, that is, to one that abstracts erroneously from the subjective valuations of individuals. But any suggestion of a causal relationship between past and present prices must be decisively rejected.

It is not disputed that there are institutional forces in operation which oppose changes in prices that would be necessitated by changes in valuations, and which are responsible when changes in prices that would have been caused by changes in supply and demand are postponed and when small or transitory changes in the relations between supply and demand lead to no corresponding change in prices at all. It is quite permissible to speak of an inertia of prices in this sense. Even the statement that the closing price forms the starting point for the transactions of the next market[7] may be accepted if it is understood in the sense suggested above. If the general conditions that determined yesterday's price have altered but little during the night, today's price should be but little different from that of yesterday, and in practice it does not seem incorrect to make yesterday's the starting point. Nevertheless, there is no causal connection between past and present prices as far as the relative exchange ratios of economic goods (not including money) are concerned. The fact that the price of beer was high yesterday cannot be of the smallest significance as far as today's price is concerned—we need only think of the effect upon the prices of alcoholic drinks that would follow a general triumph of the Prohibition movement. Anybody who devotes attention to market activities is daily aware of alterations in the exchange ratios of goods, and it is quite impossible for anybody who is well acquainted with economic phenomena to accept a theory which seeks to explain price changes by a supposed constancy of prices.

It may incidentally be remarked that to trace the determination of prices back to their supposed inertia, as even Zwiedineck in his pleadings for this assumption is obliged to admit, is to resign at the outset any hope of explaining the ultimate causes of prices and to be content with explanations from secondary causes.[8] It must unreservedly be admitted that an explanation of the earliest forms of exchange transaction that can be shown to have existed—a task to

---

[7] See Schmoller, *Grundriss der allgemeinen Volkswirtschaftslehre* (Leipzig, 1902), vol. 2, p. 110.
[8] See Zwiedineck, "Kritisches und Positives zur Preislehre," *Zeitschrift für die gesamte Staatswissenschaft*, Vol. 65, pp. 100 ff.

the solution of which the economic historian has so far contributed but little—would show that the forces that counteract sudden changes in prices were once stronger than they are now. But it must positively be denied that there is any sort of connection between those early prices and those of the present day; that is, if there really is anybody who believes it possible to maintain the assertion that the exchange ratios of economic goods (not the money prices) that prevail today on the German stock exchanges are in any sort of causal connection with those that were valid in the days of Hermann or Barbarossa. If all the exchange ratios of the past were erased from human memory, the process of market-price determination might certainly become more difficult, because everybody would have to construct a new scale of valuations for himself; but it would not become impossible. In fact, people the whole world over are engaged daily and hourly in the operation from which all prices result: the decision as to the relative significance enjoyed by specific quantities of goods as conditions for the satisfaction of wants.

It is so far as the money prices of goods are determined by *monetary* factors, that a historically continuous component is included in them, without which their actual level could not be explained. This component, too, is derived from exchange ratios which can be entirely explained by reference to the subjective valuations of the individuals taking part in the market, even though these valuations were not originally grounded upon the specifically monetary utility alone of these goods. The valuation of money by the market can only start from a value possessed by the money in the past, and this relationship influences the new level of the objective exchange value of money. The historically transmitted value is transformed by the market without regard to what has become its historical content.[9] But it is not merely the starting point for today's objective exchange value of money; it is an indispensable element in its determination. The individual must take into account the objective exchange value of money, as determined in the market yesterday, before he can form an estimate of the quantity of money that he needs today. The demand for money and the supply of it are thus influenced by the

---

[9] See Wieser, "Der Geldwert und seine Veränderungen," p. 513.

value of money in the past; but they in their turn modify this value until they are brought into equilibrium.

4

The Applicability of the Marginal-Utility Theory to Money

Demonstration of the fact that search for the determinants of the objective exchange value of money always leads us back to a point where the value of money is not determined in any way by its use as a medium of exchange, but solely by its other functions, prepares the way for developing a complete theory of the value of money on the basis of the subjective theory of value and its peculiar doctrine of marginal utility.

Until now the subjective school has not succeeded in doing this. In fact, among the few of its members who have paid any attention at all to the problem there have been some who have actually attempted to demonstrate its insolubility. The subjective theory of value has been helpless in face of the task here confronting it.

There are two theories of money which, whatever else we may think of them, must be acknowledged as having attempted to deal with the whole problem of the value of money.

The objective theories of value succeeded in introducing a formally unexceptionable theory of money into their systems, which deduces the value of money from its cost of production.[10] It is true that the abandonment of this monetary theory is not merely to be ascribed to those shortcomings of the objective theory of value in general which led to its supersession by the theory of the modern school. Apart from this fundamental weakness, the cost-of-production theory of the value of money exhibited one feature that was an easy target for criticism. While it certainly provided a theory of commodity money (even if only a *formally* correct one), it was unable to deal with the problem of credit money and fiat money. Nevertheless, it was a complete theory of money insofar as it did at least attempt to give a full explanation of the value of commodity money.

---

[10] See Senior, *Three Lectures on the Value of Money* (London, 1840; 1931), pp. 1 ff.; *Three Lectures on the Cost of Obtaining Money* (London, 1830; 1931), pp. 1 ff.

The other similarly complete theory of the value of money is that version of the quantity theory associated with the name of Davanzati.[11] According to this theory, all the things that are able to satisfy human wants are conventionally equated with all the monetary metal. From this, since what is true of the whole is also true of its parts, the exchange ratios between commodity units and units of money can be deduced. Here we are confronted with a hypothesis that is not in any way supported by facts. To demonstrate its untenability once more would nowadays be a waste of time. Nevertheless, it must not be overlooked that Davanzati was the first who attempted to present the problem as a whole and to provide a theory that would explain not merely the variations in an *existing* exchange ratio between money and other economic goods, but also the origin of this ratio.

The same cannot be said of other versions of the quantity theory. These all tacitly assume a certain value of money as given, and absolutely refuse to investigate further into the matter. They overlook the fact that what is required is an explanation of what determines the exchange ratio between money and commodities, and not merely of what causes changes in this ratio. In this respect, the quantity theory resembles various general theories of value (many versions of the doctrine of supply and demand, for example), which have not attempted to explain price as such but have been content to establish a law of price variations.[12] These forms of the quantity theory are in fact nothing but the application of the law of supply and demand to the problem of the value of money. They introduce into monetary theory all the strong points of this doctrine; and of course all its weak points as well.[13]

The revolution in economics since 1870 has not yet been any more successful in leading to an entirely satisfactory solution of this problem. Of course, this does not mean that the progress of the science has left no trace on monetary theory in general and on the theory

---

[11] See Davanzati, *Lezioni delle monete*, 1588 (in *Scrittori classici italiani di economia politica, Parte Antica* (Milan, 1804), vol. 2, p. 32. Locke and, above all, Montesquieu (*De l'Èsprit des lois*, edition Touquet [Paris, 1821], vol. 2, pp. 458 f.) share this view. See Willis, "The History and Present Application of the Quantity Theory," *Journal of Political Economy* 4 (1896): 419 ff.
[12] See Zuckerkandl, *Zur Theorie des Preises* (Leipzig, 1889), p. 124.
[13] See Wieser, "Der Geldwert und seine Veränderungen," p. 514.

of the value of money in particular. It is one of the many services of the subjective theory of value to have prepared the way for a deeper understanding of the nature and value of money. The investigations of Menger have placed the theory on a new basis. But till now one thing has been neglected. Neither Menger nor any of the many investigators who have tried to follow him have even so much as attempted to solve the fundamental problem of the value of money. Broadly speaking, they have occupied themselves with checking and developing the traditional views and here and there expounding them more correctly and precisely, but they have not provided an answer to the question: What are the determinants of the objective exchange value of money? Menger and Jevons have not touched upon the problem at all. Carver[14] and Kinley[15] have contributed nothing of real importance to its solution. Walras[16] and Kemmerer[17] assume a given value of money and develop what is merely a theory of variations in the value of money. Kemmerer, it is true, approaches very close to a solution of the problem but passes it by.

Wieser expressly refers to the incomplete nature of the previous treatment. In his criticism of the quantity theory he argues that the law of supply and demand in its older form, the application of which to the problem of money constitutes the quantity theory, has a very inadequate content, since it gives no explanation at all of the way in which value is really determined or of its level at any given time, but confines itself without any further explanation merely to stating the direction in which value will move in consequence of variations in supply or demand; that is, in an opposite direction to changes in the former and in the same direction as changes in the latter. He further argues that it is no longer possible to rest content with a theory of the economic value of money which deals so inadequately with the problem; that since the supersession of the old law of supply and demand as applied to commodities, the case for which it was originally constructed, a more searching law must also be

---

[14] See Carver, "The Value of the Money Unit," *Quarterly Journal of Economics* 11 (1897): 429 f.
[15] See Kinley, *Money* (New York, 1909), pp. 123 ff.
[16] See Walras, *Théorie de la Monnaie* (Lausanne, 1886), pp. 25 ff.
[17] See Kemmerer, *Money and Credit Instruments in Their Relation to General Prices* (New York, 1907), pp. 11 ff.

sought to apply to the case of money.[18] But Wieser does not deal
with the problem whose solution he himself states to be the object
of his investigation, for in the further course of his argument he
declares that the concepts of supply of money and demand for
money *as a medium of exchange* are useless for his purpose and puts
forward a theory which attempts to explain variations in the objective exchange value of money (*objektive innere Tauschwert des Geldes*)[19]
by reference to the relationship that exists in an economic community between money income and real income. For while it is true
that reference to the ratio between money income and real income
may well serve to explain *variations* in the objective exchange value
of money, Wieser nowhere makes the attempt to evolve a *complete*
theory of money—an attempt which, admittedly, the factors of supply and demand being excluded from consideration, would be certain to fail. The very objection that he raises against the old quantity
theory, that it affirms nothing concerning the actual determination
of value or the level at which it must be established at any time,
must also be raised against his own doctrine; and this is all the more
striking inasmuch as it was Wieser who, by revealing the historical
element in the purchasing power of money, laid the foundation for
the further development of the subjective theory of the value of
money.

The unsatisfactory results offered by the subjective theory of value
might seem to justify the opinion that this doctrine and especially
its proposition concerning the significance of marginal utility must
necessarily fall short as a means of dealing with the problem of
money. Characteristically enough, it was a representative of the new
school, Wicksell, who first expressed this opinion. Wicksell considers that the principle which lies at the basis of all modern investigation into the theory of value, namely, the concept of marginal
utility, may well be suited to explaining the determination of exchange ratios between one commodity and another, but that it has
practically no significance at all, or at most an entirely secondary
significance, in explaining the exchange ratios between money and
other economic goods. Wicksell, however, does not appear to detect
any sort of objection to the marginal-utility theory in this assertion.

[18] See Wieser, "Der Geldwert und seine Veränderungen," pp. 514 ff.
[19] [See p. 146 n. H.E.B.]

According to his argument, the objective exchange value of money is not determined at all by the processes of the market in which money and the other economic goods are exchanged. If the money price of a single commodity or group of commodities is wrongly assessed in the market, then the resulting maladjustments of the supply and demand and the production and consumption of this commodity or group of commodities will sooner or later bring about the necessary correction. If, on the other hand, all commodity prices, or the average price level, should for any reason be raised or lowered, there is no factor in the circumstances of the *commodity* market that could bring about a reaction. Consequently, if there is to be any reaction at all against a price assessment that is either too high or too low it must in some way or other originate outside the commodity market. In the further course of his argument, Wicksell arrives at the conclusion that the regulator of money prices is to be sought in the relations of the commodity market to the money market, in the broadest sense of the term. The cause which influences the demand for raw materials, labor, the use of land, and other means of production, and thus indirectly determines the upward or downward movement of commodity prices, is the ratio between the money rate of interest (*Darlehnszins*) and the "natural" or equilibrium rate of interest (*natürliche Kapitalzins*), by which we are to understand that rate of interest which would be determined by supply and demand if real capital was itself lent directly without the intermediation of money.[20]

Wicksell imagines that this argument of his provides a theory of the determination of the objective exchange value of money. In fact, however, all that he attempts to prove is that forces operate from the loan market on the commodity market which prevent the objective exchange value of money from rising too high or falling too low. He never asserts that the rate of interest on loans determines the actual level of this value in any way; in fact, to assert this would be absurd. But if we are to speak of a level of money prices that is "too high" or "too low," we must first state how the ideal level with which the actual level is compared has been established. It is in no way sufficient to show that the position of equilibrium is returned

---

[20] See Wicksell, *Geldzins und Güterpreise* (Jena, 1898), pp. iv ff, 16 ff.

to after any disturbance, if the existence of this position of equilibrium is not first explained. Indubitably, this is the primary problem, and its solution leads directly to that of the other; without it, further inquiry must remain unfruitful, for the state of equilibrium can only be maintained by those forces which first established it and continue to reestablish it. If the circumstances of the loan market can provide no explanation of the genesis of the exchange ratio subsisting between money and other economic goods, then neither can they help to explain why this ratio does not alter. The objective exchange value of money is determined in the market where money is exchanged for commodities and commodities for money. To explain its determination is the task of the theory of the value of money. But Wicksell is of the opinion that "the laws of the exchange of commodities contain in themselves nothing that could determine the absolute level of money prices."[21] This amounts to a denial of all possibility of scientific investigation in this sphere.

Helfferich also is of the opinion that there is an insurmountable obstacle in the way of applying the marginal-utility theory to the problem of money; for while the marginal-utility theory attempts to base the exchange value of goods on the degree of their utility to the individual, the degree of utility of money to the individual quite obviously depends on its exchange value, since money can have utility only if it has exchange value, and the degree of the utility is determined by the level of the exchange value. Money is valued subjectively according to the amount of consumable goods that can be obtained in exchange for it, or according to what other goods have to be given in order to obtain the money needed for making payments. The marginal utility of money to any individual, that is, the marginal utility derivable from the goods that can be obtained with the given quantity of money or that must be surrendered for the required money, presupposes a certain exchange value of the money; so the latter cannot be derived from the former.[22]

Those who have realized the significance of historically transmitted values in the determination of the objective exchange value of money will not find great difficulty in escaping from this appar-

---

[21] *Ibid.*, p. 35.
[22] See Helfferich, *Das Geld*, 6th ed. (Leipzig, 1923), p. 577.

ently circular argument. It is true that valuation of the monetary unit by the individual is possible only on the assumption that an exchange ratio already exists in the market between the money and other economic goods. Nevertheless, it is erroneous to deduce from this that a complete and satisfactory explanation of the determination of the objective exchange value of money cannot be provided by the marginal-utility theory. The fact that this theory is unable to explain the objective exchange value of money entirely by reference to its *monetary* utility; that to complete its explanation, as we were able to show, it is obliged to go back to that original exchange value which was based not on a monetary function at all but on other uses of the object that was to be used as money—this must not in any way be reckoned to the discredit of the theory, for it corresponds exactly to the nature and origin of the particular objective exchange value under discussion. To demand of a theory of the value of money that it should explain the exchange ratio between money and commodities solely with reference to the monetary function, and without the assistance of the element of historical continuity in the value of money, is to make demands of it that run quite contrary to its nature and its proper task.

The theory of the value of money as such can trace back the objective exchange value of money only to that point where it ceases to be the value of money and becomes merely the value of a commodity. At this point the theory must hand over all further investigation to the general theory of value, which will then find no further difficulty in the solution of the problem. It is true that the subjective valuation of money presupposes an existing objective exchange value; but the value that has to be presupposed is not the same as the value that has to be explained; what has to be presupposed is *yesterday's* exchange value, and it is quite legitimate to use it in an explanation of that of today. The objective exchange value of money which rules in the market today is derived from yesterday's under the influence of the subjective valuations of the individuals frequenting the market, just as yesterday's in its turn was derived under the influence of subjective valuations from the objective exchange value possessed by the money the day before yesterday.

If in this way we continually go farther and farther back we must eventually arrive at a point where we no longer find any component in the objective exchange value of money that arises from valuations based on the function of money as a common medium of exchange; where the value of money is nothing other than the value of an object that is useful in some other way than as money. But this point is not merely an instrumental concept of theory; it is an actual phenomenon of economic history, making its appearance at the moment when indirect exchange begins.

Before it was usual to acquire goods in the market, not for personal consumption, but simply in order to exchange them again for the goods that were really wanted, each individual commodity was only accredited with that value given by the subjective valuations based on its direct utility. It was not until it became customary to acquire certain goods merely in order to use them as media of exchange that people began to esteem them more highly than before, on account of this possibility of using them in indirect exchange. The individual valued them in the first place because they were useful in the ordinary sense, and then additionally because they could be used as media of exchange. Both sorts of valuation are subject to the law of marginal utility. Just as the original starting point of the value of money was nothing but the result of subjective valuations, so also is the present-day value of money.

But Helfferich manages to bring forward yet another argument for the inapplicability of the marginal-utility theory to money. Looking at the economic system as a whole, it is clear that the notion of marginal utility rests on the fact that, given a certain quantity of goods, only certain wants can be satisfied and only a certain set of utilities provided. With given wants and a given set of means, the marginal degree of utility is determined also. According to the marginal-utility theory, this fixes the value of the goods in relation to the other goods that are offered as an equivalent in exchange, and fixes it in such a manner that that part of the demand that cannot be satisfied with the given supply is excluded by the fact that it is not able to offer an equivalent corresponding to the marginal utility of the good demanded. Now Helfferich objects that while the existence of a limited supply of any goods except money is in itself sufficient to imply the limitation of their utility also, this is not true of money. The utility of a given quantity of money depends directly upon the exchange value of the money, not only from the point of view of the individual, but also for society as a whole. The higher the value of the unit in relation to other goods, the greater will be the quantity of these other goods that can be paid for by means of the same sum of money. The value of goods in general results from the limitation of the possible utilities that can be obtained from a given supply of them, and while it is usually higher according to the degree of utility which is excluded by the limitation of supply, the total utility of the supply itself cannot be increased by an increase in its value; but in the case of money, the utility of a given supply can be increased at will by an increase in the value of the unit.[23]

The error in this argument is to be found in its regarding the utility of money from the point of view of the community instead of from that of the individual. Every valuation must emanate from somebody who is in a position to dispose in exchange of the object valued. Only those who have a choice between two economic goods are able to form a judgment as to value, and they do this by preferring the one to the other. If we start with valuations from the point of view of society as a whole, we tacitly assume the existence of a socialized economic organization in which there is no exchange and in which the only valuations are those of the responsible official body. Opportunities for valuation in such a society would arise in the control of production and consumption, as, for example, in deciding how certain production goods were to be used when there were alternative ways of using them. But in such a society there would be no room at all for money. Under such conditions, a common medium of exchange would have no utility and consequently no value either. It is therefore illegitimate to adopt the point of view of the community as a whole when dealing with the value of money. All consideration of the value of money must obviously presuppose a state of society in which exchange takes place and must take as its starting point individuals acting as independent economic agents within such a society,[24] that is to say, individuals engaged in valuing things.

---

[23] *Ibid.*, p. 578.
[24] Dr. B. M. Anderson, pp. 100–110 of his excellent work *The Value of Money* (New York, 1917), has objected to the theory set forth above that instead of a logical analysis it provides merely a temporal regressus. Nevertheless, all the acute objections that he manages to bring forward are directed only against the argument that finds a historical component in the exchange ratios subsisting between commodities, an

5

*"Monetary" and "Nonmonetary" Influences Affecting the Objective
Exchange Value of Money*

Now, the first part of the problem of the value of money having
been solved, it is at last possible for us to evolve a plan of further
procedure. We no longer are concerned to explain the *origin* of the
objective exchange value of money; this task has already been performed in the course of the preceding investigation. We now have
to establish the laws which govern *variations* in existing exchange
ratios between money and the other economic goods. This part of
the problem of the value of money has occupied economists from
the earliest times, although it is the other that ought logically to
have been dealt with first. For this reason, as well as for many
others, what has been done toward its elucidation does not amount
to very much. Of course, this part of the problem is also much more
complicated than the first part.

In investigations into the nature of changes in the value of money
it is usual to distinguish between two sorts of determinants of the
exchange ratio that connects money and other economic goods;
those that exercise their effect on the money side of the ratio and
those that exercise their effect on the commodity side. This distinction is extremely useful; without it, in fact, all attempts at a solution
would have to be dismissed beforehand as hopeless. Nevertheless
its true meaning must not be forgotten.

The exchange ratios between commodities—and the same is naturally true of the exchange ratios between commodities and
money—result from determinants which affect both terms of the
exchange ratio. But existing exchange ratios between goods may be
modified by a change in determinants connected only with one of
the two sets of exchanged objects. Although all the factors that determine the valuation of a good remain the same, its exchange ratio
with another good may alter if the factors that determine the val-

---

argument with which I also [see pp. 133 ff. above] am in definite disagreement. But
Dr. Anderson recognizes the logical foundation of my theory when he declares, "I
shall maintain that value from some source other than the monetary employment is
an essential precondition of the monetary employment" (p. 126).

uation of this second good alter. If of two persons I prefer A to B, this preference may be reversed, even though my feeling for A remains unchanged, if I contract a closer friendship with B. Similarly with the relationships between goods and human beings. He who today prefers the consumption of a cup of tea to that of a dose of quinine may make a contrary valuation tomorrow, even though his liking for tea has not diminished, if he has, say, caught a fever overnight. Whereas the factors that *determine* prices always affect both sets of the goods that are to be exchanged, those of them which merely modify existing prices may sometimes be restricted to one set of goods only.[25]

(II)
Fluctuations in the Objective Exchange Value of Money Evoked by Changes in the Ratio Between the Supply of Money and the Demand for It

6

The Quantity Theory

That the objective exchange value of money as historically transmitted (*der geschichtlich überkommene objektive Tauschwert des Geldes*) is affected not only by the industrial use of the material from which it is made, but also by its monetary use, is a proposition which hardly any economist would nowadays deny. It is true that lay opinion was molded entirely by the contrary belief until very recent times. To a naive observer, money made out of precious metal was "sound money" because the piece of precious metal was an "intrins-

---

[25] See Menger, *Grundsätze der Volkswirtschaftslehre* (Vienna, 1923),pp. 304 ff. [In the German edition of this book, the above paragraph was followed by an explanation that German writers, following Menger, usually refer to "the question of the nature and extent of the influence upon the exchange ratios between money and commodities exerted by variations in those determinants of prices that lie on the monetary side" as the problem of the *innere objektive Tauschwert* of money, and to "those concerned with variations in the objective exchange value of money throughout time and space in general" as the problem of its *äussere objektive Tauschwert*. Since this distinction has not been usual in English terminology, it has been omitted from the present version; and, in what follows, wherever "the objective exchange value of money" is referred to, it is the *innere* exchange value that is meant unless the contrary is explicitly stated. H.E.B.]

ically" valuable object, while paper money was "bad money" because its value was only "artificial." But even the layman who holds this opinion accepts the money in the course of business transactions, not for the sake of its industrial use-value, but for the sake of its objective exchange value, which depends largely upon its monetary employment. He values a gold coin not merely for the sake of its industrial use-value, say because of the possibility of using it as jewelry, but chiefly on account of its monetary utility. But, of course, to do something, and to render an account to oneself of what one does and why one does it, are quite different things.[26]

Judgment upon the shortcomings of popular views about money and its value must be lenient, for even the attitude of science toward this problem has not always been free from error. Happily, the last few years have seen a gradual but definite change in popular monetary theory. It is now generally recognized that the value of money depends partly on its monetary function. This is due to the increased attention that has been devoted to questions of monetary policy since the commencement of the great controversy about the standards. The old theories proved unsatisfactory; it was not possible to explain phenomena such as those of the Austrian or Indian currency systems without invoking the assumption that the value of money originates partly in its monetary function. The naivety of the numerous writings which attacked this opinion and their complete freedom from the restraining influence of any sort of knowledge of the theory of value may occasionally lead the economist to regard them as unimportant; but they may at least claim to have performed the service of shaking deep-rooted prejudices and stimulating a general interest in the problem of prices. No doubt they are a gratifying indication of a growing interest in economic questions; if this is kept in mind, it is possible to think more generously of many erroneous monetary theories.

It is true that there has been no lack of attempts to explain the peculiar phenomena of modern monetary systems in other ways. But they have all been unsuccessful. Thus, in particular, Laughlin's theory comes to grief in failing to take account of the special aspects of the value of money that are associated with the specifically mon-

---

[26] See Wieser, *Über den Ursprung und die Hauptgesetze des wirtschaftlichen Wertes, op. cit.*, pp. iii.

etary function. Quite correctly, Laughlin stresses as the peculiar characteristic of money substitutes their constant and immediate convertibility into money.[27] Nevertheless, he would seem to be mistaken on a fundamental point when he applies the name of token money to such currencies as the rupee from 1893 to 1899 and the Russian ruble and Austrian gulden at the time of the suspension of cash payments. He accounts for the fact that a piece of paper which is not immediately convertible into gold can have any value at all, by reference to the possibility that it will nevertheless someday be converted. He compares inconvertible paper money with the shares of a concern which is temporarily not paying any dividend but whose shares may nevertheless have a certain exchange value because of the possibility of future dividends. And he says that the fluctuations in the exchange value of such paper money are consequently based upon the varying prospects of its ultimate conversion.[28]

The error in this conclusion may be most simply demonstrated by means of an actual example. Let us select for this purpose the monetary history of Austria, which Laughlin also uses as an illustration. From 1859 onward the Austrian National Bank was released from the obligation to convert its notes on demand into silver, and nobody could tell when the state paper money issued in 1866 would be redeemed, or even if it would be redeemed at all. It was not until the later 1890s that the transition to metallic money was completed by the actual resumption of cash payments on the part of the Austro-Hungarian Bank.

Now Laughlin attempts to explain the value of the Austrian currency during this period by reference to the prospect of a future conversion of the notes into metallic commodity money. He finds the basis of its value, at first in an expectation that it would be converted into silver, and afterward in an expectation that it would be converted into gold, and traces the vicissitudes of its purchasing power to the varying chances of its ultimate conversion.[29]

The inadmissibility of this argument can be demonstrated in a striking fashion. In the year 1884—the year is chosen at random—

---

[27] See Laughlin, *The Principles of Money* (London, 1903), pp. 513 f.
[28] *Ibid.*, pp. 530 f.
[29] *Ibid.*, pp. 531 ff.

the five percent Austrian government bonds were quoted on the Viennese Stock Exchange at an average rate of 95.81, or 4.19 percent below par. The quotation was in terms of Austrian paper gulden. The government bonds represented claims against the Austrian state bearing interest at five percent. Thus both the bonds and the notes were claims against the same debtor. It is true that these government bonds were not repayable, that is to say, not redeemable on the part of the creditor. Nevertheless, seeing that interest was paid on them, this could not prejudice their value in comparison with that of the *non*-interest-bearing currency notes, which also were not redeemable; furthermore, the interest on the bonds was payable in paper money, and, if the government redeemed them, it could do this also in paper money. In fact, the bonds in question were redeemed voluntarily in 1892, long before the currency notes were converted into gold. The question now arises: How could it come about that the government bonds, bearing interest at five percent, could be valued less highly than the non-interest-bearing currency notes? This could not possibly be attributed, say, to the fact that people hoped that the currency notes would be converted into gold before the bonds were redeemed. There was no suggestion of such an expectation. Quite another circumstance decided the matter.

The currency notes were common media of exchange—they were money—and consequently, besides the value that they possessed as claims against the state, they also had a value as money. It is beyond doubt that their value as claims alone would not have been an adequate basis even for a relatively large proportion of their actual exchange value. The date of repayment of the claims that were embodied in these notes was in fact quite uncertain, but in any case very distant. As claims, it was impossible for them to have a higher exchange value than corresponded to the then value of the expectation of their repayment. Now, after the cessation of free coinage of silver it was fairly obvious that the paper gulden (and incidentally the silver gulden) would not be converted at a rate appreciably in excess of the average rate at which it circulated in the period immediately preceding the conversion. In any case, after the legal determination of the conversion ratio by the Currency Regulation Law of August 2, 1892, it was settled that the conversion of the currency notes would not take place at any higher rate than this. How could it come about, then, that the gold value of the krone (the half-gulden) already fluctuated about this rate as early as the second half of the year 1892 although the date of conversion was then still quite unknown? Usually a claim to a fixed sum, the date of payment of which lies in the uncertain future, is valued considerably less highly than the sum to which it refers. To this question Laughlin's theory cannot offer an answer; only by taking account of the fact that the monetary function also contributes toward value is it possible to find a satisfactory explanation.

The attempts that have so far been made, to determine the quantitative significance of the forces emanating from the side of money that affect the exchange ratio existing between money and other economic goods, have followed throughout the line of thought of the quantity theory. This is not to say that all the exponents of the quantity theory had realized that the value of money is not determined solely by its nonmonetary, industrial employment, but also or even solely by its monetary function. Many quantity theorists have been of another opinion on this point and have believed that the value of money depends solely on the industrial employment of the monetary material. The majority have had no clear conception of the question at all; very few have approached its true solution. It is often hard to decide in which class certain of these authors should be placed; their phraseology is often obscure and their theories not seldom contradictory. All the same, let us suppose that all quantity theorists had recognized the significance of the monetary function in the determination of the value of the monetary material, and criticize the usefulness of their theory from this point of view.

When the determinants of the exchange ratios between economic goods were first inquired into, attention was early devoted to two factors whose importance for the pricing process was not to be denied. It was impossible to overlook the well-known connection between variations in the available quantity of goods and variations in prices, and the proposition was soon formulated that a good would rise in price if the available quantity of it diminished. Similarly, the importance of the total volume of transactions in the determination of prices was also realized. Thus, a mechanical theory of price determination was arrived at—the doctrine of supply and demand, which until very recently held such a prominent position in our science. Of all explanations of prices it is the oldest. We cannot dismiss it offhand as erroneous; the only valid objection to it is that it does not go back to the ultimate determinants of prices. It is correct or incorrect, according to the content given to the words *demand* and *supply*. It is correct, if account is taken of all the factors that motivate people in buying and selling. It is incorrect, if supply and demand are interpreted and compared in a merely quantitative sense.[30]

It was an obvious step to take this theory, that had been constructed to explain the reciprocal exchange ratios of commodities, and apply it to fluctuations in the relative values of commodities and money also. As soon as people became conscious of the fact of variations in the value of money at all, and gave up the naive conception of money as an invariable measure of value, they began to explain these variations also by quantitative changes in supply and demand.

It is true that the usual criticism of the quantity theory (often expressed with more resentment than is consonant with that objectivity which alone should be the distinctive mark of scientific investigation) had an easy task so far as it was leveled against the older, incomplete, version. It was not difficult to prove that the supposition that changes in the value of money must be proportionate to changes in the quantity of money, so that for example a doubling of the quantity of money would lead to a doubling of prices also, was not in accordance with facts and could not be theoretically established in any way whatever.[31] It was still simpler to show the untenability of the naive version of the theory which regarded the total *quantity* of money and the total *stock* of money as equivalent.

But all these objections do not touch the essence of the doctrine. Neither can any sort of refutation or limitation of the quantity theory be deduced from the fact that a number of writers claim validity for it only on the assumption *ceteris paribus;* not even though they state further that this supposition never is fulfilled and never could be

---

[30] See Zuckerkandl, *op. cit.,* pp. 123 ff.
[31] See Mill, *Principles of Political Economy* (London, 1867), p. 299.

fulfilled.[32] The assumption *ceteris paribus* is the self-evident appendage of every scientific doctrine and there is no economic law that can dispense with it.

Against such superficial criticism the quantity theory has been well able to defend itself triumphantly, and through the centuries, condemned by some and exalted as an indisputable truth by others, it has always been in the very center of scientific discussion. It has been dealt with in an immense literature, far beyond the power of any one person to master. It is true that the scientific harvest of these writings is but small. The theory has been adjudged "right" or "wrong," and statistical data (mostly incomplete and incorrectly interpreted) have been used both to "prove" and to "disprove" it—although sufficient care has seldom been taken to eliminate variations brought about by accidental circumstances. On the other hand, investigation on a basis of the theory of value has but seldom been attempted.

If we wish to arrive at a just appraisal of the quantity theory we must consider it in the light of the contemporary theories of value. The core of the doctrine consists in the proposition that the supply of money and the demand for it both affect its value. This proposition is probably a sufficiently good hypothesis to explain big changes in prices; but it is far from containing a complete theory of the value of money. It describes *one* cause of changes in prices; it is nevertheless inadequate for dealing with the problem exhaustively. By itself it does not comprise a theory of the value of money; it needs the basis of a general value theory. One after another, the doctrine of supply and demand, the cost-of-production theory, and the subjective theory of value have had to provide the foundations for the quantity theory.

If we make use in our discussion of only one fundamental idea contained in the quantity theory, the idea that a connection exists between variations in the value of money on the one hand and variations in the relations between the demand for money and the supply of it on the other hand, our reason is not that this is the most correct expression of the content of the theory from the historical point of view, but that it constitutes that core of truth in the theory

---

[32] Cf. Marshall, before the Indian Currency Committee, "Report" (London, 1898–99; Q. 11759), in *Official Papers* (London, 1926), p. 267.

which even the modern investigator can and must recognize as useful. Although the historian of economic theory may find this formulation inexact and produce quotations to refute it, he must nevertheless admit that it contains the correct expression of what is valuable in the quantity theory and usable as a cornerstone for a theory of the value of money.

Beyond this proposition, the quantity theory can provide us with nothing. Above all, it fails to explain the mechanism of variations in the value of money. Some of its expositors do not touch upon this question at all; the others employ an inadequate principle for dealing with it. Observation teaches us that certain relations of the kind suggested between the available stock of money and the need for money do in fact exist; the problem is to deduce these relations from the fundamental laws of value and so at last to comprehend their true significance.

7

The Stock of Money and the Demand for Money

The process, by which supply and demand are accommodated to each other until a position of equilibrium is established and both are brought into quantitative and qualitative coincidence, is the higgling of the market. But supply and demand are only the links in a chain of phenomena, one end of which has this visible manifestation in the market, while the other is anchored deep in the human mind. The intensity with which supply and demand are expressed, and consequently the level of the exchange ratio at which both coincide, depends on the subjective valuations of individuals. This is true, not only of the direct exchange ratios between economic goods other than money, but also of the exchange ratio between money on the one hand and commodities on the other.

For a long time it was believed that the demand for money was a quantity determined by objective factors and independently of subjective considerations. It was thought that the demand for money in an economic community was determined, on the one hand by the total quantity of commodities that had to be paid for during a given period, and on the other hand by the velocity of circulation of the money. There is an error in the very starting point of this way of regarding the matter, which was first successfully attacked by Menger.[33] It is inadmissible to begin with the demand for money of the community. The individualistic economic community as such, which is the only sort of community in which there is a demand for money, is not an economic agent. It demands money only insofar as its individual members demand money. The demand for money of the economic community is nothing but the sum of the demands for money of the individual economic agents composing it. But for individual economic agents it is impossible to make use of the formula: total volume of transactions ÷ velocity of circulation. If we wish to arrive at a description of the demand for money of an individual we must start with the considerations that influence such an individual in receiving and paying out money.

Every economic agent is obliged to hold a stock of the common medium of exchange sufficient to cover his probable business and personal requirements. The amount that will be required depends upon individual circumstances. It is influenced both by the custom and habits of the individual and by the organization of the whole social apparatus of production and exchange.

But all of these objective factors always affect the matter only as motivations of the individual. They are never capable of a direct influence upon the actual amount of his demand for money. Here, as in all departments of economic life, it is the subjective valuations of the separate economic agents that alone are decisive. The store of purchasing power held by two such agents whose objective economic circumstances were identical might be quite different if the advantages and disadvantages of such a store were estimated differently by the different agents.

The cash balance held by an individual need by no means consist entirely of money. If secure claims to money, payable on demand, are employed commercially as substitutes for money, being tendered and accepted in place of money, then individuals' stores of money can be entirely or partly replaced by a corresponding store of these substitutes. In fact, for technical reasons (such, for example, as the need for having money of various denominations on hand)

---

[33] See Menger, *op. cit.*, pp. 325 ff.; also Helfferich, *op. cit.*, pp. 500 ff.

this may sometimes prove an unavoidable necessity. It follows that we can speak of a demand for money in a broader and in a narrower sense. The former comprises the entire demand of an individual for money and money substitutes; the second, merely his demand for money proper. The former is determined by the will of the economic agent in question. The latter is fairly independent of individual influences, if we disregard the question of denomination referred to above. Apart from this, the question whether a greater or smaller part of the cash balance held by an individual shall consist of money substitutes is only of importance to him when he has the opportunity of acquiring money substitutes which bear interest, such as interest-bearing banknotes—a rare case—or bank deposits. In all other cases it is a matter of complete indifference to him.

The individual's demand and stock of money are the basis of the demand and stock in the whole community. So long as there are no money substitutes in use, the social demand for money and the social stock of money are merely the respective sums of the individual demands and stocks. But this is changed with the advent of money substitutes. The social demand for money in the narrower sense is no longer the sum of the individual demands for money in the narrower sense, and the social demand for money in the broader sense is by no means the sum of the individual demands for money in the broader sense. Part of the money substitutes functioning as money in the cash holdings of individuals are "covered" by sums of money held as "redemption funds" at the place where the money substitutes are cashable, which is usually, although not necessarily, the issuing concern. We shall use the term *money certificates* for those money substitutes that are completely covered by the reservation of corresponding sums of money, and the term *fiduciary media*[34] for those which are not covered in this way. The suitability of this terminology, which has been chosen with regard to the problem to be dealt with in the third part of the present work, must be demonstrated in that place. It is not to be understood in the light of banking technique or in a juristic sense; it is merely intended to serve the ends of economic argument.

Only in the rarest cases can any particular money substitutes be

---

[34] See Appendix B.

immediately assigned to the one or the other group. That is possible only for those money substitutes of which the whole species is either entirely covered by money or not covered by money at all. In the case of all other money substitutes, those the total quantity of which is partly covered by money and partly not covered by money, only an imaginary ascription of an aliquot part to each of the two groups can take place. This involves no fresh difficulty. If, for example, there are banknotes in circulation one-third of the quantity of which is covered by money and two-thirds not covered, then each individual note is to be reckoned as two-thirds fiduciary medium and one-third money certificate. It is thus obvious that a community's demand for money in the broader sense cannot be the sum of the demands of individuals for money and money substitutes, because to reckon in the demand for money certificates as well as that for the money that serves as a cover for them as the banks and elsewhere is to count the same amount twice over. A community's demand for money in the broader sense is the sum of the demands of the individual economic agents for money proper and fiduciary media (including the demand for cover). And a community's demands for money in the narrower sense are the sum of the demands of the individual economic agents for money and money certificates (this time *not* including cover).

In this part we shall ignore the existence of fiduciary media and assume that the demands for money of individual economic agents can be satisfied merely by money and money certificates, and consequently that the demand for money of the whole economic community can be satisfied merely by money proper.[35] The third part of this book is devoted to an examination of the important and difficult problems arising from the creation and circulation of fiduciary media.

The demand for money and its relations to the stock of money form the starting point for an explanation of fluctuations in the objective exchange value of money. Not to understand the nature

---

[35] Examination of the relationship of this supposition to the doctrine of the "purely metallic currency" as expounded by the Currency School would necessitate a discussion of the criticism that has been leveled at it by the Banking School; but certain remarks in the third part of the present work on fiduciary media and the clearing system will fill the gap left above.

of the demand for money is to fail at the very outset of any attempt to grapple with the problem of variations in the value of money. If we start with a formula that attempts to explain the demand for money from the point of view of the community instead of from that of the individual, we shall fail to discover the connection between the stock of money and the subjective valuations of individuals—the foundation of all economic activity. But on the other hand, this problem is solved without difficulty if we approach the phenomena from the individual agent's point of view.

No longer explanation is necessary, of the way in which an individual will behave in the market when his demand for money exceeds his stock of it. He who has more money on hand than he thinks he needs, will buy, in order to dispose of the superfluous stock of money that lies useless on his hands. If he is an entrepreneur, he will possibly enlarge his business. If this use of the money is not open to him, he may purchase interest-bearing securities; or possibly he may decide to purchase consumption goods. But in any case, he expresses by a suitable behavior in the market the fact that he regards his reserve of purchasing power as too large.

And he whose demand for money is less than his stock of it will behave in an exactly contrary fashion. If an individual's stock of money diminishes (his property or income remaining the same), then he will take steps to reach the desired level of reserve purchasing power by suitable behavior in making sales and purchases. A shortage of money means a difficulty in disposing of commodities for money. He who is obliged to dispose of a commodity by way of exchange will prefer to acquire some of the common medium of exchange for it, and only when this acquisition involves too great a sacrifice will he be content with some other economic good, which will indeed be more marketable than that which he wishes to dispose of but less marketable than the common medium of exchange. Under the present organization of the market, which leaves a deep gulf between the marketability of money on the one hand and the marketability of other economic goods on the other hand, nothing but money enters into consideration at all as a medium of exchange. Only in exceptional circumstances is any other economic good pressed into this service. In the case mentioned, therefore, every seller will be willing to accept a smaller quantity of money than he otherwise would have demanded, so as to avoid the fresh loss that he would have to suffer in again exchanging the commodity that he has acquired, which is harder to dispose of than money, for the commodity that he actually requires for consumption.

The older theories, which started from an erroneous conception of the social demand for money, could never arrive at a solution of this problem. Their sole contribution is limited to paraphrases of the proposition that an increase in the stock of money at the disposal of the community while the demand for it remains the same decreases the objective exchange value of money, and that an increase of the demand with a constant available stock has the contrary effect, and so on. By a flash of genius, the formulators of the quantity theory had already recognized this. We cannot by any means call it an advance when the formula giving the amount of the demand for money (volume of transactions ÷ velocity of circulation) was reduced to its elements, or when the attempt was made to give exact precision to the idea of a stock of money, so long as this occurred under a misapprehension of the nature of fiduciary media and of clearing transactions. No approach whatever was made toward the central problem of this part of the theory of money so long as theorists were unable to show the way in which subjective valuations are affected by variations in the ratio between the stock of money and the demand for money. But this task was necessarily beyond the power of these theories; they break down at the crucial point.[36]

Recently, Wieser has expressed himself against employing the "collective concept of the demand for money" as the starting point for a theory of fluctuations in the objective exchange value of money. He says that in an investigation of the value of money we are not concerned with the total demand for money. The demand for money to pay taxes with, for example, does not come into consideration, for these payments do not affect the value of money but only transfer purchasing power from those who pay the taxes to those who receive them. In the same way, capital and interest payments in loan transactions and the making of gifts and bequests merely involve

---

[36] It is remarkable that even investigators who otherwise take their stand upon the subjective theory of value have been able to fall into this error. So, for example, Fisher and Brown, *The Purchasing Power of Money* (New York, 1911), pp. 8 ff.

a transference of purchasing power between persons and not an augmentation or diminution of it. A functional theory of the value of money must, in stating its problem, have regard only to those factors by which the value of money is determined. The value of money is determined in the process of exchange. Consequently, the theory of the value of money must take account only of those quantities which enter into the process of exchange.[37]

But these objections of Wieser's are not only rebutted by the fact that even the surrender of money in paying taxes, in making capital and interest payments, and in giving presents and bequests, falls into the economic category of exchange. Even if we accept Wieser's narrow definition of exchange, we must still oppose his argument. It is not a peculiarity of money that its value (Wieser obviously means its objective exchange value) is determined in the process of exchange; the same is true of all other economic goods. For all economic goods it must therefore be correct to say that the theory of value has to investigate only certain quantities, namely, only those that are involved in the process of exchange. But there is no such thing in economics as a quantity that is not involved in the process of exchange. From the economic point of view, a quantity has no other relationships than those which exercise some influence upon the valuations of individuals concerned in some process or other of exchange.

This is true, even if we admit that value only arises in connection with exchange in the narrow sense intended by Wieser. But those who participate in exchange transactions, and consequently desire to acquire or dispose of money, do not value the monetary unit solely with regard to the fact that they can use it in other acts of exchange (in Wieser's narrower sense of the expression), but also because they require money in order to pay taxes, to transfer borrowed capital and pay interest, and to make presents. They consider the level of their purchasing-power reserves with a view to the necessity of having money ready for all these purposes, and their judgment as to the extent of their requirements for money is what decides the demand for money with which they enter the market.

---

[37] See Wieser, "Der Geldwert und seine Veränderungen," pp. 515 ff.

8

The Consequences of an Increase in the Quantity of Money While the Demand for Money Remains Unchanged or Does Not Increase to the Same Extent

Those variations in the ratio between the individual's demand for money and his stock of it that arise from purely individual causes cannot as a rule have a very large quantitative influence in the market. In most cases they will be entirely, or at least partly, compensated by contrary variations emanating from other individuals in the market. But a variation in the objective exchange value of money can arise only when a force is exerted in one direction that is not canceled by a counteracting force in the opposite direction. If the causes that alter the ratio between the stock of money and the demand for it from the point of view of an individual consist merely in accidental and personal factors that concern that particular individual only, then, according to the law of large numbers, it is likely that the forces arising from this cause, and acting in both directions in the market, will counterbalance each other. The probability that the compensation will be complete is the greater, the more individual economic agents there are.

It is otherwise when disturbances occur in the community as a whole, of a kind to alter the ratio existing between the individual's stock of money and his demand for it. Such disturbances, of course, cannot have an effect except by altering the subjective valuations of the individual; but they are social economic phenomena in the sense that they influence the subjective valuations of a large number of individuals, if not simultaneously and in the same degree, at least in the same direction, so that there must necessarily be some resultant effect on the objective exchange value of money.

In the history of money a particularly important part has been played by those variations in its objective exchange value that have arisen in consequence of an increase in the stock of money while the demand for it has remained unchanged or has at least not increased to the same extent. These variations, in fact, were what first attracted the attention of economists; it was in order to explain them that the quantity theory of money was first propounded. All writers have dealt most thoroughly with them. It is perhaps justifiable, therefore, to devote special attention to them and to use them to illuminate certain important theoretical points.

In whatever way we care to picture to ourselves the increase in the stock of money, whether as arising from increased production or importation of the substance of which commodity money is made, or through a new issue of fiat or credit money, the new money always increases the stock of money at the disposal of certain individual economic agents. An increase in the stock of money in a community always means an increase in the money incomes of a number of individuals; but it need not necessarily mean at the same time an increase in the quantity of goods that are at the disposal of the community, that is to say, it need not mean an increase in the national dividend. An increase in the amount of fiat or credit money is only to be regarded as an increase in the stock of goods at the disposal of society if it permits the satisfaction of a demand for money which would otherwise have been satisfied by commodity money instead, since the material for the commodity money would then have had to be procured by the surrender of other goods in exchange or produced at the cost of renouncing some other sort of production. If, on the other hand, the nonexistence of the new issue of fiat or credit money would not have involved an increase in the quantity of commodity money, then the increase of money cannot be regarded as an increase of the income or wealth of society.

An increase in a community's stock of money always means an increase in the amount of money held by a number of economic agents, whether these are the issuers of fiat or credit money or the producers of the substance of which commodity money is made. For these persons, the ratio between the demand for money and the stock of it is altered; they have a relative superfluity of money and a relative shortage of other economic goods. The immediate consequence of both circumstances is that the marginal utility to them of the monetary unit diminishes. This necessarily influences their behavior in the market. They are in a stronger position as buyers. They will now express in the market their demand for the objects they desire more intensely than before; they are able to offer more money for the commodities that they wish to acquire. It will be the obvious result of this that the prices of the goods concerned will rise, and that the objective exchange value of money will fall in comparison.

But this rise of prices will by no means be restricted to the market for those goods that are desired by those who originally have the new money at their disposal. In addition, those who have brought these goods to market will have their incomes and their proportionate stocks of money increased and, in their turn, will be in a position to demand more intensively the goods they want, so that these goods will also rise in price. Thus the increase of prices continues, having a diminishing effect, until all commodities, some to a greater and some to a lesser extent, are reached by it.[38]

The increase in the quantity of money does not mean an increase of income for all individuals. On the contrary, those sections of the community that are the last to be reached by the additional quantity of money have their incomes reduced, as a consequence of the decrease in the value of money called forth by the increase in its quantity; this will be referred to later. The reduction in the income of these classes now starts a countertendency, which opposes the tendency to a diminution of the value of money due to the increase of income of the other classes, without being able to rob it completely of its effect.

Those who hold the mechanical version of the quantity theory will be the more inclined to believe that the increase in the quantity of money must eventually lead to a uniform increase in the prices of all economic goods, the less clear their concept is of the way in which the determination of prices is affected by it. Thorough comprehension of the mechanism by means of which the quantity of money affects the prices of commodities makes their point of view altogether untenable. Since the increased quantity of money is received in the first place by a limited number of economic agents only and not by all, the increase of prices at first embraces only those goods that are demanded by these persons; further, it affects these goods more than it afterward affects any others. When the increase of prices spreads farther, if the increase in the quantity of

---

[38] See Hume, *Essays,* ed. Frowde (London), pp. 294 ff.; Mill, *op. cit.,* pp. 298 ff.; Cairnes, *Essays in Political Economy, Theoretical and Applied* (London, 1873), pp. 57 ff.; Spiethoff, "Die Quantitätstheorie insbesondere in ihrer Verwertbarkeit als Haussetheorie," *Festgaben für Adolf Wagner* (Leipzig, 1905), pp. 250 ff.

money is only a single transient phenomenon, it will not be possible for the differential increase of prices of these goods to be completely maintained; a certain degree of adjustment will take place. But there will not be such a complete adjustment of the increases that all prices increase in the same proportion. The prices of commodities after the rise of prices will not bear the same relation to each other as before its commencement; the decrease in the purchasing power of money will not be uniform with regard to different economic goods.

Hume, it may be remarked, bases his argument concerning this matter on the supposition that every Englishman is miraculously endowed with five pieces of gold during the night.[39] Mill rightly remarks on this, that it would not lead to a uniform increase in the demand for separate commodities; the luxury articles of the poorer classes would rise more in price than the others. All the same, he believes that a uniform increase in the prices of all commodities, and this exactly in proportion to the increase in the quantity of money, would occur, if "the wants and inclinations of the community collectively in respect to consumption" remained the same. He assumes, no less artificially than Hume, that "to every pound, or shilling, or penny, in the possession of any one, another pound, shilling, or penny were suddenly added."[40] But Mill fails to see that even in this case a uniform rise of prices would not occur, even supposing that for each member of the community the proportion between stock of money and total wealth was the same, so that the addition of the supplementary quantity of money did not result in an alteration of the relative wealth of individuals. For, even in this quite impossible case, every increase in the quantity of money would necessarily cause an alteration in the conditions of demand, which would lead to a disparate increase in the prices of the individual economic goods. Not all commodities would be demanded more intensively, and not all of those that were demanded more intensively would be affected in the same degree.[41]

There is no justification whatever for the widespread belief that

---

[39] Hume, *op. cit.*, p. 307
[40] Mill, *op. cit.*, p. 299.
[41] See Conant, "What Determines the Value of Money?" *Quarterly Journal of Economics* 18 (1904): 559 ff.

variations in the quantity of money must lead to inversely proportionate variations in the objective exchange value of money, so that, for example, a doubling of the quantity of money must lead to a halving of the purchasing power of money.

Even assuming that in some way or other—it is confessedly difficult to imagine in what way—every individual's stock of money were to be increased so that his relative position as regards other holders of property was unaltered, it is not difficult to prove that the subsequent variation in the objective exchange value of money would not be proportioned to the variation in the quantity of money. For, in fact, the way in which an individual values a variation in the quantity of money at his disposal is by no means directly dependent on the amount of this variation; but we should have to assume that it was, if we wished to conclude that there would be a proportionate variation in the objective exchange value of money. If the possessor of a units of money receives b additional units, then it is not at all true to say that he will value the total stock $a + b$ exactly as highly as he had previously valued the stock a alone. Because he now has disposal over a larger stock, he will now value each unit less than he did before; but *how much* less will depend upon a whole series of individual circumstances, upon subjective valuations that will be different for each individual. Two individuals who are equally wealthy and who each possess a stock of money a, will not by any means arrive at the same variation in their estimation of money after an increase of b units in each of their stocks of money. It is nothing short of absurdity to assume that, say, doubling the amount of money at the disposal of an individual must lead to a halving of the exchange value that he ascribes to each monetary unit. Let us, for example, imagine an individual who is in the habit of holding a stock of a hundred kronen and assume that a sum of a further hundred kronen is paid by somebody or other to this individual. Mere consideration of this example is sufficient to show the complete unreality of all the theories that ascribe to variations in the quantity of money a uniformly proportionate effect on the purchasing power of money. For it involves no essential modification of this example to assume that similar increases in the quantity of money are experienced by all the members of the community at once.

The mistake in the argument of those who suppose that a variation in the quantity of money results in an inversely proportionate variation in its purchasing power lies in its starting point. If we wish to arrive at a correct conclusion, we must start with the valuations of separate individuals; we must examine the way in which an increase or decrease in the quantity of money affects the value scales of individuals, for it is from these alone that variations in the exchange ratios of goods proceed. The initial assumption in the arguments of those who maintain the theory that changes in the quantity of money have a proportionate effect on the purchasing power of money is the proposition that if the value of the monetary unit were doubled, half of the stock of money at the disposal of the community would yield the same utility as that previously yielded by the whole stock. The correctness of this proposition is not disputed; nevertheless, it does not prove what it is meant to prove.

In the first place, it must be pointed out that the levels of the total stock of money and of the value of the money unit are matters of complete indifference as far as the utility obtained from the use of the money is concerned. Society is always in enjoyment of the maximum utility obtainable from the use of money. Half of the money at the disposal of the community would yield the same utility as the whole stock, even if the variation in the value of the monetary unit was not proportioned to the variation in the stock of money. But it is important to note that it by no means follows from this that doubling the quantity of money means halving the objective exchange value of money. It would have to be shown that forces emanate from the valuations of individual economic agents which are able to bring about such a proportionate variation. This can never be proved; in fact, its contrary is likely. We have already given a proof of this for the case in which an increase of the quantity of money held by individual economic agents involves at the same time an increase of their income or wealth. But even when the increase in the quantity of money does not affect the wealth or income of the individual economic agents, the effect is still the same.

Let us assume that a man gets half his income in the form of interest-bearing securities and half in the form of money; and that he is in the habit of saving three-quarters of his income, and does this by retaining the securities and using that half of his income which he receives in cash in equal parts for paying for current consumption and for the purchase of further securities. Now let us assume that a variation in the composition of his income occurs, so that he receives three-quarters of it in cash and only one-quarter in securities. From now on this man will use two-thirds of his cash receipts for the purchase of interest-bearing securities. If the price of the securities rises or, which is the same thing, if their rate of interest falls, then in either case he will be less willing to buy and will reduce the sum of money that he would otherwise have employed for their purchase; he is likely to find that the advantage of a slightly increased reserve exceeds that which could be obtained from the acquisition of the securities. In the second case he will doubtless be inclined to pay a higher price, or more correctly, to purchase a greater quantity at the higher price, than in the first case. But he will certainly not be prepared to pay *double* as much for a unit of securities in the second case as in the first case.

As far as the earlier exponents of the quantity theory are concerned, the assumption that variations in the quantity of money would have an inversely proportionate effect on its purchasing power may nevertheless be excusable. It is easy to go astray on this point if the attempt is made to explain the value phenomena of the market by reference to exchange value. But it is inexplicable that those theorists also who suppose they are taking their stand on the subjective theory of value could fall into similar errors. The blame here can only be laid to the account of a mechanical conception of market processes. Thus even Fisher and Brown, whose concept of the quantity theory is a mechanical one, and who attempt to express in mathematical equations the law according to which the value of money is determined, necessarily arrive at the conclusion that variations in the ratio between the quantity of money and the demand for it lead to proportionate variations in the objective exchange value of money.[42] How and through what channels this comes about is not disclosed by the formula, for it contains no reference at all to the only factors that are decisive in causing variations of the exchange ratios, that is, variations in the subjective valuations of individuals.

Fisher and Brown give three examples to prove the correctness

---

[42] See Fisher and Brown, *op. cit.*, pp. 28 ff., 157 ff.

of their conclusions. In the first, they start with the supposition that the government changes the denomination of the money, so that, for example, what was previously called a half-dollar is now called a whole dollar. It is obvious, they say, that this will cause an increase in the number of dollars in circulation and that prices reckoned in the new dollars will have to be twice as high as they were previously. Fisher and Brown may be right so far, but not in the conclusions that they proceed to draw. What their example actually deals with is not an increase in the quantity of money but merely an alteration in its name. What does the "money" referred to in this example really consist of? Is it the stuff of which dollars are made, the claim that lies behind a credit dollar, the token that is used as money, or is it the word *dollar*?

The second example given by Fisher and Brown is no less incorrectly interpreted. They start from the assumption that the government divides each dollar into two and mints a new dollar from each half. Here again all that occurs is a change of name.

In their third example they do at least deal with a real increase in the quantity of money. But this example is just as artificial and misleading as those of Hume and Mill which we have already dealt with in some detail. They suppose that the government gives everybody an extra dollar for each dollar that he already possesses. We have already shown that even in this case a proportionate change in the objective exchange value of money cannot follow.

One thing only can explain how Fisher is able to maintain his mechanical quantity theory. To him the quantity theory seems a doctrine peculiar to the value of money; in fact, he contrasts it outright with the laws of value of other economic goods. He says that if the world's stock of sugar increases from a million pounds to a million hundredweight, it would not follow that a hundredweight would have the value that is now possessed by a pound. Money only is peculiar in this respect, according to Fisher. But he does not give a proof of this assertion. With as much justification as that of Fisher and Brown for their mechanical formula for the value of money, a similar formula could be set out for the value of any commodity, and similar conclusions drawn from it. That nobody attempts to do this is to be explained simply and solely by the circumstance that such a formula would so clearly contradict our experience of the demand curves for most commodities, that it could not be maintained even for a moment.

If we compare two static economic systems, which differ in no way from one another except that in one there is twice as much money as in the other, it appears that the purchasing power of the monetary unit in the one system must be equal to half that of the monetary unit in the other. Nevertheless, we may not conclude from this that a doubling of the quantity of money must lead to a halving of the purchasing power of the monetary unit; for every variation in the quantity of money introduces a dynamic factor into the static economic system. The new position of static equilibrium that is established when the effects of the fluctuations thus set in motion are completed cannot be the same as that which existed before the introduction of the additional quantity of money. Consequently, in the new state of equilibrium the conditions of demand for money, given a certain exchange value of the monetary unit, will also be different. If the purchasing power of each unit of the doubled quantity of money were halved, the unit would not have the same significance for each individual under the new conditions as it had in the static system before the increase in the quantity of money. All those who ascribe to variations in the quantity of money an inverse proportionate effect on the value of the monetary unit are applying to dynamic conditions a method of analysis that is only suitable for static conditions.

It is also entirely incorrect to think of the quantity theory as if the characteristics in question affecting the determination of value were peculiar to money. Most of both the earlier and the later adherents of the theory have fallen into this error, and the fierce and often unfair attacks that have been directed against it appear in a better light when we know of this and other errors of a like kind of which its champions have been guilty.

9

Criticism of Some Arguments Against the Quantity Theory

We have already examined one of the objections that have been brought against the quantity theory: the objection that it only holds good *ceteris paribus*. No more tenable as an objection against the determinateness of our conclusions is reference to the possibility that an additional quantity of money may be hoarded. This argument has played a prominent role in the history of monetary theory; it was one of the sharpest weapons in the armory of the opponents of the quantity theory. Among the arguments of the opponents of the currency theory it immediately follows the proposition relating to the elasticity of cash-economizing methods of payment, to which it also bears a close relation as far as its content is concerned. We shall deal with it here separately; nevertheless all that we can say about it in the present place needs to be set in its proper light by the arguments contained in the third part of this book, which is devoted to the doctrine of fiduciary media.

For Fullarton, hoards are the regular *deus ex machina*. They absorb the superfluous quantity of money and prevent it from flowing into circulation until it is needed.[43] Thus they constitute a sort of reservoir which accommodates the ebb and flow of money in the market to the variations in the demand for money. The sums of money collected in hoards lie there idle, waiting for the moment when commerce needs them for maintaining the stability of the objective exchange value of money; and all those sums of money, that might threaten this stability when the demand for money decreases, flow back out of circulation into these hoards to slumber quietly until they are called forth again. This tacitly assumes [44] the fundamental correctness of the arguments of the quantity theory, but asserts that there is nevertheless a principle inherent in the economic system that always prevents the working out of the processes that the quantity theory describes.

But Fullarton and his followers unfortunately neglected to indicate the way in which variations in the demand for money set in motion the mechanism of the hoards. Obviously they supposed this to proceed without the will of the transacting parties entering into the matter at all. Such a view surpasses the naivest versions of the quantity theory in its purely mechanical conception of market trans-

---

[43] See Fullarton, *On the Regulation of Currencies*, 2d ed. (London, 1845), pp. 69 ff., 138 f.; Wagner, *Die Geld- und Kredittheorie der Peelschen Bankakte* (Vienna, 1862), pp. 97 ff.
[44] Elsewhere, explicitly as well. See Fullarton, *op. cit.*, pp. 57 f.; Wagner, *op. cit.*, p. 70.

actions. Even the most superficial investigation into the problem of
the demand for money could not have failed to demonstrate the
untenability of the doctrine of hoards.

In the first place, it must be recognized that from the economic
point of view there is no such thing as money lying idle. All money,
whether in reserves or literally in circulation (that is, in process of
changing hands at the very moment under consideration), is devoted in exactly the same way to the performance of a monetary
function.[45] In fact, since money that is surrendered in an exchange
is immediately transferred from the ownership of the one party to
that of the other, and no period of time can be discovered in which
it is actually in movement, all money must be regarded as at rest in
the cash reserve of some individual or other. The stock of money of
the community is the sum of the stocks of individuals; there is no
such thing as errant money, no money which even for a moment
does not form part of somebody's stock. All money, that is to say,
lies in some individual's stock, ready for eventual use. It is a matter
of indifference how soon the moment occurs when a demand for
money next arises and the sum of money in question is paid out.
In every household or family the members of which are at least
moderately prosperous there is a minimum reserve whose level is
constantly maintained by replenishment. (The fact has already been
mentioned, that besides objective conditions, subjective factors influencing the individual economic agent help to determine the
amount of the individual demand for money.) What is called storing
money is a way of using wealth. The uncertainty of the future makes
it seem advisable to hold a larger or smaller part of one's possessions
in a form that will facilitate a change from one way of using wealth
to another, or transition from the ownership of one good to that of
another, in order to preserve the opportunity of being able without
difficulty to satisfy urgent demands that may possibly arise in the
future for goods that will have to be obtained by way of exchange.
So long as the market has not reached a stage of development in
which all, or at least certain, economic goods can be sold (that is,
turned into money) at any time under conditions that are not too
unfavorable, this aim can be achieved only by holding a stock of

---

[45] See also Knies, *Geld und Kredit* (Berlin, 1876), vol. 2, 1st half, pp. 284 ff.

money of a suitable size. The more active the life of the market becomes, the more can this stock be diminished. At the present day, the possession of certain sorts of securities which have a large market so that they can be realized without delay and without very considerable loss, at least in normal times, may make the holding of large cash reserves to a certain extent unnecessary.

The demand for money for storage purposes is not separable from the demand for money for other purposes. Hoarding money is nothing but the custom of holding a greater stock of it than is usual with other economic agents, at other times, or in other places. The hoarded sums of money do not lie idle, whether they are regarded from the social or from the individual point of view. They serve to satisfy a demand for money just as much as any other money does. Now the adherents of the banking principle seem to hold the opinion that the demand for storing purposes is elastic and conforms to variations in the demand for money for other purposes in such a way that the total demand for money, that is, that for storing purposes and that for other purposes taken together, adjusts itself to the existing stock of money without any variation in the objective exchange value of the monetary unit. This view is entirely mistaken. In fact, the conditions of demand for money, including the demand for storage purposes, is independent of the circumstances of the supply of money. The contrary supposition can be supported only by supporting a connection between the quantity of money and the rate of interest,[46] that is, by asserting that the variations arising from changes in the ratio between the demand for money and the supply of it, influence to a different degree the prices of goods of the first order and those of goods of higher orders, so that the proportion between the prices of these two classes of goods is altered. The question of the tenability of this proposition, which is based on the view that the rate of interest is dependent on the greater or lesser quantity of money, will have to be brought up again in part three. There the opportunity will also arise for showing that the cash reserves of the banks that issue fudiciary media no more act as a buffer in this way than these mythical hoards do. There is no such thing as a "reserve store" of money out of which commerce can at any

---

[46] See Fullarton, *op. cit.*, p. 71.

time supply its extra requirements or into which it can direct its
surpluses.

The doctrine of the importance of hoards for stabilizing the objective exchange value of money has gradually lost its adherents
with the passing of time. Nowadays its supporters are few. Even
Diehl's membership of this group is only apparent. He agrees, it is
true, with the criticism directed by Fullarton against the currency
theory. On the other hand, he concedes that Fullarton's expressions
inert and *dormant* are erroneously applied to reserves of money, since
these reserves are not idle but merely serve a different purpose from
that served by circulating money; he also agrees that sums of money
in such reserves and sums used for purposes of payment are not
sharply distinguishable, and that the same sums serve now one
purpose and now the other. In spite of this, however, he supports
Fullarton as against Ricardo. He says that, even if the sums taken
out of the reserves must again be replaced out of the stocks of money
present in the community, this need not occur immediately; a long
period may elapse before it is necessary; and that in any case it
follows that the mechanical connection which Ricardo assumes to
exist between the quantity of money *in circulation* and the prices of
commodities cannot be accepted, even with regard to hoards.[47]
Diehl does not show in greater detail *why* a long period may elapse
before the sums supposed to be taken from the reserves are replaced. But he does admit the fundamental correctness of the criticism leveled at Fullarton's arguments; it is possible to grant the sole
reservation that he makes if we interpret it as meaning that time
may and must elapse before changes in the quantity of money express themselves all over the market in a variation of the objective
exchange value of money. For that the increase in individuals' stocks
of money which results from the inflow of the additional quantity
of money must bring about a change in the subjective valuations of
the individuals, and that this occurs immediately and begins immediately to have an effect in the market, can hardly be denied. On
the other hand, an increase in an individual's demand for money
while his stock remains the same, or a decrease of his stock while
his demand remains the same, must lead at once to changes in

[47] See Diehl, *Sozialwissenschaftliche Erläuterungen zu David Ricardos Grundsätzen der
Volkswirtschaft und Besteuerung*, 3d ed. (Leipzig, 1922), Part 2, p. 230.

subjective valuations which must be expressed in the market, even if not all at once, in an increase of the objective exchange value of money. It may be admitted that every variation in the quantity of money will impel the individual to check his judgment as to the extent of his requirements for money and that this may result in a reduction of his demand in the case of a diminishing stock of money and an augmentation of it in the case of an increasing stock, but the assumption that such a limitation or extension *must* occur has no logical foundation, not to speak of the assumption that it must occur in such a degree as to keep the objective exchange value of money stable.

A weightier objection is the denial of the practical importance of the quantity theory, that is implied in the attribution to the present organization of the money, payment, and credit system of a tendency to cancel out variations in the quantity of money and prevent them from becoming effective. It is said that the fluctuating velocity of circulation of money, and the elasticity of methods of payment made possible by the credit system and the progressive improvement of banking organization and technique, that is, the facility with which methods of payment can be adjusted to expanded or contracted business, have made the movement of prices as far as is possible independent of variations in the quantity of money, especially since there exists no quantitative relation between money and its substitutes, that is, between the stock of money and the volume of transactions and payments. It is said that if in such circumstances we still wish to preserve the quantity theory we must not base it merely upon current money but "extend it to embrace all money whatever, including not only all the tangible money substitutes that are capable of circulation, but also every transaction of the banking system or agreement between two parties to a contract that replaces a payment of money." It is admitted that this would make the theory quite useless in practice, but it would secure its theoretical universality. And it is not denied that this raises an almost insoluble problem—that of the conditions under which credit comes into being and of the manner in which it affects the determination of values and prices.[48]

---

[48] See Spiethoff, *op. cit.,* pp. 263 ff.; Kemmerer, *op. cit.,* pp. 67 ff.; Mill, *op. cit.,* pp, 316 ff.

The answer to this is contained in the third part of the present work, where the problem of the alleged elasticity of credit is discussed.[49]

10

Further Applications of the Quantity Theory

In general the quantity theory has not been used for investigating the consequences that would follow a *decrease* in the demand for money while the stock of money remained the same. There has been no historical motive for such an investigation. The problem has never been a live one; for there has never been even a shadow of justification for attempting to solve controversial questions of economic policy by answering it. Economic history shows us a continual increase in the demand for money. The characteristic feature of the development of the demand for money is its intensification; the growth of division of labor and consequently of exchange transactions, which have constantly become more and more indirect and dependent on the use of money, have helped to bring this about, as well as the increase of population and prosperity. The tendencies which result in an increase in the demand for money became so strong in the years preceding the war that even if the increase in the stock of money had been very much greater than it actually was, the objective exchange value of money would have been sure to increase. Only the circumstance that this increase in the demand for money was accompanied by an extraordinarily large expansion of credit, which certainly exceeded the increase in the demand for money in the broader sense, can serve to explain the fact that the objective exchange value of money during this period not only failed to increase, but actually decreased. (Another factor that was concerned in this is referred to later in this chapter.)

If we were to apply the mechanical version of the quantity theory to the case of a decrease in the demand for money while the stock of money remained unaltered, we should have to conclude that there would be a uniform increase in all commodity prices, arithmetically proportional to the change in the ratio between the stock

---

[49] See pp. 336 ff. below.

of money and the demand for it. We should expect the same results as would follow upon an increase of the stock of money while the demand for it remained the same. But the mechanical version of the theory, based as it is upon an erroneous transference of static law to the dynamic sphere, is just as inadequate in this case as in the other. It cannot satisfy us because it does not explain what we want to have explained. We must build up a theory that will show us how a decrease in the demand for money while the stock of it remains the same affects prices by affecting the subjective valuations of money on the part of individual economic agents. A diminution of the demand for money while the stock remained the same would in the first place lead to the discovery by a number of persons that their cash reserves were too great in relation to their needs. They would therefore enter the market as buyers with their surpluses. From this point, a general rise in prices would come into operation, a diminution of the exchange value of money. More detailed explanation of what would happen then is unnecessary.

Very closely related to this case is another, whose practical significance is incomparably greater. Even if we think of the demand for money as constantly increasing it may happen that the demand for *particular kinds* of money diminishes, or even ceases altogether so far as it depends upon their characteristics as general media of exchange, and this is all we have to deal with here. If any given kind of money is deprived of its monetary characteristics, then naturally it also loses the special value that depends on its use as a common medium of exchange, and only retains that value which depends upon its other employment. In the course of history this has always occurred when a good has been excluded from the constantly narrowing circle of common media of exchange. Generally speaking, we do not know much about this process, which to a large extent took place in times about which our information is scanty. But recent times have provided an outstanding example: the almost complete demonetization of silver. Silver, which previously was widely used as money, has been almost entirely expelled from this position, and there can be no doubt that at a time not very far off, perhaps even in a few years only, it will have played out its part as money altogether. The result of the demonetization of silver has been a diminution of its objective exchange value. The price of silver in London fell from 60 9/10d. on an average in 1870 to 23 12/16d. on an average in 1909. Its value was bound to fall, because the sphere of its employment had contracted. Similar examples can be provided from the history of credit money also. For instance, the notes of the southern states in the American Civil War may be mentioned, which as the successes of the northern states increased, lost *pari passu* their monetary value as well as their value as claims.[50]

More deeply than with the problem of the consequences of a diminishing demand for money while the stock of it remains the same, which possesses only a small practical importance, the adherents of the quantity theory have occupied themselves with the problem of a diminishing stock of money while the demand for it remains the same and with that of an increasing demand for money while the stock of it remains the same. It was believed that complete answers to both questions could easily be obtained in accordance with the mechanical version of the quantity theory, if the general formula, which appeared to embrace the essence of the problems, was applied to them. Both cases were treated as inversions of the case of an increase in the quantity of money while the demand for it remained the same; and from this the corresponding conclusions were drawn. Just as the attempt was made to explain the depreciation of credit money simply by reference to the enormous increase in the quantity of money, so the attempt was made to explain the depression of the seventies and eighties by reference to an increase of the demand for money while the quantity of money did not increase sufficiently. This proposition lay at the root of most of the measures of currency policy of the nineteenth century. The aim was to regulate the value of money by increasing or diminishing the quantity of it. The effects of these measures appeared to provide an inductive proof of the correctness of this superficial version of the quantity theory, and incidentally concealed the weaknesses of its logic. This supposition alone can explain why no attempt was ever made to exhibit the mechanism of the increase of the value of money as a result of the decrease in the volume of circulation. Here again the old theory needs to be supplemented, as has been done in our argument above.

[50] See White, *Money and Banking Illustrated by American History* (Boston, 1895), pp. 166 ff.

Normally, the increase in the demand for money is slow, so that any effect on the exchange ratio between money and commodities is discernible only with difficulty. Nevertheless, cases do occur in which the demand for money in the narrower sense increases suddenly and to an unusually large degree, so that the prices of commodities drop suddenly. Such cases occur when the public loses faith in an issuer of fiduciary media at a time of crisis, and the fiduciary media cease to be capable of circulation. Many examples of this sort are known to history (one of them is provided by the experiences of the United States in the late autumn of 1907), and it is possible that similar cases may occur in the future.

(III)

A Special Cause of Variations in the Objective Exchange Value
of Money Arising from the Peculiarities of Indirect Exchange

11

"Dearness of Living"

Those determinants of the objective exchange value of money that have already been considered exhibit no sort of special peculiarity. So far as they are concerned, the exchange value of money is determined no differently from the exchange value of other economic goods. But there are other determinants of variations in the objective exchange value of money which obey a special law.

No complaint is more widespread than that against "dearness of living." There has been no generation that has not grumbled about the "expensive times" that it lives in. But the fact that "everything" is becoming dearer simply means that the objective exchange value of money is falling. It is extraordinarily difficult, if not impossible, to subject such assertions as this to historical and statistical tests. The limits of our knowledge in this direction will have to be referred to in the chapter dealing with the problem of the measurability of variations in the value of money. Here we must be content to anticipate the conclusions of this chapter and state that we can expect no support from investigations into the history of prices or from the methods employed in such investigations. The statements of the average man, even though it may very easily happen that these are

founded on self-deception and even though they are so much at the
mercy of variations in the subjective valuations of the individual,
would almost form a better substantiation of the fact of a progressive
fall in the objective exchange value of money than can be provided
by all the contents of voluminous statistical publications. Certainty
can be afforded only by demonstration that chains of causes exist,
which are capable of evoking this sort of movement in the objective
exchange value of money and would evoke it unless they were
cancelled by some counteracting force. This path, which alone can
lead to the desired goal, has already been trodden by many investigators—with what success, we shall see.

12

*Wagner's Theory: The Influence of the Permanent
Predominance of the Supply Side over the
Demand Side on the Determination of Prices*

With many others, and in agreement with general popular opinion, Wagner assumes the predominance of a tendency toward the
diminution of the objective exchange value of money. He holds that
this phenomenon can be explained by the fact that the supply side
is almost invariably the stronger and the most capable of pursuing
its own acquisitive interest. Even apart from actual cartels, rings,
and combinations, and in spite of all the competition of individual
sellers among themselves, he claims that the supply side has more
solidarity than the opposing demand side. He argues further that
the tradesmen engaged in retail trade are more interested in an
increase of prices than their customers are in the continuance of the
old prices or in price reductions; for the amount of the tradesmen's
earnings, and consequently their whole economic and social position, depends largely on the prices they obtain, while as a rule only
special, and therefore relatively unimportant, interests of the customers are involved. Hence the growth on the supply side of a
tendency toward the maintenance and raising of prices, which acts
as a kind of permanent pressure in the direction of higher prices,
more energetically and more universally than the opposing tendency on the demand side. Prices certainly are kept down and re-

duced in retail trade with the object of maintaining and expanding sales and increasing total profits, and competition may, and often does, make this necessary. But neither influence, according to Wagner, is in the long run so generally and markedly effective as the interest in and striving for higher prices, which is in fact able to compete with and overcome their resistance. In this permanent predominance of the supply side over the demand side, Wagner sees one of the causes of the general increases in prices.[51]

Wagner, that is to say, attributes the progressive fall in the objective exchange value of money to a series of factors which have no effect on the determination of wholesale prices but only in the determination of retail prices. Now it is a well-known phenomenon that the retail prices of consumption goods are affected by numerous influences which prevent them from responding rapidly and completely to movements of wholesale prices. And, among the peculiar determinants of retail prices, those predominate which tend to keep them above the level corresponding to wholesale prices. It is, for instance, well known that retail prices adapt themselves more slowly to decreases in wholesale prices than to increases. But it must not be overlooked that the adjustment must eventually take place, all the same, and that the retail prices of consumption goods always participate in the movements of the prices of production goods, even if they lag behind them; and that it is only small, transient movements in wholesale trade that have no effect on retail trade.

Even if we were willing to admit the existence of a permanent predominance of the supply side over the demand side, it would still be decidedly questionable whether we could deduce a tendency toward a general increase of dearness from it. If no further cause could be shown to account for an increase of wholesale prices—and Wagner does not attempt this at all—then we can argue a progressive increase of retail prices only if we are prepared to assume that the time lag between the movements of retail and of wholesale prices is continually increasing. But Wagner makes no such assumption; and it would be very difficult to support it, if he did. It may be said, in fact, that modern commercial development has brought about a tendency toward a *more* rapid adjustment of retail prices to whole-

---

[51] See Wagner, *Theoretische Sozialökonomik* (Leipzig, 1909), vol. 2, p, 245.

sale and manufacturers' prices. Multiple and chain stores and co-operative societies follow the movements of wholesale prices much more closely than peddlers and small shopkeepers.

It is entirely incomprehensible why Wagner should connect this tendency to a general rise of prices, arising from the predominance of the supply side over the demand side, with the individualistic system of free competition or freedom of trade, and declare that it is under such a system that the tendency is clearest and operates with the greatest force and facility. No proof is given of this assertion, which is probably a consequence of Wagner's antipathy to economic liberalism; neither could one easily be devised. The more developed the freedom of trade, the more easily and quickly are movements in wholesale prices reflected in retail prices, especially downward movements. Where legislative and other limitations on freedom of trade place small producers and retailers in a favored position, the adjustment is slower and sometimes complete adjustment may even be prevented altogether.

A striking example of this is afforded by the Austrian attempts during the last generation to favor craftsmen and small shopkeepers in their competition against factories and large stores, together with the subsequent considerable rise in prices between 1890 and 1914. It is not under free competition that the conditions which Wagner calls the permanent predominance of the supply side over the demand side are most strongly in evidence, but in those circumstances where the development of free competition is opposed by the greatest obstacles.

13

*Wieser's Theory: The Influence on the Value of Money
Exerted by a Change in the Relations Between
Natural Economy and Money Economy*

Wieser's attempt[52] to explain an increase in the money prices of goods unaccompanied by any considerable change in their value in

---

[52] See Wieser, "Der Geldwert und seine geschichtlichen Veränderungen," pp. 57 ff.; "Der Geldwert und seine Veränderungen," pp. 527 ff.; "Theorie der gesellschaftlichen Wirtschaft," in *Grundriss der Sozialökonomik* (Tübingen, 1914), Part I pp. 327 ff.

terms of other goods, is not entirely satisfactory either. He holds the opinion that most of the changes in the value of money that have actually occurred are to be attributed to changes in the relations between the "natural economy" (*Naturalwirtschaft*) and the "money economy" (*Geldwirtschaft*). When the money economy flourishes, the value of money is reduced; when it decays, the value of money rises again. In the early stages of a money economy most wants are still satisfied by the methods of the natural economy. The family is self-supporting; it lives in its own house, and itself produces the greater part of what it needs; the sale of its products constitutes only a supplementary source of income. Consequently, the cost of living of the producer, or, what comes to the same thing, the value of his labor, is not fully allowed for or not allowed for at all in the cost of the products that are sold; all that is included is the cost of the raw materials used and the wear and tear of those tools or other instruments that have had to be specially constructed, which in any case do not amount to much under conditions of extensive production. So it is with the buyer also; the wants that he satisfies by purchase are not among his more important wants and the use-values that he has to estimate are not very great.

Then gradually all this changes. The extension of the sphere of the money economy introduces into cost calculations factors that were not included before but were dealt with on "natural economic" principles. The list of the costs that are reckoned in monetary terms grows longer, and each new element in the cost calculation is estimated by comparison with the factors already expressed in money, and added to them, with the effect of raising prices. Thus a general rise of prices occurs, but this is not interpreted as a consequence of changes in supply conditions, but as a fall in the value of money.

According to Wieser, if it is not possible to explain the increasing rise in the prices of commodities as originating in monetary factors alone (that is, in variations in the relations between the supply of money and the demand for it), then we must seek another reason for these changes in the general level of prices. Now it is impossible to find the reason by reference to such fluctuations in the values of commodities as are caused by factors belonging to the commodity side of the price ratio; for nowadays we are not worse supplied with goods than our forefathers were. But, to Wieser, no other explanation seems more natural than that which attributes the diminution of the purchasing power of money to the extension of the money economy which was its historical accompaniment. For Wieser, in fact, it is this very inertia of prices which has helped to bring about the change in the value of money during each period of fresh progress; it must have been this that caused the older prices to be raised by the amount of the additional values involved whenever new factors were co-opted into that part of the process of production that was regulated by the money economy. But the higher the money prices of commodities rise, the lower must the value of money fall in comparison. Increasing dearness thus appears as an inevitable symptom of the development of a growing money economy.

It cannot be denied that this argument of Wieser's reveals important points in connection with the market and the determination of prices, which, if followed up, have important bearings on the determination of the exchange ratios between the various economic goods other than money. Nevertheless, so far as Wieser's conclusions relate to the determination of money prices, they exhibit serious shortcomings. In any case, before his argument could be accepted as correct, it would have to be proved that, not forces emanating from the money side, but only forces emanating from the commodity side, are here involved. Not the valuation of money, but only that of the commodities, could have experienced the transformation supposed to be manifested in the alteration of the exchange ratio.

But the chain of reasoning as a whole must be rejected. The development of facilities for exchanging means that the new recruits to the economy increase their subjective valuations of those goods which they wish to dispose of. Goods which they previously valued solely as objects of personal use are now valued additionally on account of their exchangeability for other goods. This necessarily involves a rise in their subjective value in the eyes of those who possess them and are offering them for exchange. Goods which are to be disposed of in exchange are now no longer valued in terms of the use-value that they would have had for their owners if consumed by them, but in terms of the use-value of the goods that may be obtained in exchange for them. The latter value is always higher than the former, for exchanges only occur when they are profitable to both of the parties concerned.

But on the other hand—and Wieser does not seem to have thought of this—the subjective value of the goods *acquired* in exchange sinks. The individuals acquiring them no longer ascribe to them the significance corresponding to their position in a subjective scale of values (*Wertskala*) or utilities (*Nutzenskala*), they ascribe to them only the smaller significance that belongs to the other goods that have to be surrendered in order to get them.

Let us suppose that the scale of values of the possessor of an apple, a pear, and a glass of lemonade, is as follows:

1. An apple
2. A piece of cake
3. A glass of lemonade
4. A pear

If now this man is given the opportunity of exchanging his pear for a piece of cake, this opportunity will increase the significance that he attaches to the pear. He will now value the pear more highly than the lemonade. If he is given the choice between relinquishing either the pear or the lemonade, he will regard the loss of the lemonade as the lesser evil. But this is balanced by his reduced valuation of the cake. Let us assume that our man possesses a piece of cake, as well as the pear, the apple, and the lemonade. Now if he is asked whether he could better put up with the loss of the cake or of the lemonade, he will in any case prefer to lose the cake, because he can make good this loss by surrendering the pear, which ranks below the lemonade in his scale of values. The possibility of exchange introduces considerations of the objective exchange value of goods into the economic decisions of every individual; the original primary scale of use-values is replaced by the derived secondary scale of exchange values and use-values, in which economic goods are ranked not only with regard to their use-values, but also according to the value of the goods that can be obtained for them in exchange. There has been a transposition of the goods; the order of their significance has been altered. But if one good is placed higher, then—there can be no question of it—some other must be placed lower. This arises simply from the very nature of the scale of values, which constitutes nothing but an arrangement of the subjective valuations in order of the significance of the objects valued.

The extension of the sphere of exchange has the same effects on objective exchange values as on subjective values. Here also every increase of value on the one side must be opposed by a decrease of value on the other side. In fact the alteration of an exchange ratio between two goods in such a way that both become dearer is inconceivable. And this cannot be avoided by the interposition of money. When it is asserted that the objective exchange value of money has experienced an alteration, some special cause for this must be demonstrated, apart from the bare fact of the extension of the sphere of exchange. But nobody has ever provided this demonstration.

Wieser commences by contrasting, after the fashion of economic historians, the natural economy and the money economy. These terms fail to provide that scientific abstraction of concepts that is the indispensable basis of all theoretical investigation. It remains uncertain whether the contrast of an exchangeless state with an order of society based upon exchange is intended, or a contrast between conditions of direct exchange and of indirect exchange based upon the use of money. It seems most likely that Wieser intends to contrast an exchangeless state with one of exchange through money. This is certainly the sense in which the expressions natural economy and money economy are used by economic historians; and this definition corresponds to the actual course of economic history after the full development of the institution of money. Nowadays, when new geographical areas or new spheres of consumption are brought within the scope of exchange, there is a direct transition from the exchangeless state to that of the money economy; but this has not always been so. And in any case the economist must make a clear distinction.

Wieser speaks of the townsman who is in the habit of spending his summer holiday in the country and of always finding cheap prices there. One year, when this townsman goes on holiday he finds that prices have suddenly become higher all round; the village has meanwhile been brought within the scope of the money economy. The farmers now sell their milk and eggs and poultry in the town and demand from their summer visitors the prices that they can hope to get at market. But what Wieser describes here is only half the process. The other half is worked out in the town, where the milk, eggs, and poultry coming on the market from the newly tapped sources of supply in the village exhibit a tendency toward a reduction of price. The inclusion of what has hitherto been a natural economy within the scope of an exchange system involves no one-sided rise of prices, but a leveling of prices. The contrary effect would be evoked by any contraction of the scope of the exchange system; it would have an inherent tendency to increase the differences between prices. Thus we should not use this phenomenon, as Wieser does, to substantiate propositions about variations in the objective exchange value of money.

14

The Mechanism of the Market as a Force Affecting the Objective Exchange Value of Money

Nevertheless, the progressive rise of prices and its complement, the fall in the value of money, may quite well be explained from the monetary side, by reference to the nature of money and monetary transactions.

The modern theory of prices has stated all its propositions with a view to the case of direct exchange. Even where it does include indirect exchange within the scope of its considerations, it does not take sufficient account of the peculiarity of that kind of exchange which is dependent upon the help of the common medium of exchange, or money. This, of course, does not constitute an objection to the modern theory of prices. The laws of price determination which it has established for the case of direct exchange are also valid for the case of indirect exchange, and the nature of an exchange is not altered by the use of money. Nevertheless, the monetary theorist has to contribute an important addition to the general theory of prices.

If a would-be buyer thinks that the price demanded by a would-be seller is too high, because it does not correspond to his subjective valuations of the goods in question, a direct exchange will not be feasible unless the would-be seller reduces his demands. But by indirect exchange, with money entering into the case, even without such a reduction there is still a possibility that the transaction may take place. In certain circumstances the would-be buyer may decide to pay the high price demanded, if he can hope similarly to obtain a better price than he had reckoned upon for those goods and services that he himself has to dispose of. In fact, this would very often be the best way for the would-be buyer to obtain the greatest possible advantage from the transaction. Of course, this will not be true, as in the case of transactions like those of the stock exchange, or in individual bargaining, when both parties cooperate immediately in the determination of prices and consequently are able to give direct expression to their subjective estimates of commodity and medium of exchange. But there are cases in which prices appear to be determined one-sidedly by the seller, and the buyer is obliged to abstain from purchase when the price demanded is too high. In such a case, when the abstention of the purchaser indicates to the seller that he has overreached his demand, the seller may reduce his price again (and, of course, in so doing, may possibly go too far, or not far enough). But under certain conditions a different procedure may be substituted for this roundabout process. The buyer may agree to the price demanded and attempt to recoup himself elsewhere by screwing up the prices of the goods that he himself has for sale. Thus a rise in the price of food may cause the laborers to demand higher wages. If the entrepreneurs agree to the laborers' demands, then they in turn will raise the prices of their products, and then the food producers may perhaps regard this rise in the price of manufactured goods as a reason for a new rise in the price of food. Thus increases in prices are linked together in an endless chain, and nobody can indicate where the beginning is and where the end, or which is cause and which effect.

In modern selling policies "fixed prices" play a large part. It is customary for cartels and trusts and in fact all monopolists, including the state, to fix the prices of their products independently, without consulting the buyers; they appear to prescribe prices to the buyer. The same is often true in retail trade. Now this phenomenon is not accidental. It is an inevitable phenomenon of the unorganized market. In the unorganized market, the seller does not come into contact with all of the buyers, but only with single individuals or groups. Bargaining with these few persons would be useless, for it is not their valuations alone but those of all the would-be purchasers of the good in question that are decisive for price determination. Consequently the seller fixes a price that in his opinion corresponds approximately to what the price ought to be (in which it is understandable that he is more likely to aim too high than too low), and waits to see what the buyers will do. In all of those cases in which he alone appears to fix prices, he lacks exact knowledge of the buyers' valuations. He can make more or less correct assumptions about them, and there are merchants who by close observation of the market and of the psychology of buyers have become quite remarkably expert at this; but there can be no certainty. In fact, estimates often have to be made of the effects of uncertain and future processes. The sole way by which sellers can arrive at reliable knowledge about the valuations of consumers is the way of trial and error. Therefore they raise prices until the abstention of the buyers shows them that they have gone too far. But even though the price may seem too high, given the current value of money the buyer may still pay it if he can hope in the same way to raise the price which he "fixes" and believes that this will lead more quickly to his goal than abstention from purchasing, which might not have its full effect for a long time and might also involve a variety of inconveniences to him. In such circumstances the seller is deprived of his sole reliable check upon the reasonableness of the prices he demands. He sees that these prices are paid, thinks that the profits of his business are increasing proportionately, and only gradually discovers that the fall in the purchasing power of money deprives him of part of the advantage he has gained. Those who have carefully traced the history of prices must agree that this phenomenon repeats itself a countless number of times. It cannot be denied that much of this passing on of price increases has indeed reduced the value of money, but has by no means altered the exchange ratios between other economic goods in the intended degree.

In order to guard against any possible misunderstanding, it should be explicitly stated that there is no justification for drawing the conclusion from this that all increases of prices can be passed on in this way, and so perhaps for assuming that there is a fixed exchange ratio between the different economic goods and human

efforts. To be consistent, we should then have to ascribe the rise in
the money prices of goods to the vain efforts of human greed. A rise
in the money price of a commodity does as a rule modify its exchange ratio to the other commodities, although not always in the
same degree as that in which its exchange ratio to money has been
altered.

The champions of the mechanical version of the quantity theory
may perhaps admit the fundamental correctness of this line of argument, but still object that every variation in the objective exchange value of money that does not start from changes in the
relations between the supply of money and the demand for it must
be automatically self-correcting. If the objective exchange value of
money falls, then the demand for money must necessarily increase,
since in order to cope with the volume of transactions a larger sum
of money is necessary. If it were permissible to regard a community's
demand for money as the quotient obtained by dividing the volume
of transactions by the velocity of circulation, this objection would
be justified. But the error in it has already been exposed. The dependence of the demand for money on objective conditions, such
as the number and size of the payments that have to be coped with,
is only an indirect dependence through the medium of the subjective valuations of individuals. If the money prices of commodities
have risen and each separate purchase now demands more money
than before, this need not necessarily cause individuals to increase
their stocks of money. It is quite possible, despite the rise of prices,
that individuals will form no intention of increasing their reserves,
that they will not increase their demand for money. They will probably endeavor to increase their money incomes; in fact this is one
way in which the general rise of prices expresses itself. But increase
of money incomes is by no means identical with increase of money
reserves. It is of course possible that individuals' demands for
money may rise with prices; but there is not the least ground for
assuming that this *will* occur, and in particular for assuming that
such an increase will occur in such a degree that the effect of the
decrease in the purchasing power of money is completely canceled.
Quite as justifiably, the contrary assumption might also be haz-
arded, namely, that the avoidance of unnecessary expenditure
forced upon the individual by the rise of prices would lead to a

revision of views concerning the necessary level of cash reserves and that the resultant decision would certainly be not for an increase, but rather for even a decrease, in the amount of money to be held.

But here again it must be observed that this is a matter of a variation brought about through dynamic agencies. The static state, for which the contention attributed to the adherents of the mechanical version of the quantity theory would be valid, is disturbed by the fact that the exchange ratios between individual commodities are necessarily modified. Under certain conditions, the technique of the market may have the effect of extending this modification to the exchange ratio between money and other economic goods also.[53]

(IV)

Excursuses

15

The Influence of the Size of the Monetary Unit and Its Subdivisions on the Objective Exchange Value of Money

The assertion is often encountered that the size of the monetary unit exerts a certain influence on the determination of the exchange ratio between money and the other economic goods. In this connection the opinion is expressed that a large monetary unit tends to raise the money prices of commodities while a small monetary unit is likely to increase the purchasing power of money. Considerations of this sort played a notable part in Austria at the time of the currency regulation of the year 1892 and were decisive in causing the new krone, or half-gulden, to be substituted for the previous, larger, unit, the gulden. So far as this assertion touches the determination of wholesale prices, it can hardly be seriously maintained. But in retail trade the size of the monetary unit admittedly has a certain significance, which, however, must not be overestimated.[54]

Money is not indefinitely divisible. Even with the assistance of money substitutes for expressing fractional sums that for technical

---

[53] See also my article "Die allgemeine Teuerung im Lichte der theoretischen Nationalökonomie, *Archiv für Sozialwissenschaft* 37: 563 ff.
[54] Menger, *Beiträge zur Währungsfrage in Österreich-Ungarn* (Jena, 1892), pp. 53 ff.

reasons cannot conveniently be expressed in the actual monetary material (a method that has been brought to perfection in the modern system of token coinage), it seems entirely impossible to provide commerce with every desired fraction of the monetary unit in a form adapted to the requirements of a rapid and safe transaction of business. In retail trade, rounding off must necessarily be resorted to. The retail prices of the less valuable commodities—and among these are the prices of the most important articles of daily use and those of certain services such as the carriage of letters and passenger transport on railways and tramways—must be adjusted in some way to the available coinage. The coinage can only be disregarded in the case of commodities whose nature allows *them* to be subdivided to any desired extent. In the case of commodities that are not so divisible, the prices of the smallest quantity of them that is offered for independent sale must coincide with the value of one or more of the available coins. But in the case of both groups of commodities, continual subdivision of quantities for retail sale is hindered by the fact that small values cannot be expressed in the available coinage. If the smallest available fractional coin is too large to express exactly the price of some commodity, then the matter may be adjusted by exchanging several units of the commodity on the one hand against one or more coins on the other. In the retail market for fruit, vegetables, eggs, and other similar commodities, prices such as two for three heller, five for eight heller, and so on, are everyday phenomena. But in spite of this there remain a large number of fine shades of value that are inexpressible. Ten pfennigs of the currency of the German Reich (equivalent to $\frac{1}{27900}$ kg. of gold) could not be expressed in coins of the Austrian krone currency; eleven heller (equivalent to $\frac{11}{328000}$ kg. of gold) were too little, twelve heller (equivalent to $\frac{3}{82000}$ kg. of gold) were too much. Consequently there had to be small differences between prices which otherwise would have been kept equal in both countries.[55]

This tendency is intensified by the circumstance that the prices of particularly common goods and services are usually expressed, not merely in such fractions of the monetary unit as can be expressed

---

[55] For example, the letter postage rates of the member countries of the International Postal Union.

in coins, but in amounts corresponding as nearly as possible to the denominations of the coinage. Everybody is familiar with the tendency toward "rounding off" which retail prices exhibit, and this is based almost entirely on the denominations of money and money substitutes. Still greater is the significance of the denominations of the coinage in connection with certain prices for which custom prescribes payment "in round figures." The chief examples of this are tips, fees, and the like.

16

A Methodological Comment

In a review devoted to the first edition of this book,[56] Professor Walter Lotz deals with the criticism that I have brought forward against Laughlin's explanation of the value of the Austrian silver gulden in the years 1879–92.[57] His arguments are particularly interesting, inasmuch as they offer an excellent opportunity of exemplifying the difference that exists between the conception and solution of problems in modern economic theory based on the subjective theory of value on the one hand, and under the empirico-realistic treatment of the historically and sociopolitically oriented schools of Schmoller and Brentano on the other.

According to Professor Lotz it is "a question of taste" whether my arguments are "recognized as having any value." He does not "find them impressive." He says that he himself was not at first able to agree with Laughlin's view, until "Laughlin mentioned information, which makes his arguments at least very probable." Laughlin, in fact, told him that "in the eighties he received the information from the leading house of Viennese high finance, that people were reckoning with the fact that the paper gulden would be eventually converted at some rate or other." Professor Lotz adds to this: "Certainly it was also of importance that the circulation of paper gulden and silver gulden was quantitatively very moderate, and that these means of payment were accepted by the public banks at their nominal value. All the same, the expectations for the future that the

---

[56] *Jahrbücher für Nationalökonomie und Statistik*, 3d Series, vol. 47, pp. 86–93.
[57] See pp. 148 ff. above.

leading house of Viennese high finance had reason to nurse cannot have been quite without effect on the international valuation of the Austrian paper gulden. Consequently it may be justifiable in view of this information to ascribe some weight to Laughlin's argument, in spite of von Mises."

The mysterious communication made to Laughlin by "the leading house of Viennese high finance," and handed on by him to Professor Lotz, was a *secret de Polichinelle*. The innumerable articles devoted to the question of the standard that appeared during the eighties in the Austrian and Hungarian papers, especially in the *Neue Freie Presse*, always assumed that Austria-Hungary would go over to the gold standard. Preparation for this step had been made as early as 1879 by the suspension of the free coinage of silver. All the same, proof of this fact, which is denied by nobody (or at least not by me), in no way solves the problem we are concerned with, as Professor Lotz apparently supposes it to do. It merely indicates the problem that we have to solve. The fact that the gulden was "eventually" to be converted into gold "at some rate or other" does not explain why it was at that time valued at a certain amount and not higher or lower. If the gulden were to be converted into gold, and the national debt certificates into gulden, how did it come about that the interest-bearing national debt bonds were valued less highly than the gulden notes and coined gulden which did not bear interest? That is what we have to explain. It is obvious that our problem is only just beginning at the point where it is finished with for Professor Lotz.

It is true that Professor Lotz is prepared to admit that it was "also of importance" that the circulation of paper gulden and silver gulden was "quantitatively very moderate"; and he grants the validity of yet a third explanation in addition, namely, that this means of payment was accepted by the Treasury at its nominal value. But the relationship of these explanations to each other remains obscure. Possibly it has not occurred to Professor Lotz that the first and second are difficult to reconcile. For if the gulden was valued only in consideration of its eventual conversion into gold, it is fair to assume that it could have made no difference whether more or fewer gulden were in circulation, so long, say, as the funds available for conversion were not limited to a given amount. The third attempt at an explanation is altogether invalid, since the "nominal value" of the gulden was only the "gulden" over again and the very point at issue is to account for the purchasing power of the gulden.

The sort of procedure that Professor Lotz adopts here for solving a problem of economic science must necessarily end in failure. It is not enough to collect the opinions of businessmen—even if they are "leading" men or belong to "leading" houses—and then serve them up to the public, garnished with a few *on the one hand's* and *on the other hand's*, an *admittedly* or so, and a sprinkling of *all the same's*. The collection of "facts" is not science, by a long way. There are no grounds for ascribing authoritative significance to the opinions of businessmen; for economics, these opinions are nothing more than material, to be worked upon and evaluated. When the businessman tries to explain anything he becomes as much a "theorist" as anybody else; and there is no reason for giving a preference to the theories of the practical merchant or farmer. It is, for instance, impossible to prove the cost-of-production theory of the older school by invoking the innumerable assertions of businessmen that "explain" variations in prices by variations in costs of production.

Nowadays there are many who, busied with the otiose accumulation of material, have lost their understanding for the specifically *economic* in the statement and solution of problems. It is high time to remember that economics is something other than the work of the reporter whose business it is to ask X the banker and Y the commercial magnate what they think of the economic situation.

CHAPTER 9

The Problem of the Existence of Local Differences in the Objective Exchange Value of Money

1

Interlocal Price Relations

Let us at first ignore the possibility of various kinds of money being employed side by side, and assume that in a given district one kind of money serves exclusively as the common medium of exchange. The problem of the reciprocal exchange ratios of different kinds of money will then form the subject matter of the next chapter. In this chapter, however, let us imagine an isolated geographical area of any size whose inhabitants engage in mutual trade and use a single good as common medium of exchange. It makes no immediate difference whether we think of this region as composed of several states, or as part of one large state, or as a particular individual state. It will not be necessary until a later stage in our argument to mention certain incidental modifications of the general formula which result from differences in the legal concepts of money in different states.

It has already been mentioned that two economic goods, which are of similar constitution in all other respects, are not to be regarded as members of the same species if they are not both ready for consumption at the same place. For many purposes it seems more convenient to regard them as goods of different species related to one another as goods of higher and lower orders.[1] Only in the case of money is it permissible in certain circumstances to ignore the factor of position in space. For the utility of money, in contrast to that of other economic goods, is to a certain extent free from the limitations of geographical distance. Checks and clearing systems, and similar institutions, have a tendency to make the use of money more or less independent of the difficulties and costs of transport. They have had the effect of permitting gold stored in the cellars of the Bank of England, for instance, to be used as a common medium of exchange anywhere in the world. We can easily imagine a monetary organization which, by the exclusive use of notes or clearinghouse methods, allows all transfers to be made with the instrumentality of sums of money that never change their position in space. If we assume, further, that the costs associated with every transaction are not influenced by the distance between the two parties to the contract and between each of them and the place where the money is (it is well known that this condition is already realized in some cases; for example, in the charges made for postal and money-order services), then there is sufficient justification for ignoring differences in the geographical situation of money. But a corresponding abstraction with regard to other economic goods would be inadmissible. No institution can make it possible for coffee in Brazil to be consumed in Europe. Before the consumption good "coffee in Europe" can be made out of the production good "coffee in Brazil," this production good must first be combined with the complementary good "means of transport."

If differences due to the geographical position of money are disregarded in this way, we get the following law for the exchange ratio between money and other economic goods: every economic good, that is ready for consumption (in the sense in which that phrase is usually understood in commerce and technology), has a subjective use-value *qua* consumption good at the place where it is and *qua* production good at those places to which it may be brought for consumption. These valuations originate independently of each other; but, for the determination of the exchange ratio between money and commodities, both are equally important. The money price of any commodity in any place, under the assumption of com-

---

[1] See pp. 97 above.

pletely unrestricted exchange and disregarding the differences arising from the time taken in transit, must be the same as the price at
any other place, augmented or diminished by the money cost of
transport.

Now there is no further difficulty in including in this formula
the cost of transport of money, or a further factor, on which the
banker and exchange dealer lay great weight, namely, the costs
arising from the recoinage which may be necessary. All these factors,
which it is not necessary to enumerate in further detail, have a
combined effect on the foreign exchange rate (cable rate, etc.) the
resultant of which must be included in our calculation as a positive
or negative quantity. To prevent any possible misunderstanding, it
should once more be explicitly remarked that we are concerned here
only with the rate of exchange between places in which the same
kind of money is in use, although it is a matter of indifference
whether the same *coins* are legal tender in both places. The essentially different problems of the rate of exchange between different
kinds of money will not occupy us until the following chapter.

2

Alleged Local Differences in the Purchasing Power of Money

In contrast to the law of interlocal price relations that has just
been explained is the popular belief in local variations in the purchasing power of money. The assertion is made again and again
that the purchasing power of money may be different in different
markets at the same time, and statistical data are continually being
brought forward to support this assertion. Few economic opinions
are so firmly rooted in the lay mind as this. Travelers are in the habit
of bringing it home with them, usually as a piece of knowledge
gained by personal observation. Few visitors to Austria from Germany at the beginning of the twentieth century had any doubts that
the value of money was higher in Germany than in Austria. That
the objective exchange value of gold, our commodity money κατ'
ἐξοχὴν, stood at different levels in different parts of the world,
passed for established truth in even economic literature.[2]

We have seen where the fallacy lies in this, and may spare our-

_____

[2] See Senior, *Three Lectures on the Cost of Obtaining Money*, pp. 1 ff.

selves unnecessary repetition. It is the leaving out of account of the *positional* factor in the nature of economic goods, a relic of the crudely materialist conception of the economic problem, that is to blame for this confusion of ideas. All the alleged local differences in the purchasing power of money can easily be explained in this way. It is not permissible to deduce a difference in the purchasing power of money in Germany and in Russia from the fact that the price of wheat is different in these countries, for wheat in Russia and wheat in Germany represent two different species of goods. To what absurd conclusions should we not come if we regarded goods lying in bond in a customs or excise warehouse and goods of the same technological species on which the duty or tax had already been paid as belonging to the same species of goods in the economic sense? We should then apparently have to suppose that the purchasing power of money could vary from building to building or from district to district within a single town. Of course, if there are those who prefer to retain commercial terminology, and think it better to distinguish species of goods merely by their external characteristics, we cannot say that they shall not do this. To contend over terminological questions would be an idle enterprise. We are not concerned with words, but with facts. But if this form of expression, in our opinion the less appropriate, is employed, care must be taken in some way to make full allowance for distinctions based on differences in the places at which the commodities are situated ready for consumption. It is not sufficient merely to take account of costs of transport and of customs duties and indirect taxes. The effect of direct taxes, for example, the burden of which is to a large extent transferable also, must be included in the calculation.

It seems better to us to use the terminology suggested above, which stresses with greater clearness that the purchasing power of money shows a tendency to come to the same level throughout the world, and that *the alleged differences in it are almost entirely explicable by differences in the quality of the commodities offered and demanded,* so that there is only a small and almost negligible remainder left over, that is due to differences in the quality of the offered and demanded money.

The existence of the tendency itself is hardly questioned. But the force which it exerts, and hence its importance also, are estimated variously, and the old classical proposition, that money like every other commodity always seeks out the market in which it has the highest value, is said to be mistaken. Wieser has said in this connection that the monetary transactions involved in exchange are induced by the commodity transactions; that they constitute an auxiliary movement, which proceeds only so far as is necessary to permit the completion of the principal movement. But the international movement of commodities, Wieser declares, is even nowadays noticeably small in comparison with domestic trade. The transmitted national equilibrium of prices is broken through for relatively few commodities whose prices are world prices. Consequently, the transmitted value of money is still for the most part as significant as ever. It will not be otherwise until, in place of the national organization of production and labor which still prevails today, a complete world organization has been established; but it will be a long while before this happens. At present the chief factor of production, labor, is still subject to national limitations everywhere; a nation adopts foreign advances in technique and organization only to the degree permitted by its national characteristics, and, in general, does not very easily avail itself of opportunities of work abroad, whereas within the nation entrepreneurs and wage laborers move about to a considerable extent. Consequently, wages everywhere retain the national level at which they have been historically determined, and thus the most important element in costs remains nationally determined at this historical level; and the same is true of most other cost elements. On the whole, the transmitted value of money forms the basis of further social calculations of costs and values. Meanwhile, the international contacts are not yet strong enough to raise national methods of production on to a single world level and to efface the differences in the transmitted national exchange values of money.[3]

It is hardly possible to agree with these arguments, which smack a little too much of the cost-of-production theory of value and are certainly not to be reconciled with the principles of the subjective theory. Nobody would wish to dispute the fact that costs of production differ greatly from one another in different localities. But it

---

[3] See Wieser, "Der Geldwert und seine Veränderungen," *Schriften des Vereins für Sozialpolitik* 132: 531 f.

must be denied that this exercises an influence on the price of commodities and on the purchasing power of money. The contrary follows too clearly from the principles of the theory of prices, and is too clearly demonstrated day by day in the market, to need any special proof in addition. The consumer who seeks the cheapest supply and the producer who seeks the most paying sale concur in the endeavor to liberate prices from the limitations of the local market. Intending buyers do not bother much about the national costs of production when those abroad are lower. (And because this is so, the producer working with higher costs of production calls for protective duties.) That differences in the wages of labor in different countries are unable to influence the price levels of commodities is best shown by the circumstance that even the countries with high levels of wages are able to supply the markets of the countries with low levels of wages. Local differences in the prices of commodities whose natures are technologically identical are to be explained on the one hand by differences in the cost of preparing them for consumption (expenses of transport, cost of retailing, etc.) and on the other hand by the physical and legal obstacles that restrict the mobility of commodities and human beings.

3

Alleged Local Differences in the Cost of Living

There is a certain connection between the assertion of local differences in the purchasing power of money and the widespread belief in local differences in the cost of living. It is supposed to be possible "to live" more cheaply in some places than in others. It might be supposed that both statements come to the same thing, and that it makes no difference whether we say that the Austrian crown was "worth" less in 1913 than the eighty-five pfennigs which corresponded to its gold value, or that "living" was dearer in Austria than in Germany. But this is not correct. The two propositions are by no means identical. The opinion that living is more expensive in one place than in another in no way implies the proposition that the purchasing power of money is different. Even with complete equality of the exchange ratio between money and other economic goods it may happen that an individual is involved in unequal costs in securing the same level of satisfaction in different places. This is especially likely to be the case when residence in a certain place awakens wants which the same individual would not have been conscious of elsewhere. Such wants may be social or physical in nature. Thus, the Englishman of the richer classes is able to live more cheaply on the Continent, because he is obliged to fulfill a series of social duties at home that do not exist for him abroad. Again, living in a large town is dearer than in the country if only because the immediate propinquity in town of so many possibilities of enjoyment stimulates desires and calls forth wants that are unknown to the provincial. Those who often visit theaters, concerts, art exhibitions, and similar places of entertainment, naturally spend more money than those who live in otherwise similar circumstances, but have to go without these pleasures. The same is true of the physical wants of human beings. In tropical areas, Europeans have to take a series of precautions for the protection of health which would be unnecessary in the temperate zones. All those wants whose origin is dependent on local circumstances demand for their satisfaction a certain stock of goods which would otherwise be used for the satisfaction of other wants, and consequently they diminish the degree of satisfaction that a given stock of goods can afford.

Hence, the statement that the cost of living is different in different localities only means that the same individual cannot secure the same degree of satisfaction from the same stock of goods in different places. We have just given one reason for this phenomenon. But, besides this, the belief in local differences in the cost of living is also supported by reference to local differences in the purchasing power of money. It would be possible to prove the incorrectness of this view. It is no more appropriate to speak of a difference between the purchasing power of money in Germany and in Austria than it would be justifiable to conclude from differences between the prices charged by hotels on the peaks and in the valleys of the Alps that the objective exchange value of money is different in the two situations and to formulate some such proposition as that the purchasing power of money varies inversely with the height above sea level. *The purchasing power of money is the same everywhere; only the commodities offered are not the same.* They differ in a quality that is eco-

nomically significant—the position in space of the place at which
they are ready for consumption.

But although the exchange ratios between money and economic
goods of completely similar constitution in all parts of a unitary
market area in which the same sort of money is employed are at any
time equal to one another, and all apparent exceptions can be traced
back to differences in the *spatial quality* of the commodities, it is
nevertheless true that price differentials evoked by the difference in
position (and hence in economic quality) of the commodities may
under certain circumstances constitute a subjective justification of
the assertion that there are differences in the cost of living. He who
voluntarily visits Karlsbad on account of his health would be wrong
in deducing from the higher price of houses and food there that it
is impossible to get as much enjoyment from a given sum of money
in Karlsbad as elsewhere and that consequently living is dearer
there. This conclusion does not allow for the difference in quality
of the commodities whose prices are being compared. It is just because of this difference in quality, just because it has a certain value
for him, that the visitor comes to Karlsbad. If he has to pay more in
Karlsbad for the same quantity of satisfactions, this is due to the
fact that in paying for them he is also paying the price of being able
to enjoy them in the immediate neighborhood of the medicinal
springs. The case is different for the businessman and laborer and
official who are merely tied to Karlsbad by their occupations. The
propinquity of the waters has no significance for the satisfaction of
their wants, and so their having to pay extra on account of it for
every good and service that they buy will, since they obtain no
additional satisfaction from it, appear to them as a reduction of the
possibilities of the enjoyment that they might otherwise have. If
they compare their standard of living with that which they could
achieve with the same expenditure in a neighboring town, they will
arrive at the conclusion that living is really dearer at the spa than
elsewhere. They will then only transfer their activity to the dearer
spa if they believe that they will be able to secure there a sufficiently
higher money income to enable them to achieve the same standard
of living as elsewhere. But in comparing the standards of satisfaction
attainable they will leave out of account the advantage of being able
to satisfy their wants in the spa itself because this circumstance has

no value in their eyes. Every kind of wage will therefore, under the assumption of complete mobility, be higher in the spa than in other, cheaper, places. This is generally known as far as it applies to contract wages; but it is also true of official salaries. The government pays a special bonus to those of its employees who have to take up their duties in "dear" places, in order to put them on a level with those functionaries who are able to live in cheaper places. The laborers too have to be compensated by higher wages for the higher cost of living.

This also is the clue to the meaning of the sentence, "Living is dearer in Austria than in Germany," a sentence which has a certain meaning even though there is no difference between the purchasing power of money in the two countries. The differences in prices in the two areas do not refer to commodities of the same nature; what are supposed to be identical commodities really differ in an essential point; they are available for consumption in different places. Physical causes on the one hand, social causes on the other, give to this distinction a decisive importance in the determination of prices. He who values the opportunity of working in Austria as an Austrian among Austrians, who has been brought up to work and earn money in Austria, and cannot get a living anywhere else on account of language difficulties, national customs, economic conditions, and the like, would nevertheless be wrong in concluding from a comparison of domestic and foreign commodity prices that living was dearer at home. He must not forget that part of every price he pays is for the privilege of being able to satisfy his wants in Austria. An independent rentier with a free choice of domicile is in a position to decide whether he prefers a life of apparently limited satisfactions in his native country among his own kindred to one of apparently more abundant satisfaction among strangers in a foreign land. But most people are spared the trouble of such a choice; for most, staying at home is a matter of necessity, emigration an impossibility.

To recapitulate: the exchange ratio subsisting between commodities and money is everywhere the same. But men and their wants are not everywhere the same, and neither are commodities. Only if these distinctions are ignored is it possible to speak of local differences in the purchasing power of money or to say that living is dearer in one place than in another.

CHAPTER 10

The Exchange Ratio Between Money of Different Kinds

1

The Twofold Possibility of the Coexistence of Different Kinds of Money

The existence of an exchange ratio between two sorts of money is dependent upon both being used side by side, at the same time, by the same economic agents, as common media of exchange. We could perhaps conceive of two economic areas, not connected in any other way, being linked together only by the fact that each exchanged the commodity it used for money against that used for money by the other, in order then to use the acquired monetary commodity otherwise than as money. But this would not be a case of an exchange ratio between different kinds of money simply arising from their monetary employment. If we wish successfully to conduct our investigation as an investigation into the theory of money, then even in the present chapter we must disregard the nonmonetary uses of the material of which commodity money is made; or, at least, take account of them only where this is necessary for the complete clarification of all the processes connected with our problem. Now the assertion that, apart from the effects of the industrial use of the monetary material, an exchange ratio can be established between two sorts of money only when both are used as money simultaneously and side by side, is not the usual view. That is to say, prevailing opinion distinguishes two cases: that in which two or more domestic kinds of money exist side by side in the parallel standard, and that in which the money in exclusive use at home is of a kind different from the money used abroad. Both cases are dealt with separately, although there is no theoretical difference between them as far as the determination of the exchange ratio between the two sorts of money is concerned.

If a gold-standard country and a silver-standard country have business relations with each other and constitute a unitary market for certain economic goods, then it is obviously incorrect to say that the common medium of exchange consists of gold only for the inhabitants of the gold-standard country, and of silver only for those of the silver-standard country. On the contrary, from the economic point of view both metals must be regarded as money for each area. Until 1873, gold was just as much a medium of exchange for the German buyer of English commodities as silver was for the English buyer of German commodities. The German farmer who wished to exchange corn for English steel goods could not do so without the instrumentality of both gold and silver. Exceptional cases might arise, where a German sold in England for gold and bought again with gold, or where an Englishman sold in Germany for silver and bought with silver; but this merely demonstrates more clearly still the monetary characteristic of both metals for the inhabitants of both areas. Whether the case is one of an exchange through the instrumentality of money used once or used more than once, the only important point is that the existence of international trade relations results in the consequence that the money of each of the single areas concerned is money also for all the other areas

It is true that there are important differences between that money which plays the chief part in domestic trade, is the instrument of most exchanges, predominates in the dealings between consumers and sellers of consumption goods, and in loan transactions, and is recognized by the law as legal tender, and that money which is employed in relatively few transactions, is hardly ever used by consumers in their purchases, does not function as an instrument of loan operations, and is not legal tender. In popular opinion, the former money only is domestic money, the latter foreign money.

Although we cannot accept this if we do not want to close the way to an understanding of the problem that occupies us, we must nevertheless emphasize that it has great significance in other connections. We shall have to come back to it in the chapter which deals with the social effects of fluctuations in the objective exchange value of money.

2

The Static or Natural Exchange Ratio Between Different Kinds of Money

For the exchange ratio between two or more kinds of money, whether they are employed side by side in the same country (the parallel standard) or constitute what is popularly called foreign money and domestic money, it is the exchange ratio between individual economic goods and the individual kinds of money that is decisive. The different kinds of money are exchanged in a ratio corresponding to the exchange ratios existing between each of them and the other economic goods. If 1 kg. of gold is exchanged for m kg. of a particular sort of commodity, and 1 kg. of silver for $\frac{m}{15\frac{1}{2}}$ kg. of the same sort of commodity, then the exchange ratio between gold and silver will be established at $15\frac{1}{2}$. If some disturbance tends to alter this ratio between the two sorts of money, which we shall call the static or natural ratio, then automatic forces will be set in motion that will tend to reestablish it.[1]

Let us consider the case of two countries each of which carries on its domestic trade with the aid of one sort of money only, which is different from that used in the other country. If the inhabitants of two areas with different currencies who have previously exchanged their commodities directly without the intervention of money begin to make use of money in the transaction of their business, they will base the exchange ratio between the two kinds of money on the exchange ratio between each kind of money and the commodities. Let us assume that a gold-standard country and a silver-standard

---

[1] The theory put forward above, which comes from Ricardo, is advocated with particular forcefulness nowadays by Cassel, who uses the name purchasing-power parity for the static exchange ratio. See Cassel, *Money and Foreign Exchange After 1914* (London, 1922), p. 181 f.

country had exchanged cloth directly for wheat on such terms that one meter of cloth was given for one bushel of wheat. Let the price of cloth in the country of its origin be one gram of gold per meter; that of wheat, 15 grams of silver per bushel. If international trade is now put on a monetary basis, then the price of gold in terms of silver must be established at 15. If it were established higher, say at 16, then indirect exchange through the instrumentality of money would be disadvantageous from the point of view of the owners of the wheat as compared with direct exchange; in indirect exchange for a bushel of wheat they would obtain only fifteen-sixteenths of a meter of cloth as against a whole meter in direct exchange. The same disadvantage would arise for the owners of the cloth if the price of gold was established at anything lower, say at 14 grams of silver. This, of course, does not imply that the exchange ratios between the different kinds of money have actually developed in this manner. It is to be understood as a logical, not a historical, explanation. Of the two precious metals gold and silver it must especially be remarked that their reciprocal exchange ratios have slowly developed with the development of their monetary position.

If no other relations than those of barter exist between the inhabitants of two areas, then balances in favor of one party or the other cannot arise. The objective exchange values of the quantities of commodities and services surrendered by each of the contracting parties must be equal, whether present goods or future goods are involved. Each constitutes the price of the other. This fact is not altered in any way if the exchange no longer proceeds directly but indirectly through the intermediaryship of one or more common media of exchange. The surplus of the balance of payments that is not settled by the consignment of goods and services but by the transmission of money was long regarded merely as a consequence of the state of international trade. It is one of the great achievements of Classical political economy to have exposed the fundamental error involved in this view. It demonstrated that international movements of money are not consequences of the state of trade; that they constitute not the effect, but the cause, of a favorable or unfavorable trade balance. The precious metals are distributed among individuals and hence among nations according to the extent and intensity of their demands for money. No individual and no nation need fear at any time to have less money than it needs. Government measures designed to regulate the international government of money in order to ensure that the community shall have the amount it needs, are just as unnecessary and inappropriate as, say, intervention to ensure a sufficiency or corn or iron or the like. This argument dealt the Mercantilist theory its death blow.[2]

Nevertheless statesmen are still greatly exercised by the problem of the international distribution of money. For hundreds of years, the Midas theory, systematized by Mercantilism, has been the rule followed by governments in taking measures of commercial policy. In spite of Hume, Smith, and Ricardo, it still dominates men's minds more than would be expected. Phoenixlike, it rises again and again from its own ashes. And indeed it would hardly be possible to overcome it with objective argument; for it numbers its disciples among that great host of the half-educated who are proof against any argument, however simple, if it threatens to rob them of long-cherished illusions that have become too dear to part with. It is only regrettable that these lay opinions not only predominate in discussions of economic policy on the part of legislators, the press—even the technical journals—and businessmen, but still occupy much space even in scientific literature. The blame for this must again be laid to the account of obscure notions concerning the nature of fiduciary media and their significance as regards the determination of prices. The reasons which, first in England and then in all other countries, were urged in favor of the limitation of the fiduciary note issue have never been understood by modern writers, who know them only at secondhand or thirdhand. That they in general plead for their retention, or only demand such modifications as leave the principle untouched, merely expresses their reluctance to replace an institution which on the whole has indubitably justified itself by a system whose effects they, to whom the phenomena of the market constitute an insoluble riddle, are naturally least of all able to foresee. When these writers seek for a motive in present-day banking policy, they can find none but that characterized by the slogan, "Protection of the national stock of the precious metals." We can pass the more lightly over these views in the present place since we

[2] See Senior, *Three Lectures on the Transmission of the Precious Metals from Country to Country and the Mercantile Theory of Wealth* (London, 1828), pp. 5 ff.

shall have further opportunity in part three to discuss the true meaning of the bank laws that limit the note issue.

Money does not flow to the place where the rate of interest is highest; neither is it true that it is the richest nations that attract money to themselves. The proposition is as true of money as of every other economic good, that its distribution among individual economic agents depends on its marginal utility. Let us first completely abstract from all geographical and political concepts, such as country and state, and imagine a state of affairs in which money and commodities are completely mobile within a unitary market area. Let us further assume that all payments, other than those cancelled out by offsetting or mutual balancing of claims, are made by transferring money, and not by the cession of fiduciary media; that is to say, that uncovered notes and deposits are unknown. This supposition, again, is similar to that of the "purely metallic currency" of the English Currency School, although with the help of our precise concept of fiduciary media we are able to avoid the obscurities and shortcomings of their point of view. In a state of affairs corresponding to these suppositions of ours, all economic goods, including of course money, tend to be distributed in such a way that a position of equilibrium between individuals is reached, when no further act of exchange that any individual could undertake would bring him any gain, any increase of subjective value. In such a position of equilibrium, the total stock of money, just like the total stocks of commodities, is distributed among individuals according to the intensity with which they are able to express their demand for it in the market. Every displacement of the forces affecting the exchange ratio between money and other economic goods brings about a corresponding change in this distribution, until a new position of equilibrium is reached. This is true of individuals, but it is also true of all the individuals in a given area taken together. For the goods possessed and the goods demanded by a nation are only the sums of the goods possessed and the goods demanded by all the economic agents, private as well as public, which make up the nation, among which the state as such admittedly occupies an important position, but a very far from dominant one.

Trade balances are not causes but merely concomitants of movements of money. For if we look beneath the veil with which the forms of monetary transactions conceal the nature of exchanges of goods, then it is clear that, even in international trade, commodities are exchanged for commodities, through the instrumentality of money. Just as the single individual does, so also all the individuals in an economic community taken together, wish in the last analysis to acquire not money, but other economic goods. If the state of the balance of payments is such that movements of money would have to occur from one country to the other, independently of any altered estimation of money on the part of their respective inhabitants, then operations are induced which reestablish equilibrium. Those persons who receive more money than they need will hasten to spend the surplus again as soon as possible, whether they buy production goods or consumption goods. On the other hand, those persons whose stock of money falls below the amount they need will be obliged to increase their stock of money, either by restricting their purchases or by disposing of commodities in their possession. The price variations, in the markets of the countries in question, that occur for these reasons, give rise to transactions which must always reestablish the equilibrium of the balance of payments. A credit or debit balance of payments that is not dependent upon an alteration in the conditions of demand for money can only be transient.[3]

Thus international movements of money, so far as they are not of a transient nature and consequently soon rendered ineffective by movements in the contrary direction, are always called forth by variations in the demand for money. Now it follows from this that a country in which fiduciary media are not employed is never in danger of losing its stock of money to other countries. Shortage of money and superabundance of money can no more be a permanent experience for a nation than for an individual. Ultimately they are spread out uniformly among all economic agents using the same economic good as common medium of exchange, and naturally their effects on the objective exchange value of money which bring about the adjustment between the stock of money and the demand

---

[3] See Ricardo, "Principles of Political Economy and Taxation," in *Works*, ed. Mc-Culloch, 2d ed. (London, 1852), pp. 213 ff.; Hertzka, *Das Wesen des Geldes* (Leipzig, 1887), pp. 42 ff.; Kinley, *Money* (New York, 1909), pp. 78 ff.; Wieser, "Der Geldwert und seine Veränderungen," *Schriften des Vereins für Sozialpolitik* 132: 530 ff.

for it are finally uniform for all economic agents. Measures of economic policy which aim at increasing the quantity of money circulating in a country could be successful so far as the money circulates in other countries also, only if they brought about a displacement in relative demands for money. Nothing is fundamentally altered in all this by the employment of fiduciary media. So far as there remains a demand for money in the narrower sense despite the use of fiduciary media, it will express itself in the same way.

There are many gaps in the Classical doctrine of international trade. It was built up at a time when international exchange relations were largely limited to dealings in present goods. No wonder, then, that its chief reference was to such goods or that it left out of account the possibility of an international exchange of services, and of present goods for future goods. It remained for a later generation to undertake the expansion and correction here necessary, a task that was all the easier since all that was wanted was a consistent expansion of the same doctrine to cover these phenomena as well. The classical doctrine had further restricted itself to that part of the problem presented by international metallic money. The treatment with which credit money had to be content was not satisfactory, and this shortcoming has not been entirely remedied yet. The problem has been regarded too much from the point of view of the technique of the monetary system and too little from that of the theory of exchange of goods. If the latter point of view had been adopted, it would have been impossible to avoid commencing the investigation with the proposition that the balance of trade between two areas with different currencies must always be in equilibrium, without the emergence of a balance needing to be corrected by the transport of money.[4] If we take a gold-standard and a silver-standard country as an example, then there still remains the possibility that the money of the one country will be put to a nonmonetary use in the other. Such a possibility must naturally be ruled out of account. The relations between two countries with fiat money would be the best example to take; if we merely make our example more general by

---

[4] Transitory displacements are possible, if foreign money is acquired in the speculative anticipation of its appreciating.

supposing that metallic money may be in use, then only the monetary use of the metallic money must be considered. It is then immediately clear that goods and services can only be paid for with other goods and services; that in the last analysis there can be no question of payment in money.

CHAPTER 11

The Problem of Measuring the Objective Exchange Value of Money and Variations in It

1

The History of the Problem

The problem of measuring the objective exchange value of money and its variations has attracted much more attention than its significance warrants. If all the columns of figures and tables and curves that have been prepared in this connection could perform what has been promised of them, then we should certainly have to agree that the tremendous expenditure of labor upon their construction would not have been in vain. In fact, nothing less has been hoped from them than the solution of the difficult questions connected with the problem of the objective exchange value of money. But it is very well known, and has been almost ever since the methods were discovered, that such aids cannot avail here.

The fact that, in spite of all this, the improvement of methods of calculating index numbers is still worked at most zealously, and that they have even been able to achieve a certain popularity that is otherwise denied to economic investigation, may well appear puzzling. It becomes explicable if we take into account certain peculiarities of the human mind. Like the king in Rückert's *Weisheit des Brahmanen*, the layman always tends to seek for formulae that sum up the results of scientific investigation in a few words. But the briefest and most pregnant expression for such summaries is in figures. Simple numerical statement is sought for even where the nature of the case excludes it. The most important results of research in the social sciences leave the multitude apathetic, but any set of figures awakens its interest. Its history becomes a series of dates, its economics a collection of statistical data. No other objection is more often brought against economics by laymen than that there are no economic laws; and if an attempt is made to meet this objection, then almost invariably the request is made that an example of such a law should be named and expounded—as if fragments of systems, whose study demands years of thought on the part of the expert, could be made intelligible to the novice in a few minutes. Only by letting fall morsels of statistics is it possible for the economic theorist to maintain his prestige in the face of questions of this sort.

Great names in the history of economics are associated with various systems of index numbers. Indeed, it was but natural that the best brains should have been the most attracted by this extraordinarily difficult problem. But in vain. Closer investigation shows us how little the inventors of the various index-number methods themselves thought of their attempts, how justly, as a rule, they were able to estimate their importance. He who cares to go to the trouble of demonstrating the uselessness of index numbers for monetary theory and the concrete tasks of monetary policy will be able to select a good proportion of his weapons from the writings of the very men who invented them.

2

The Nature of the Problem

The objective exchange value of the monetary unit can be expressed in units of any individual commodity. Just as we are in the habit of speaking of a money price of the other exchangeable goods, so we may conversely speak of the commodity price of money, and have then so many expressions for the objective exchange value of money as there are commercial commodities that are exchanged for money. But these expressions tell us little; they leave unanswered the questions that we want to solve. There are two parts to the problem of measuring the objective exchange value of money. First we have to obtain numerical demonstration of the fact of variations in the objective exchange value of money; then the question must be decided whether it is possible to make a quantitative examination of the causes of particular price movements, with special reference to the question whether it would be possible to produce evidence of such variations in the purchasing power of money as lie on the monetary side of the ratio.[1]

So far as the first-named problem is concerned, it is self-evident that its solution must assume the existence of a good, or complex of goods, of unchanging objective exchange value. The fact that such goods are inconceivable needs no further elucidation. For a good of this sort could exist only if all the exchange ratios between all goods were entirely free from variations. With the continually varying foundations on which the exchange ratios of the market ultimately rest, this presumption can never be true of a social order based upon the free exchange of goods.[2]

To measure is to determine the ratio of one quantity to another which is invariable or assumed to be invariable. Invariability in respect of the property to be measured, or at least the legitimacy of assuming such invariability, is a *sine qua non* of all measurement. Only when this assumption is admissible is it possible to determine the variations that are to be measured. Then, if the ratio between the measure and the object to be measured alter, this can only be referred to causes directly affecting the latter. Thus the problems of measuring the two kinds of variation in the objective exchange value of money go together. If the one is proved to be soluble, then so also is the other; and proof of the insolubility of the one is also proof of the insolubility of the other.

3

Methods of Calculating Index Numbers

Nearly all the attempts that have hitherto been made to solve the problem of measuring the objective exchange value of money have

[1] [Following Menger, we should call the first of these two problems the problem of the measurability of the *äussere* objective exchange value of money, the second that of the measurability of its *innere* objective exchange value. See also p. 146 n. H.E.B.]
[2] See Menger, *Grundsätze der Volkswirtschaftslehre*, 2d ed. (Vienna, 1923), pp. 298 ff.

started from the idea that if the price movements of a large number of commodities were combined by a particular method of calculation, the effects of those determinants of the price movements which lie on the side of the commodities would largely cancel one another out, and consequently, that such calculations would make it possible to discover the direction and extent of the effects of those determinants of price movements that lie on the monetary side. This assumption would prove correct, and the inquiries instituted with its help could led to the desired results, if the exchange ratios between the other economic goods were constant among themselves. Since this assumption does not hold good, refuge must be taken in all sorts of artificial hypotheses in order to obtain at least some sort of an idea of the significance of the results gained. But to do this is to abandon the safe ground of statistics and enter into a territory in which, in the absence of any reliable guidance (such as could be provided only by a complete understanding of all the laws governing the value of money), we must necessarily go astray. So long as the determinants of the objective exchange value of money are not satisfactorily elucidated in some other way, the sole possible reliable guide through the tangle of statistical material is lacking. But even if investigation into the determinants of prices and their fluctuations, and the separation of these determinants into single factors, could be achieved with complete precision, statistical investigation of prices would still be thrown on its own resources at the very point where it most needs support. That is to say, in monetary theory, as in every other branch of economic investigation, it will never be possible to determine the quantitative importance of the separate factors. Examination of the influence exerted by the separate determinants of prices will never reach the stage of being able to undertake numerical imputation among the different factors. All determinants of prices have their effect only through the medium of the subjective estimates of individuals; and the extent to which any given factor influences these subjective estimates can never be predicted. Consequently, the evaluation of the results of statistical investigations into prices, even if they could be supported by established theoretical conclusions, would still remain largely dependent on the rough estimates of the investigator, a circumstance that is apt to reduce their value considerably. Under certain conditions, index numbers may do very useful service as an aid to investigation into the history and statistics of prices; for the extension of the theory of the nature and value of money they are unfortunately not very important.

4

Wieser's Refinement of the Methods of Calculating Index Numbers

Very recently Wieser has made a new suggestion which constitutes an improvement of the budgetary method of calculating index numbers, notably employed by Falkner.[3] This is based on the view that when nominal wages change but continue to represent the same real wages, then the value of money has changed, because it expresses the same real quantity of value differently from before, or because the ratio of the monetary unit to the unit of real value has changed. On the other hand, the value of money is regarded as unchanged when nominal wages go up or down, but real wages move exactly parallel with them. If the contrast between money income and real income is substituted for that between nominal and real wages and the whole sum of the individuals in the community substituted for the single individual, then it is said to follow that such variations of the total money income as are accompanied by corresponding variations of the total real income do not indicate variations in the value of money at all, even if at the same time the prices of goods have changed in accordance with the altered conditions of supply. Only when the same real income is expressed by a different money income has the specific value of money changed. Thus to measure the value of money, a number of typical kinds of income should be chosen and the real expenditure corresponding to each determined, that is, the quantity of each kind of thing on which the incomes are spent. The money expenditure corresponding to this real expenditure is also to be shown, all for a particular base year; and then for each year the sums of money are to be evaluated in which the same quantities of real value were represented, given the prices ruling at the time. The result, it is claimed,

---

[3] On Falkner's method, see Laughlin, *The Principles of Money* (London, 1903), pp. 213–21; Kinley, *Money* (New York, 1909), pp. 253 ff.

would be the possibility of working out an average which would give for the whole country the monetary expression, as determined year by year in the market, of the real income taken as base. Thus it would be discovered whether a constant real value had a constant, a higher, or a lower, money expression year by year, and so a measure would be obtained of variations in the value of money.[4]

The technical difficulties in the way of employing this method, which is the most nearly perfect and the most deeply thought out of all methods of calculating index numbers, are apparently insurmountable. But even if it were possible to master them, this method could never fulfill the purpose that it is intended to serve. It could attain its end only under the same supposition that would justify all other methods; namely, the supposition that the exchange ratios between the individual economic goods excluding money are constant, and that only the exchange ratio between money and each of the other economic goods is liable to fluctuation. This would naturally involve an inertia of all social institutions, of population, of the distribution of wealth and income, and of the subjective valuations of individuals. Where everything is in a state of flux the supposition breaks down completely.

It was impossible for this to escape Wieser, who insists on allowance for the fact that the types of income and the classes into which the community is divided gradually alter, and that in the course of time certain kinds of consumption are discontinued and new kinds begun. For short periods, Wieser is of the opinion that this involves no particular difficulty; that it would be easy to retain the comparability of the totals by eliminating expenditures that did not enter into both sets of budgets. For long periods, he recommends Marshall's chain method of always including a sufficient number of transitional types and restricting comparisons to any given type and that immediately preceding or following it. This hardly does away with the difficulty. The farther we went back in history, the more we should have to eliminate; ultimately it seems that only those portions of real income would remain that serve to satisfy the most

---

[4] See Wieser, "Über die Messung der Veränderungen des Geldwerts," *Schriften des Vereins für Sozialpolitik* 132 (Leipzig, 1910): 544 ff. Joseph Lowe seems to have made a similar proposal as early as 1822; on this, see Walsh, *The Measurement of General Exchange Value* (New York, 1901), p. 84.

fundamental needs of existence. Even within this limited scope, comparisons would be impossible, as, say, between the clothing of the twentieth century and that of the tenth century. It is still less possible to trace back historically the typical incomes, which would necessarily involve consideration of the existing division of society into classes. The progress of social differentiation constantly increases the number of types of income. And this is by no means simply due to the splitting up of single types; the process is much more complicated. Members of one group break off and intermingle with other groups or portions of other groups in a most complicated manner. With what type of income of the past can we compare that, say, of the modern factory worker?

But even if we were to ignore all these considerations, other difficulties would arise. It is quite possible, even most probable, that subjective valuations of equal portions of real income have altered in the course of time. Changes in ways of living, in tastes, in opinions concerning the objective use value of individual economic goods, evoke quite extraordinarily large fluctuations here, even in short periods. If we do not take account of this in estimating the variations of the money value of these portions of income, then new sources of error arise that may fundamentally affect our results. On the other hand, there is no basis at all for taking account of them.

All index-number systems, so far as they are intended to have a greater significance for monetary theory than that of mere playing with figures, are based upon the idea of measuring the utility of a certain quantity of money.[5] The object is to determine whether a gram of gold is more or less useful today than it was at a certain time in the past. As far as objective use value is concerned, such an investigation may perhaps yield results. We may assume the fiction, if we like, that, say, a loaf of bread is always of the same utility in the objective sense, always comprises the same food value. It is not necessary for us to enter at all into the question of whether this is permissible or not. For certainly this is not the purpose of index numbers; their purpose is the determination of the subjective significance of the quantity of money in question. For this, recourse

---

[5] See Weiss, *Die moderne Tendenz in der Lehre vom Geldwert, Zeitschrift für Volkswirtschaft, Sozialpolitik und Verwaltung*, vol. 19, p. 546.

must be had to the quite nebulous and illegitimate fiction of an eternal human with invariable valuations. In Wieser's typical incomes that have to be traced back through the centuries may be seen an attempt to refine this fiction and to free it from its limitations. But even this attempt cannot make the impossible possible, and was necessarily bound to fail. It represents the most perfect conceivable development of the index-number system, and the fact that this also leads to no practical result condemns the whole business. Of course, this could not escape Wieser. If he neglected to lay particular stress upon it, this is probably due solely to the circumstance that his concern was not so much to indicate a way of solving this insoluble problem, as to extract from a usual method all that could be got from it.

5

The Practical Utility of Index Numbers

The inadmissibility of the methods proposed for measuring variations in the value of money does not obtrude itself too much if we only want to use them for solving practical problems of economic policy. Even if index numbers cannot fulfill the demands that theory has to make, they can still, in spite of their fundamental shortcomings and the inexactness of the methods by which they are actually determined, perform useful workaday services for the politician.

If we have no other aim in view than the comparison of points of time that lie close to one another, then the errors that are involved in every method of calculating numbers may be so far ignored as to allow us to draw certain rough conclusions from them. Thus, for example, it becomes possible to a certain extent to span the temporal gap that lies, in a period of variation in the value of money, between movements of stock exchange rates and movements of the purchasing power that is expressed in the prices of commodities.[6]

In the same way we can follow statistically the progress of vari-

---

[6] See also pp. 243 ff. below.

ations in purchasing power from month to month. The practical utility of all these calculations for certain purposes is beyond doubt; they have proved their worth in quite recent events. But we should beware of demanding more from them than they are able to perform.

CHAPTER 12

The Social Consequences of Variations in the Objective Exchange Value of Money

1

The Exchange of Present Goods for Future Goods

Variations in the objective exchange value of money evoke displacements in the distribution of income and property, on the one hand because individuals are apt to overlook the variability of the value of money, and on the other hand because variations in the value of money do not affect all economic goods and services uniformly and simultaneously.

For hundreds, even thousands, of years, people completely failed to see that variations in the objective exchange value of money could be induced by monetary factors. They tried to explain all variations of prices exclusively from the commodity side. It was Bodin's great achievement to make the first attack upon this assumption, which then quickly disappeared from scientific literature. It long continued to dominate lay opinion, but nowadays it appears to be badly shaken even here. Nevertheless, when individuals are exchanging present goods against future goods they do not take account in their valuations of variations in the objective exchange value of money. Lenders and borrowers are not in the habit of allowing for possible future fluctuations in the objective exchange value of money.

Transactions in which present goods are exchanged for future goods also occur when a future obligation has to be fulfilled, not in money, but in other goods. Still more frequent are transactions in which the contracts do not have to be fulfilled by either party until a later point of time. All such transactions involve a risk, and this fact is well known to all contractors. When anybody buys (or sells) corn, cotton, or sugar futures, or when anybody enters into a long-term contract for the supply of coal, iron, or timber, he is well aware of the risks that are involved in the transaction. He will carefully weigh the chances of future variations in prices, and often take steps, by means of insurance or hedging transactions such as the technique of the modern exchange has developed, to reduce the aleatory factor in his dealings.

In making long-term contracts involving money, the contracting parties are generally unconscious that they are taking part in a speculative transaction. Individuals are guided in their dealings by the belief that money is stable in value, that its objective exchange value is not liable to fluctuations, at least so far as its monetary determinants are concerned. This is shown most clearly in the attitude assumed by legal systems with regard to the problem of the objective exchange value of money.

In law, the objective exchange value of money is stable. It is sometimes asserted that legal systems adopt the *fiction* of the stability of the exchange value of money; but this is not true. In setting up a fiction, the law requires us to take an actual situation and imagine it to be different from what it really is, either by thinking of nonexistent elements as added to it or by thinking of existing elements as removed from it, so as to permit the application of legal maxims which refer only to the situation as thus transformed. Its purpose in doing this is to make it possible to decide cases according to analogy when a direct ruling does not apply. The whole nature of legal fictions is determined by this purpose, and they are sustained only so far as it requires. The legislator and the judge always remain aware that the fictitious situation does not correspond to reality. So it is also with the so-called dogmatic fiction that is employed in jurisprudence to permit legal facts to be systematically classified and related to each other. Here again, the situation is thought of *as* existing, but it is not assumed *to* exist.[1]

The attitude of the law to money is quite a different matter. The jurist is totally unacquainted with the problem of the value of money; he knows nothing of fluctuations in its exchange value. The naive popular belief in the stability of the value of money has been admitted, with all its obscurity, into the law, and no great historical cause of large and sudden variations in the value of money has ever provided a motive for critical examination of the legal attitude toward the subject. The system of civil law had already been completed when Bodin set the example of attempting to trace back variations in the purchasing power of money to causes exerting their influence from the monetary side. In this matter, the discoveries of more modern economists have left no trace on the law. For the law, the invariability of the value of money is not a fiction, but a fact.

All the same, the law does devote its attention to certain incidental questions of the value of money. It deals thoroughly with the question of how existing legal obligations and indebtednesses should be reckoned as affected by a transition from one currency to another. In earlier times, jurisprudence devoted the same attention to the royal debasement of the coinage as it was later to devote to the problems raised by the changing policies of states in choosing first between credit money and metallic money and then between gold and silver. Nevertheless, the treatment that these questions have received at the hands of the jurists has not resulted in recognition of the fact that the value of money is subject to continual fluctuation. In fact, the nature of the problem, and the way in which it was dealt with, made this impossible from the very beginning. It was treated, not as a question of the attitude of the law toward variations in the value of money, but as a question of the power of the prince or state arbitrarily to modify existing obligations and thus to destroy existing rights. At one time, this gave rise to the question whether the legal validity of the money was determined by the stamp of the ruler of

---

[1] See Dernburg, *Pandekten*, 6th ed. (Berlin, 1900), vol. 1, p. 84. On the fact that one of the chief characteristics of a fiction is the explicit consciousness of its fictitiousness, see also Vaihinger, *Die Philosophie des Als ob*, 6th ed. (Leipzig, 1920), p. 173; English trans., *The Philosophy of "As If"* (London: Kegan Paul, 1924).

the country or by the metal content of the coin; later, to the question whether the command of the law or the free usage of business was to settle if the money was legal tender or not. The answer of public opinion, grounded on the principles of private property and the protection of acquired rights, ran the same in both cases: "Prout quidque contractum est, ita et solvi debet; ut cum re contraximus, re solvi debet, veluti cum mutuum dedimus, ut retro pecuniae tantundem solvi debeat."[2] The proviso in this connection, that nothing was to be regarded as money except what passed for such at the time when the transaction was entered into and that the debt must be repaid not merely in the metal but in the currency that was specified in the contract, followed from the popular view, regarded as the only correct one by all classes of the community but especially by the tradesmen, that what was essential about a coin was its metallic content, and that the stamp had no other significance than as an authoritative certificate of weight and fineness. It occurred to nobody to treat coins in business transactions any differently from other pieces of metal of the same weight and fineness. In fact, it is now removed beyond doubt that the standard was a metallic one.

The view that in the fulfillment of obligations contracted in terms of money the metallic content alone of the money was to be taken into account prevailed against the nominalistic doctrine expounded by the minting authorities. It is manifested in the legal measures taken for stabilizing the metal content of the coinage, and since the end of the seventeenth century when currencies developed into systematic monetary standards it has provided the criterion for determining the ratio between different coins of the same metal (when current simultaneously or successively), and for the attempts, admittedly unsuccessful, to combine the two precious metals in a uniform monetary system.

Even the coming of credit money, and the problems that it raised, could not direct the attention of jurisprudence to the question of the

---

[2] L. 80, *Dig. de solutionibus et liberationibus* 46, 3. *Pomponius libro quarto ad Quintum Mucium.* See further Seidler, "Die Schwankungen des Geldwertes und die juristische Lehre von dem Inhalt der Geldschulden," *Jahrbücher für Nationalökonomie und Statistik* (1894), 3d series, vol. 7, pp. 685 ff.; Endemann, *Studien in der romanische-kanonistischen Wirtschafts- und Rechtslehre bis gegen Ende des 17 Jahrhunderts* (Berlin, 1874), vol. 2, p. 173.

value of money. A system of *paper* money was thought of as according with the spirit of the law only if the paper money remained constantly equivalent to the metallic money to which it was originally equivalent and which it had replaced or if the metal content or metal value of the claims remained decisive in contracts of indebtedness. But the fact that the exchange value of even *metallic* money is liable to variation has continued to escape explicit legal recognition and public opinion, at least as far as gold is concerned (and no other metal need nowadays be taken into consideration); there is not a single legal maxim that takes account of it, although it has been well known to economists for more than three centuries.

In its naive belief in the stability of the value of money the law is in complete harmony with public opinion. When any sort of difference arises between law and opinion, a reaction must necessarily follow; a movement sets in against that part of the law that is felt to be unjust. Such conflicts always tend to end in a victory of opinion over the law; ultimately the views of the ruling class become embodied in the law. The fact that it is nowhere possible to discover a trace of opposition to the attitude of the law on this question of the value of money shows clearly that its provisions relating to this matter cannot possibly be opposed to general opinion. That is to say, not only the law but public opinion also has never been troubled with the slightest doubt whatever concerning the stability of the value of money; in fact, so free has it been from doubts on this score that for an extremely long period money was regarded as the *measure* of value. And so when anybody enters into a credit transaction that is to be fulfilled in money it never occurs to him to take account of future fluctuations in the purchasing power of money.

Every variation in the exchange ratio between money and other economic goods shifts the position initially assumed by the parties to credit transactions in terms of money. An increase in the purchasing power of money is disadvantageous to the debtor and advantageous to the creditor; a decrease in its purchasing power has the contrary significance. If the parties to the contract took account of expected variations in the value of money when they exchanged present goods against future goods, these consequences would not occur. (But it is true that neither the extent nor the direction of these variations can be foreseen.)

The variability of the purchasing power of money is only taken into account when attention is drawn to the problem by the coexistence of two or more sorts of money whose exchange ratio is liable to big fluctuations. It is generally known that possible future variations in foreign-exchange rates are fully allowed for in the terms of credit transactions of all kinds. The part played by considerations of this sort, both in trade within countries where more than one sort of money is in use and in trade between countries with different currencies, is well known. But the allowance for the variability of the value of money in such cases is made in a fashion that is still not incompatible with the supposition that the value of money is stable. The fluctuations in value of one kind of money are measured by the equivalent of one of its units in terms of units of another kind of money, but the value of this other kind of money is for its part assumed to be stable. The fluctuations of the currency whose stability is in question are measured in terms of gold; but the fact that gold currencies are also liable to fluctuation is not taken into account. In their dealings individuals allow for the variability of the objective exchange value of money, so far as they are conscious of it; but they are conscious of it only with regard to certain kinds of money, not with regard to all. Gold, the principal common medium of exchange nowadays, is thought of as stable in value.[3]

So far as variations in the objective exchange value of money are foreseen, they influence the terms of credit transactions. If a future fall in the purchasing power of the monetary unit has to be reckoned with, lenders must be prepared for the fact that the sum of money which a debtor repays at the conclusion of the transaction will have a smaller purchasing power than the sum originally lent. Lenders, in fact, would do better not to lend at all, but to buy other

---

[3] In a review of the first edition (*Die Neue Zeit*, 30th year, vol. 2, p. 1024–1027), Hilferding criticized the above arguments as "merely funny." Perhaps it is demanding too much to expect this detached sense of humor to be shared by those classes of the German nation who have suffered in consequence of the depreciation of the mark. Yet only a year or two ago even these do not appear to have understood the problem any better. Fisher (*Hearings Before the Committee on Banking and Currency of the House of Representatives*, 67th Cong., 4th sess., on H.R. 11788 [Washington, D.C., 1923], pp. 5 ff., 25 ff.) gives typical illustrations. It was certainly an evil fate for Germany that its monetary and economic policy in recent years should have been in the hands of men like Hilferding and Havenstein, who were not qualified even for dealing with the depreciation of the mark in relation to gold.

goods with their money. The contrary is true for debtors. If they buy commodities with the money they have borrowed and sell them again after a time, they will retain a surplus over and above the sum that they have to pay back. The credit transaction results in a gain for them. Consequently it is not difficult to understand that, so long as continued depreciation is to be reckoned with, those who lend money demand higher rates of interest and those who borrow money are willing to pay the higher rates. If, on the other hand, it is expected that the value of money will increase, then the rate of interest will be lower than it would otherwise have been.[4]

Thus if the direction and extent of variations in the exchange value of money could be foreseen, they would not be able to affect the relations between debtor and creditor; the coming alterations in purchasing power could be sufficiently allowed for in the original terms of the credit transaction.[5] But since this assumption, even so far as fluctuations in credit money or fiat money relatively to gold money are concerned, never holds good except in a most imperfect manner, the allowance made in debt contracts for future variations in the value of money is necessarily inadequate; while even now-adays, after the big and rapid fluctuations in the value of gold that have occurred since the outbreak of the world war, the great majority of those concerned in economic life (one might, in fact, say all of them, apart from the few who are acquainted with theoretical economics) are completely ignorant of the fact that the value of gold is variable. The value of gold currencies is still regarded as stable.

Those economists who have recognized that the value of even the best money is variable have recommended that in settling the terms of credit transactions, that is to say, the terms on which present goods are exchanged for future goods, the medium of exchange should not be one good alone, as is usual nowadays, but a "bundle" of goods; it is possible in theory if not in practice to include *all* economic goods in such a bundle. If this proposal were adopted, money would still be used as a medium for the exchange of present goods; but in credit transactions the outstanding obligation would

---

[4] See Knies, *Geld und Kredit*, (Berlin, 1876), vol. 2, Part I, pp. 105 ff.; Fisher, *The Rate of Interest* (New York, 1907), pp. 77 ff., 257 ff., 327 ff., 356 ff.
[5] See Clark, *Essentials of Economic Theory* (New York, 1907), pp. 541 ff.

be discharged, not by payment of the nominal sum of money specified in the contract, but by payment of a sum of money with the purchasing power that the original sum had at the time when the contract was made. Thus, if the objective exchange value of money rises during the period of the contract, a correspondingly smaller sum of money will be payable; if it falls, a correspondingly larger sum.

The arguments devoted above to the problem of measuring variations in the value of money show the fundamental inadequacy of these recommendations. If the prices of the various economic goods are given equal weight in the determination of the parity coefficients without consideration of their relative quantities, then the evils for which a remedy is sought may merely be aggravated. If variations in the prices of such commodities as wheat, rye, cotton, coal, and iron are given the same significance as variations in the prices of such commodities as pepper, opium, diamonds, or nickel, then the establishment of the tabular standard would have the effect of making the content of long-term contracts even more uncertain than at present. If what is called a weighted average is used, in which individual commodities have an effect proportioned to their significance,[6] then the same consequences will still follow as soon as the conditions of production and consumption alter. For the subjective values attached by human beings to different economic goods are just as liable to constant fluctuation as are the conditions of production; but it is impossible to take account of this fact in determining the parity coefficients, because these must be invariable in order to permit connection with the past.

It is probable that the immediate associations of any mention nowadays of the effects of variations in the value of money on existing debt relations will be in terms of the results of the monstrous experiments in inflation that have characterized the recent history of Europe. In all countries, during the latter part of this period, the jurists have thoroughly discussed the question of whether it would have been possible or even whether it was still possible, by means of the existing law, or by creating new laws, to offset the injury done to creditors. In these discussions it was usually overlooked that the

---

[6] See Walsh, *The Measurement of General Exchange Value* (New York, 1901), pp. 80 ff.; Zižek, *Die statistischen Mittelwerte* (Leipzig, 1908), pp. 183 ff.

variations in the content of debt contracts that were consequent upon the depreciation of money were due to the attitude toward the problem taken by the law itself. It is not as if the legal system were being invoked to remedy an inconvenience for which it was not responsible. It was just its own attitude that was felt to be an inconvenience—the circumstance that the government had brought about depreciation. For the legal maxim by which an inconvertible banknote is legal tender equally with the gold money that was in circulation before the outbreak of the war, with which it has nothing in common but the name *mark*, is a part of the whole system of legal rules which allow the state to exploit its power to create new money as a source of income. It can no more be dissociated from this system than can the laws canceling the obligation of the banks to convert their notes and obliging them to make loans to the government by the issue of new notes.

When jurists and businessmen assert that the depreciation of money has a very great influence on all kinds of debt relations, that it makes all kinds of business more difficult, or even impossible, that it invariably leads to consequences that nobody desires and that everybody feels to be unjust, we naturally agree with them. In a social order that is entirely founded on the use of money and in which all accounting is done in terms of money, the destruction of the monetary system means nothing less than the destruction of the basis of all exchange. Nevertheless, this evil cannot be counteracted by *ad hoc* laws designed to remove the burden of the depreciation from single persons, or groups of persons, or classes of the community, and consequently to impose it all the more heavily on others. If we do not desire the pernicious consequences of depreciation, then we must make up our minds to oppose the inflationary policy by which the depreciation is created.

It has been proposed that monetary liabilities should be settled in terms of gold and not according to their nominal amount. If this proposal were adopted, for each mark that had been borrowed that sum would have to be repaid that could at the time of repayment buy the same weight of gold as one mark could at the time when the debt contract was entered into.[7] The fact that such proposals are

---

[7] See Mügel, *Geldentwertung und Gesetzgebung* (Berlin, 1923), p. 24.

now put forward and meet with approval shows that etatism has already lost its hold on the monetary system and that inflationary policies are inevitably approaching their end.[8] Even only a few years ago, such a proposal would either have been ridiculed or else branded as high treason. (It is, by the way, characteristic that the first step toward enforcing the idea that the legal tender of paper money should be restricted to its market value was taken without exception in directions that were favorable to the national exchequer.)

To do away with the consequences of unlimited inflationary policy one thing only is necessary—the renunciation of all inflationary measures. The problem which the proponents of the tabular standard seek to solve by means of a "commodity currency" supplementing the metallic currency, and which Irving Fisher seeks to solve by his proposals for stabilizing the purchasing power of money, is a different one—that of dealing with variations in the value of *gold*.

2

Economic Calculation and Accountancy

The naive conception of money as stable in value or as a measure of value is also responsible for economic calculation being carried out in terms of money.

Even in other respects, accountancy is not perfect. The precision of its statements is only illusory. The valuations of goods and rights with which it deals are always based on estimates depending on more or less uncertain and unknown factors. So far as this uncertainty arises from the commodity side of the valuations, commercial practice, sanctioned by the law, attempts to get over the difficulty by the exercise of the greatest possible caution. With this purpose it demands conservative estimates of assets and liberal estimates of liabilities, so that the merchant may be preserved from self-deceit about the success of his enterprises and his creditors protected.

But there are also shortcomings in accountancy that are due to the uncertainty in its valuations that results from the liability to

---

[8] [It should be remembered that all this was written in 1924. H.E.B.]

variation of the value of money itself. Of this, the merchant, the accountant, and the commercial court are alike unsuspicious. They hold money to be a measure of price and value, and they reckon as freely in monetary units as in units of length, area, capacity, and weight. And if an economist happens to draw their attention to the dubious nature of this procedure, they do not even understand the point of his remarks.[9]

This disregard of variations in the value of money in economic calculation falsifies accounts of profit and loss. If the value of money falls, ordinary bookkeeping, which does not take account of monetary depreciation, shows apparent profits, because it balances against the sums of money received for sales a cost of production calculated in money of a higher value, and because it writes off from book values originally estimated in money of a higher value items of money of a smaller value. What is thus improperly regarded as profit, instead of as part of capital, is consumed by the entrepreneur or passed on either to the consumer in the form of price reductions

---

[9] At Vienna in March 1892 at the sessions of the Currency Inquiry Commission, which was appointed in preparation for the regulation of the Austrian currency, Carl Menger remarked: "I should like to add that not only legislators, but all of us in our everyday life, are in the habit of disregarding the fluctuations in the purchasing power of money. Even such distinguished bankers as yourselves, gentlemen, draw up your balance sheet at the end of the year without inquiring whether by any chance the sum of money representing the share capital has gained or lost in purchasing power." These remarks of Menger's were not understood by the director of the Bodenkreditanstalt, Theodor von Taussig, the most outstanding of all Austrian bankers. He replied: "A balance sheet is a balancing of the property or assets of a company or individual against its liabilities, both expressed in terms of the accepted measure of value or monetary standard, that is, for Austria in gulden. Now I cannot see how, when we are thus expressing property and indebtedness in terms of the standard (which we have assumed to be homogeneous), we are to take account of variations in the standard of measurement instead of taking account of variations in the object to be measured, as is customary." Taussig completely failed to see that the point at issue concerned the estimation of the value of goods and the amount of depreciation to be written off, and not the balancing of monetary claims and monetary obligations, or that a profit and loss account, if it is not to be hopelessly inexact, must take account of variations in the value of money. Menger had no occasion to raise this point in his reply, since he was rather concerned to show that his remarks were not to be interpreted, as Taussig was inclined to interpret them, as an accusation of dishonest practice on the part of the bank directors. Menger added: "What I said was merely that *all* of us, not *only* the directors of the banks (I said *even* such men as are at the head of the banks), make the mistake of not taking account in everyday life of changes in the value of money" (*Stenographische Protokolle über die vom 8. bis 17. März 1892 abgehaltenen Sitzungen der nach Wien einberufenen Währungs-Enquete-Kommission* [Vienna, 1892], pp. 211, 257, 270).

that would not otherwise have been made or to the laborer in the form of higher wages, and the government proceeds to tax it as income or profits. In any case, consumption of capital results from the fact that monetary depreciation falsifies capital accounting. Under certain conditions the consequent destruction of capital and increase of consumption may be partly counteracted by the fact that the depreciation also gives rise to genuine profits, those of debtors, for example, which are not consumed but put into reserves. But this can never more than partly balance the destruction of capital induced by the depreciation.[10]

The consumers of the commodities that are sold too cheaply as a result of the false reckoning induced by the depreciation need not be inhabitants of the territory in which the depreciating money is used as the national currency. The price reductions brought about by currency depreciation encourage export to countries the value of whose money is either not falling at all or at least falling less rapidly. The entrepreneur who is reckoning in terms of a currency with a stable value is unable to compete with the entrepreneur who is prepared to make a quasi-gift of part of his capital to his customers. In 1920 and 1921, Dutch traders who had sold commodities to Austria could buy them back again after a while much more cheaply than they had originally sold them, because the Austrian traders completely failed to see that they were selling them for less than they had cost.

So long as the true state of the case is not recognized, it is customary to rejoice in a naive Mercantilistic fashion over the increase of exports and to see in the depreciation of money a welcome "export premium." But once it is discovered that the source whence this premium flows is the capital of the community, then the "selling off" procedure is usually regarded less favorably. Again, in importing countries the public attitude wavers between indignation against "dumping" and satisfaction with the favorable conditions of purchase.

Where the currency depreciation is a result of government inflation carried out by the issue of notes, it is possible to avert its disastrous effect on economic calculation by conducting all book-

---

[10] See my book, *Nation, Staat und Wirtschaft* (Vienna, 1919), pp. 129 ff. A whole series of writings dealing with these questions has since appeared in Germany and Austria.

keeping in a stable money instead. But so far as the depreciation is a depreciation of gold, the world money, there is no such easy way out.[11]

3

Social Consequences of Variations in the Value of Money When Only One Kind of Money Is Employed

If we disregard the exchange of present goods for future goods, and restrict our considerations for the time being to those cases in which the only exchanges are those between present goods and present money, we shall at once observe a fundamental difference between the effects of an isolated variation in a single commodity price, emanating solely from the commodity side, and the effects of a variation in the exchange ratio between money and other economic goods in general, emanating from the monetary side. Variations in the price of a single commodity influence the distribution of goods among individuals primarily because the commodity in question, if it plays a part in exchange transactions at all, is *ex definitione* not distributed among individuals in proportion to their demands for it. There are economic agents who produce it (in the broadest sense of the word, so as to include dealers) and sell it, and there are economic agents who merely buy it and consume it. And it is obvious what effects would result from a displacement of the exchange ratio between this particular good and the other economic goods (including money); it is clear who would be likely to benefit by them and who to be injured.

The effects in the case of money are different. As far as money is concerned, all economic agents are to a certain extent dealers.[12] Every separate economic agent maintains a stock of money that corresponds to the extent and intensity with which he is able to express his demand for it in the market. If the objective exchange value of all the stocks of money in the world could be instantaneously and in equal proportion increased or decreased, if all at once the money prices of all goods and services could rise or fall

---

[11] Cf. further pp. 440 ff. below.
[12] See Ricardo, *Letters to Malthus,* ed. Bonar (Oxford, 1887), p. 10.

uniformly, the relative wealth of individual economic agents would not be affected. Subsequent monetary calculation would be in larger or smaller figures; that is all. The variation in the value of money would have no other significance than that of a variation of the calendar or of weights and measures.

The social displacements that occur as consequences of variations in the value of money result solely from the circumstance that this assumption never holds good. In the chapter dealing with the determinants of the objective exchange value of money it was shown that variations in the value of money always start from a given point and gradually spread out from this point through the whole community. And this alone is why such variations have an effect on the social distribution of income.

It is true that the variations in market exchange ratios that emanate from the commodity side are also not as a rule completed all at once; they also start at some particular point and then spread with greater or less rapidity. And because of this, price variations of this sort too are followed by consequences that are due to the fact that the variations in prices do not occur all at once but only gradually. But these are consequences that are encountered in a marked degree by a limited number of economic agents only, namely, those who, as dealers or producers, are sellers of the commodity in question. And further, this is not the sum of the consequences of variations in the objective exchange value of a commodity. When the price of coal falls because production has increased while demand has remained unaltered, then, for example, those retailers are involved who have taken supplies from the wholesale dealers at the old higher price but are now able to dispose of them only at the new and lower price. But this alone will not account for all the social changes brought about by the increase of production of coal. The increase in the supply of coal will have improved the economic position of the community. The fall in the price of coal does not merely amount to a rearrangement of income and property between producer and consumer; it also expresses an increase in the national dividend and national wealth. Many have gained what none have lost. The case of money is different.

The most important of the causes of a diminution in the value of money of which we have to take account is an increase in the stock of money while the demand for it remains the same, or falls off, or, if it increases, at least increases less than the stock. This increase in the stock of money, as we have seen, starts with the original owners of the additional quantity of money and then transfers itself to those that deal with these persons, and so forth. A lower subjective valuation of money is then passed on from person to person because those who come into possession of an additional quantity of money are inclined to consent to pay higher prices than before. High prices lead to increased production and rising wages, and, because all of this is generally regarded as a sign of economic prosperity, a fall in the value of money is, and always has been, considered an extraordinarily effective means of increasing economic welfare.[13] This is a mistaken view, for an increase in the quantity of money results in no increase of the stock of consumption goods at people's disposal. Its effect may well consist in an alteration of the *distribution* of economic goods among human beings but in no case, apart from the incidental circumstance referred to on page 161 above, can it directly increase the *total* amount of goods possessed by human beings, or their welfare. It is true that this result may be brought about *indirectly,* in the way in which any change in distribution may affect production as well; that is, by those classes in whose favor the redistribution occurs using their additional command of money to accumulate more capital than would have been accumulated by those people from whom the money was withdrawn. But this does not concern us here. What we are concerned with is whether the variation in the value of money has any other economic significance than its effect on distribution. If it has no other economic significance, then the increase of prosperity can only be apparent; for it can only benefit a part of the community at the cost of a corresponding loss by the other part. And thus in fact the matter is. The cost must be borne by those classes or countries that are the last to be reached by the fall in the value of money.

Let us, for instance, suppose that a new gold mine is opened in an isolated state. The supplementary quantity of gold that streams from it into commerce goes at first to the owners of the mine and then by turns to those who have dealings with them. If we sche-

---

[13] See Hume, *Essays,* ed. Frowde (London), p. 294 ff.

matically divide the whole community into four groups, the mine owners, the producers of luxury goods, the remaining producers, and the agriculturalists, the first two groups will be able to enjoy the benefits resulting from the reduction in the value of money, the former of them to a greater extent than the latter. But even as soon as we reach the third group, the situation is altered. The profit obtained by this group as a result of the increased demands of the first two will already be offset to some extent by the rise in the prices of luxury goods which will have experienced the full effect of the depreciation by the time it begins to affect other goods. Finally, for the fourth group, the whole process will result in nothing but loss. The farmers will have to pay dearer for all industrial products before they are compensated by the increased prices of agricultural products. It is true that when at last the prices of agricultural products do rise, the period of economic hardship for the farmers is over; but it will no longer be possible for them to secure profits that will compensate them for the losses they have suffered. That is to say, they will not be able to use their increased receipts to purchase commodities at prices corresponding to the old level of the value of money; for the increase of prices will already have gone through the whole community. Thus the losses suffered by the farmers at the time when they still sold their products at the old low prices but had to pay for the products of others at the new and higher prices remain uncompensated. It is these losses of the groups that are the last to be reached by the variation in the value of money which ultimately constitute the source of the profits made by the mine owners and the groups most closely connected with them.

There is no difference between the effects on the distribution of income and wealth that are evoked by the fact that variations in the objective exchange value of money do not affect different goods and services at the same time and in the same degree, whether the case is that of metallic money or that of fiat or credit money. When the increase of money proceeds by way of issue of currency notes or inconvertible banknotes, at first only certain economic agents benefit and the additional quantity of money only spreads gradually through the whole community. If, for example, there is an issue of paper money in time of war, the new notes will first go into the pockets of the war contractors. "As a result, these persons' demands for certain articles will increase and so also the price and the sale of these articles, but especially in so far as they are luxury articles. Thus the position of the producers of these articles will be improved, their demand for other commodities will also increase, and thus the increase of prices and sales will go on, distributing itself over a constantly augmented number of articles, until at last it has reached them all."[14] In this case, as before, there are those who gain by inflation and those who lose by it. The sooner anybody is in a position to adjust his money income to its new value, the more favorable will the process be for him. Which persons, groups, and classes fare better in this, and which worse, depends upon the actual data of each individual case, without knowledge of which we are not in a position to form a judgment.

Let us now leave the example of the isolated state and turn our attention to the international movements that arise from a fall in the value of money due to an increase in its amount. Here, again, the process is the same. There is no increase in the available stock of goods; only its distribution is altered. The country in which the new mines are situated and the countries that deal directly with it have their position bettered by the fact that they are still able to buy commodities from other countries at the old lower prices at a time when depreciation at home has already occurred. Those countries that are the last to be reached by the new stream of money are those which must ultimately bear the cost of the increased welfare of the other countries. Thus Europe made a bad bargain when the newly discovered gold fields of America, Australia, and South Africa evoked a tremendous boom in these countries. Palaces rose over night where there was nothing a few years before but virgin forest and wilderness; the prairies were intersected with railways; and anything and everything in the way of luxury goods that could be produced by the Old World found markets in territories which a little earlier had been populated by naked nomads and among people who in many cases had previously been without even the barest necessaries of existence. All of this wealth was imported from the old industrial countries by the new colonists, the fortunate diggers, and paid for in gold that was spent as freely as it had been received.

---

[14] Auspitz and Lieben, *Untersuchungen über die Theorie des Preises* (Leipzig, 1889), p. 65.

It is true that the prices paid for these commodities were higher than would have corresponded to the earlier purchasing power of money; nevertheless, they were not so high as to make full allowance for the changed circumstances. Europe had exported ships and rails, metal goods and textiles, furniture and machines, for gold which it little needed or did not need at all, for what it had already was enough for all its monetary transactions.

A diminution of the value of money brought about by any other kind of cause has an entirely similar effect. For the economic consequences of variations in the value of money are determined, not by their causes, but by the nature of their slow progress, from person to person, from class to class, and from country to country. If we consider in particular those variations in the value of money which arise from the action of sellers in increasing prices, as described in the second chapter of this part, we shall find that the resultant gradual diminution of the value of money constitutes one of the motives of the groups which apparently dictate the rise of prices. The groups which begin the rise have it turned to their own disadvantage when the other groups eventually raise their prices too; but the former groups receive their higher prices at a time when the prices of the things they buy are still at the lower level. This constitutes a permanent gain for them. It is balanced by the losses of those groups who are the last to raise the prices of their goods or services; for these already have to pay the higher prices at a time when they are still receiving only the lower prices for what they sell. And when they eventually raise their prices also, being the last to do this they can no longer offset their earlier losses at the expense of other classes of the community. Wage laborers used to be in this situation, because as a rule the price of labor did not share in the earlier stages of upward price movements. Here the entrepreneurs gained what the laborers lost. For a long time, civil servants were in the same situation. Their multitudinous complaints were partly based on the fact that, since their money incomes could not easily be increased, they had largely to bear the cost of the continual rise in prices. But recently this state of affairs has been changed through the organization of the civil servants on trade-union lines, which has enabled them to secure a quicker response to demands for increases of salaries.

The converse of what is true of a depreciation in the value of money holds for an increase in its value. Monetary appreciation, like monetary depreciation, does not occur suddenly and uniformly throughout a whole community, but as a rule starts from single classes and spreads gradually. If this were not the case, and if the increase in the value of money took place almost simultaneously in the whole community, then it would not be accompanied by the special kind of economic consequences that interest us here. Let us assume, for instance, that bankruptcy of the credit-issuing institutions of a country leads to a panic and that everybody is ready to sell commodities at any price whatever in order to put himself in possession of cash, while on the other hand buyers cannot be found except at greatly reduced prices. It is conceivable that the increase in the value of money that would arise in consequence of such a panic would reach all persons and commodities uniformly and simultaneously. As a rule, however, an increase in the value of money spreads only gradually. The first of those who have to content themselves with lower prices than before for the commodities they sell, while they still have to pay the old higher prices for the commodities they buy, are those who are injured by the increase in the value of money. Those, however, who are the last to have to reduce the prices of the commodities they sell, and have meanwhile been able to take advantage of the fall in the prices of other things, are those who profit by the change.

4

*The Consequences of Variations in the Exchange Ratio Between
Two Kinds of Money*

Among the consequences of variations in the value of money it is those of variations in the exchange ratio between two different kinds of money in which economic science has been chiefly interested. This interest has been aroused by the events of monetary history. In the course of the nineteenth century, international trade developed in a hitherto undreamed-of manner, and the economic connections between countries became extraordinarily close. Now just at this time when commercial relations were beginning to grow more active, the monetary standards of the individual states were becoming more diverse. A number of countries went over for a shorter or longer period to credit money, and the others, which were partly on gold and partly on silver, were soon in difficulties, because the ratio between the values of these two precious metals, which had changed but slowly during centuries, suddenly began to exhibit sharp variations. And in recent years this problem has been given a much greater practical significance still by monetary happenings in the war and postwar periods.

Let us suppose that one kilogram of silver had been exchangeable for ten quintals of wheat, and that upon the objective exchange value of silver being halved, owing, say, to the discovery of new and prolific mines, one kilogram of it was no longer able to purchase more than five bushels of wheat. From what has been said on the natural exchange ratio of different kinds of money, it follows that the objective exchange value of silver in terms of other kinds of money would now also be halved. If it had previously been possible to purchase one kilogram of gold with fifteen kilograms of silver, thirty kilograms would now be needed to make the same purchase; for the objective exchange value of gold in relation to commodities would have remained unchanged, while that of silver had been halved. Now this change in the purchasing power of silver over commodities will not occur all at once, but gradually. A full account has been given of the way in which it will start from a certain point and gradually spread outward, and of the consequences of this process. Until now we have investigated these consequences only so far as they occur within an area with a uniform monetary standard; but now we must trace up the further consequences involved in commercial relations with areas in which other sorts of money are employed. One thing that was found to be true of the former case can be predicated of this also: if the variations in the objective exchange value of the money occurred uniformly and simultaneously throughout the whole community, then such social consequences could not appear at all. The fact that these variations always occur *one after another* is the sole reason for their remarkable economic effects.

Variations in the objective exchange value of a given kind of money do not affect the determination of the exchange ratio between this and other kinds of money until they begin to affect commodities that either are already objects of commercial relations between the two areas or at least are able to become such upon a moderate change in prices. The point of time at which this situation arises determines the effects upon the commercial relations of the two areas that will result from variations in the objective exchange value of money. These vary according as the prices of the commodities concerned in international trade are adjusted to the new value of money before or after those of other commodities. Under the modern organization of the monetary system this adjustment is usually first made on the stock exchanges. Speculation on the foreign-exchange and security markets anticipates coming variations in the exchange ratios between the different kinds of money at a time when the variations in the value of money have by no means completed their course through the community, perhaps when they have only just begun it, but in any case before they have reached the commodities that play a decisive part in foreign trade. He would be a poor speculator who did not grasp the course of events in time and act accordingly. But as soon as the variation in the foreign-exchange rate has been brought about, it reacts upon foreign trade in a peculiar manner until the prices of all goods and services have been adjusted to the new objective exchange value of money. During this interval the margins between the different prices and wages constitute a fund that somebody must receive and somebody surrender. In a word, we are here again confronted with a redistribution, which is noteworthy in that its influence extends beyond the area where the good whose objective exchange value is changing is employed as domestic money. It is clear that this is the only sort of consequence that can follow from variations in the value of money. The social stock of goods has in no way been increased; the total quantity that can be distributed has remained the same.

As soon as an uncompleted change in the objective exchange value of any particular kind of money becomes expressed in the foreign-exchange rates, a new opportunity of making a profit is opened up, either for exporters or for importers according as the purchasing power of money is decreasing or increasing. Let us take the former case, that of a diminution in the value of money. Since, according to our assumptions, the changes in domestic prices are not yet finished, exporters derive an advantage from the circumstance that the commodities that they market already fetch the new higher prices whereas the commodities and services that they want themselves and, what is of particular importance, the material and personal factors of production that they employ, are still obtainable at the old lower prices. Who the "exporter" is who pockets this gain, whether it is the producer or the dealer, is impertinent to our present inquiry; all that we need to know is that in the given circumstances transactions will result in profit for some and loss for others.

In any case the exporter shares his profit with the foreign importer and foreign consumer. And it is even possible—this depends upon the organization of the export trade—that the profits which the exporter retains are only apparent, not real.

Thus the result is always that the gains of foreign buyers, which in certain cases are shared with home exporters, are counterbalanced by losses that are borne entirely at home. It is clear that what was said of the promotion of exportation by the falsification of monetary accounting applies also to the "export premium" arising from a diminution of the value of money.

CHAPTER 13

Monetary Policy

1

Monetary Policy Defined[1]

The economic consequences of fluctuations in the objective exchange value of money have such important bearings on the life of the community and of the individual that as soon as the state had abandoned the attempt to exploit for fiscal ends its authority in monetary matters, and as soon as the large-scale development of the modern economic community had enabled the state to exert a decisive influence on the kind of money chosen by the market, it was an obvious step to think of attaining certain sociopolitical aims by influencing these consequences in a systematic manner. Modern currency policy is something essentially new; it differs fundamentally from earlier state activity in the monetary sphere. Previously, good government in monetary matters—from the point of view of the citizen—consisted in conducting the business of minting so as to furnish commerce with coins which could be accepted by everybody at their face value; and bad government in monetary matters—again from the point of view of the citizen—amounted to the be-

[1] [The author uses the term *Geldwertpolitik* in the technical sense defined in the above section. I have reserved the term *monetary policy* for this special meaning. *Currency policy* is the term I have used to translate *Währungspolitik*. H.E.B.]

247

trayal by the state of the general confidence in it. But when states did debase the coinage, it was always from purely fiscal motives. The government needed financial help, that was all; it was not concerned with questions of currency policy.

Questions of currency policy are questions of the objective exchange value of money. The nature of the monetary system affects a currency policy only insofar as it involves these particular problems of the value of money; it is only insofar as they bear upon these questions that the legal and technical characteristics of money are pertinent. Measures of currency policy are intelligible only in the light of their intended influence on the objective exchange value of money. They consequently comprise the antithesis of those acts of economic policy which aim at altering the money prices of single commodities or groups of commodities.

Not every value problem connected with the objective exchange value of money is a problem of currency policy. In conflicts of currency policy there are also interests involved which are not primarily concerned with the alteration of the value of money for its own sake. In the great struggle that was involved in the demonetization of silver and the consequent movement of the relative exchange ratio of the two precious metals gold and silver, the owners of the silver mines and the other protagonists of the double standard or of the silver standard were not actuated by the same motives. While the latter wanted a change in the value of money in order that there might be a general rise in the prices of commodities, the former merely wished to raise the price of *silver as a commodity* by securing, or more correctly regaining, an extensive market for it. Their interests were in no way different from those of producers of iron or oil in trying to extend the market for iron or oil so as to increase the profitability of their businesses. It is true that this is a value problem, but it is a *commodity*-value problem—that of increasing the exchange value of the metal silver—and not a problem of the value of money.[2]

---

[2] Similar interests, say those of the printers, lithographers, and the like, may play a part in the production of paper money also. Perhaps such motives had something to do with Benjamin Franklin's recommendation of an increase of paper money in his first political writing, which was published (anonymously) in Philadelphia in 1729: "A Modest Inquiry into the Nature and Necessity of a Paper Currency" (in *The Works of Benjamin Franklin*, ed. Sparks [Chicago, 1882], vol. 2, pp. 253–77). Shortly before—as he relates in his autobiography (*ibid.*, vol. 1, p. 73)—he had printed the notes for New Jersey, and when his pamphlet led to the decision to issue more notes

But although this motive has played a part in currency controversy, it has been a very subordinate part. Even in the United States, the most important silver-producing area, it has been of significance only inasmuch as the generous practical encouragement of the silver magnates has been one of the strongest supports of the bimetallistic agitation. But most of the recruits to the silver camp were attracted, not by the prospect of an increase in the value of the mines, which was a matter of indifference to them, but by the hope of a fall in the purchasing power of money, from which they promised themselves miraculous results. If the increase in the price of silver could have been brought about in any other way than through the extension of its use as money, say by the creation of a new industrial demand, then the owners of the mines would have been just as satisfied; but the farmers and industrialists who advocated a silver currency would not have benefited from it in any way. And then they would undoubtedly have transferred their allegiance to other currency policies. Thus, in many states, paper inflationism was advocated, partly as a forerunner of bimetallism and partly in combination with it.

But even though questions of currency policy are never more than questions of the value of money, they are sometimes disguised so that their true nature is hidden from the uninitiated. Public opinion is dominated by erroneous views on the nature of money and its value, and misunderstood slogans have to take the place of clear and precise ideas. The fine and complicated mechanism of the money and credit system is wrapped in obscurity, the proceedings on the stock exchange are a mystery, the function and significance of the banks elude interpretation. So it is not surprising that the arguments brought forward in the conflict of the different interests often missed the point altogether. Counsel was darkened with cryptic phrases whose meaning was probably hidden even from those who uttered them. Americans spoke of "the dollar of our fathers" and Austrians of "our dear old gulden note"; silver, the money of the common man, was set up against gold, the money of the aristocracy. Many a tribune of the people, in many a passionate dis-

---

in Pennsylvania, despite the opposition of the "rich men," he got the order to print the notes. He remarks on this in his autobiography: "A very profitable job, and a great help to me. This was another advantage gained by me being able to write" (*ibid.*, p. 92).

course, sounded the loud praises of silver, which, hidden in deep mines, lay awaiting the time when it should come forth into the light of day to ransom miserable humanity, languishing in its wretchedness. And while some thus regarded gold as nothing less than the embodiment of the very principle of evil, all the more enthusiastically did others exalt the glistening yellow metal which alone was worthy to be the money of rich and mighty nations. It did not seem as if men were disputing about the distribution of economic goods; rather it was as if the precious metals were contending among themselves and against paper for the lordship of the market. All the same, it would be difficult to claim that these Olympic struggles were engendered by anything but the question of altering the purchasing power of money.

2

The Instruments of Monetary Policy

The principal instrument of monetary policy at the disposal of the state is the exploitation of its influence on the choice of the *kind* of money. It has been shown above that the position of the state as controller of the mint and as issuer of money substitutes has allowed it in modern times to exert a decisive influence over individuals in their choice of the common medium of exchange. If the state uses this power systematically in order to force the community to accept a particular sort of money whose employment it desires for reasons of monetary policy, then it is actually carrying through a measure of monetary policy. The states which completed the transition to a gold standard a generation ago, did so from motives of monetary policy. They gave up the silver standard or the credit-money standard because they recognized that the behavior of the value of silver or of credit money was unsuited to the economic policy they were following. They adopted the gold standard because they regarded the behavior of the value of gold as relatively the most suitable for carrying out their monetary policies.

If a country has a metallic standard, then the *only* measure of currency policy that it can carry out by itself is to go over to another kind of money. It is otherwise with credit money and fiat money.

Here the state is able to influence the movement of the objective exchange value of money by increasing or decreasing its quantity. It is true that the means is extremely crude, and that the extent of its consequences can never be foreseen. But it is easy to apply and popular on account of its drastic effects.

3

Inflationism

Inflationism is that monetary policy that seeks to increase the quantity of money.

Native inflationism demands an increase in the quantity of money without suspecting that this will diminish the purchasing power of the money. It wants more money because in its eyes the mere abundance of money is wealth. *Fiat* money! Let the state "create" money, and make the poor rich, and free them from the bonds of the capitalists! How foolish to forgo the opportunity of making everybody rich, and consequently happy, that the state's right to create money gives it! How wrong to forgo it simply because this would run counter to the interests of the rich! How wicked of the economists to assert that it is not within the power of the state to create wealth by means of the printing press!—*You statesmen want to build railways, and complain of the low state of the exchequer? Well, then, do not beg loans from the capitalists and anxiously calculate whether your railways will bring in enough to enable you to pay interest and amortization on your debt. Create money, and help yourselves.* [3]

Other inflationists realize very well that an increase in the quantity of money reduces the purchasing power of the monetary unit. But they endeavor to secure inflation nonetheless, *because* of its effect on the value of money; they want depreciation, because they want to favor debtors at the expense of creditors and because they want to encourage exportation and make importation difficult. Others, again, recommend depreciation for the sake of its supposed property of stimulating production and encouraging the spirit of enterprise.

---

[3] On the naive inflationary proposals that have been made in recent years by the motor-car manufacturer Henry Ford, the famous inventor Edison, and the American senator Ladd, see Yves Guyot, *Les problèmes de la déflation* (Paris, 1923), pp. 281 f.

Depreciation of money can benefit debtors only when it is unforeseen. If inflationary measures and a reduction of the value of money are expected, then those who lend money will demand higher interest in order to compensate their probable loss of capital, and those who seek loans will be prepared to pay the higher interest because they have a prospect of gaining on capital account. Since, as we have shown, it is never possible to foresee the extent of monetary depreciation, creditors in individual cases may suffer losses and debtors make profits, in spite of the higher interest exacted. Nevertheless, in general it will not be possible for any inflationary policy, unless it takes effect suddenly and unexpectedly, to alter the relations between creditor and debtor in favor of the latter by increasing the quantity of money.[4] Those who lend money will feel obliged, in order to avoid losses, either to make their loans in a currency that is more stable in value than the currency of their own country, or to include in the rate of interest they ask, over and above the compensation that they reckon for the probable depreciation of money and the loss to be expected on that account, an additional premium for the risk of a *less* probable further depreciation. And if those who were seeking credit were inclined to refuse to pay this additional compensation, the diminution of supply in the loan market would force them to it. During the inflation after the war it was seen how savings deposits decreased because savings banks were not inclined to adjust interest rates to the altered conditions of the variations in the purchasing power of money.

It has already been shown in the preceding chapter that it is a mistake to think that the depreciation of money stimulates production. If the particular conditions of a given case of depreciation are such that wealth is transferred to the rich from the poor, then admittedly saving (and consequently capital accumulation) will be encouraged, production will consequently be stimulated, and so the welfare of posterity increased. In earlier epochs of economic history a moderate inflation may sometimes have had this effect. But the more the development of capitalism has made money loans (bank and savings-bank deposits and bonds, especially bearer bonds and

---

[4] This had been urged as early as 1740 by William Douglass in his anonymous writing *A Discourse Concerning the Currencies in the British Plantations in America* (Boston, 1740). See also Fisher, *The Rate of Interest*, p. 356.

mortgage bonds) the most important instruments of saving, the more has depreciation necessarily imperiled the accumulation of capital, by decreasing the motive for saving. How the depreciation of money leads to capital consumption through falsification of economic calculation, and how the appearance of a boom that it creates is an illusion, and how the depreciation of the money really reacts on foreign trade have similarly been explained already in the preceding chapter.

A third group of inflationists do not deny that inflation involves serious disadvantages. Nevertheless, they think that there are higher and more important aims of economic policy than a sound monetary system. They hold that although inflation may be a great evil, yet it is not the greatest evil, and that the state might under certain circumstances find itself in a position where it would do well to oppose greater evils with the lesser evil of inflation. When the defense of the fatherland against enemies, or the rescue of the hungry from starvation is at stake, then, it is said, let the currency go to ruin whatever the cost.

Sometimes this sort of conditional inflation is supported by the argument that inflation is a kind of taxation that is advisable in certain circumstances. Under some conditions, according to this argument, it is better to meet public expenditure by a fresh issue of notes than by increasing the burden of taxation or by borrowing. This was the argument put forward during the war when the expenditure on the army and navy had to be met; and this was the argument put forward in Germany and Austria after the war when a part of the population had to be provided with cheap food, the losses on the operation of the railways and other public undertakings met, and reparations payments made. The assistance of inflation is invoked whenever a government is unwilling to increase taxation or unable to raise a loan; that is the truth of the matter. The next step is to inquire *why* the two usual methods of raising money for public purposes cannot or will not be employed.

It is only possible to levy high taxes when those who bear the burden of the taxes assent to the purpose for which the resources so raised are to be expended. It must be observed here that the greater the total burden of taxation becomes, the harder it is to deceive public opinion as to the impossibility of placing the whole burden of taxation upon the small richer class of the community. The taxation of the rich or of property affects the whole community, and its ultimate consequences for the poorer classes are often more severe than those of taxation levied throughout the community. These implications may perhaps be harder to grasp when taxation is low; but when it is high they can hardly fail to be recognized. There can, moreover, be no doubt that it is scarcely possible to carry the system of relying chiefly upon "taxation of ownership" any farther than it has been carried by the inflating countries, and that the incidence of further taxation could not have been concealed in the way necessary to guarantee continued popular support.

Who has any doubt that the belligerent peoples of Europe would have tired of war much more quickly if their governments had clearly and candidly laid before them at the time the account of their war expenditure? In no European country did the war party dare to impose taxation on the masses to any considerable extent for meeting the cost of the war. Even in England, the classical country of "sound money," the printing presses were set in motion. Inflation had the great advantage of evoking an appearance of economic prosperity and of increase of wealth, of falsifying calculations made in terms of money, and so of concealing the consumption of capital. Inflation gave rise to the pseudo-profits of the entrepreneur and capitalist which could be treated as income and have specially heavy taxes imposed upon them without the public at large—or often even the actual taxpayers themselves—seeing that portions of capital were thus being taxed away. Inflation made it possible to divert the fury of the people to "speculators" and "profiteers." Thus it proved itself an excellent psychological resource of the destructive and annihilist war policy.

What war began, revolution continued. The socialistic or semi-socialistic state needs money in order to carry on undertakings which do not pay, to support the unemployed, and to provide the people with cheap food. It also is unable to secure the necessary resources by means of taxation. It dare not tell the people the truth. The state-socialist principle of running the railways as a state institution would soon lose its popularity if it was proposed, say, to levy a special tax for covering their running losses. And the German and Austrian people would have been quicker in realizing where the resources came from that made bread cheaper if they themselves had had to supply them in the form of a bread tax. In the same way, the German government that decided for the "policy of fulfillment" in opposition to the majority of the German people, was unable to provide itself with the necessary means except by printing notes. And when passive resistance in the Ruhr district gave rise to a need for enormous sums of money, these, again for political reasons, were only to be procured with the help of the printing press.

A government always finds itself obliged to resort to inflationary measures when it cannot negotiate loans and dare not levy taxes, because it has reason to fear that it will forfeit approval of the policy it is following if it reveals too soon the financial and general economic consequences of that policy. Thus inflation becomes the most important psychological resource of any economic policy whose consequences have to be concealed; and so in this sense it can be called an instrument of *unpopular,* that is, of antidemocratic, policy, since by misleading public opinion it makes possible the continued existence of a system of government that would have no hope of the consent of the people if the circumstances were clearly laid before them. That is the political function of inflation. It explains why inflation has always been an important resource of policies of war and revolution and why we also find it in the service of socialism. When governments do not think it necessary to accommodate their expenditure to their revenue and arrogate to themselves the right of making up the deficit by issuing notes, their ideology is merely a disguised absolutism.

The various aims pursued by inflationists demand that the inflationary measures shall be carried through in various special ways. If depreciation is wanted in order to favor the debtor at the expense of the creditor, then the problem is to strike unexpectedly at creditor interests. As we have shown, to the extent to which it could be foreseen, an expected depreciation would be incapable of altering the relations between creditors and debtors. A policy aiming at a progressive diminution of the value of money does not benefit debtors.

If, on the other hand, the depreciation is desired in order to "stimulate production" and to make exportation easier and importation more difficult in relation to other countries, then it must be borne in mind that the absolute level of the value of money—its purchasing power in terms of commodities and services and its exchange ratio against other kinds of money—is without significance for external (as for internal) trade; the variations in the objective exchange value of money have an influence on business only so long as they are in progress. The "beneficial effects" on trade of the depreciation of money only last so long as the depreciation has not affected all commodities and services. Once the adjustment is completed, then these "beneficial effects" disappear. If it is desired to retain them permanently, continual resort must be had to fresh diminutions of the purchasing power of money. It is not enough to reduce the purchasing power of money by one set of measures only, as is erroneously supposed by numerous inflationist writers; only the progressive diminution of the value of money could permanently achieve the aims which they have in view.[5] But a monetary system that corresponds to these requirements can never be actually realized.

Of course, the real difficulty does not lie in the fact that a progressive diminution of the value of money must soon reach amounts so small that they would no longer meet the requirements of commerce. Since the decimal system of calculation is customary in the majority of present-day monetary systems, even the more stupid sections of the public would find no difficulty in the new reckoning when a system of higher units was adopted. We could quite easily imagine a monetary system in which the value of money was constantly falling at the same proportionate rate. Let us assume that the purchasing power of this money, through variations in the determinants that lie on the side of money, sinks in the course of a year by one-hundredth of its amount at the beginning of the year. The levels of the value of the money at each new year then constitute a diminishing geometrical series. If we put the value of the money at the beginning of the first year as equivalent to 100, then the ratio of diminution is equivalent to 0.99, and the value of money at the end of the nth year is equivalent to $100 \times 0.99^{n-1}$. Such a convergent geometrical progression gives an infinite series, any member of which is always to the next following member in the ratio of 100:99.

---

[5] See Hertzka, *Währung und Handel* (Vienna, 1876), p. 42.

We could quite easily imagine a monetary system based on such a principle; perhaps even more easily still if we increased the ratio, say, to 0.995 or even 0.9975.

But however clearly we may be able to imagine such a monetary system, it certainly does not lie in our power actually to create one like it. We know the determinants of the value of money, or think we know them. But we are not in a position to bend them to our will. For we lack the most important prerequisite for this; we do not so much as know the quantitative significance of variations in the quantity of money. We cannot calculate the intensity with which definite quantitative variations in the ratio of the supply of money and the demand for it operate upon the subjective valuations of individuals and through these indirectly upon the market. This remains a matter of very great uncertainty. In employing any means to influence the value of money we run the risk of giving the wrong dose. This is all the more important since in fact it is not possible even to *measure* variations in the purchasing power of money. Thus even though we can roughly tell the direction in which we should work in order to obtain the desired variation, we still have nothing to tell us how far we should go, and we can never find out where we are already, what effects our intervention has had, or how these are proportioned to the effects we desire.

Now the danger involved in overdoing an arbitrary influence—a political influence; that is, one arising from the conscious intervention of human organizations—upon the value of money must by no means be underestimated, particularly in the case of a diminution of the value of money. Big variations in the value of money give rise to the danger that commerce will emancipate itself from the money which is subject to state influence and choose a special money of its own. But without matters going so far as this it is still possible for all the consequences of variations in the value of money to be eliminated if the individuals engaged in economic activity clearly recognize that the purchasing power of money is constantly sinking and act accordingly. If in all business transactions they allow for what the objective exchange value of money will probably be in the future, then all the effects on credit and commerce are finished with. In proportion as the Germans began to reckon in terms of gold, so was further depreciation rendered incapable of altering the relationship between creditor and debtor or even of influencing trade. By going over to reckoning in terms of gold, the community freed itself from the inflationary policy, and eventually even the government was obliged to acknowledge gold as a basis of reckoning.

A danger necessarily involved in all attempts to carry out an inflationary policy is that of excess. Once the principle is admitted that it is possible, permissible, and desirable, to take measures for "cheapening" money, then immediately the most violent and bitter controversy will break out as to how far this principle is to be carried. The interested parties will differ not merely about the steps still to be taken, but also about the results of the steps that have been taken already. It would be impossible for any inflationary measures to be taken without violent controversy. It would be practically impossible so much as to consider counsels of moderation. And these difficulties arise even in the case of an attempt to secure what the inflationists call the beneficial effects of a single and isolated depreciation. Even in the case, say, of assisting "production" or debtors after a serious crisis by a single depreciation of the value of money, the same problems remain to be solved. They are difficulties that have to be reckoned with by every policy aiming at a reduction of the value of money.

Consistently and uninterruptedly continued inflation must eventually lead to collapse. The purchasing power of money will fall lower and lower, until it eventually disappears altogether. It is true that an endless process of depreciation can be *imagined*. We can imagine the purchasing power of money getting continually lower without ever disappearing altogether, and prices getting continually higher without it ever becoming impossible to obtain commodities in exchange for notes. Eventually this would lead to a situation in which even retail transactions were in terms of millions and billions and even higher figures; but the monetary system itself would remain.

But such an imaginary state of affairs is hardly within the bounds of possibility. In the long run, a money which continually fell in value would have no commercial utility. It could not be used as a standard of deferred payments. For all transactions in which commodities or services were not exchanged for cash, another medium would have to be sought. In fact, a money that is continually depreciating becomes useless even for cash transactions. Everybody attempts to minimize his cash reserves, which are a source of continual loss. Incoming money is spent as quickly as possible, and in the purchases that are made in order to obtain goods with a stable value in place of the depreciating money even higher prices will be agreed to than would otherwise be in accordance with market conditions at the time. When commodities that are not needed at all or at least not at the moment are purchased in order to avoid the holding of notes, then the process of extrusion of the notes from use as a general medium of exchange has already begun. It is the beginning of the "demonetization" of the notes. The process is hastened by its paniclike character. It may be possible once, twice, perhaps even three or four times, to allay the fears of the public; but eventually the affair must run its course and then there is no longer any going back. Once the depreciation is proceeding so rapidly that sellers have to reckon with considerable losses even if they buy again as quickly as is possible, then the position of the currency is hopeless.

In all countries where inflation has been rapid, it has been observed that the decrease in the value of the money has occurred faster than the increase in its quantity. If m represents the nominal amount of money present in the country before the beginning of the inflation, P the value of the monetary unit then in terms of gold, M the nominal amount of money at a given point of time during the inflation, and p the value in gold of the monetary unit at this point of time; then, as has often been shown by simple statistical investigations, $mP > Mp$. It has been attempted to prove from this that the money has depreciated "too rapidly" and that the level of the rate of exchange is not "justified." Many have drawn from it the conclusion that the quantity theory is obviously not true and that depreciation of money cannot be a result of an increase in its quantity. Others have conceded the truth of the quantity theory in its primitive form and argued the permissibility or even the necessity of continuing to increase the quantity of money in the country until its total gold value is restored to the level at which it stood before the beginning of the inflation, that is, until $Mp = mP$.

The error that is concealed in all of this is not difficult to discover.

We may completely ignore the fact already referred to that the exchange rates (including the bullion rate) move in advance of the purchasing power of the money unit as expressed in the prices of commodities, so that the gold value must not be taken as a basis of operations, but purchasing power in terms of commodities, which as a rule will not have decreased to the same extent as the gold value. For this form of calculation too, in which P and p do not represent value in terms of gold but purchasing power in terms of commodities, would still as a rule give the result $mP > Mp$. But it must be observed that as the depreciation of money proceeds, the demand for money (that is, for the kind of money in question) gradually begins to fall. When loss of wealth is suffered in proportion to the length of time money is kept on hand, endeavors are made to reduce cash holdings as much as possible. Now if every individual, even if his circumstances are otherwise unchanged, no longer wishes to maintain his cash holding at the same level as before the beginning of the inflation, the demand for money in the whole community, which can only be the sum of the individuals' demands, decreases too. There is also the additional fact that as commerce gradually begins to use foreign money and actual gold in place of notes, individuals begin to hold part of their reserves in foreign money and in gold and no longer in notes.

An expected fall in the value of money is anticipated by speculation so that the money has a lower value in the present than would correspond to the relationship between the immediate supply of it and demand for it. Prices are asked and given that are not related to the present amount of money in circulation nor to present demands for money, but to future circumstances. The panic prices paid when the shops are crowded with buyers anxious to pick up something or other while they can, and the panic rates reached on the exchange when foreign currencies and securities that do not represent a claim to fixed sums of money rise precipitously, anticipate the march of events. But there is not enough money available to pay the prices that correspond to the presumable future supply of money and demand for it. And so it comes about that commerce suffers from a shortage of notes, that there are not enough notes on hand for fulfilling commitments that have been entered into. The mechanism of the market that adjusts the total demand and the total supply to each other by altering the exchange ratio no longer functions as far as the exchange ratio between money and other economic goods is concerned. Business suffers sensibly from a shortage of notes. This bad state of affairs, once matters have gone as far as this, can in no way be helped. Still further to increase the note issue (as many recommend) would only make matters worse. For, since this would accelerate the growth of the panic, it would also accentuate the maladjustment between depreciation and circulation. Shortage of notes for transacting business is a symptom of an advanced stage of inflation; it is the reverse aspect of panic purchases and panic prices, the reflection of the "bullishness" of the public that will finally lead to catastrophe.

The emancipation of commerce from a money which is proving more and more useless in this way begins with the expulsion of the money from hoards. People begin at first to hoard other money instead so as to have marketable goods at their disposal for unforeseen future needs—perhaps precious-metal money and foreign notes, and sometimes also domestic notes of other kinds which have a higher value because they cannot be increased by the state (for example, the Romanoff ruble in Russia or the "blue" money of communist Hungary); then ingots, precious stones, and pearls; even pictures, other objects of art, and postage stamps. A further step is the adoption of foreign currency or metallic money (that is, for all practical purposes, gold) in credit transactions. Finally, when the domestic currency ceases to be used in retail trade, wages as well have to be paid in some other way than in pieces of paper which are then no longer good for anything.

The collapse of an inflation policy carried to its extreme—as in the United States in 1781 and in France in 1796—does not destroy the monetary system, but only the credit money or fiat money of the state that has overestimated the effectiveness of its own policy. The collapse emancipates commerce from etatism and establishes metallic money again.

It is not the business of science to criticize the political aims of inflationism. Whether the favoring of the debtor at the expense of the creditor, whether the facilitation of exports and the hindrance of imports, whether the stimulation of production by transferring wealth and income to the entrepreneur, are to be recommended or not, are questions which economics cannot answer. With the instruments of monetary theory alone, these questions cannot even be elucidated as far as is possible with other parts of the apparatus of economics. But there are nevertheless three conclusions that seem to follow from our critical examination of the possibilities of inflationary policy.

In the first place, all the aims of inflationism can be secured by other sorts of intervention in economic affairs, and secured better, and without undesirable incidental effects. If it is desired to relieve debtors, moratoria may be declared or the obligation to repay loans may be removed altogether; if it is desired to encourage exportation, export premiums may be granted; if it is desired to render importation more difficult, simple prohibition may be resorted to, or import duties levied. All these measures permit discrimination between classes of people, branches of production, and districts, and this is impossible for an inflationary policy. Inflation benefits all debtors, including the rich, and injures all creditors, including the poor; adjustment of the burden of debts by special legislation allows of differentiation. Inflation encourages the exportation of all commodities and hinders all importation; premiums, duties, and prohibitions can be employed discriminatingly.

Second, there is no kind of inflationary policy the extent of whose effects can be foreseen. And finally, continued inflation must lead to a collapse.

Thus we see that, considered purely as a political instrument, inflationism is inadequate. It is, technically regarded, bad policy, because it is incapable of fully attaining its goal and because it leads to consequences that are not, or at least are not always, part of its aim. The favor it enjoys is due solely to the circumstance that it is a policy concerning whose aims and intentions public opinion can be longest deceived. Its popularity, in fact, is rooted in the difficulty of fully understanding its consequences.

4

Restrictionism or Deflationism

That policy which aims at raising the objective exchange value of money is called, after the most important means at its disposal, restrictionism or deflationism. This nomenclature does not really embrace all the policies that aim at an increase in the value of money. The aim of restrictionism may also be attained by not increasing the quantity of money when the demand for it increases, or by not increasing it enough. This method has quite often been adopted as a way of increasing the value of money in face of the problems of a depreciated credit-money standard; further increase of the quantity of money has been stopped, and the policy has been to wait for the effects on the value of money of an increasing demand for it. In the following discussion, following a widespread custom, we shall use the terms restrictionism and deflationism to refer to *all* policies directed to raising the value of money.

The existence and popularity of inflationism is due to the circumstance that it taps new sources of public revenue. Governments had inflated from fiscal motives long before it occurred to anybody to justify their procedure from the point of view of monetary policy. Inflationistic arguments have always been well supported by the fact that inflationary measures not only do not impose any burden on the national exchequer, but actually bring resources to it. Looked at from the fiscal point of view, inflationism is not merely the cheapest economic policy; it is also at the same time a particularly good remedy for a low state of the public finances. Restrictionism, however, demands positive sacrifices from the national exchequer when it is carried out by the withdrawal of notes from circulation (say through the issue of interest-bearing bonds or through taxation) and their cancellation; and at the least it demands from it a renunciation of potential income by forbidding the issue of notes at a time when the demand for money is increasing. This alone would suffice to explain why restrictionism has never been able to compete with inflationism.

Nevertheless, the unpopularity of restrictionism has other causes as well. Attempts to raise the objective exchange value of money, in the circumstances that have existed, have necessarily been limited either to single states or to a few states and at the best have had only a very small prospect of simultaneous realization throughout the whole world. Now as soon as a single country or a few countries go over to a money with a rising purchasing power, while the other countries retain a money with a falling or stationary exchange value, or one which although it may be rising in value is not rising to the same extent, then, as has been demonstrated above, the conditions of international trade are modified. In the country whose money is rising in value, exportation becomes more difficult and importation easier. But the increased difficulty of exportation and the increased facility of importation, in brief the deterioration of the balance of trade, have usually been regarded as an unfavorable situation and consequently been avoided. This alone would provide an adequate explanation of the unpopularity of measures intended to raise the purchasing power of money.

But furthermore, quite apart from any consideration of foreign trade, an increase in the value of money has not been to the advantage of the ruling classes. Those who get an immediate benefit from such an increase are all those who are entitled to receive fixed sums of money. Creditors gain at the expense of debtors. Taxation, it is true, becomes more burdensome as the value of money rises; but the greater part of the advantage of this is secured, not by the state, but by its creditors. Now policies favoring creditors at the expense of debtors have never been popular. Lenders of money have been held in odium, at all times and among all peoples.[6]

Generally speaking, the class of persons who draw their income exclusively or largely from the interest on capital lent to others has not been particularly numerous or influential at any time in any country. A not insignificant part of the total income from the lending of capital is received by persons whose incomes chiefly arise from other sources, and in whose budgets it plays only a subordinate part. This is the case, for instance, not only of the laborers, peasants, small industrialists, and civil servants, who possess savings that are invested in savings deposits or in bonds, but also of the numerous big industrialists, wholesalers, or shareholders, who also own large amounts of bonds. The interests of all of these as lenders of money are subordinate to their interests as landowners, merchants, manufacturers, or employees. No wonder, then, that they are not very enthusiastic about attempts to raise the level of interest.[7]

Restrictionistic ideas have never met with any measure of popular sympathy except after a time of monetary depreciation when it has

[6] See Bentham, *Defense of Usury*, 2d ed. (London, 1790), pp. 102 ff.
[7] See Wright and Harlow, *The Gemini Letters* (London, 1844), pp. 51 ff.

been necessary to decide what should take the place of the abandoned inflationary policy. They have hardly ever been seriously entertained except as part of the alternative: "Stabilization of money at the present value or revaluation at the level that it had before the inflation."

When the question arises in this form, the reasons that are given for the restoration of the old metal parity start from the assumption that notes are essentially promises to pay so much metallic money. Credit money has always originated in a suspension of the convertibility into cash of Treasury notes or banknotes (sometimes the suspension was even extended to token coins or to bank deposits) that were previously convertible at any time on the demand of the bearer and were already in circulation. Now whether the original obligation of immediate conversion was expressly laid down by the law or merely founded on custom, the suspension of conversion has always taken on the appearance of a breach of the law that could perhaps be excused, but not justified; for the coins or notes that became credit money through the suspension of cash payment could never have been put into circulation otherwise than as money substitutes, as secure claims to a sum of commodity money payable on demand. Consequently, the suspension of immediate convertibility has always been decreed as a merely temporary measure, and a prospect held out of its future rescission. But if credit money is thought of only as a promise to pay, "devaluation" cannot be regarded as anything but a breach of the law, or as meaning anything less than national bankruptcy.

Yet credit money is not merely an acknowledgment of indebtedness and a promise to pay. As money, it has a different standing in the transactions of the market. It is true that it could not have become a money-substitute unless it had constituted a claim. Nevertheless, at the moment when it became actual money—credit money—(even if through a breach of the law), it ceased to be valued with regard to the more or less uncertain prospect of its future full conversion and began to be valued for the sake of the monetary function that it performed. Its far lower value as an uncertain claim to a future cash payment has no significance so long as its higher value as a common medium of exchange is taken into account.

It is therefore quite beside the point to interpret devaluation as national bankruptcy. The stabilization of the value of money at its present—lower—level is, even when regarded merely with a view to its effects on existing debt relations, something other than this; it is both more and less than national bankruptcy. It is more, for it affects not merely public debts, but also all private debts; it is less, for one thing because it also affects those *claims* of the state that are in terms of credit money while *not* affecting such of its obligations as are in terms of cash (metallic money) or foreign currency, and for another thing because it involves no modification of the relations of the parties to any contract of indebtedness in terms of credit money made at a time when the currency stood at a low level, without the parties having reckoned on an increase of the value of money. When the value of money is increased, then those are enriched who at the time possess credit money or claims to credit money. Their enrichment must be paid for by debtors, among them the state (that is, the taxpayers). Yet those who are enriched by the increase in the value of money are not the same as those who were injured by the depreciation of money in the course of the inflation; and those who must bear the cost of the policy of raising the value of money are not the same as those who benefited by its depreciation. To carry out a deflationary policy is not to do away with the consequences of inflation. You cannot make good an old breach of the law by committing a new one. And as far as debtors are concerned, restriction is a breach of the law.

If it is desired to make good the injury which has been suffered by creditors during the inflation, this can certainly not be done by restriction. In the simpler circumstances of an undeveloped credit system, the attempt has been made to find a way out of the difficulty by conversion of the debts contracted before and during the period of inflation, every debt being recalculated in the devaluated money according to the value of the credit money in terms of metallic money on the day of origin. Supposing, for instance, that the metallic money had been depreciated to one-fifth of its former value, a borrower of 100 gulden before the inflation would have to pay back after the stabilization, not 100 gulden, but 500, together with interest on the 500; and a borrower of 100 gulden at a time when the credit money had already sunk to half of its nominal value, would have to pay interest on and pay back 250 gulden.[8] This, however, only covers debt obligations which are still current; the debts which have already been settled in the depreciated money are not affected. No notice is taken of sales and purchases of bonds and other claims to fixed sums of money; and, in an age of bearer bonds, this is a quite particularly serious shortcoming. Finally, this sort of regulation is inapplicable to current-account transactions.

It is not our business here to discuss whether something better than this could have been thought of. In fact, if it is possible to make any sort of reparation of the damage suffered by creditors at all, it must clearly be sought by way of some such methods of recalculation. But in any case, increasing the purchasing power of money is not a suitable means to this end.

Considerations of credit policy also are adduced in favor of increasing the value of money to the metal parity that prevailed before the beginning of the period of inflation. A country that has injured its creditors through depreciation brought about by inflation, it is said, cannot restore the shattered confidence in its credit otherwise than by a return to the old level of prices. In this way alone can those from whom it wishes to obtain new loans be satisfied as to the future security of their claims; the bondholders will be able to assume that any possible fresh inflation would not ultimately reduce their claims, because after the inflation was over the original metal parity would presumably be returned to. This argument has a peculiar significance[9] for England, among whose most important sources of income is the position of the city of London as the world's banker. All those who availed themselves of the English banking system, it is said, ought to be satisfied as to the future security of the English deposits, in order that the English banking business should not be diminished by mistrust in the future of the English currency. As always in the case of considerations of credit policy like this, a good deal of rather dubious psychology is assumed in this argument. It

[8] See Hofmann, "Die Devalvierung des österreichischen Papiergeldes im Jahre 1811," *Schriften des Vereins für Sozialpolitik* 165, Part I.
[9] [It should be remembered that the German edition from which the present version is translated was published in 1926. See, however, the discussion of British policy, pp. 23–26 above. H.E.B.]

may be there are more effectual ways of restoring confidence in the future than by measures that do not benefit some of the injured creditors at all—those who have already disposed of their claims— and do benefit many creditors who have not suffered any injury— those who acquired their claims after the depreciation began.

In general, therefore, it is impossible to regard as decisive the reasons that are given in favor of restoring the value of money at the level that it had before the commencement of the inflationary policy, especially as consideration of the way in which trade is affected by a rise in the value of money suggests a need for caution. Only where and so far as prices are not yet completely adjusted to the relationship between the stock of money and the demand for it which has resulted from the increase in the quantity of money, is it possible to proceed to a restoration of the old parity without encountering a too violent opposition.

5

Invariability of the Objective Exchange Value of Money as the Aim of Monetary Policy

Thus, endeavors to increase or decrease the objective exchange value of money prove impracticable. A rise in the value of money leads to consequences which as a rule seem to be desired by only a small section of the community; a policy with this aim is contrary to interests which are too great for it to be able to hold its own against them in the long run. The kinds of intervention which aim at decreasing the value of money seem more popular; but their goal can be more easily and more satisfactorily reached in other ways, while their execution meets with quite insuperable difficulties.

Thus nothing remains but to reject both the augmentation and the diminution of the objective exchange value of money. This suggests the ideal of a money with an invariable exchange value, so far as the monetary influences on its value are concerned. *But,* this is the ideal money of enlightened statesmen and economists, not that of the multitude. The latter thinks in far too confused a manner to be able to grasp the problems here involved. (It must be confessed that they are the most difficult in economics.) For most people (so far as they do not incline to inflationistic ideas), that money seems to be the best whose objective exchange value is not subject to any variation at all, *whether originating on the monetary side or on the commodity side.*

The ideal of a money with an exchange value that is not subject to variations due to changes in the ratio between the supply of money and the need for it—that is, a money with an invariable *innere objektive Tauschwert*[10]—demands the intervention of a regulating authority in the determination of the value of money; and its continued intervention. But here immediately most serious doubts arise from the circumstance, already referred to, that we have no useful knowledge of the quantitative significance of given measures intended to influence the value of money. More serious still is the circumstance that we are by no means in a position to determine with precision whether variations have occurred in the exchange value of money from any cause whatever, and if so to what extent, quite apart from the question of whether such changes have been effected by influences working from the monetary side. Attempts to stabilize the exchange value of money in this sense must therefore be frustrated at the outset by the fact that both their goal and the road to it are obscured by a darkness that human knowledge will never be able to penetrate. But the uncertainty that would exist as to whether there was any need for intervention to maintain the stability of the exchange value of money, and as to the necessary extent of such intervention, would inevitably give full license again to the conflicting interests of the inflationists and restrictionists. Once the principle is so much as admitted that the state may and should influence the value of money, even if it were only to guarantee the stability of its value, the danger of mistakes and excesses immediately arises again.

These possibilities, and the remembrance of very recent experiments in public finance and inflation, have subordinated the unrealizable ideal of a money with an invariable exchange value to the demand that the state should at least refrain from exerting any sort of influence on the value of money. A metallic money, the augmentation or diminution of the quantity of metal available for which is

---

[10] [See p. 146 n above.]

independent of deliberate human intervention, is becoming the modern monetary ideal.

The significance of adherence to a metallic-money system lies in the freedom of the value of money from state influence that such a system guarantees. Beyond doubt, considerable disadvantages are involved in the fact that not only fluctuations in the ratio of the supply of money and the demand for it, but also fluctuations in the conditions of production of the metal and variations in the industrial demand for it, exert an influence on the determination of the value of money. It is true that these effects, in the case of gold (and even in the case of silver), are not immoderately great, and these are the only two monetary metals that need be considered in modern times. But even if the effects were greater, such a money would still deserve preference over one subject to state intervention, since the latter sort of money would be subject to still greater fluctuations.

6

The Limits of Monetary Policy

The results of our investigation into the development and significance of monetary policy should not surprise us. That the state, after having for a period used the power which it nowadays has of influencing to some extent the determination of the objective exchange value of money in order to affect the distribution of income, should have to abandon its further exercise, will not appear strange to those who have a proper appreciation of the economic function of the state in that social order which rests upon private property in the means of production. The state does not govern the market; in the market in which products are exchanged it may quite possibly be a powerful party, but nevertheless it is only one party of many, nothing more than that. All its attempts to transform the exchange ratios between economic goods that are determined in the market can only be undertaken with the instruments of the market. It can never foresee exactly what the result of any particular intervention will be. It cannot bring about a desired result in the degree that it wishes, because the means that the influencing of demand and supply place at its disposal only affect the pricing process through the medium of the subjective valuations of individuals; but no judgment as to the intensity of the resulting transformation of these valuations can be made except when the intervention is a small one, limited to one or a few groups of commodities of lesser importance, and even in such a case only approximately. All monetary policies encounter the difficulty that the effects of any measures taken in order to influence the fluctuations of the objective exchange value of money can neither be foreseen in advance, nor their nature and magnitude be determined even after they have already occurred.

Now the renunciation of intervention on grounds of monetary policy that is involved in the retention of a metallic commodity currency is not complete. In the regulation of the issue of fiduciary media there is still another possibility of influencing the objective exchange value of money. The problem that this gives rise to must be investigated (in the following part) before we can discuss certain plans that have recently been announced for the establishment of a monetary system under which the value of money would be more stable than that of a gold currency.

7

Excursus: The Concepts Inflation and Deflation

Observant readers may perhaps be struck by the fact that in this book no precise definition is given of the terms *inflation* and *deflation* (or restriction or contraction); that they are in fact hardly employed at all, and then only in places where nothing in particular depends upon their precision. Only inflationism and deflationism (or restrictionism) are spoken of, and an exact definition is given of the concepts implied by these expressions.[11] Obviously this procedure demands special justification.

I am by no means in agreement with those unusually influential voices that have been raised against the employment of the expression *inflation* altogether.[12] But I do think that it is an expression that it is possible to do without, and that it would be highly dangerous, on account of a serious difference between its meaning in the pure

---

[11] Cp. pp. 251 and 262–63 above.
[12] Esp. Pigou, *The Economics of Welfare* (London, 1921), pp. 665 ff.

economic theory of money and banking and its meaning in every-day discussions of currency policy, to make use of it where a sharp scientific precision of the words employed is desirable.

In theoretical investigation there is only one meaning that can rationally be attached to the expression *inflation:* an increase in the quantity of money (in the broader sense of the term, so as to include fiduciary media as well), that is not offset by a corresponding increase in the need for money (again in the broader sense of the term), so that a fall in the objective exchange value of money must occur. Again, deflation (or restriction, or contraction) signifies a diminution of the quantity of money (in the broader sense) which is not offset by a corresponding diminution of the demand for money (in the broader sense), so that an increase in the objective exchange value of money must occur. If we so define these concepts, it follows that either inflation or deflation is constantly going on, for a situation in which the objective exchange value of money did not alter could hardly ever exist for very long. The theoretical value of our definition is not in the least reduced by the fact that we are not able to measure the fluctuations in the objective exchange value of money, or even by the fact that we are not able to discern them at all except when they are large.

If the variations in the objective exchange value of money that result from these causes are so great that they can no longer remain unobserved, it is usual in discussions of economic policy to speak of inflation and deflation (or restriction, or contraction). Now in these discussions, whose practical significance is extraordinarily great, it would be very little to the purpose to use those precise concepts which alone come up to a strictly scientific standard. It would be ridiculous pedantry to attempt to provide an economist's contribution to the controversy as to whether in this or the other country inflation has occurred since 1914 by saying: "Excuse me, there has probably been inflation throughout the whole world since 1896, although on a small scale." In politics, the question of degree is sometimes the whole point, not, as in theory, the question of principle.

But once the economist has acknowledged that it is not entirely nonsensical to use the expressions *inflation* and *deflation* to indicate such variations in the quantity of money as evoke *big* changes in the objective exchange value of money, he must renounce the employment of these expressions in pure theory. For the point at which a change in the exchange ratio begins to deserve to be called big is a question for political judgment, not for scientific investigation.

It is incontrovertible that ideas are bound up with the popular usage of the terms *inflation* and *deflation* that must be combated as altogether inappropriate when they creep into economic investigation. In everyday usage, these expressions are based upon an entirely untenable idea of the stability of the value of money, and often also on conceptions that ascribe to a monetary system in which the quantity of money increases and decreases *pari passu* with the increase and decrease of the quantity of commodities the property of maintaining the value of money stable. Yet however worthy of condemnation this mistake may be, it cannot be denied that the first concern of those who wish to combat popular errors with regard to the causes of the recent tremendous variations in prices should not so much be the dissemination of correct views on the problems of the nature of money in general, as the contradiction of those fundamental errors which, if they continue to be believed, must lead to catastrophic consequences. Those who in the years 1914–24 contested the balance-of-payments theory in Germany in order to oppose the continuation of the policy of inflation may claim the indulgence of their contemporaries and successors if they were not always quite strictly scientific in their use of the word *inflation*. In fact, it is this very indulgence that we are bound to exercise toward the pamphlets and articles dealing with monetary problems that obliges us to refrain from using these misleading expressions in scientific discussion.

CHAPTER 14

The Monetary Policy of Etatism

1

The Monetary Theory of Etatism

Etatism, as a theory, is the doctrine of the omnipotence of the state, and, as a policy, the attempt to regulate all mundane affairs by authoritative commandment and prohibition. The ideal society of etatism is a particular sort of socialistic community; it is usual in discussions involving this ideal society to speak of state socialism, or, in some connections, of Christian socialism. Superficially regarded, the etatistic ideal society does not differ very greatly from the outward form assumed by the capitalistic organization of society. Etatism by no means aims at the *formal* transformation of all ownership of the means of production into state ownership by a complete overthrow of the established legal system. Only the biggest industrial, mining, and transport enterprises are to be nationalized; in agriculture, and in medium- and small-scale industry, private property is nominally to continue. Nevertheless, all enterprises are to become state undertakings in fact. Owners are to be left the title and dignity of ownership, it is true, and to be given a right to the receipt of a "reasonable" income, "in accordance with their position"; but, in fact, every business is to be changed into a government office and every livelihood into an official profession. There is no room at all for independent enterprise under any variety of state socialism. Prices are to be regulated authoritatively; authority is to fix what is to be produced, and how, and in what quantities. There is to be no speculation, no "excessive" profit, no loss. There is to be no innovation unless it be decreed by authority. The official is to direct and supervise everything.[1]

It is one of the peculiarities of etatism that it is unable to conceive of human beings living together in society otherwise than in accordance with its own particular socialistic ideal. The superficial similarity that exists between the socialist state that is its ideal and pattern and the social order based upon private property in the means of production causes it to overlook the fundamental differences that separate the two. Everything that contradicts the assumption that the two kinds of social order are similar is regarded by the etatist as a transient anomaly and a culpable transgression of authoritative decrees, as evidence that the state has let slip the reins of government and only needs to take them more firmly in hand for everything to be beautifully in order again. That the social life of human beings is subject to definite limitations; that it is governed by a set of laws that are comparable with those of Nature; these are notions that are unknown to the etatist. For the etatist, everything is a question of *Macht*—power, force, might. And his conception of *Macht* is crudely materialistic.

Every word of etatistic thought is contradicted by the doctrines of sociology and economics; this is why etatists endeavor to prove that these sciences do not exist. In their opinion, social affairs are shaped by the state. To the law, all things are possible; and there is no sphere in which state intervention is not omnipotent.

For a long time the modern etatists shrank from an explicit application of their principles to the theory of money. It is true that some, Adolf Wagner and Lexis in particular, expressed views on the domestic and foreign value of money and on the influence of the balance of payments on the condition of the exchanges that contained all the elements of an etatistic theory of money; but always with great caution and reserve. The first to attempt an explicit application of etatistic principles in the sphere of monetary doctrine, was Knapp.

---

[1] On this, see my book, *Die Gemeinwirtschaft*, 2d ed., (Jena, 1922), pp. 211 ff.

The policy of etatism had its heyday during the period of the world war, which itself was the inevitable consequence of the dominance of etatistic ideology. In the "war economy" the postulates of etatism were realized.[2] The war economy and the transition economy showed what etatism is worth and what the policy of etatism is able to achieve.

An examination of etatistic monetary doctrine and monetary policy has a significance that is not limited to the history of ideas. For in spite of all its ill success, etatism is still the ruling doctrine, at least on the continent of Europe. It is, at any rate, the doctrine of the rulers; its ideas prevail in monetary policy. However convinced we may be that it is scientifically valueless, it will not do for us nowadays to ignore it.[3]

2

National Prestige and the Rate of Exchange

For the etatist, money is a creature of the state, and the esteem in which money is held is the economic expression of the respect or prestige enjoyed by the state. The more powerful and the richer the state, the better its money. Thus, during the war, it was asserted that "the monetary standard of the victors" would ultimately be the best money. Yet victory and defeat on the battlefield can exercise only an indirect influence on the value of money. Generally speaking, a victorious state is more likely than a conquered one to be able to renounce the aid of the printing press, for it is likely to find it easier to limit its expenditure on the one hand and to obtain credit on the other hand. But the same considerations suggest that increasing prospects of peace will lead to a more favorable estimation of the currency even of the defeated country. In October 1918 the mark and the krone rose; it was believed that even in Germany and

---

[2] See my book, *Nation, Staat und Wirtschaft* (Vienna, 1919), pp. 108 ff.

[3] Cassel rightly says: "A perfectly clear understanding of the monetary problem, brought about by the world war, can never be attained until officialdom's interpretation of affairs has been disproved point by point, and full light thrown on all the delusions with which the authorities attempted as long as possible to obsess the public mind" (Cassel, *Money and Foreign Exchange After 1914* [London, 1922], pp. 7 ff.). See Gregory's criticism of the most important etatistic arguments in his *Foreign Exchange Before, During and After the War* (London, 1921), esp. pp. 65 ff.

Austria a cessation of inflation might be counted upon—an expectation which admittedly was not fulfilled.

History likewise shows that sometimes the "monetary standard of the victors" can prove to be very bad. There have seldom been more brilliant victories than those eventually achieved by the American insurgents under Washington against the English troops. But the American "continental" dollar did not benefit from them. The more proudly the star-spangled banner rose on high, the lower did the exchange rate fall, until, at the very moment when the victory of the rebels was secured, the dollar became entirely valueless. The course of events was no different not long afterward in France. In spite of the victories of the revolutionary army, the metal premium rose continually, until at last in 1796 the value of money touched zero point. In both cases the victorious state had carried inflation to its extreme.

Neither has the *wealth* of a country any bearing on the valuation of its money. Nothing is more erroneous than the widespread habit of regarding the monetary standard as something in the nature of the shares of the state or the community. When the German mark was quoted at ten centimes in Zurich, bankers said: "Now is the time to buy marks. The German community is indeed poorer nowadays than before the war, so that a low valuation of the mark is justified. Nevertheless, the wealth of Germany is certainly not reduced to a twelfth of what it was before the war; so the mark is bound to rise." And when the Polish mark had sunk to five centimes in Zurich, other bankers said: "This low level is inexplicable. Poland is a rich country; it has a flourishing agriculture, it has wood, coal and oil; so its rate of exchange ought to be incomparably higher."[4] Such observers fail to recognize that the valuation of the monetary unit depends not upon the wealth of the country, but upon the ratio between the quantity of money and the demand for it, so that even the richest country may have a bad currency and the poorest country a good one.

---

[4] A leader of the Hungarian Soviet republic said to the author in the spring of 1919: "The paper money issued by the Soviet republic ought really to have the highest exchange rate next to the Russian money, for, through the socialization of the private property of all Hungarians, the Hungarian state has become next to Russia the richest state in the world, and consequently the most deserving of credit."

3

The Regulation of Prices by Authoritative Decree

The oldest and most popular instrument of etatistic monetary policy is the official fixing of maximum prices. High prices, thinks the etatist, are not a consequence of an increase in the quantity of money, but a consequence of reprehensible activity on the part of "bulls" and "profiteers"; it will suffice to suppress their machinations in order to ensure the cessation of the rise of prices. Thus it is made a punishable offense to demand, or even to pay, "excessive" prices.

Like most other governments, the Austrian government during the war began this kind of criminal-law contest with price raising on the same day that it put the printing press in motion in the service of the national finances. Let us suppose that it had at first been successful in this. Let us completely disregard the fact that the war had also diminished the supply of commodities, and suppose that there had been no forces at work on the commodity side to alter the exchange ratio between commodities and money. We must further disregard the fact that the war, by increasing the period of time necessary for transporting money, and by limiting the operation of the clearing system, and also in other ways, had increased the demand for money of individual economic agents. Let us merely discuss the question, what consequences would necessarily follow if, *ceteris paribus*, with an increasing quantity of money, prices were restricted to the old level by official compulsion?

An increase in the quantity of money leads to the appearance in the market of new desire to purchase, which had previously not existed; "new purchasing power," it is usual to say, has been created. If the new would-be purchasers compete with those that are already in the market, then, so long as it is not permissible to raise prices, only part of the total purchasing power can be exercised. This means that there are would-be purchasers who leave the market without having effected their object although they were ready to agree to the price demanded, would-be purchasers who return home with the money with which they set out in order to purchase. Whether or not a would-be purchaser who is prepared to pay the official price gets the commodity that he desires depends upon all sorts of circumstances, which are, from the point of view of the market, quite inessential; for example, upon whether he was on the spot in time, or has personal relations with the seller, or other similar accidents. The mechanism of the market no longer works to make a distinction between the would-be purchasers who are still able to buy and those who are not; it no longer brings about a coincidence between supply and demand through variations in price. Supply lags behind demand. The play of the market loses its meaning; other forces have to take its place.

But the government that puts the newly created notes in circulation does so because it wishes to draw commodities and services out of their previous avenues in order to direct them into some other desired employment. It wishes to buy these commodities and services; not, as is also a quite conceivable procedure, to commandeer them by force. It must, therefore, desire that everything should be obtainable for money and for money alone. It is not to the advantage of the government that a situation should arise in the market that makes some of the would-be purchasers withdraw without having effected their object. The government desires to purchase; it desires to use the market, not to disorganize it. But the officially fixed price does disorganize the market in which commodities and services are bought and sold for money. Commerce, so far as it is able, seeks relief in other ways. It redevelops a system of direct exchange, in which commodities and services are exchanged without the instrumentality of money. Those who are forced to dispose of commodities and services at the fixed prices do not dispose of them to everybody, but merely to those to whom they wish to do a favor. Would-be purchasers wait in long queues in order to snap up what they can get before it is too late; they race breathlessly from shop to shop, hoping to find one that is not yet sold out.

For once the commodities have been sold that were already on the market when their price was authoritatively fixed at a level below that demanded by the situation of the market, then the emptied storerooms are not filled again. Charging more than a certain price is prohibited, but producing and selling have not been made compulsory. There are no longer any sellers. The market ceases to function. But this means that economic organization based on division of labor becomes impossible. The level of money prices cannot be fixed without overthrowing the system of social division of labor.

Thus official fixing of prices, which is intended to establish them and wages generally below the level that they would attain in a free market, is completely impracticable. If the prices of individual kinds of commodities and services are subjected to such restrictions, then disturbances occur that are settled again by the capacity for adjustment possessed by the economic order based on private property sufficiently to make the continuance of the system possible. If such regulations are made general and really put into force, then their incompatibility with the existence of a social order based upon private property becomes obvious. The attempt to restrain prices within limits has to be given up. A government that sets out to abolish market prices is inevitably driven toward the abolition of private property; it has to recognize that there is no middle way between the system of private property in the means of production combined with free contract, and the system of common ownership of the means of production, or socialism. It is gradually forced toward compulsory production, universal obligation to labor, rationing of consumption, and, finally, official regulation of the whole of production and consumption.

This is the road that was taken by economic policy during the war. The etatist, who had jubilantly proclaimed the state's ability to do everything it wanted to do, discovered that the economists had nevertheless been quite right and that it was not possible to manage with price regulation alone. Since they wished to eliminate the play of the market, they had to go farther than they had originally intended. The first step was the rationing of the most important necessaries; but soon compulsory labor had to be resorted to and eventually the subordination of the whole of production and consumption to the direction of the state. Private property existed in name only; in fact, it had been abolished.

The collapse of militarism was the end of wartime socialism also. Yet no better understanding of the economic problem was shown under the revolution than under the old regime. All the same experiences had to be gone through again.

The attempts that were made with the aid of the police and the criminal law to prevent a rise of prices did not come to grief because officials did not act severely enough or because people found ways of avoiding the regulations. They did not suffer shipwreck because the entrepreneurs were not public spirited, as the socialist-etatistic legend has it. They were bound to fail because the economic organization based upon division of labor and private property in the means of production can function only so long as price determination in the market is free. If the regulation of prices had been successful, it would have paralyzed the whole economic organism. They only thing that made possible the continued functioning of the social apparatus of production was the incomplete enforcement of the regulations that was due to the paralysis of the efforts of those who ought to have executed them.

During thousands of years, in all parts of the inhabited earth, innumerable sacrifices have been made to the chimera of just and reasonable prices. Those who have offended against the laws regulating prices have been heavily punished; their property has been confiscated, they themselves have been incarcerated, tortured, put to death. The agents of etatism have certainly not been lacking in zeal and energy. But, for all this, economic affairs cannot be kept going by magistrates and policemen.

4

The Balance-of-Payments Theory as a Basis of Currency Policy

According to the current view, the maintenance of sound monetary conditions is only possible with a "credit balance of payments." A country with a "debit balance of payments" is supposed to be unable permanently to stabilize the value of its money; the depreciation of the currency is supposed to have an organic basis and to be irremediable except by the removal of the organic defects.

The confutation of this and related objections is implicit in the quantity theory and in Gresham's law. The quantity theory shows that money can never permanently flow abroad from a country in which only metallic money is used (the "purely metallic currency" of the currency principle). The tightness in the domestic market called forth by the efflux of part of the stock of money reduces the prices of commodities, and so restricts importation and encourages exportation, until there is once more enough money at home. The precious metals which perform the function of money are distributed among individuals, and consequently among separate countries, according to the extent and intensity of the demand of each for money. State intervention to assure to the community the necessary quantity of money by regulating its international movements is supererogatory. An undesired efflux of money can never be anything but a result of state intervention endowing money of different values with the same legal tender. All that the state need do, and can do, in order to preserve the monetary system undisturbed, is to refrain from such intervention. That is the essence of the monetary theory of the Classical economists and their immediate successors, the Currency School. It is possible to refine and amplify this doctrine with the aid of the modern subjective theory; but it is impossible to overthrow it, and impossible to put anything else in its place. Those who are able to forget it only show that they are unable to think as economists.

When a country has substituted credit money or fiat money for metallic money, because the legal equating of the overissued paper and the metallic money sets in motion the mechanism described by Gresham's law, it is often asserted that the balance of payments determines the rate of exchange. But this also is a quite inadequate explanation. The rate of exchange is determined by the purchasing power possessed by a unit of each kind of money; it must be determined at such a level that it makes no difference whether commodities are purchased directly with the one kind of money or indirectly, through money of the other kind. If the rate of exchange moves away from the position that is determined by the purchasing-power parity, which we call the natural or equilibrium rate, then certain sorts of transaction would become profitable. It would become lucrative to purchase commodities with the money that was undervalued by the rate of exchange as compared with the ratio given by its purchasing power, and to sell them for the money that was overvalued in the rate of exchange in comparison with its purchasing power. And because there were such opportunities of profit, there would be a demand on the foreign-exchange market for the money that was undervalued by the exchanges and this would raise the rate of exchange until it attained its equilibrium position. Rates of exchange vary because the quantity of money varies and the prices of commodities vary. As has already been remarked, it is solely owing to market technique that this basic relationship is not actually expressed in the temporal sequence of events. In fact, the determination of foreign-exchange rates, under the influence of speculation, anticipates the expected variations in the prices of commodities.

The balance-of-payments theory forgets that the volume of foreign trade is completely dependent upon prices; that neither exportation nor importation can occur if there are no differences in prices to make trade profitable. The theory clings to the superficial aspects of the phenomena it deals with. It cannot be doubted that if we simply look at the daily or hourly fluctuations on the exchanges we shall only be able to discover that the state of the balance of payments at any moment *does* determine the supply and the demand in the foreign-exchange market. But this is a mere beginning of a proper investigation into the determinants of the rate of exchange. The next question is, What determines the state of the balance of payments at any moment? And there is no other possible answer to this than that it is the price level and the purchases and sales induced by the price margins that determine the balance of payments. Foreign commodities can be imported, at a time when the rate of exchange is rising, only if they are able to find purchasers despite their high prices.

One variety of the balance-of-payments theory attempts to distinguish between the importation of necessaries and the importation of articles that can be dispensed with. Necessaries, it is said, have to be bought whatever their price is, simply because they cannot be done without. Consequently there must be a continual depreciation in the currency of a country that is obliged to import necessaries from abroad and itself is able to export only relatively dispensable articles. To argue thus is to forget that the greater or less necessity or dispensability of individual goods is fully expressed in the intensity and extent of the demand for them in the market, and thus in the amount of money which is paid for them. However strong the desire of the Austrians for foreign bread, meat, coal, or sugar may be, they can only get these things if they are able to pay for them. If they wish to import more, they must export more; if they cannot export manufactured and semimanufactured goods, then they must export shares, bonds, and securities of various kinds. If the note circulation were not increased, then the prices of the objects that were offered for sale would have to decrease if the demand for import goods and hence their prices were to rise. Or else the upward movement of the prices of necessaries would have to be opposed by a fall in the price of the dispensable articles the purchase of which was restricted so as to permit the purchase of the necessaries. There could be no question of a general rise of prices. And the balance of payments would be brought into equilibrium, either by the export of securities and the like, or by an increased export of dispensable goods. It is only when the above assumption does not hold good, only when the quantity of notes in circulation is increased, that foreign commodities can still be imported in the same quantities in spite of a rise in the foreign exchange; it is only because this assumption does not hold good that the rise in the foreign exchange does not throttle importation and encourage exportation until there is again a credit balance of payments.

Ancient Mercantilist error therefore involved a specter of which we need not be afraid. No country, not even the poorest, need abandon the hope of sound currency conditions. It is not the poverty of individuals and the community, not indebtedness to foreign nations, not the unfavorableness of the conditions of production, that force up the rate of exchange, but inflation.

It follows that all the means that are employed for hindering a rise in the exchange rate are useless. If the inflationary policy continues, they remain ineffective; if there is no inflationary policy, then they are superfluous. The most important of these methods is the prohibition or limitation of the importation of certain goods that are deemed dispensable, or at least less indispensable than others. This causes the sums of domestic money that would have been used for the purchase of these commodities to be used for other purchases and naturally the only goods here concerned are those that would otherwise have been sold abroad. These will now be purchased at home for prices that are higher than those offered for them abroad. Thus the reduction of imports and so of the demand for foreign exchange is balanced on the other side by an equal reduction of exports and so of the supply of foreign exchange. Imports are in fact paid for by exports and not by money, as Neo-Mercantilist dilettantism still continues to believe. If it is really desired to dam up the demand for foreign exchange, then the amount of money to the extent of which it is desired to stop importation must be taken away from those at home—say by taxation—and kept out of circulation altogether; that is, not used for state purposes, but destroyed. That is to say, a deflationary policy must be followed. Instead of the importation of chocolate, wine, and lemonade being limited, the members of the community must be deprived of the money that they would otherwise spend on these commodities. Then they must limit their consumption either of these or of some other commodities. In the former case, less foreign exchange will be wanted, in the latter more foreign exchange offered, than previously.

5

The Suppression of Speculation

It is not easy to determine whether there are any who still adhere in good faith to the doctrine that traces back the depreciation of money to the activity of speculators. The doctrine is an indispensable instrument of the lowest form of demagogy; it is the resource of governments in search of a scapegoat. There are scarcely any independent writers nowadays who defend it; those who support it are paid to do so. Nevertheless, a few words must be devoted to it, for the monetary policy of the present day is based largely upon it.

Speculation does not determine prices; it has to accept the prices that are determined in the market. Its efforts are directed to correctly estimating future price situations, and to acting accordingly. The influence of speculation cannot alter the average level of prices over a given period; what it can do is to diminish the gap between the highest and the lowest prices. Price fluctuations are reduced by speculation, not aggravated, as the popular legend has it.

It is true that the speculator may happen to go astray in his estimate of future prices. What is usually overlooked in considering this possibility is that under the given conditions it is far beyond the capacities of most people to foresee the future any more correctly. If this were not so, the opposing group of buyers or sellers would have got the upper hand in the market. The fact that the opinion accepted by the market has later proved to be false is lamented by nobody with more genuine sorrow than by the speculators who held it. They do not err of malice prepense; after all, their object is to make profits, not losses.

Even prices that are established under the influence of speculation result from the cooperation of two parties, the bulls and the bears. Each of the two parties is always equal to the other in strength and in the extent of its commitments. Each has an equal responsibility for the determination of prices. Nobody is from the outset and for all time bull or bear; a dealer becomes a bull or a bear only on the basis of a summing up of the market situation, or, more correctly, on the basis of the dealings that follow on such a summing up. Anybody can change his role at any moment. The price is determined at that level at which the two parties counterbalance each other. The fluctuations of the foreign-exchange rate are not determined solely by bears selling but just as much by bulls buying.

The etatistic view traces back the rise in the price of foreign currencies to the machinations of enemies of the state at home and abroad. These enemies, it is asserted, dispose of the national currency with a speculative intent and purchase foreign currencies with a speculative intent. Two cases are conceivable. Either these enemies are actuated in their dealings by the hope of making a profit, when the same is true of them as of all other speculators. Or they wish to damage the reputation of the state of which they are enemies by depressing the value of its currency, even though they themselves are injured by the operations that lead to this end. To consider the possibility of such enterprises is to forget that they are hardly practicable. The sales of the bears, if they ran against the feeling of the market, would immediately start a contrary movement; the sums disposed of would be taken up by the bulls in expectation of a coming reaction without any effect on the rate of exchange worth mentioning.

In truth, these self-sacrificing bear maneuvers that are undertaken, not to make a profit, but to damage the reputation of the state, belong to the realm of fables. It is true that operations may well be undertaken on foreign-exchange markets that have as their aim, not the securing of a profit, but the creation and maintenance of a rate that does not correspond to market conditions. But this sort of intervention always proceeds from governments, who hold themselves responsible for the currency and always have in view the establishment and maintenance of a rate of exchange above the equilibrium rate. These are artificial bull, not bear, maneuvers. Of course, such intervention also must remain ineffective in the long run. In fact, there is only one way in the last resort to prevent a further fall in the value of money—ceasing to increase the note circulation; and only one way of raising the value of money—reducing the note circulation. Any intervention, such as that of the German Reichsbank in the spring of 1923, in which only a small part of the increasing note expansion was recovered by the banks through the sale of foreign bills, would necessarily be unsuccessful.

Led by the idea of opposing speculation, inflationistic governments have allowed themselves to become involved in measures whose meaning is hardly intelligible. Thus at one time the importation of notes, then their exportation, then again both their exportation and importation, have been prohibited. Exporters have been forbidden to sell for their own country's notes, importers to buy *with* them. All trade in terms of foreign money and precious metals has been declared a state monopoly. The quotation of rates for foreign money on home exchanges has been forbidden, and the communication of information concerning the rates determined at home outside the exchanges and the rates negotiated on foreign exchanges made severely punishable. All these measures have proved useless and would probably have been more quickly set aside than actually was the case if there had not been important factors in favor of their retention. Quite apart from the political significance already referred to attaching to the maintenance of the proposition that the fall in the value of money was only to be ascribed to wicked speculators, it must not be forgotten that every restriction of trade creates vested interests that are from then onward opposed to its removal.

An attempt is sometimes made to demonstrate the desirability of measures directed against speculation by reference to the fact that there are times when there is nobody in opposition to the bears in the foreign-exchange market so that they alone are able to determine the rate of exchange. That, of course, is not correct. Yet it must be noticed that speculation has a peculiar effect in the case of a currency whose progressive depreciation is to be expected while it is impossible to foresee when the depreciation will stop, if at all. While, in general, speculation reduces the gap between the highest and lowest prices without altering the average price level, here, where the movement will presumably continue in the same direction, this naturally cannot be the case. The effect of speculation here is to permit the fluctuation, which would otherwise proceed more uniformly, to proceed by fits and starts with the interposition of pauses. If foreign-exchange rates begin to rise, then, to those speculators who buy in accordance with their own view of the circumstances, are added large numbers of outsiders. These camp followers strengthen the movement started by the few that trust to an independent opinion and send it farther than it would have gone under the influence of the expert professional speculators alone. For the reaction cannot set in so quickly and effectively as usual. Of course, it is the *general* assumption that the depreciation of money will go still farther. But eventually sellers of foreign money must make an appearance, and then the rising movement of the exchanges comes to a standstill; perhaps even a backward movement sets in for a time. Then, after a period of "stable money," the whole thing begins again.

The reaction admittedly begins late, but it must begin as soon as rates of exchange have run too far ahead of commodity prices. If the gap between the equilibrium rate of exchange and the market rate is big enough to give play for profitable commodity transactions, then there will also arise a speculative demand for the domestic paper money. Not until the scope for such transactions has again disappeared owing to a rise in commodity prices will a new rise in the price of foreign exchange set in.

Etatism eventually comes to regard the possession of foreign money, balances as such, and foreign bills, as behavior reprehensible in itself. From this point of view, it is the duty of citizens—not that this is asserted in so many words, but it is the tone of all official declarations—to put up with the harmful consequences of the depreciation of money to their private property and to make no attempt to avoid this by acquiring such possessions as are not eaten up by the depreciation of money. From the point of view of the individual, they declare, it may indeed appear profitable for him to save himself from impoverishment by a flight from the mark, but from the point of view of the community this is harmful and therefore to be condemned. This demand really comes to a cool request on the part of those who enjoy the benefits of the inflation that everybody else should render up his wealth for sacrifice to the destructive policy of the state. In this case, as in all others in which similar assertions are made, it is not true that there exists an opposition between the interests of the individual and the interests of the community. The national capital is composed of the capital of the individual members of the state, and when the latter is consumed nothing remains of the former either. The individual who takes steps to invest his property in such a way that it cannot be eaten up by the depreciation of money does not injure the community; on the contrary, in taking steps to preserve his private property from destruction he also preserves some of the property of the community from destruction. If he surrendered it without opposition to the effects of the inflation all he would do would be to further the destruction of part of the national wealth and enrich those to whom the inflationary policy brings profit.

It is true that not inconsiderable sections of the best classes of the German people have given credit to the asseverations of the inflationists and their press. Many thought that they were doing a patriotic act when they did not get rid of their marks or kronen and mark or kronen securities, but retained them. By so doing, they did not serve the fatherland. That they and their families have as a consequence sunk into poverty only means that some of the members of those classes of the German people from which the cultural reconstruction of the nation was to be expected are reduced to a condition in which they are able to help neither the community nor themselves.

PART THREE

MONEY AND BANKING

CHAPTER 15

The Business of Banking

1

Types of Banking Activity

The business of banking falls into two distinct branches: the negotiation of credit through the loan of other people's money and the
granting of credit through the issue of fiduciary media, that is, notes
and bank balances that are not covered by money. Both branches of
business have always been closely connected. They have grown up
on a common historical soil, and nowadays are still often carried on
together by the same firm. This connection cannot be ascribed to
merely external and accidental factors; it is founded on the peculiar
nature of fiduciary media, and on the historical development of the
business of banking. Nevertheless, the two kinds of activity must be
kept strictly apart in economic theory; for only by considering each of
them separately is it possible to understand their nature and functions.
The unsatisfactory results of previous investigations into the theory
of banking are primarily attributable to inadequate consideration of
the fundamental difference between them.

Modern banks, beside their banking activities proper, carry on
various other more or less closely related branches of business. There
is, for example, the business of exchanging money, on the basis of
which the beginnings of the banking system in the Middle Ages were

developed, and to which the bill of exchange, one of the most important instruments of banking activity, owes its origin. Banks still carry on this business nowadays, but so do exchange bureaus, which perform no banking functions; and these also devote themselves to such business as the purchase and sale of securities.

The banks have also taken over a number of functions connected with the general management of the property of their customers. They accept and look after securities as "open" deposits, detach interest and dividend coupons as they fall due, and receive the sums concerned. They superintend the allotment of shares, attend to the renewal of coupon sheets, and see to other similar matters. They carry out stock exchange dealings for their customers and also the purchase and sale of securities that are not quoted on the exchange. They let out strong rooms which are used for the secure disposal of articles of value under the customer's seal. All of these activities, whatever their bearing in individual cases upon the profitability of the whole undertaking, and however great their economic significance for the community as a whole, yet have no inherent connection with banking proper as we have defined it above.

The connection between banking proper and the business of speculation and flotation is similarly loose and superficial. This is the branch of their activities on which the general economic importance of the banks nowadays depends, and by means of which on the continent of Europe and in the United States they secured control of production, no less than of the provision of credit. It would not be easy to overestimate the influence on the organization of economic life that has been exerted by the change in the relation of the banks to industry and commerce; perhaps it would not be an exaggeration to describe it as the most important event in modern economic history. But in connection with the influence of banking on the exchange ratio between money and other economic goods, which alone concerns us here, it has no significance at all.

2

The Banks as Negotiators of Credit

The activity of the banks as negotiators of credit is characterized by the lending of other people's, that is, of borrowed, money. Banks borrow money in order to lend it; the difference between the rate of interest that is paid to them and the rate that they pay, less their working expenses, constitutes their profit on this kind of transaction. Banking is negotiation between granters of credit and grantees of credit. Only those who lend the money of others are bankers; those who merely lend their own capital are capitalists, but not bankers.[1] Our use of this definition of the Classical School should not furnish any ground for terminological controversy. The expression *banking* may be extended or contracted as one likes, although there seems little reason for departing from a terminology that has been usual since Smith and Ricardo. But one thing is essential: that activity of the banks that consists in lending other people's money must be sharply distinguished from all other branches of their business and subjected to separate consideration.

For the activity of the banks as negotiators of credit the golden rule holds, that an organic connection must be created between the credit transactions and the debit transactions. The credit that the bank grants must correspond quantitatively and qualitatively to the credit that it takes up. More exactly expressed, "The date on which the bank's obligations fall due must not precede the date on which its corresponding claims can be realized."[2] Only thus can the danger of insolvency be avoided. It is true that a risk remains. Imprudent granting of credit is bound to prove just as ruinous to a bank as to any other merchant. That follows from the legal structure of their business; there is no legal connection between their credit transactions and their debit transactions, and their obligation to pay back the money they have borrowed is not affected by the fate of their investments; the obligation continues even if the investments prove dead losses. But it is just the existence of this risk which makes it worthwhile for the bank to play the part of an intermediary between the granter of credit and the grantee of it. It is from the acceptance of this risk that the bank derives its profits and incurs its losses.

That is all that needs to be said here about this branch of the business of banking. For as far as money and monetary theory are

---

[1] See Bagehot, *Lombard Street* (London, 1906), p. 21.
[2] Knies, *Geld und Kredit*, (Berlin, 1876), vol. 2, Part II, p. 242. See further, Weber, *Depositen- und Spekulationsbanken* (Leipzig, 1902), pp. 106 f.; Sayous, *Les banques de dépôt, les banques de crédit et les sociétés financières*, 2d ed. (Paris, 1907), pp. 219 ff.; Jaffé, *Das englische Bankwesen*, 2d ed. (Leipzig, 1910), p. 203.

concerned, even the function of the banks as negotiators of credit is of significance only so far as it is able to influence the issue of fiduciary media, which alone will be discussed in the rest of the present work.

3

The Banks as Issuers of Fiduciary Media

To comprehend the significance of fiduciary media, it is necessary to examine the nature of credit transactions.

Acts of exchange, whether direct or indirect, can be performed either in such a way that both parties fulfill their parts of the contract at the same time, or in such a way that they fulfill them at different times. In the first case we speak of cash transactions; in the second, of credit transactions. A credit transaction is an exchange of present goods for future goods.

Credit transactions fall into two groups, the separation of which must form the starting point for every theory of credit and especially for every investigation into the connection between money and credit and into the influence of credit on the money prices of goods. On the one hand are those credit transactions which are characterized by the fact that they impose a sacrifice on that party who performs his part of the bargain before the other does—the forgoing of immediate power of disposal over the exchanged good, or, if this version is preferred, the forgoing of power of disposal over the surrendered good until the receipt of that for which it is exchanged. This sacrifice is balanced by a corresponding gain on the part of the other party to the contract—the advantage of obtaining earlier disposal over the good acquired in exchange, or, what is the same thing, of not having to fulfill his part of the bargain immediately. In their respective valuations both parties take account of the advantages and disadvantages that arise from the difference between the times at which they have to fulfill the bargain. The exchange ratio embodied in the contract contains an expression of the value of time in the opinions of the individuals concerned.

The second group of credit transactions is characterized by the fact that in them the gain of the party who receives before he pays is balanced by no sacrifice on the part of the other party. Thus the difference in time between fulfillment and counterfulfillment, which is just as much the essence of this kind of transaction as of the other, has an influence merely on the valuations of the one party, while the other is able to treat it as insignificant. This fact at first seems puzzling, even inexplicable; it constitutes a rock on which many economic theories have come to grief. Nevertheless, the explanation is not very difficult if we take into account the peculiarity of the goods involved in the transaction. In the first kind of credit transactions, what is surrendered consists of money or goods, disposal over which is a source of satisfaction and renunciation of which a source of dissatisfaction. In the credit transactions of the second group, the granter of the credit renounces for the time being the ownership of a sum of money, but this renunciation (given certain assumptions that in this case are justifiable) results for him in no reduction of satisfaction. If a creditor is able to confer a loan by issuing claims which are payable on demand, then the granting of the credit is bound up with no economic sacrifice for him. He could confer credit in this form free of charge, if we disregard the technical costs that may be involved in the issue of notes and the like. Whether he is paid immediately in money or only receives claims at first, which do not fall due until later, remains a matter of indifference to him.[3]

It seems desirable to choose special names for the two groups of credit transactions in order to avoid any possible confusion of the concepts. For the first group the name *commodity credit* (*Sachkredit*) is suggested, for the second the name *circulation credit* (*Zirkulationskredit*). It must be admitted that these expressions do not fully indicate the essence of the distinction that they are intended to characterize. This objection, however, which can in some degree be urged against all technical terms, is not of very great importance. A sufficient reply to it is contained in the fact that there are no better and more apt expressions in use to convey the distinction intended, which, generally speaking, has not received the consideration it

---

[3] See Macleod, *The Elements of Banking* (London, 1904), p. 153.

merits. In any case the expression *circulation credit* gives occasion for fewer errors than the expression *emission credit* (*Emissionskredit*), which is sometimes used and has been chosen merely with regard to the issue of notes. Besides, what applies to all such differences of opinion is also true of this particular terminological controversy— the words used do not matter; what does matter is what the words are intended to mean.

Naturally, the peculiarities of circulation credit have not escaped the attention of economists. It is hardly possible to find a single theorist who has devoted serious consideration to the fundamental problems of the value of money and credit without having referred to the peculiar circumstances in which notes and checks are used. That this recognition of the individuality of certain kinds of credit transactions has not led to the distinction of commodity credit and circulation credit is probably to be ascribed to certain accidents in the history of our science. The criticism of isolated dogmatic and economico-political errors of the Currency principle that constituted the essence of most nineteenth-century investigation into the theory of banking and credit led to an emphasis being placed on all the factors that could be used to demonstrate the essential similarity of notes and other media of bank credit, and to the oversight of the important differences that exist between the two groups of credit characterized above, the discovery of which constitutes one of the permanent contributions of the Classical School and its successors, the Currency theorists.

The peculiar attitude of individuals toward transactions involving circulation credit is explained by the circumstance that the claims in which it is expressed can be used in every connection instead of money. He who requires money, in order to lend it, or to buy something, or to liquidate debts, or to pay taxes, is not first obliged to convert the claims to money (notes or bank balances) into money; he can also use the claims themselves directly as means of payment. For everybody they therefore are really money substitutes; they perform the monetary function in the same way as money; they are "ready money" to him, that is, present, not future, money. The practice of the merchant who includes under cash not merely the notes and token coinage which he possesses but also any bank balances which he has constantly at his immediate disposal by means of

checks or otherwise is just as correct as that of the legislator who
endows these fiduciary media with the legal power of settling all
obligations contracted in terms of money—in doing which he only
confirms a usage that has been established by commerce.

In all of this there is nothing special or peculiar to money. The
objective exchange value of an indubitably secure and mature claim,
which embodies a right to receive a definite individual thing or a
definite quantity of fungible things, does not differ in the least from
the objective exchange value of the thing or quantity of things to
which the claim refers. What is significant for us lies in the fact that
such claims to money, if there is no doubt whatever concerning
either their security or their liquidity, are, simply on account of their
equality in objective exchange value to the sums of money to which
they refer, commercially competent to take the place of money entirely. Anyone who wishes to acquire bread can achieve his aim by
obtaining in the first place a mature and secure claim to bread. If he
only wishes to acquire the bread in order to give it up again in
exchange for something else, he can give this claim up instead and
is not obliged to liquidate it. But if he wishes to consume the bread,
then he has no alternative but to procure it by liquidation of the
claim. With the exception of money, all the economic goods that
enter into the process of exchange necessarily reach an individual
who wishes to consume them; all claims which embody a right to
the receipt of such goods will therefore sooner or later have to be
realized. A person who takes upon himself the obligation to deliver
on demand a particular individual good, or a particular quantity of
fungible goods (with the exception of money), must reckon with
the fact that he will be held to its fulfillment, and probably in a very
short time. Therefore he dare not promise more than he can be
constantly ready to perform. A person who has a thousand loaves
of bread at his immediate disposal will not dare to issue more than
a thousand tickets each of which gives its holder the right to demand
at any time the delivery of a loaf of bread. It is otherwise with money.
Since nobody wants money except in order to get rid of it again,
since it never finds a consumer except on ceasing to be a common
medium of exchange, it is quite possible for claims to be employed
in its stead, embodying a right to the receipt on demand of a certain
sum of money and unimpugnable both as to their convertibility in

general and as to whether they really would be converted on the demand of the holder; and it is quite possible for these claims to pass from hand to hand without any attempt being made to enforce the right that they embody. The obligee can expect that these claims will remain in circulation for so long as their holders do not lose confidence in their prompt convertibility or transfer them to persons who have not this confidence. He is therefore in a position to undertake greater obligations than he would ever be able to fulfill; it is enough if he takes sufficient precautions to ensure his ability to satisfy promptly that proportion of the claims that is actually enforced against him.

The fact that is peculiar to money alone is not that mature and secure claims to money are as highly valued in commerce as the sums of money to which they refer, but rather that such claims are complete substitutes for money, and, as such, are able to fulfill all the functions of money in those markets in which their essential characteristics of maturity and security are recognized. It is this circumstance that makes it possible to issue more of this sort of substitute than the issuer is always in a position to convert. And so the fiduciary medium comes into being in addition to the money certificate.

Fiduciary media increase the supply of money in the broader sense of the word; they are consequently able to influence the objective exchange value of money. To the investigation of this influence the following chapters are devoted.

4

Deposits as the Origin of Circulation Credit

Fiduciary media have grown up on the soil of the deposit system; deposits have been the basis upon which notes have been issued and accounts opened that could be drawn upon by checks. Independently of this, coins, at first the smaller and then the medium-sized, have developed into fiduciary media. It is usual to reckon the acceptance of a deposit which can be drawn upon at any time by means of notes or checks as a type of credit transaction and juristically this view is, of course, justified; but economically, the case is not one of a credit transaction. If *credit* in the economic sense means the exchange of a present good or a present service against a future good or a future service, then it is hardly possible to include the transactions in question under the conception of credit. A depositor of a sum of money who acquires in exchange for it a claim convertible into money at any time which will perform exactly the same service for him as the sum it refers to, has exchanged no present good for a future good. The claim that he has acquired by his deposit is also a present good for him. The depositing of the money in no way means that he has renounced immediate disposal over the utility that it commands.

Therefore the claim obtained in exchange for the sum of money is equally valuable to him whether he converts it sooner or later, or even not at all; and because of this it is possible for him, without damaging his economic interests, to acquire such claims in return for the surrender of money without demanding compensation for any difference in value arising from the difference in time between payment and repayment, such, of course, as does not in fact exist. That this could be so repeatedly overlooked is to be ascribed to the long accepted and widely accepted view that the essence of credit consists in the confidence which the lender reposes in the borrower. The fact that anybody hands money over to a bank in exchange for a claim to repayment on demand certainly shows that he has confidence in the bank's constant readiness to pay. But this is not a credit transaction, because the essential element, the exchange of present goods for future goods, is absent. But another circumstance that has helped to bring about the mistaken opinion referred to is the fact that the business performed by banks in exchanging money for claims to money payable on demand which can be transferred in the place of money, is very closely and intimately connected with that particular branch of their credit business that has most influenced the volume of money and entirely transformed the whole monetary system of the present day, namely, the provision of circulation credit. It is with this sort of banking business alone, the issue of notes and the opening of accounts that are not covered by money, that we are concerned. For this sort of business alone is of significance in connection with the function and value of money; the volume of money is affected by no other credit transactions than these.

While all other credit transactions may occur singly and be performed on both sides by persons who do not regularly occupy themselves with such transactions, the provision of credit through the issue of fiduciary media is only possible on the part of an undertaking which conducts credit transactions as a matter of regular business. Deposits must be accepted and loans granted on a fairly considerable scale before the necessary conditions for the issue of fiduciary media are fulfilled. Notes cannot circulate unless the person who issues them is known and trustworthy. Moreover, payment by transfer from one account to another presupposes either a large circle of customers of the same bank or such a union of several banking undertakings that the total number of participants in the system is large. Fiduciary media can therefore be created only by banks and bankers; but this is not the only business that can be carried on by banks and bankers.

One branch of banking business deserves particular mention because, although closely related to that circle of banking activities with which we have to deal, it is quite without influence on the volume of money. This is that deposit business which does not serve the bank as a basis for the issue of fiduciary media. The activity carried on here by the bank is merely that of an intermediary, concerning which the English definition of a banker as a man who lends other people's money is perfectly apt. The sums of money handed over to the bank by its customers in this branch of business are not a part of their reserves, but investments of money which are not necessary for day-to-day transactions. As a rule the two groups of deposits are distinguished even by the form they have in banking technique. The current accounts can be withdrawn on demand, that is to say, without previous notice. Often no interest at all is paid upon them, but when interest is paid, it is lower than that on the investment deposits. On the other hand, the investment deposits always bear interest and are usually repayable only on notice being given in advance. In the course of time, the differences in banking technique between the two kinds of deposit have been largely obliterated. The development of the savings-deposit system has made it possible for the banks to undertake the obligation to pay out small amounts of savings deposits at any time without notice. The larger the sums which are brought to the banks in the investment-deposit business, the greater, according to the law of large numbers, is the probability that the sums paid in on any particular day will balance those whose repayment is demanded, and the smaller is the reserve which will guarantee the bank the possibility of not having to break any of its promises. Such a reserve is all the easier to maintain inasmuch as it is combined with the reserve of the current-account business. Small business people or not very well-to-do private individuals, whose monetary affairs are too insignificant to be transferred as a whole to a bank, now make use of this development by trusting part of their reserve to the banks in the form of savings deposits. On the other hand, the circumstance that competition among banks has gradually raised the rate of interest on current accounts causes sums of money that are not needed for current-account purposes, and therefore might be invested, to be left on current account as a temporary investment. Nevertheless, these practices do not alter the principle of the matter; it is not the formal technical aspect of a transaction but its economic character that determines its significance for us.

From the point of view of the banks there does exist a connection between the two kinds of deposit business inasmuch as the possibility of uniting the two reserves permits of their being maintained at a lower level than their sum would have to be if they were completely independent. This is extremely important from the point of view of banking technique, and explains to some degree the advantage of the deposit banks, which carry on both branches of business, over the savings banks, which only accept savings deposits (the savings banks being consequently driven to take up current-account business also). For the organization of the banking system this circumstance is of importance; for the theoretical investigation of its problems it is negligible.

The essential thing about that branch of banking business which alone needs to be taken into consideration in connection with the volume of money is this: the banks that undertake current-account business for their customers are, for the reasons referred to above, in a position to lend out part of the deposited sums of money. It is a matter of indifference how they do this, whether they actually lend out a portion of the deposited money or issue notes to those who want credit or open a current account for them. The only circumstance that is of importance here is that the loans are granted out of a fund *that did not exist before the loans were granted.* In all other circumstances, whenever loans are granted they are granted out of existing and available funds of wealth. A bank which neither possesses the right of note issue nor carries on current-account business for its customers can never lend out more money than the sum of its own resources and the resources that other persons have entrusted to it. It is otherwise with those banks that issue notes or open current accounts. They have a fund from which to grant loans, over and above their own resources and those resources of other people that are at their disposal.

5

The Granting of Circulation Credit

According to the prevailing opinion, a bank which grants a loan in its own notes plays the part of a credit negotiator between the borrowers and those in whose hands the notes happen to be at any time. Thus in the last resort bank credit is not granted by the banks but by the holders of the notes. The intervention of the banks is said to have the single object of permitting the substitution of its well-known and indubitable credit for that of an unknown and perhaps less trustworthy debtor and so of making it easier for a borrower to get a loan taken up by "the public." It is asserted, for example, that if bills are discounted by the bank and the discounted equivalent paid out in notes, these notes only circulate in place of the bills, which would otherwise be passed directly from hand to hand in lieu of cash. It is thought that this can also be proved historically by reference to the fact that before the development of the bank-of-issue system, especially in England, bills circulated to a greater extent than afterward; that in Lancashire, for example, until the opening of a branch of the Bank of England in Manchester, nine-tenths of the total payments were made in bills and only one-tenth in money or banknotes.[4] Now this view by no means describes the essence of the matter. A person who accepts and holds notes, grants no credit; he exchanges no present good for a future good. The

---

[4] See Fullarton, *On the Regulation of Currencies,* 2d ed. (London, 1845), p. 39; Mill, *Principles of Political Economy* (London, 1867), p. 314; Jaffé, *op. cit.,* p. 175.

immediately convertible note of a solvent bank is employable every-where as a fiduciary medium instead of money in commercial trans-actions, and nobody draws a distinction between the money and the notes which he holds as cash. The note is a present good just as much as the money.

Notes might be issued by banks in either of two ways. One way is to exchange them for money. According to accounting principles, the bank here enters into a debit transaction and a credit transaction; but the transaction is actually a matter of indifference, since the new liability is balanced by an exactly corresponding asset. The bank cannot make a profit out of such a transaction. In fact such a trans-action involves it in a loss, since it brings in nothing to balance the expense of manufacturing the notes and storing the stocks of money. The issue of fully backed notes can therefore only be carried on in conjunction with the issue of fiduciary media. This is the second possible way of issuing notes, to issue them as loans to persons in search of credit. According to the books, this, like the other, is a case of a credit and a debit transaction only.[5] It is true that this is not shown by the bank's balance sheet. On the credit side of the balance sheet are entered the loans granted and the state of the till, and on the debit side, the notes. We approach a better under-standing of the true nature of the whole process if we go instead to the profit-and-loss account. In this account there is recorded a profit whose origin is suggestive—"profit on loans." When the bank lends other people's money as well as its own resources, part of this profit arises from the difference between the rates of interest that it pays its depositors and the rates that it charges its borrowers. The other part arises from the granting of circulation credit. It is the bank that makes this profit, not the holders of the notes. It is possible that the bank may retain the whole of it; but sometimes it shares it, either with the holders of the notes or, more probably, with the depositors. But in either case there is a profit.[6]

Let us imagine a country whose monetary circulation consists in 100 million ducats. In this country a bank-of-issue is established. For the sake of simplicity, let us assume that the bank's own capital

---

[5] See Jaffé, *op. cit.*, p. 153.
[6] This is the "surplus profit" (*Übergewinn*) of the business of banking, referred to by Hermann (*op. cit.*, pp. 500 f.).

is invested as a reserve outside the banking business, and that it
has to pay the annual interest on this capital to the state in return
for the concession of the right of note issue—an assumption that
does correspond closely with the actual situation of some banks-of-
issue. Now let the bank have fifty million ducats paid into it and
issue fifty million ducats' worth of one-ducat notes against this sum.
But we must suppose that the bank does not allow the whole sum
of fifty million ducats to remain in its vaults; it lends out forty million
on interest to foreign businessmen. The interest on these loans con-
situtes its gross profit which is reduced only by the cost of manufacture of the notes, by administrative expenses, and the like. Is it
possible in this case to say that the holders of the notes have granted
credit to the foreign debtors of the bank, or to the bank itself?

Let us alter our example in a nonessential point. Let the bank
lend the forty million not to foreigners but to persons within the
country. One of these, A, is indebted to B for a certain sum, say the
cost of goods which he has bought from him. A has no money at
his disposal, but is ready to cede to B a claim maturing in three
months, which he himself holds against P. Can B agree to this?
Obviously only if he himself does not need for the next three months
the sum of money which he could demand immediately, or if he has
a prospect of finding somebody who can do without a corresponding sum of money for three months and is therefore ready to take
over the claim against P. Or the situation might arise in which B
wished to buy goods immediately from C, who was willing to permit postponement of payment for three months. In such a case, if
C was really in agreement with the postponement, this could only
be for one of the three reasons that might also cause B to be content
with payment after the lapse of three months instead of immediate
payment. All these, in fact, are cases of genuine credit transactions,
of the exchange of present goods for future goods. Now the number
and extent of these transactions is dependent on the quantity of
present goods available; the total of the possible loans is limited by
the total quantity of money and other goods available for this purpose. Loans can be granted only by those who have disposal over
money or other economic goods which they can do without for a
period. Now when the bank enters the arena by offering forty million ducats on the loan market, the fund available for lending pur-

poses is increased by exactly this sum; what immediate influence this must have on the rate of interest, should not need further explanation. Is it then correct to say that when the bank discounts bills it does nothing but substitute a convenient note currency for an inconvenient bill currency?[7] Is the banknote really nothing but a handier sort of bill of exchange? By no means. The note that embodies the promise of a solvent bank to pay a sum to the bearer on demand at any time, that is, immediately if desired, differs in an important point from the bill that contains the promise to pay a sum of money after the passage of a period of time. The sight bill, which (as is well known) plays no part in the credit system, is comparable with the note; but not the time bill, which is the form regularly assumed by the bills that are usual in credit transactions. A person who pays the price of a purchased commodity in money, in notes, or by the transfer of any other claim payable on demand, has carried through a cash transaction; a person who pays the purchase price by the acceptance of a three-month bill has carried through a credit transaction.[8]

Let us introduce a further unessential variation into our example, which will perhaps help to make the matter clearer. Let us assume that the bank has first issued notes to the value of fifty million ducats and received for them fifty million ducats in money; and now let us suppose it to place a further forty million ducats in its own notes on the loan market. This case is in every way identical with the two considered above.

The activity of note issue cannot in any way be described as increasing the demand for credit in the same sense as, say, an increase in the number of bills current. Quite the contrary. The bank-of-issue does not demand credit; it grants it. When an additional quantity of bills comes on to the market, this increases the demand for credit, and therefore raises the rate of interest. The placing of an additional quantity of notes on the loan market at first has the opposite effect; it constitutes an increase in the supply of credit and has therefore an immediate tendency to diminish the rate of interest.[9]

---

[7] As, for example, even Wicksell does (*Geldzins und Güterpreise* [Jena, 1898], p. 57).
[8] See Torrens, *The Principles and Practical Operation of Sir Robert Peel's Act of 1844 Explained and Defended*, 2d ed. (London, 1857), pp. 16 ff.
[9] *Ibid.*, p. 18.

It is one of the most remarkable phenomena in the history of political economy that this fundamental distinction between notes and bills could have passed unnoticed. It raises an important problem for investigators into the history of economic theory. And in solving this problem it will be their principal task to show how the beginnings of a recognition of the true state of affairs that are to be found even in the writings of the Classical School and were further developed by the Currency School, were destroyed instead of being continued by the work of those who came after.[10]

6

Fiduciary Media and the Nature of Indirect Exchange

It should be sufficiently clear from what has been said that the traditional way of looking at the matter is but little in harmony with the peculiarities of fiduciary media. To regard notes and current accounts, whether they are covered by money or not, as constituting the same phenomenon, is to bar the way to an adequate conception of the nature of these peculiarities. To regard noteholders or owners of current accounts as granters of credit is to fail to recognize the meaning of a credit transaction. To treat both notes and bills of exchange in general (that is, not merely sight bills) as "credit instruments" alike is to renounce all hope of getting to the heart of the matter.

On the other hand, it is a complete mistake to assert that the nature of an act of exchange is altered by the employment of fiduciary media. Not only those exchanges that are carried through by the cession of notes or current-account balances covered by money, but also those exchanges that are carried through by the employment of fiduciary media, are indirect exchanges involving the use of money. Although from the juristic point of view it may be significant whether a liability incurred in an act of exchange is dis-

---

[10] Since the appearance of the first edition of the present work numerous books have been published that still do not recognize the problem of circulation credit. Among the works that have grasped the nature of this problem the following should be mentioned: Schumpeter, *Theorie der wirtschaftlichen Entwicklung* (Leipzig, 1912), pp. 219 ff.; Schlesinger, *Theorie der Geld- und Kreditwirtschaft* (Munich and Leipzig, 1914), pp. 133 ff.; Hahn, *Volkswirtschaftliche Theorie des Bankkredits* (Tübingen, 1920), pp. 52 ff.

charged by physical transference of pieces of money or by cession of a claim to the immediate delivery of pieces of money, that is, by cession of a money substitute, this has no bearing upon the economic nature of the act of exchange. It would be incorrect to assert, for instance, that when payment is made by check, commodities are really exchanged against commodities, only without any of the crude clumsiness of primitive barter.[11] Here, just as in every other indirect exchange made possible by money, and in contrast to direct exchange, money plays the part of an intermediary between commodity and commodity. But money is an economic good with its own fluctuations in value. A person who acquires money or money substitutes will be affected by all the variations in their objective exchange value. This is just as true of payment by notes or checks as of the physical transference of pieces of money. But this is the only point that matters, and not the accidental circumstance whether money physically "enters into" the transaction as a whole. Anybody who sells commodities and is paid by means of a check and then immediately uses either the check itself or the balance that it puts at his disposal to pay for commodities that he has purchased in another transaction, has by no means exchanged commodities directly for commodities. He has undertaken two independent acts of exchange, which are connected no more intimately than any other two purchases.

It is possible that the terminology proposed is not the most suitable that could be found. This must be freely admitted. But it may at least be claimed for it that it opens the way to a better comprehension of the nature of the phenomena under discussion than those that have been previously employed. For if it is not quite true to say that inexact and superficial terminology has been chiefly responsible for the frequently unsatisfactory nature of the results of investigations into the theory of banking, still a good deal of the ill success of such investigations is to be laid to that account.

That economic theory puts questions of law and banking technique in the background and draws its boundaries differently from

---

[11] Thus Lexis, *Allegemeine Volkswirtschaftslehre* (Berlin, 1910) (Hinnenberg, *Die Kultur der Gegenwart*, section II, vol. 10, Part 1), p. 122; Lexis, *Geld und Preise* (Riesser-Festgabe, Berlin, 1913), pp. 83 f. Similarly, with regard to the clearinghouse business, Schumacher, *Weltwirtschaftliche Studien* (Leipzig, 1911), pp. 53 f. and the writings there referred to.

those drawn by jurisprudence or business administration is or should be self-evident. Reference to discrepancies between the above theory and the legal or technical nature of particular procedures is therefore no more relevant as an argument against the theory than economic considerations would be in the settlement of controversial juristic questions.

CHAPTER 16

The Evolution of Fiduciary Media

1

The Two Ways of Issuing Fiduciary Media

Thus fiduciary media are claims to the payment of a given sum on demand, which are not covered by a fund of money, and whose legal and technical characteristics make them suitable for tender and acceptance instead of money in fulfillment of obligations that are in terms of money. As has already been suggested, it is not the dead letter of the law so much as actual business practice that counts, so that some things function as fiduciary media, although they cannot be regarded as promises to pay money from the juristic point of view, because they nevertheless are in fact honored as such by somebody or other. We were able to show that, so far as they are not money certificates, even modern token coins and such kinds of money as the German thaler during the period from the establishment of the gold standard until its abolition, constitute fiduciary media and not money.

Fiduciary media may be issued in two ways: by banks, and otherwise. Bank fiduciary media are characterized by being dealt with as constituting a debt of the issuing body. They are entered as liabilities, and the issuing body does not regard the sum issued as an increase of its income or capital, but as an increase on the debit side

311

of its account, which must be balanced by a corresponding increase on the credit side if the whole transaction is not to figure as a loss. This way of dealing with fiduciary media makes it necessary for the issuing body to regard them as part of its trading capital and never to spend them on consumption but always to invest them in business. These investments need not always be loans; the issuer may himself carry on a productive enterprise with the working capital that is put into his hands by the issue of fiduciary media. It is known that some deposit banks sometimes open deposit accounts without a money cover not only for the purpose of granting loans, but also for the purpose of directly procuring resources for production on their own behalf. More than one of the modern credit and commercial banks has invested a part of its capital in this manner, and the question of the right attitude in this case of the holders of the money substitutes, and of the state legislature that feels itself called upon to protect them, remains an open one. In earlier times there was a similar problem concerning banks issuing notes[1] until banking practice or the law prescribed short-term loans as "cover."

The issuer of fiduciary media may, however, regard the value of the fiduciary media put into circulation as an addition to his income or capital. If he does this, he will not take the trouble to cover the increase in his obligations due to the issue by setting aside a special credit fund out of his capital. He will pocket the profits of the issue, which in the case of token coinage is called seigniorage, as composedly as any other sort of income.

The only difference between the two ways of putting fiduciary media into circulation lies in the attitude of the issuer. Naturally, this cannot have any significance for the determination of the value of the fiduciary media. The difference between the methods of issue is a result of historical factors. Fiduciary media have sprung from two different roots: from the activities of the deposit and giro banks on the one hand, and from the state prerogative of minting on the other hand. The former is the source of notes and current accounts; the latter, that of convertible Treasury notes, token coins, and that current money of which the coinage is restricted, but which can be regarded neither as credit money nor as fiat money because it is

---

[1] See Lotz, *Geschichte und Kritik des deutschen Bankgesetzes vom 14. März 1875* (Leipzig, 1888), pp. 72 f.

actually convertible into money on demand to its full amount. Today the difference between the two methods of issuing is gradually disappearing, all the more as the state endeavors to act in the same way as the banks in issuing fiduciary media. Some states are already in the habit of devoting the profits of their coinage to special purposes and of refusing to treat them in any way as an increase of wealth.[2]

Of the two types of money substitutes issued by the banks, the current account is the older. The banknote, in fact, is only a development of it. It is true that the two are different in the eyes of the law and the banker, but they do not differ at all in the eyes of the economist. The only distinctions between them are in those legal or banking or commercial peculiarities of the banknote which give it a special capacity of circulation. It is easily transferable and very like money in the way in which it is transferred. Banknotes were therefore able to outstrip the older money substitute, the current account, and penetrate into commerce with extraordinary rapidity. For medium and small payments they offer such great advantages that the current account was hardly able to maintain its ground beside them. It was not until the second half of the nineteenth century that the current account once more became important along with the banknote. In large transactions, check and clearing payments are often superior to notes. But the chief reason why the current account was able in part to expel the banknote must by no means be sought in any inherent requirements of business. The current account is not, as it is sometimes the fashion to assert without any reason or proof, a "higher" form of money substitute than the banknote. The banknote has been supplanted by the current account in many countries because its development was artificially hindered and that of the current account artificially encouraged, the reason for this being that acceptance of the doctrines of the Currency principle led people to see danger for the stability of the exchange ratio between money and other economic goods only in the overissue of notes, and not in the excessive increase of bank deposits.

---

[2] See for example on the Swiss currency reserve fund established by article 8 of the Currency Act of January 31, 1860, Altherr, *Eine Betrachtung über neue Wege der schweizerischen Münzpolitik* (Bern, 1908), pp. 61 ff.

For the study of the credit system from the economic point of view, the contrast between notes and deposits is of minor importance. There are payments for which one or other form is the more suitable, and payments for which both forms are suitable. If their development had been allowed to take its own course, this fact would undoubtedly have been more evident than it is today, when the attempt is sometimes made to bring about the employment of one or other kind of fiduciary medium by artificial means in circumstances where it appears the less appropriate technically.

2

Fiduciary Media and the Clearing System

That want of clarity concerning the nature of fiduciary media which constitutes the chief characteristic of the writings of the banking theorists and their *epigoni*, the modern writers on problems of banking theory, leads to a perpetual confusion between money substitutes and a series of institutions which reduce the demand for money in the narrower sense, and also to relative neglect of the differences that exist between money certificates and fiduciary media within the group of money substitutes proper.

The economic effect of an exchange that is carried out with the help of a certain quantity of a fungible good, can sometimes, if several persons have to transact business at the same time, be attained more indirectly in ways which, while they are formally of a more complicated legal structure, nevertheless fundamentally simplify the technical transaction and make it possible to dispense in particular instances with the physical presence of pieces of the medium of exchange. If A has to deliver a piece of cloth to B and receive a sheep from him for it, and if A at the same time has to give a sheep to C and receive from him a horse, these two exchanges can also be transacted if B gives a sheep to C on behalf and on account of A, so freeing himself from the obligation that he is under to give A a sheep in return for the cloth and A from the obligation that he is under to give C a sheep in return for the horse. Whereas the direct transaction of these two exchanges would have necessitated four transfers, this procedure necessitates only three.

The possibility of facilitating exchanges in this way is extraordinarily increased by extension of the custom of using certain goods as common media of exchange. For the number of cases in which anybody simultaneously owes and has a claim to a certain fungible good will increase with the number of cases in which one and the same fungible good—the common medium of exchange—is the object of exchange in individual transactions. Full development of the use of money leads at first to a splitting up into two acts of indirect exchange even of such transactions as could in any case have been carried through by direct exchange. The butcher and the baker, who could also exchange their products directly, often prefer to have their mutual relations take the form of an exchange carried through with the help of money which their other transactions assume also. The butcher sells meat to the baker for money and the baker sells bread to the butcher for money. This gives rise to reciprocal money claims and money obligations. But it is clear that a settlement can be arrived at here, not only by each party actually handing money over to the other, but also by means of offsetting, in which merely the balance remaining over is settled by payment of money. To complete the transaction in this way by full or partial cancellation of counterclaims offers important advantages in comparison with direct exchange: all the freedom connected with the use of money is combined with the technical simplicity that characterizes direct exchange transactions.

This method of carrying through indirect exchanges by cancellation of counterclaims is very greatly stimulated at the time when the cases where its employment is possible are increased by the fact that credit transactions, or the exchange of present goods for future goods, are becoming customary. When all exchanges have to be settled in ready cash, then the possibility of performing them by means of cancellation is limited to the case exemplified by the butcher and baker and only then on the assumption, which of course only occasionally holds good, that the demands of both parties are simultaneous. At the most, it is possible to imagine that several other persons might join in and so a small circle be built up within which drafts could be used for the settlement of transactions without the actual use of money. But even in this case simultaneity would still be necessary, and, several persons being involved, would be still seldomer achieved.

These difficulties could not be overcome until credit set business free from dependence on the simultaneous occurrence of demand and supply. This, in fact, is where the importance of credit for the monetary system lies. But this could not have its full effect so long as all exchange was still direct exchange, so long even as money had not established itself as a common medium of exchange. The instrumentality of credit permits transactions between two persons to be treated as simultaneous for purposes of settlement even if they actually take place at different times. If the baker sells bread to the cobbler daily throughout the year and buys from him a pair of shoes on one occasion only, say at the end of the year, then the payment on the part of the baker, and naturally on that of the cobbler also, would have to be made in cash, if credit did not provide a means first for delaying the one party's liability and then for settling it by cancellation instead of by cash payment.

Exchanges made with the help of money can also be settled in part by offsetting if claims are transferred within a group until claims and counterclaims come into being between the same persons, these being then canceled against each other, or until the claims are acquired by the debtors themselves and so extinguished. In interlocal and international dealing in bills, which has been developed in recent years by the addition of the use of checks and in other ways which have not fundamentally changed its nature, the same sort of thing is carried out on an enormous scale. And here again credit increases in a quite extraordinary fashion the number of cases in which such offsetting is feasible.[3] In all these cases we have an exchange made with the help of money which is nevertheless transacted without the actual *use* of money or money substitutes simply by means of a process of offsetting between the parties. Money in these cases is still a medium of exchange, but its employment in this capacity is independent of its physical existence. Use is made of money, but not *physical* use of actually existing money or money substitutes. Money which is not present performs an economic function; it has its effect solely by reason of the possibility of its being *able* to be present.

---

[3] See Knies, *Geld und Kredit*, (Berlin, 1876), vol. 2, Part I, pp. 268 ff.

The reduction of the demand for money in the broader sense which is brought about by the use of offsetting processes for settling exchanges made with the help of money, without affecting the function performed by money as a medium of exchange, is based upon the reciprocal cancellation of claims to money. The use of money is avoided because claims to money are transferred instead of actual money. This process is continued until claim and debt come together, until creditor and debtor are united in the same person. Then the claim to money is extinguished, since nobody can be his own creditor or his own debtor.[4] The same result may be reached at an earlier stage by reciprocal cancellation, that is by the liquidation of counterclaims by a process of offsetting.[5] In either case the claim to money ceases to exist, and then, and not until then, is the act of exchange which gave birth to the claim finally completed.

Any transfer of a claim which does not bring it nearer to being extinguished by cancellation or offsetting cannot decrease the demand for money. In fact, if the transfer of the claim is not instead of payment in money, then it is on the contrary the source of a fresh demand for money. Now cession of claims instead of payment in money has, apart from the use of money substitutes, never been of very great commercial importance. As far as claims that are already due are concerned, the holder will as a rule prefer to call in the outstanding sums of money, because he will invariably find it easier to buy (and carry through other transactions in the market) with money or money substitutes than with claims whose goodness has not been indisputably established. But if the holder does in exceptional cases transfer such a claim by way of payment, then the new holder will be in the same position. A further hindrance to the transfer of claims to money that are not yet due instead of payment in money is the fact that such claims can be accepted only by such persons as are able to agree to postponement of payment; to rest content with a claim that is not yet due, when immediate payment could be enforced, is to grant credit.

Commercial requirements had previously made use of the legal

---

[4] See l. 21, sec. 1 D. de liberatione legata 34, 3. Terentius Clemens *libro XII ad legem Juliam et Papiam*.
[5] See l. 1 D. der compensationibus 16, 2. Modestinus libro sexto pandectarum.

institution of the bill in a way that caused it to circulate in a manner fairly similar to that of fiduciary media. Toward the end of the eighteenth and at the beginning of the nineteenth century bills were current in the European commercial centers which were endorsed by the merchants in place of payment in money.[6] Since it was the general custom to make payments in this way, anybody could accept a bill that still had some time to run even when he wanted cash immediately; for it was possible to reckon with a fair amount of certainty that those to whom payments had to be made would also accept a bill not yet mature in place of ready money. It is perhaps hardly necessary to add that in all such transactions the element of time was of course taken into consideration, and discount consequently allowed for. Now it is true that this might increase the technical difficulties in handling the circulatory apparatus, which was already not an easy matter to deal with for other reasons, such, for example, as the different amounts of the bills. But, on the other hand, it offered a profit to any holder who did not pass the bill on immediately but kept it for a while, even if only for a very short while, in his portfolio. Used in this way, the bill was able to make up to a certain extent for the lack of fiduciary media. Even though it might not be due for a long time ahead, the holder could regard it as liquid, because he could pass it on at any time.

Despite this, bills of this sort were not fiduciary media in the sense in which notes or deposits are. They lack the characteristic features and properties which enabled the fiduciary medium, the indefinitely augmentable product of the arbitrary issuing activity of the banks, to become a complete substitute for money for business purposes. It is true that the cooperation of issuers and acceptors can give the circulation of bills the capacity of unlimited augmentation and unlimited lease of life through the agency of bill jobbing and regular prolongation, even if technical difficulties alone are sufficient to prevent the bills from ever being used in business to the same extent as money substitutes. But every increase in the amount of bills in circulation makes negotiation of individual bills more difficult. It reduces the resources of the market. In fact, the holder of a bill, as distinct from the holder of a note or of a current account,

---

[6] See Thornton, *An Enquiry into the Nature and Effects of the Paper Credit of Great Britain* (London, 1802), pp. 39 ff.

is a creditor. A person who accepts a bill must examine the standing of the previous endorser, and also that of the issuer and the others who are liable for the bill, but in particular the primary acceptor. Whoever passes a bill on, in endorsing it undertakes responsibility for the payment of the amount of the bill. The endorsement of the bill is in fact not a final payment; it liberates the debtor to a limited degree only. If the bill is not paid then his liability is revived in a greater degree than before. But the peculiar rigor of the law relating to its enforcement and the responsibility of its signatories could not be eliminated, for it was these very characteristics alone that had made the bill a suitable instrument for the cession, in place of money payment, of unmatured claims for which the common-law provisions regarding indebtedness are little suited. To whatever extent the custom of issuing or endorsing bills in place of payment in money may have established itself, every single payment that was made in this way nevertheless retained the character of a credit transaction. It was necessary in each individual case for the parties to the transaction to begin by coming to a special agreement as to the present price to be paid for the claim that would not fall due until some future time; if the amount of bills in circulation increased greatly, or if doubts happened to arise concerning the solidity of the position of any of the signatories, then it became more difficult to place the bill even on fairly tolerable terms. Issuer and acceptor had then in addition to make arrangements for covering the bill before it fell due, even if only by negotiating a prolongation bill. There is none of this in the case of fiduciary media, which pass like money from hand to hand without any sort of friction.

The modern organization of the payment system makes use of institutions for systematically arranging the settlement of claims by offsetting processes. There were beginnings of this as early as the Middle Ages, but the enormous development of the clearinghouse belongs to the last century. In the clearinghouse, the claims continuously arising between members are subtracted from one another and only the balances remain for settlement by the transfer of money or fiduciary media. The clearing system is the most important institution for diminishing the demand for money in the broader sense.

In the literature of the banking system it is not as a rule customary

to draw a sufficient distinction between the diminution of the demand for money in the broader sense which is due to the operations
of the clearinghouses and the diminution of the demand for money
in the narrower sense which is due to the extension of the use of
fiduciary media. This is the cause of much obscurity.

3

Fiduciary Media in Domestic Trade

In the domestic trade of most civilized countries, the actual *use*
of money for transacting exchanges made with the *help* of money
has been very largely superseded by the use of money substitutes.
And among the money substitutes, fiduciary media play a constantly increasing part. At the same time, the number of exchanges
made with the help of money which are settled by the offsetting of
counterclaims is growing also. There are countries in which nearly
all the internal payments that are not settled by the clearing process
are made without the use of money merely with the aid of banknotes
and deposits that are not covered by money, of token coins in the
proper sense of the word, and of other coins convertible on demand
into money. In other countries, again, the fiduciary medium has not
yet been developed to a like extent; but if we disregard those countries in which the insecurity of the law hinders the birth of that
confidence in the soundness of the issuer which is the *sine qua non*
for the circulation of money substitutes, then we shall find no part
of the world in which a large proportion of the internal payments
are not made by means of the use of fiduciary media alone, without
the actual transference of money. It is only in medium-sized transactions that there is still room for the transference of actual money.
In Germany and England before the war it was usual to make payments of twenty to one hundred marks and £1 and £5 by the transference of gold coins. Smaller and larger payments were made
almost exclusively by the cession of token coins or notes or deposits
which were only partly covered by money. It was the same in other
countries.

The fact that money continued to be in actual circulation at all in
a series of states, like Germany and England, and was not entirely

superseded by fiduciary media and money certificates, was due solely to legislative intervention. For reasons which were connected with certain views on the nature of notes, it was thought that the circulation of notes of small denominations ought to be opposed.[7] The battle against the one-pound note in England ended with the complete victory of the sovereign, and this victory had a significance outside England, too, for the disfavor in which small banknotes were held for decades on the continent of Europe was based upon English opinion. It is certain that in those states which have a sound administration of justice and a developed banking system, the employment of actual money in commerce could be replaced without difficulty by the issue of a corresponding quantity of small notes.

In some countries in which the actual transfer of money has been completely superseded by fiduciary media and money certificates, this end has been systematically sought and attained in a peculiar fashion and under very peculiar conditions. The silver-standard countries—India, primarily, but the situation was similar in other Asiatic states—after the great controversy about the standards had been decided in favor of monometallism, were forced to accept the world gold standard. But there were extraordinary difficulties in the way of the transition to a monetary system in imitation of English or German institutions. To introduce gold money in the circulation of these countries would have necessitated the conveyance of enormous quantities of gold to them, which would not have been practicable without serious convulsion of the European money market and would have meant great sacrifice. The governments of these countries, however, had to endeavor at all costs on the one hand not to raise the value of gold (so as not to disturb the European markets), and on the other hand not to reduce the value of silver any more than was necessary. The English government in India did not dare to undertake anything which might have had an unfavorable influence on the London money market; but, having regard to India's Asiatic competitors, which presumably would remain on the

---

[7] See Baird, *The One Pound Note, Its History, Place and Power in Scotland, and Its Adaptability for England*, 2d ed. (Edinburgh, 1901), pp. 9 ff.; Graham, *The One Pound Note in the History of Banking in Great Britain*, 2d ed. (Edinburgh, 1911), pp. 195 ff.; Nicholson, *A Treatise on Money and Essays on Present Monetary Problems* (Edinburgh, 1888), pp. 177 ff.; Jevons, *Investigations in Currency and Finance* (London, 1909), pp. 275 ff.

silver standard, neither did it dare to take any steps which would expedite the fall in the price of silver and consequently weaken for a time, even if only in appearance, the ability of India to compete with China, Japan, the Straits Settlements, and the other silver countries. It therefore had the task of conducting India's transition to the gold standard without buying gold in considerable quantities or selling silver.

The problem was not insoluble. Within limits, the circumstances were similar to those of the bimetallic countries which had discontinued the free coinage of silver at the end of the seventies. And besides, careful scientific consideration of the problem showed that it was possible to create a gold standard without a gold currency; that it was enough to discontinue the free coinage of silver and to announce its convertibility into gold at a specific rate, making this effective by establishing a suitable conversion fund, in order to give the country a gold standard which would differ from that of England only in the lower level of the stock of gold. It was only necessary to go back to the writings of Ricardo in order to find the plan for such a currency system already worked out in detail. Lindsay[8] and Probyn[9] followed this path and, building upon Ricardo, worked out plans for this kind of currency regulation. Both wanted to close the mints to silver and to make the rupee convertible into gold at a fixed ratio. For the future, only the rupee was to be legal tender. The two proposals differed on some minor points, of which the most important was that while Probyn held it necessary that the rupee should be convertible into gold in India itself, Lindsay was of the opinion that it would suffice if the conversion were to be in London from a gold reserve to be established there. Both proposals were rejected, by the Indian government and by the commissions appointed to inquire into the Indian monetary system. The opinion was expressed that a normal gold standard necessitates an actual

---

[8] See Lindsay, *A Gold Standard Without a Gold Coinage in England and India* (Edinburgh, 1879), pp. 12 ff. I have not been able to obtain access to a second pamphlet by the same author which appeared anonymously in 1892 under the title *Ricardo's Exchange Remedy*.

[9] See Probyn, *Indian Coinage and Currency* (London, 1897), pp. 1 ff.

gold currency, and that the lack of such a currency would awaken mistrust.[10]

The report of the commission of 1898 was signed by the most eminent experts of the day; its comments on the recommendations of Probyn and Lindsay were supported on the decisive point by the expert opinions of the biggest bankers in the British Empire. The course of events vindicated the theorists, however, not the statesmen and great financiers who had regarded them with amused commiseration. What was ultimately done in India corresponded roughly and on the whole to the recommendations of Probyn and Lindsay, even if there were variations in detail. And the monetary systems of other countries that had previously been on a silver standard were organized in a precisely similar manner. The present currency system of India, of the Straits Settlements, of the Philippines, and of the other Asiatic countries which have followed their example, is superficially characterized by the fact that in domestic trade, payments in money, that is, in gold, do not occur at all or at least are far rarer than in the gold-standard countries of Europe and America, and even in these the actual circulation of gold is only quite small in proportion to the total of all the payments made with the help of money. Under the system in India, payments are made, along with notes, checks, and giro transfers, chiefly in silver coins, which are partly relics of the time of the silver standard, and partly minted by the government for the account of the state and to the benefit of the Treasury, which receives the considerable profits of the coinage. A conversion fund, which is set up and administered by the government, exchanges these silver coins at a fixed ratio for gold, gold securities, or other claims to money, payable on demand, while, on the other hand, it issues such silver coins in exchange for gold in unlimited quantities at the same rate, allowance being made for the expenses of storage, transportation, etc. The minor details of this arrangement differ in different countries; but the differences

---

[10] See *Report of the Indian Currency Committee 1898* (in *Stability of International Exchange, Report on the Introduction of the Gold-Exchange Standard into China and Other Silver-using Countries* submitted to the Secretary of State, October 1, 1903, by the Commission on International Exchange [Washington, D.C., 1903], Appendix G), pp. 315 ff.; Heyn, *Die indische Währungsreform*, (Berlin, 1903), pp. 54 ff.; Bothe, *Die indische Währungsreform seit 1893* (Stuttgart, 1906), pp. 199 ff.

in its legal or banking technique are insignificant as far as its nature is concerned. It is, for example, of no further significance, whether or not the silver coins are converted on the basis of a legal obligation. All that matters is whether the conversion actually does take place on demand.[11]

There exists no fundamental difference at all between the currency system of these Asiatic and American countries and that that the European gold-standard countries once had. Under both systems, payments are made without the actual transference of money by the aid of the surrender of fiduciary media. The fact that in England and Germany the actual transference of money also played a certain part for medium-sized payments, whereas in India and in the Philippines the number of actual transfers of money is scarcely worth mentioning, or that in the former countries the proportion of the circulation that was not covered by money was smaller than in the latter, is quite inessential; it is a difference that is merely quantitative, not qualitative. Of no great relevance is the circumstance that the fiduciary media were in the one case predominantly banknotes and checks and are in the other case predominantly silver coins. The silver rupee is in truth nothing but a metallic note, for the conversion of which its issuer, the state, is responsible.[12]

Following up a train of thought of Ricardo's, who was the first to develop the plan of this monetary system more than a hundred years ago,[13] it is customary to speak of it as the gold-exchange standard. The aptness of this designation can only be conceded if it is intended to stress the peculiarities in banking and currency technique that characterize the system. But it is a name that must be rejected if it is intended to indicate the existence of a fundamental difference from what used to be the English and German type of gold standard. It is not correct to assert that in these countries gold functions merely as a measure of prices while the silver coins are

[11] On the fate of the Indian currency in the period of inflation during the Great War, see Spalding, *Eastern Exchange, Currency and Finance*, 3d ed. (London, 1920), pp. 31 ff.

[12] See Conant, "The Gold Exchange Standard in the Light of Experience," *The Economic Journal* 19 (1909): 200.

[13] In the pamphlet published in 1816, "Proposals for an Economical and Secure Currency with Observations on the Profits of the Bank of England," in *Works*, ed. McCulloch, 2d ed. (London, 1852), pp. 404 ff.

used as a common medium of exchange. We know what little justification there is for speaking of a price-measuring function of
money. In Ricardo's sense, it was possible to speak of measurement
and measures of value; from the point of view of the subjective
theory of value these and similar concepts are untenable. In India
and Austria-Hungary and in all other countries with similar currency and banking systems, gold is or was just as much a common
medium of exchange as in prewar England or Germany; the difference between the two systems is only one of degree, not one of
kind.

4

Fiduciary Media in International Trade

The practice of making payments by the writing off or reciprocal
balancing of claims is not restricted by the boundaries of states or
countries. It was in fact in trade between different areas that the
need for it was earliest and most strongly felt. The transportation
of money always involves not inconsiderable cost, loss of interest,
and risk. If the claims arising out of various transactions are liquidated not by the actual transference of money, but by balancing or
offsetting, then all these expenses and dangers can be avoided. This
provided an extraordinarily effective motive for developing those
methods of making payments over long distances which saved the
transference of sums of money. Quite early we find the use of bills
established for interlocal payments; then in addition we later find
checks, and ordinary and cable transfers, all forming the basis of an
interlocal clearing system which worked through the ordinary free
play of the market without the help of a special clearinghouse.
When making payments *within* a given locality the advantages for
the individual of the method of settling transactions by the clearing
process and therefore without the use of cash are smaller than those
when making payments *between* localities, and therefore it was a
longer time before the system of reciprocal cancellation came into
full operation with the establishment of clearinghouses.

If the clearing system has without difficulty transcursed political boundaries and created for itself a world-embracing organization in the international bill and check system, the validity of the fiduciary media, like that of all money substitutes, is nationally limited. There are no money substitutes, and so no fiduciary media, that are recognized internationally and consequently able to take the place of money in international trade for settling the balances that remain over after the clearing process. That is often overlooked in discussions of the present position of the international system of payments and the possibilities of its future development. Here again, in fact, the confusion creeps in, that has already been criticized adversely, between the system of reciprocal cancellation and the circulation of fiduciary media. This is most clear in the usual arguments about international giro transactions. In domestic giro transactions, payments are effected by the transfer of money substitutes, which are often fiduciary media, namely, the balances of the members at the giro bank. In international transactions, the money substitute is lacking, and even the international clearing system that is recommended in various quarters is not intended to introduce one. Rather it should be pointed out that this so-called international giro system—which incidentally was done away with again by the inflation during the war—while it may have changed the external form of the traditional manner of settling international monetary claims, has not changed in nature. When banks of various countries agree to give their clients the right to undertake direct transference from their balances to the balances of the clients of foreign banks, this may quite well constitute a new and additional method of international settlement of accounts. A Viennese desirous of paying a sum of money to somebody in Berlin was previously able either to use an international money order or to go to the exchange and buy a bill on Berlin and send it to his creditor. As a rule he would have made use of the intermediate services of a bank, which for its part would perform the transaction through the purchase of a foreign bill or a check. Later, if he was a member of the check system of the Austrian Post Office Savings Bank and his creditor belonged to that of the German post office, he would have been able to make the transfer more simply by sending the appropriate order on the Vienna office of the Post Office Savings Bank. This might well be more convenient and better suited to the demands of business than the only method that was once usual; but, however excellent a method, it was not a new method of international monetary intercourse. For the balances of this international giro system, if they could not be paid by bills, had to be paid by the actual transference of money. It is not true that the international giro system has decreased the international transportation of money. Even before its introduction, the Viennese who wanted to pay money to somebody in Berlin did not buy twenty-mark pieces and send them to Berlin in a parcel.

The only thing calculated to create international money substitutes and subsequently international fiduciary media would be the establishment of an international giro bank or bank-of-issue. When it became possible to use the notes issued by the world bank and the accounts opened by it for the settlement of money claims of all kinds, there would no longer be any need to settle the national balances of payments by transportation of money. The actual transference of money could be superseded by the transference of the notes issued by the world bank or of checks giving disposal over the issuer's account with the world bank, or even by simple entries in the books of the world bank. The balances of the international "clearinghouse," which already exists today although it is not concentrated in any one locality and has not the rigid organization of the national clearinghouses, would then be paid off in the same way as those of the national clearinghouses are at present.

Proposals have been made again and again for the creation of international fiduciary media through the establishment of an interstate bank. It is true that this must not be taken to include every project for extending the international giro system in the sense in which this word is commonly used. Nevertheless, in certain writings which demand the foundation of a world bank, or at least of an interstate banking organization, there gleams the idea of an international fiduciary medium.[14] The problems of organization raised by the establishment of such an international institution could be solved in various ways. The establishment of the world bank as a special form of organization and as an independent legal

---

[14] See Patterson, *Der Krieg der Banken*, trans. from the English by Holtzendorff (Berlin, 1867), pp. 17 ff.; Wolf, *Verstaatlichung der Silberproduktion und andere Vorschläge zur Währungsfrage* (Zurich, 1892), pp. 54 ff.; Wolf, "Eine international Banknote," in *Zietschrift für Sozialwissenschaft* (1908), vol 11, pp. 44 ff.

body would probably be the simplest form for the new creation. It would, however, also be possible, apart from this, to establish a special central authority for administering and investing the sums of money paid in to open the accounts, and for issuing the money substitutes. An attempt could be made to avoid the obstructions which the susceptibilities of national vanity would probably oppose to the local concentration of the business of the bank by leaving the reserves of the world giro authority and the world issuing authority in the keeping of the separate national banks. In the reserves of every central bank a distinction would then have to be made between two sums: one, which would have to serve as a basis for the world organization of the system of payments, and over which only the authorities of the latter would have power of disposal; and a second, which would continue to be at the service of the national monetary system. It would even be possible to go still further and leave the issue of international notes and other money substitutes to the individual banks, which would only be required in doing this to follow the instructions given by the authorities of the world organization. It is not our task to investigate which of the various possibilities is the most practical; it is its nature alone that interests us, not the actual form it might take.

Special reference must nevertheless be made to one point. If the balances in the books of the world bank are to be acquired only by cash payment of the full sum in money, or by transfer from some other account that has been acquired by cash payment of the full sum in money, and if the world bank is to issue notes only in exchange for money, then its establishment may certainly render unnecessary the transportation of quantities of money (which still plays a large part nowadays in the international payments system), but it would not have the effect of economizing money payments. It is true that it would be able to reduce the demand for money, because transferences would perhaps be completed more quickly and with less friction. But, as before, the payments that were made through the bank would involve the actual use of money. Of course, the money would remain in the vaults of the world bank and only the right to demand its surrender would be transferred. But the amount of the payments would be arithmetically limited by the amount of the money deposits in the bank. The possibility of transferring sums of money would be bound up with the existence of these sums of money in actual monetary shape. In order to free the international monetary system from these fetters the world bank would have to be granted the right of issuing notes as loans also and of opening accounts on credit; that is to say, the right of partly lending out its reserves of money. Then, and not until then, would the interstate system of payments be given a fiduciary medium such as is already possessed by the domestic system; it would become independent of the quantity of money in existence.

The realization of a world-bank project developed in this way is opposed by tremendous obstacles which it would hardly be possible to surmount in the near future. The least of these obstacles is constituted by the variety of the kinds of money that are in use in the individual states. Nevertheless, in spite of the inflation that was created by the world war and its consequences, we are every day approaching nearer and nearer to the situation of having a world monetary unit based on the metallic money gold. More important are the difficulties due to political considerations. The establishment of a world bank might come to grief owing to the uncertainty of its position in international law. No state would wish to incur the danger of the accounts of its citizens being impounded by the world bank in case of war. This involves questions of primary importance and therefore no provisions of international law, however surrounded with precautions they might be, could satisfy the individual states so far as to overcome their opposition to membership in such an organization.[15]

Nevertheless, the biggest difficulty in the way of issuing international credit instruments lies in the circumstance that it would scarcely be possible for the states that had joined the world-banking system to come to an agreement concerning the policy to be followed by the bank in issuing the credit instruments. Even the question of determining the quantity of them to be issued would disclose irreconcilable antagonisms. Under present conditions, therefore, proposals for the establishment of a world bank with power of issuing fiduciary media attract hardly any notice.[16]

---

[15] These words, written in 1911, need no addition today.
[16] See De Greef, "La monnaie, le crédit et le change dans le commerce international," *Revue economique internationale* 4 (1911): 58 ff.

CHAPTER 17

Fiduciary Media and the Demand for Money

1

The Influence of Fiduciary Media on the Demand for Money in the Narrower Sense

The development of the clearing system, especially the extension of the clearinghouse proper, reduces the demand for money in the broader sense: part of the exchanges made with the help of money can be carried through without the actual physical circulation of money or money substitutes. Thus a tendency has arisen toward the reduction of the objective exchange value of money, which has counteracted the tendency for it to rise which was bound to result from the enormous increase in the demand for money in consequence of the progressive extension of the exchange economy. The development of fiduciary media has the same sort of effect; fiduciary media, which can, as money substitutes, take the place of money in commerce, reduce the demand for money in the narrower sense. This constitutes the great significance of fiduciary media, in this their effect on the exchange ratio between money and other economic goods is to be sought.

The development of fiduciary media, the most important institution for reducing the need for money in the narrower sense, equally with the establishment and development of clearinghouses, the most important institution for reducing the need for money in the broader sense, has not been merely left to the free play of economic forces. The demand for credit on the part of merchants and manufacturers and princes and states, and the endeavor to make a profit on the part of the bankers, were not the sole forces affecting its development. Intervention took place with the object of furthering and expediting the process. As the naive Midas-like trust in the usefulness of a large stock of precious metals disappeared and was replaced by sober consideration of the monetary problem, so the opinion gained strength that a reduction of the national demand for money in the narrower sense constituted an outstanding economic interest. Adam Smith suggested that the expulsion of gold and silver by paper, that is to say notes, would substitute for an expensive means of exchange a less expensive, which, however, would perform the same service. He compares gold and silver which is circulating in a country with a road over which all the corn has to be brought to market but on which nevertheless nothing grows. The issue of notes, he says, creates, as it were, a path through the air and makes it possible to turn a large part of the roads into fields and meadows and in this way considerably to increase the annual yield of land and labor.[1] Similar views are entertained by Ricardo. He also sees the most fundamental advantage of the use of notes in the diminution of the cost to the community of the apparatus of circulation. His ideal monetary system is one which would ensure to the community with the minimum cost the use of a money of invariable value. Starting from this point of view, he formulates his recommendations, which aim at expelling money composed of the precious metal from actual domestic circulation.[2]

The views on the nature of methods of payment which diminish the demand for money, which were developed by the Classical economists, were already known in the eighteenth century. Their acceptance in the writings of the Classical economists and the brilliant way in which they were expounded, ensured general recognition for them in the nineteenth and twentieth centuries also. The opposition which they occasionally called forth, has now sunk into silence. In

[1] See Smith, *The Wealth of Nations,* Cannan's ed. (London, 1930), vol. 2, pp. 28, 78.
[2] See Ricardo, "The High Price of Bullion a Proof of the Depreciation of Bank Notes," in *Works,* ed. McCulloch, 2d ed. (London, 1852), pp. 263 ff.; "Proposals for an Economical and Secure Currency," in *ibid.*, pp. 397 ff.; see pp. 324–25 above and 467–68 below.

all countries the aim of banking policy is to secure the greatest possible extension of money-economizing means of payment.

If metallic money is employed, then the advantages of a diminution of the demand for money due to the extension of such other means of payment are obvious. In fact, the development of the clearing system and of fiduciary media has at least kept pace with the potential increase of the demand for money brought about by the extension of the money economy, so that the tremendous increase in the exchange value of money, which otherwise would have occurred as a consequence of the extension of the use of money, has been completely avoided, together with its undesirable consequences. If it had not been for this the increase in the exchange value of money, and so also of the monetary metal, would have given an increased impetus to the production of the metal. Capital and labor would have been diverted from other branches of production to the production of the monetary metal. This would undoubtedly have meant increased returns to certain individual undertakings; but the welfare of the community would have suffered. The increase in the stock of precious metals which serve monetary purposes would not have improved the position of the individual members of the community, would not have increased the satisfaction of their wants; for the monetary function could also have been fulfilled by a smaller stock. And, on the other hand, a smaller quantity of economic goods would have been available for the direct satisfaction of human wants if a part of the capital and labor power that otherwise would have been used for their production had been diverted to mining precious metals. Even apart from the diversion of production, a decrease of prosperity would result from the fact that as a consequence of the rise in value of the precious metals caused by the use for monetary purposes the stock available for industrial employment would decrease, since certain quantities would be transferred from the latter employment to the former. This all becomes particularly clear if we think of an economic community which does not itself produce the precious metals, but imports them. Here the amount of their cost is expressed by the quantity of commodities that must be surrendered to foreign countries in order to obtain the supplementary quantity of monetary metal in exchange. In a country that itself produces the precious metals, the matter is the same in principle; all that is different is the way of reckoning the loss of welfare through the sacrifice of the other branches of production and the preference for mining the precious metals; it is perhaps less perceptible, but it is just as comprehensible in theory. The measure of the additional harm done by the diversion of metal to monetary uses is always given by the quantity of metal that is withdrawn from other uses in favor of the monetary use.

Where fiat or credit money is employed, these reasons in favor of the extension of clearing methods of payment and of the use of fiduciary media do not arise. The only thing in their favor is that they would avoid an increase in the value of money; although this consideration is decisive. Where they are employed, the principle of establishing the national monetary apparatus and maintaining it in working order with the minimum cost must be attained in another way. It must be an object of policy, for example, to manufacture the paper notes with the minimum cost of production. It is immediately obvious that nothing like the same quantitative significance can be attributed to this problem as to that of decreasing the monetary demand for precious metals. However great the care taken in producing the notes, their cost of production could never be anything near so great as that of the precious metals. If we take into further consideration the fact that the artistic production of the notes also constitutes a precautionary measure against counterfeiting, so that merely on this ground, economizing in this sphere is not worth considering, it follows that the problem of diminishing the cost of the circulatory apparatus when fiat or credit money is employed must be of an entirely different nature from what it is when commodity money is employed.

2

The Fluctuations in the Demand for Money

In order to be able to make an accurate estimate of the bearing of clearing methods of payment and of fiduciary media on the development of the demand for money, it is necessary to be clear about the nature of variations in the demand for money.

Fluctuations in the demand for money, insofar as the objective conditions of its development are concerned, are governed in all communities by the same law. An extension of the procedure of exchange mediated by money increases the demand for money; a decrease of indirect exchange, a return to exchange *in natura*, decreases it. But even apart from variations in the extent of indirect exchange which are insignificant nowadays, large variations in the demand for money occur which are determined by factors of general economic development. Increase of population, and progress in division of labor, together with the extension of exchange which goes hand in hand with it, increase the demand for money of individuals, and also therefore the demand for money of the community, which consists merely in the sum of the demands for money of individuals. Decrease of population and retrogression of the exchange economy, bring about a contraction in it. These are the determinants of the big changes in the demand for money. Within these large variations, it is possible to observe smaller periodical movements. Such are in the first place brought about by commercial and industrial fluctuations, by the alternation of boom and depression peculiar to modern economic life, by good and bad business.[3] The crest and the trough of the wave always cover a period of several years. But also within single years, quarters, months, and weeks, even within single days, there are considerable fluctuations in the level of the demand for money. The transactions involving the use of money are concentrated together at particular points of time; and even where this is not the case, the demand for money is differentiated by the practice on the part of buyers of settling their share of transactions on particular dates. On the daily markets it may perhaps seldom happen that the demand for money during the hours of the market is greater than before or after. The periodical rise and fall of the demand for money can be seen much more clearly where transactions are concentrated in weekly, monthly and annual markets. A similar effect results from the custom of not paying wages and salaries daily, but weekly, monthly, or quarterly. Rents, interest, and repayment installments, are as a rule paid on particular days. The accounts of the tailor, the shoemaker, the butcher, the baker, the bookseller, the doctor, and so forth, are often settled not daily but periodically. The tendency in all these arrangements is

---

[3] On the question of the dependence of economic fluctuations on credit policy, see pp. 445 f. below.

enormously strengthened by the mercantile practice of establishing certain days as days of settlement, or paydays. The middle and last days of the month have gained a special significance in this connection, and among the last days of the month, particularly the last day of the quarters. But, above all, the payments that have to be made in a community during the year are concentrated in the autumn, the decisive circumstance being that agriculture, for natural reasons, has its chief business period in the autumn. All of these facts have been repeatedly and exhaustively illustrated by statistics; nowadays they are the common property of all discussions on the nature of banks and money.[4]

3

The Elasticity of the System of Reciprocal Cancellation

It is usual to ascribe to the payment system elasticity that is said to be attained by means of the credit system and the continual improvements in banking organization and technique, the capacity of adjusting the available stock of money to the level of the demand for money at any time without exerting any influence on the exchange ratio between money and other economic goods. Between the volume of fiduciary media and the bank transactions or private arrangements that can take the place of a transfer of money, on the one hand, and the quantity of money, on the other hand, there is said to be no fixed relationship which could make the former rigidly dependent upon the latter. Instead of there being a fixed quantitative relationship between money and its substitutes, that is to say, between the stock of money and the various exchange and payment transactions, it is said that the organization of banking institutions and the credit system has made commerce in the highest degree independent of the quantity of money available. The present-day organization of the money, clearing, and credit system is said to have the tendency to balance out variations in the quantity of money and render them ineffective, and so to make prices as far as possible

---

[4] See Jevons, *Investigations in Currency and Finance*, pp. 8, 151 ff.; Palgrave, *Bank Rate and the Money Market in England, France, Germany, Holland and Belgium 1844–1900* (London, 1903), pp. 106 ff.; 138; J. Laughlin, *The Principles of Money* (London, 1903), pp. 409 ff.

independent of the stock of money.[5] By others, this adjusting capacity is ascribed only to fiduciary media, uncovered banknotes,[6] or unbacked deposits.[7]

Before the soundness of these assertions can be tested, they must be brought out of the obscurity that is due to a confusion between the effects of the clearing system and those of the issue of fiduciary media. The two must be considered separately.

The reduction in the demand for money in the broader sense that results from the practice of settling counterclaims by balancing them against each other is limited in the first place by the number and amount of the claims and counterclaims falling due on the same date. No greater number or amount of claims can be reciprocally canceled between two parties than exist between them at the given moment. If, instead of payment in money, claims on third persons are transferred which are canceled by the transferee and the debtor by means of claims held by the latter against the former, the sphere of the offsetting process can be extended. The clearinghouses which nowadays exist in all important commercial centers are able to avoid the technical and legal difficulties in the way of such transfers, and have thus performed a quite extraordinary service in the extension of the system of reciprocal cancellation. Nevertheless, the clearing system is still capable of further improvement. Very many payments that could be settled by way of cancellation are still made by the actual transfer of money.

If we imagine the clearing system fully developed, so that all payments are first attempted to be settled by balancing, even those in everyday retail trade (which, for practical reasons, would not appear to be easy of accomplishment), then we are faced with a second limit to the extension of the clearing system, although this, unlike the first, is not surmountable. Even if the community were in a stable condition in which there were no variations in the relative incomes and wealth of individuals and in the sizes of their reserves, complete reciprocal cancellation of all the transfers of money that have to be made at a given moment would be possible, only if the

---

[5] See Spiethoff, "Die Quantitätstheorie insbesondere in ihrer Verwertbarkeit als Haussetheorie," *Festgaben für Adolf Wagner* (Leipzig, 1905), pp. 263 f.
[6] See Helfferich, *Studien über Geld- und Bankwesen* (Berlin, 1900), pp. 151 f.; Schumacher, *Weltwirtschaftliche Studien* (Leipzig, 1911), pp. 5 ff.
[7] See White, *An Elastic Currency* (New York, 1893), p. 4.

money received by individuals was spent again immediately and nobody wanted to hold a sum of money in reserve against unforeseen and indefinite expenditure. But since these assumptions do not hold good, and in fact never could hold good, so long as money is in demand at all as a common medium of exchange, it follows that there is a rigid maximum limit to the transactions that can be settled through the clearing system. A community's demand for money in the broader sense, even with the fullest possible development of the system of reciprocal cancellation, cannot be forced below a minimum which will be determined according to circumstances.

Now the degree in which a clearing system is actually developed within the limits which the circumstances of the time allow for it, is in no way dependent upon the ratio between the demand for money and the stock of money. A relative decline in the one or the other can of itself exercise neither a direct nor an indirect influence on the development of the clearing system. Such development is invariably due to special causes. It is no more justifiable to assume that progressive extension of settlement on the clearing principle reduces the demand for money precisely in the degree in which the increasing development of commerce augments it, than to suppose that the growth of the clearing system can never outstrip the increase in the demand for money. The truth is rather that the two lines of development are completely independent of one another. There is a connection between them only insofar as deliberate attempts to counteract an increase in the exchange value of money by reducing the demand of money through a better development of the clearing system may be made with greater vigor during a period of rising prices; assuming, of course, that the aim of currency policy is to prevent an increase in the purchasing power of money. But this is no longer a case of an automatic adjustment of the forces acting upon the objective exchange value of money, but one of political experiments in influencing it, and the extent to which these measures are accompanied by success remains a matter of doubt.

Thus it is easy to see what little justification there is for ascribing to the clearing system the property, without affecting the objective exchange value of money, of correcting the disparities that may arise between the stock of money and the demand for it, and which could otherwise be eliminated only by suitable automatic variations in the exchange ratio between money and other economic goods. The development of the clearing system is independent of the other factors that determine the ratio between the supply of money and the demand for it. The effect on the demand for money of an expansion or contraction of the system of reciprocal cancellation thus constitutes an independent phenomenon which is just as likely to strengthen as to weaken the tendencies which for other reasons have an influence in the market on the exchange ratio between money and commodities. It seems self-evident that an increase in the number and size of payments cannot be the sole determinant of the demand for money. Part of the new payments will be settled by the clearing system; for this, too, *ceteris paribus*, will be extended in such a way as thenceforward to be responsible for the settlement of the same proportion of all payments as before. The rest of the payments could only be settled by clearing processes if there was an extension of the clearing system beyond the customary degree; but such an extension can never be called forth automatically by an increase in the demand for money.

4

The Elasticity of a Credit Circulation Based on Bills, Especially on Commodity Bills

The doctrine of the elasticity of fiduciary media, or more correctly expressed, of their automatic adjustment at any given time to the demand for money in the broader sense, stands in the very center of modern discussions of banking theory. We have to show that this doctrine does not correspond to the facts, or at least not in the form in which it is generally expounded and understood; and the proof of this will at the same time refute one of the most important arguments of the opponents of the quantity theory.[8]

Tooke, Fullarton, Wilson, and their earlier English and German disciples, teach that it does not lie in the power of the banks-of-issue to increase or diminish their note circulation. They say that the quantity of notes in circulation is settled by the demand within

---

[8] See pp. 173 ff. above.

the community for media of payment. If the number and amount of the payments are increasing, then, they say, the media of payment must also increase in number and amount; if the number and amount of the payments are diminishing, then, they say, the number and amount of the media of payment must also diminish. Expansion and contraction of the quantity of notes in circulation are said to be never the cause, always only the effect, of fluctuations in business life. It therefore follows that the behavior of the banks is merely passive; they do not influence the circumstances which determine the amount of the total circulation, but are influenced by them. Every attempt to extend the issue of notes beyond the limits set by the general conditions of production and prices is immediately frustrated by the reflux of the surplus notes, because they are not needed for making payments. Conversely, it is said, the only result of any attempt at an arbitrary reduction of the note circulation of a bank is the immediate filling of the gap by a competing bank; or, if this is not possible, as for instance because the issue of notes is legally restricted, then commerce will create for itself other media or circulation, such as bills, which will take the place of the notes.[9]

It is in harmony with the views expounded by the Banking theorists on the essential similarity of deposits and notes to apply what they say on this point about notes to deposits also. It is in this sense that the doctrine of the elasticity of fiduciary media is generally understood today;[10] it is in this sense alone that it is possible to defend it even with only an appearance of justification. We may further suppose, as being generally admitted, that it is not because of lack of public confidence in the issuing bank that the fiduciary media are returned to it, whether in the form of notes presented for conversion into cash or as demands for the withdrawal of deposits. This assumption also agrees with the teachings of Tooke and his followers.

The fundamental error of the Banking School lies in its failure to

---

[9] See Tooke, *An Inquiry into the Currency Principle* (London, 1844), pp. 60 ff.; 122 f.; Fullarton, *On the Regulation of Currencies*, 2d ed. (London, 1845), pp. 82 ff.; Wilson, *Capital, Currency and Banking* (London, 1847), pp. 67 ff.; Mill, *Principles of Political Economy* (London, 1867), pp. 395 ff.; Wagner, *Geld- und Kredittheorie der Peelschen Bankakte* (Vienna, 1862), pp. 135 ff. On Mill's lack of consistency in this question, see Wicksell, *Geldzins und Güterpreise* (Jena, 1898), pp. 78 f.

[10] See Laughlin, *The Principles of Money* (London, 1903), p. 412.

understand the nature of the issue of fiduciary media. When the bank discounts a bill or grants a loan in some other way, it exchanges a present good for a future good. Since the issuer creates the present good that it surrenders in the exchange—the fiduciary media—practically out of nothing, it would only be possible to speak of a natural limitation of the quantity of fiduciary media if the quantity of future goods that are exchanged in the loan market against present goods was limited to a fixed amount. But this is by no means the case. The quantity of future goods is indeed limited by external circumstances, but not that of the future goods that are offered on the market in the form of money. The issuers of the fiduciary media are able to induce an extension of the demand for them by reducing the interest demanded to a rate below the natural rate of interest, that is below that rate of interest that would be established by supply and demand if the real capital were lent *in natura* without the mediation of money,[11] whereas on the other hand the demand for fiduciary media would be bound to cease entirely as soon as the rate asked by the bank was raised above the natural rate. The demand for money and money substitutes that is expressed on the loan market is in the last resort a demand for capital goods or, when consumption credit is involved, for consumption goods. He who tries to borrow "money" needs it solely for procuring other economic goods. Even if he only wishes to supplement his reserve, he has no other object in this than to secure the possibility of acquiring other goods in exchange at the given moment. The same is true if he needs the money for making payments that have fallen due; in this case it is the person receiving the payment who intends to purchase other economic goods with the money received.

That demand for money and money substitutes which determines the exchange ratio between money and other economic goods achieves expression only in the behavior of individuals when buying and selling other economic goods. Only when, say, money is being exchanged for bread is the position of the economic goods, money and commodity, in the value scales of the individual parties to the transaction worked out and used as a basis of action; and from this the precise arithmetical exchange ratio is determined. But when

[11] See Wicksell, *op. cit.,* p. v.

what is demanded is a money loan that is to be paid back in money again, then such considerations do not enter into the matter. Then only the difference in value between present goods and future goods is taken into account, and this alone has an influence on the determination of the exchange ratio, that is, on the determination of the level of the rate of interest.

For this reason the Banking principle is unable to prove that no more fiduciary media can be put into circulation than an amount determined by fixed circumstances not dependent on the will of the issuer. It has therefore directed its chief attention to the proof of the assertion that any superfluous quantity of fiduciary media will be driven out of circulation back to the issuing body. Unlike money, fiduciary media do not come on to the market as payments, but as loans, Fullarton teaches; they must therefore automatically flow back to the bank when the loan is repaid.[12] This is true. But Fullarton overlooks the possibility that the debtor may procure the necessary quantity of fiduciary media for the repayment by taking up a new loan.

Following up trains of thought that are already to be found in Fullarton and the other writers of his circle, and in support of certain institutions of the English and Continental banking system, which, it must be said, have quite a different significance in practice than that which is erroneously ascribed to them, the more recent literature of banking theory has laid stress upon the significance of the short-term commodity bill for the establishment of an elastic credit system. The system by which payments are made could, it is said, be made capable of the most perfect adjustment to the changing demands upon it, if it were brought into immediate causal connection with the demand for media of payment. According to Schumacher, that can only be done through banknotes, and has been done in Germany by basing the banknotes on the commodity bills, the quantity of which increases and decreases with the intensity of economic life. Through the channel of the discounting business, in place of interest-bearing commodity bills (which have only a limited capacity of circulation because their amounts are always different, their validity of restricted duration, and their soundness dependent

---

[12] See Fullarton, *op. cit.*, p. 64.

on the credit of numerous private persons), banknotes are issued (which are put into circulation in large quantities by a well-known semipublic institution and always refer to the same sums without limitation as to time, and therefore possess a much wider capacity of circulation, comparable to that of metallic money). Then on the redemption of the discounted bill an exchange in the contrary direction is said to take place: the banknotes, or instead of them metallic money, flow back to the bank, diminishing the quantity of media of payment in circulation. It is argued that if money is correctly defined as a draft on a consideration for services rendered, then a banknote based on an accepted commodity bill corresponds to this idea to the fullest extent, since it closely unites the service and the consideration for it and regularly disappears again out of circulation after it has negotiated the latter. It is claimed that through such an organic connection between the issue of banknotes and economic life, created by means of the commodity bill, the quantity of the means of payment in circulation is automatically adjusted to variations in the need for means for payment. And that the more completely this is attained, the more out of the question is it that the money itself will experience the variations in value affecting prices, and the more will the determination of prices be subject to the supply and demand on the commodity market.[13]

In the face of this, we must first of all ask how it is possible to justify the drawing of a fundamental distinction between banknotes and other money substitutes, between banknotes not covered by money and other fiduciary media. Deposits which can be drawn upon at any time by check, apart from certain minor technical and juristic details which make them unusable in retail trade and for certain other payments, are just as good a money substitute as the banknote. It is a matter of indifference from the economic point of view whether the bank discounts a bill by paying out currency in notes or by a credit on a giro account. From the point of view of banking technique there may be certain differences of importance to the bank official; but whether the bank issues credit in the business of discounting only or whether it also grants other short-term loans cannot be a very fundamental issue. A bill is only a form of

---

[13] See Schumacher, *op. cit.*, pp. 122 f.

promissory note with a special legal and commercial qualification. No economic difference can be found between a claim in the form of a bill and any other claim of equal goodness and identical time of maturity. And the commodity bill, again, differs only juristically from an open book debt that has come into being through a credit-purchase transaction. Thus it comes to the same thing in the end whether we talk of the elasticity of the note circulation based on commodity bills or of the elasticity of a circulation of fiduciary media resulting from the cession of short-term claims arising out of credit sales.

Now the number and extent of purchases and sales on credit are by no means independent of the credit policy followed by the banks, the issuers of fiduciary media. If the conditions under which credit is granted are made more difficult, their number must decrease; if the conditions are made easier, their number must increase. When there is a delay in the payment of the purchase price, only those can sell who do not need money immediately; but in this case bank credit would not be requisitioned at all. Those, however, who want money immediately can only make sales on credit if they have a prospect of immediately being able to turn into money the claims which the transaction yields them. Other granters of credit can only place just so many present goods at the disposal of the loan market as they possess; but it is otherwise with the banks, which are able to procure additional present goods by the issue of fiduciary media. They are in a position to satisfy all the requests for credit that are made to them. But the extent of these requests depends merely upon the price that they demand for granting the credit. If they demand less than the natural rate of interest—and they must do this if they wish to do any business at all with the new issue of fiduciary media; it must not be forgotten that they are offering an additional supply of credit to the market—then these requests will increase.

When the loans granted by the bank through the issue of fiduciary media fall due for repayment, then it is true that a corresponding sum of fiduciary media returns to the bank, and the quantity in circulation is diminished. But fresh loans are issued by the bank at the same time and new fiduciary media flow into circulation. Of course, those who hold the commodity-bill theory will object that a further issue of fiduciary media can take place only if new commodity bills come into existence and are presented for discounting. This is quite true. But whether new commodity bills come into existence depends upon the credit policy of the banks.

Let us just picture to ourselves the life history of a commodity bill, or, more correctly, of a chain of commodity bills. A cotton dealer has sold raw cotton to a spinner. He draws on the spinner and has the three-month bill discounted that the latter has accepted. After three months have passed, the bill will be presented by the bank to the spinner and redeemed by him. The spinner provides himself with the necessary sum of cash, having meanwhile spun the cotton and sold the yarn to a weaver, by negotiating a bill drawn on the weaver and accepted by him. Whether these two sale-and-purchase transactions come to pass depends now chiefly upon the level of the bank discount rate. The seller, in the one case the cotton dealer, in the second case the spinner, needs the money immediately; he can only make the sale with a delay in the payment of the purchase price if the sum due in three months *less discount* at least equals the sum under which he is not inclined to sell his commodity. It is unnecessary to give any further explanation of the significance attaching to the level of the bank discount rate in this calculation. Our example proves our point just as well even if we assume that the commodity that is sold reaches the consumers in the course of the three months during which the bill circulates and is paid for by them without direct requisitioning of credit. For the sums which the consumers use for this purpose have come to them as wages or profits out of transactions that were only made possible through the granting of credit on the part of the banks.

When we see that the quantity of the commodity bills presented for discount increases at certain times and decreases again at other times, we must not conclude that these fluctuations are to be explained by variations in the demands for money of individuals. The only admissible conclusion is that under the conditions made by the banks at the time there is no greater number of people seeking credit. If the banks-of-issue bring the rate of interest they charge in their creditor transactions near to the natural rate of interest, then the demands upon them decrease; if they reduce their rate of interest so that it falls lower than the natural rate of interest, then these demands increase. The cause of fluctuations in the demand for the credit of the banks-of-issue is to be sought nowhere else than in the credit policy they follow.

By virtue of the power at their disposal of granting bank credit through the issue of fiduciary media the banks are able to increase indefinitely the total quantity of money and money substitutes in circulation. By issuing fiduciary media, they can increase the stock of money in the broader sense in such a way that an increase in the demand for money which otherwise would lead to an increase in the objective value of money would have its effects on the determination of the value of money nullified. They can, by limiting the granting of loans, so reduce the quantity of money in the broader sense in circulation as to avoid a diminution of the objective exchange value of money which would otherwise occur for some reason or other. In certain circumstances, as has been said, this *may* occur. But in all the mechanism of the granting of bank credit and in the whole manner in which fiduciary media are created and return again to the place whence they were issued, there is nothing which must *necessarily* lead to such a result. It may quite as well happen, for instance, that the banks increase the issue of fiduciary media at the very moment when a reduction in the demand for money in the broader sense or an increase in the stock of money in the narrower sense is leading to a reduction of the objective exchange value of money; and their intervention will strengthen the existing tendency to a variation in the value of money. The circulation of fiduciary media is in fact not elastic in the sense that it automatically accommodates the demand for money to the stock of money without influencing the objective exchange value of money, as is erroneously asserted. It is only elastic in the sense that it allows of any sort of extension of the circulation, even completely unlimited extension, just as it allows of any sort of restriction. The quantity of fiduciary media in circulation has no natural limits. If for any reason it is desired that it should be limited, then it must be limited by some sort of deliberate human intervention—that is by banking policy.

Of course, all of this is true only under the assumption that all banks issue fiduciary media according to uniform principles, or that there is only one bank that issues fiduciary media. A single bank carrying on its business in competition with numerous others is not in a position to enter upon an independent discount policy. If regard to the behavior of its competitors prevents it from further reducing the rate of interest in bank-credit transactions, then—apart from an extension of its clientele—it will be able to circulate more fiduciary media only if there is a demand for them even when the rate of interest charged is not lower than that charged by the banks competing with it Thus the banks may be seen to pay a certain amount of regard to the periodical fluctuations in the demand for money. They increase and decrease their circulation *pari passu* with the variations in the demand for money, so far as the lack of a uniform procedure makes it impossible for them to follow an independent interest policy. But in doing so, they help to stabilize the objective exchange value of money. To this extent, therefore, the theory of the elasticity of the circulation of fiduciary media is correct; it has rightly apprehended one of the phenomena of the market, even if it has also completely misapprehended its cause. And just because it has employed a false principle for explaining the phenomenon that it has observed, it has also completely closed the way to understanding of a second tendency of the market, that emanates from the circulation of fiduciary media. It was possible for it to overlook the fact that so far as the banks proceed uniformly, there must be a continual augmentation of the circulation of fiduciary media, and consequently a fall of the objective exchange value of money.

5

The Significance of the Exclusive Employment of Bills as Cover for Fiduciary Media

The German Bank Act of March 14, 1875, required that the notes issued in excess of the gold cover should be covered by bills of exchange; but in practice this provision has been understood to refer only to commodity bills. The significance of this prescription differs from that popularly attributed to it. It does not make the note issue elastic; it does not even bring it, as is erroneously believed, into an organic connection with the conditions of demand for money; these are all illusions, which should long ago have been destroyed. Neither has it the significance for maintaining the possibility of conversion of the notes that is ascribed to it; this will have to be referred to in greater detail later.

The limitation of the note issue not covered by metal, that is of fiduciary media in the form of banknotes, is the fundamental principle of the German act, which is based upon Peel's Act. And among the numerous and multiform obstacles that have been set up with this aim, the strict provision concerning the investment of the assets backing the note issue takes a not altogether unimportant place. That these must consist not merely in claims, but in claims in the form of bills; that the bills must have at the most three months to run; that they should bear the names, preferably of three, but at least of two, parties known to be solvent—all these conditions limit the note issue. At the very beginning, a considerable part of the national credit is kept away from the banks. A similar effect results from the further limitation of the note cover merely to commodity bills, as was undoubtedly intended by the legislature even though express provision for it was omitted from the Bank Act, probably because of the impossibility of giving a legal definition of the concept of a commodity bill. That this limitation did in fact amount to a restriction of the issue of fiduciary media is best shown by the fact that when the Bank Act was passed the number of commodity bills was already limited, and that since then, in spite of a considerable increase in the demand for credit, their number has decreased to such an extent that the Reichsbank meets with difficulties when it attempts to select such bills only for purposes of investing without decreasing the amount of credit granted.[14]

6

The Periodical Rise and Fall in the Extent to Which Bank Credit Is Requisitioned

The requests made to the banks are requests, not for the transfer of money, but for the transfer of other economic goods. Would-be borrowers are in search of capital, not money. They are in search of capital *in the form of money*, because nothing other than power of

---

[14] See Prion, *Das deutsche Wechseldiskontgeschäft* (Leipzig, 1907), pp. 120 ff., 291 ff.

disposal over money can offer them the possibility of being able to acquire in the market the real capital which is what they really want. Now the peculiar thing, which has been the source of one of the most difficult puzzles in economics for more than a hundred years, is that the would-be borrower's demand for capital is satisfied by the banks through the issue of money substitutes. It is clear that this can only provide a provisional satisfaction of the demands for capital. The banks cannot evoke capital out of nothing. If the fiduciary media satisfy the desire for capital, that is if they really procure disposition over capital goods for the borrowers, then we must first seek the source from which this supply of capital comes. It will not be particularly difficult to discover it. If the fiduciary media are perfect substitutes for money and do all that money could do, if they add to the social stock of money in the broader sense, then their issue must be accompanied by appropriate effects on the exchange ratio between money and other economic goods. The cost of creating capital for borrowers of loans granted in fiduciary media is borne by those who are injured by the consequent variation in the objective exchange value of money; but the profit of the whole transaction goes not only to the borrowers, but also to those who issue the fiduciary media, although these admittedly have sometimes to share their gains with other economic agents, as when they hold interest-bearing deposits, or the state shares in their profits.

The entrepreneurs who approach banks for loans are suffering from shortage of capital; it is never shortage of money in the proper sense of the word that drives them to present their bills for discounting. In some circumstances this shortage of capital may be only temporary; in other circumstances it may be permanent. In the case of the many undertakings which constantly draw upon short-term bank credit, year in, year out, the shortage of capital is a permanent one.

For the problem with which we are concerned, the circumstances causing the shortage of capital on the part of entrepreneurs do not matter. We may even provisionally disregard, as of minor importance, the question whether the shortage is one of investment capital or working capital. Sometimes the view is propounded that it is unjustified to procure investment capital partly by way of bank credit although this is less undesirable as a way of procuring working capital. Such arguments as these have played an important part in recent discussions of banking policy. The banks have been adversely criticized on the ground of their having used a considerable part of the credit issued by them for granting loans to industrial enterprises in search not of fixed but of working capital and of having thus endangered their liquidity. Legislation has been demanded to limit to liquid investments only the assets backing the liabilities arising from the issue of fiduciary media. Provisions of this sort are designed to deal with fiduciary media in the form of deposits in the same way as the note issue has been dealt with under the influence of the doctrines of the Currency School. We have already commented on their significance and have shown, as further discussion will remind us, that the only practical value of these, as of all similar restrictions, lies in the obstacles they oppose to unlimited expansion of credit.

The cash reserve which is maintained by every business enterprise also is a part of its working capital. If an enterprise feels for any reason obliged to increase its reserve this must be regarded as an increase of its capital. If it requisitions credit for this purpose, its action cannot be regarded as any different from a demand for credit that arises from any other cause—say, on account of an extension of plant or the like.

But attention must now be drawn to a phenomenon which, even if it adds nothing new to what has been said already, may serve to set some important processes of the money-and-capital market in a clearer light. It has been repeatedly mentioned already that commercial practice concentrates all kinds of settlements on particular days of the year so that there is bound to be a bigger demand for money on these days than on others. The concentration of days of settlement at the end of the week, the fortnight, the month, and the quarter, is a factor which considerably increases the demand for money, and so of course the demand for capital, on the part of undertakings. Even though an entrepreneur could reckon safely on sufficient receipts on a given day to meet the obligations falling due on that or the following day, still it would only be in the rarest cases that he could use the former directly for paying the latter. The technique of payment is not so far developed that it would always be possible to fulfill obligations punctually without having secured some days beforehand free disposal over the necessary means. A person who has to redeem a bill that falls due at his bank on September 30 will usually have to take steps, before that date, for covering it; sums which do not reach him until the very day of maturity of the bill will mostly prove useless for this purpose. In any case it is completely impracticable to use the receipts on any given day for making payments that fall due on the same day at distant places. On the days of settlement there must therefore necessarily be an increased demand for money on the part of the individual undertaking, and this will disappear again just as quickly as it arose. Of course, this demand for money too is a demand for capital. Hypercritical theorists, following Mercantile usage, are accustomed to draw a subtle distinction between the demand for money and the demand for capital; they contrast the demand for short-term credit, as a demand for money, with the demand for long-term credit, as a demand for capital. There is little reason for retaining this terminology, which has been responsible for much confusion. What is here called the demand for money is nothing but a real demand for capital; this must never be forgotten. If the undertaking takes up a short-term loan to supplement its cash reserve, then the case is one of a genuine credit transaction, of an exchange of future goods for present goods.

The increased demand of the entrepreneur for money and consequently for capital which occurs on these days of settlement, expresses itself in an increase of the requests for loans that are made to credit-issuing banks. In those countries where notes and not deposits are the chief kind of fiduciary media, this is perceptible in an increase in the quantity of bills handed in at the banks-of-issue for discounting and, if these bills are actually discounted, in the quantity of notes in circulation.[15] Now this regular rise and fall of the level of the note circulation round about the days of settlement can in no way be explained by an increase in the total quantity of bills in existence in the community. No new bills, particularly no new short-term bills, are drawn and handed in to the banks to be discounted. It is bills that have the normal period to run, that are negotiated shortly before maturity. Until then they are retained in

---

[15] Part of the rediscounting done at the Reichsbank by the private banks shortly before the critical days of settlement is done not so much because the banks are short of capital but because they desire to pass on nearly matured bills to be called in by the Reichsbank, which is able to perform this task more cheaply than they are, thanks to its extensive network of branches. See *ibid.*, pp. 138 ff.

the portfolios either of nonbankers or of banks whose issue of fiduciary media is limited, whether because they have a small clientele or because of legal obstacles. It is not until the demand for money increases that the bills reach the large banks-of-issue. It is clear how little justification there is for the assertion that the amount of the note issue of central European banks-of-issue is organically connected with the quantity of bills drawn in the community. Only some of the bills are discounted at the banks by the issue of fiduciary media; the others complete their term without calling bank credit into use. But the proportion between the two amounts depends entirely on the credit policy that the credit-issuing banks follow.

Bank legislation has taken particular account of the extraordinary increase in the demand for money round about quarter-day. Article two of the German Bank (Amendment) Act of June 1, 1909, extends the usual tax-free quota of notes of 550 million marks to 750 million marks for the tax accounts based on information concerning the last days of March, June, September, and December in each year, thus sanctioning a procedure that the banks had been in the habit of following for decades. On every day of settlement, the entrepreneur's demand for credit increases, and therefore the natural rate of interest also. But the credit-issuing banks have endeavored to counteract the increase in interest on loans either by not raising the rate of discount at all, or by not raising it to an extent corresponding to the increase in the natural rate of interest. Of course, the consequence of this has necessarily been to swell their circulation of fiduciary media. State banking policy has in general put no obstacles in the way of this practice of the banks, which undoubtedly helps to stabilize the objective exchange value of money. The German Bank Act of 1909 was the first which took steps to give it direct support.

7

The Influence of Fiduciary Media on Fluctuations in the Objective Exchange Value of Money

Thus there is no such thing as an automatic adjustment of the quantity of fiduciary media in circulation to fluctuations in the demand for money without an effect on the objective exchange value of money. Consequently all those arguments are ill founded which seek to deny practical significance to the quantity theory by reference to the alleged elasticity of the circulation of money. The increase and decrease of the stock of fiduciary media in a free banking system have no greater natural connection, direct or indirect, with the rise and fall of the demand for money in the broader sense, than the increase and decrease of the stock of money have with the rise and fall of the demand for money in the narrower sense. Such a connection exists only insofar as the credit banks deliberately try to bring it about. Apart from this, the only connection that can be established between the two sets of variations, which are in themselves independent of each other, is like that of the policy which, say, in a period of increasing demand for money in the broader sense aims at an increase of fiduciary media in order to counteract the rise in the objective exchange value of money which might otherwise be expected. Since it is impossible to measure fluctuations in the objective exchange value of money, even only approximately, we are not able to judge whether the increase of fiduciary media that has occurred during the last century in nearly all the countries of the world has together with the increase in the quantity of money kept pace with the increase in the demand for money in the broader sense, or fallen behind it, or outstripped it. All that we can be sure of is that at least a part of the increase in the demand for money in the broader sense has been robbed of its influence on the purchasing power of money by the increase in the quantity of money and fiduciary media in circulation.

CHAPTER 18

The Redemption of Fiduciary Media

1

The Necessity for Complete Equivalence Between Money and Money Substitutes

There is nothing remarkable in the fact that money substitutes, as completely liquid claims to money against persons whose capacity to pay is beyond all doubt, have a value as great as the sums of money to which they refer. Admittedly, the question does arise: *Are* there any persons whose capacity to pay is so completely certain as to be quite beyond all doubt? And it may be pointed out that more than one bank, whose solvency nobody had dared to call in question even the day before, has collapsed ignominiously; and that so long as the remembrance of events of this sort has not entirely vanished from human memory, it must evoke at least a small difference between the valuation of money and that of claims to money payable at any time, even if, as far as human foresight goes, these latter are to be regarded as completely sound.

It is undeniable that such questions reveal a possible source of a certain lack of confidence in notes and checks, which would necessarily result in money substitutes having a lower value than money. But, on the other hand, there are reasons which might cause individuals to value money substitutes *more* highly than money, even if demands for the conversion of money into money substitutes were not always satisfied immediately. We shall have to speak of this later. Furthermore, quite apart from all these circumstances, it should be clearly pointed out that doubts as to the quality of fiduciary media are hardly tenable nowadays. In the case of money substitutes of medium and small denominations, among which token coins occupy the most important place, doubts of this nature do not come into consideration at all. But in the case also of the money substitutes that are used to meet the requirements of large-scale business, the possibility of loss is as good as nonexistent under present conditions; at least the possibility of loss is no greater in connection with the money substitutes issued by the large central banks than is the danger of demonetization that threatens the holders of any particular kind of money.

Now the complete equivalence of sums of money and secure claims to immediate payment of the same sums gives rise to a consequence that has extremely important bearings on the whole monetary system; namely, the possibility of tendering or accepting claims of this sort wherever money might be tendered or accepted. Exchanges are made through the medium of money; this fact remains unaltered. Buyers buy with money, and sellers sell for it. But exchanges are not always made by the *transfer* of a sum of money. They may also be made by the transfer or assignment of a claim to money. Now claims to money which fulfill the conditions mentioned above pass from hand to hand without those who acquire them feeling any need for actually enforcing them. They completely perform all the functions of money. Why then should the bidders burden themselves with the trouble of redeeming them? The claim which has been set in circulation remains in circulation, and becomes a money substitute. So long as confidence in the soundness of the bank is unshaken, and so long as the bank does not issue more money substitutes than its customers require for their dealings with one another (and everybody is to be regarded as a customer of the bank who accepts its money substitutes in place of money), then the situation in which the right behind the money substitute is enforced by presentation of notes for redemption or by withdrawal of deposits simply does not arise. The bank-of-issue may therefore assume that its money substitutes will remain in circulation until the necessity of dealing with persons outside the circle of customers forces holders to redeem them. This, in fact, is the very thing which enables the bank to issue fiduciary media at all, that is, to put money substitutes in circulation without maintaining in readiness the sum that would be necessary to keep the promise of immediate conversion that they represent.

The body which issues the fiduciary media and is responsible for maintaining their equivalence with the sums of money to which they refer must nevertheless be able to redeem promptly those fiduciary media which their holders present for conversion into money when they have to make payments to persons who do not recognize these fiduciary media as money substitutes. This is the only way in which a difference between the value of money on the one hand and of the notes and deposits on the other hand can be prevented from coming into existence.

2

The Return of Fiduciary Media to the Issuer on Account of Lack of Confidence on the Part of the Holders

The view has sometimes been expressed that if an issuing body wishes to secure equivalence between its fiduciary media and the money to which they refer, it should take precautions so as to be able to redeem those fiduciary media that are returned to it through lack of confidence on the part of the holders. It is impossible to subscribe to this view; for it completely fails to recognize the significance and object of a conversion fund. It cannot be the function of a conversion fund to enable the issuing body to redeem its fiduciary media when its counters are besieged by holders who have lost confidence in them. Confidence in the capacity of circulation of fiduciary media is not an individual phenomenon; either it is shared by everybody, or it does not exist at all. Fiduciary media can fulfill their function only on the condition that they are fully equivalent to the sums of money to which they refer. They cease to be equivalent to these sums of money as soon as confidence in the issuer is shaken even if only among a part of the community. The yokel who presents his note for redemption in order to convince himself of the bank's capacity to pay, which nobody else doubts, is only a comic figure that the bank has no need to fear. It need not make any special arrangements or take any special precautions on his account. But any bank that issues fiduciary media is forced to suspend payments if *everybody* begins to present notes for redemption or to withdraw deposits. Any such bank is powerless against a panic; no system and no policy can help it then. This follows necessarily from the very nature of fiduciary media, which imposes upon those who issue them the obligation to pay a sum of money which they cannot command.[1]

The history of the last two centuries contains more than one example of such catastrophes. Those banks that have succumbed to the onslaughts of noteholders and depositors have been reproached with bringing about the collapse by granting credit imprudently, by tying up their capital, or by advancing loans to the state; extremely serious charges have been brought against their directors. Where the state itself has been the issuer of the fiduciary media, the impossibility of maintaining their redeemability has usually been ascribed to their having been issued in defiance of precepts based on banking experience. It is obvious that this attitude is due to a misunderstanding. Even if the banks had put all their assets in short investments, that is, in investments that could have been realized in a relatively short time, they would not have been able to meet the demands of their creditors. This follows merely from the fact that the banks' claims fall due only after notice has been given, while those of their creditors are payable on demand. Thus there lies an irresolvable contradiction in the nature of fiduciary media. Their equivalence to money depends on the promise that they will at any time be converted into money at the demand of the person entitled to them and on the fact that proper precautions are taken to make this promise effective. But—and this is likewise involved in the nature of fiduciary media—what is promised is an impossibility insofar as the bank is never able to keep its loans perfectly liquid. Whether the fiduciary media are issued in the course of bank-

---

[1] See Ricardo, "Proposals," in *Works*, ed. McCulloch, 2d ed. (London, 1852), p. 406; Walras, *Études d'économie politique appliquée* (Lausanne, 1898), pp. 365 f.

ing operations or not, immediate redemption is always impracticable if the confidence of the holders has been lost.

3
The Case Against the Issue of Fiduciary Media

Recognition of the fact, which had been pointed out before the
time of Ricardo, that there is no way in which an issuer of fiduciary
media can protect itself against the consequences of a panic or avoid
succumbing to any serious run, may lead, if one likes, to a demand
that the creation of fiduciary media should be prohibited. Many
writers have adopted this attitude. Some have demanded the prohibition of the issue of such notes as have no metal backing; others,
the prohibition of all clearing transactions except with full metallic
cover; others again, and this is the only logical position, have combined both demands.[2]

Such demands as these have not been fulfilled. The progressive
extension of the money economy would have led to an enormous
extension in the demand for money if its efficiency had not been
extraordinarily increased by the creation of fiduciary media. The
issue of fiduciary media has made it possible to avoid the convul-
sions that would be involved in an increase in the objective exchange value of money, and reduced the cost of the monetary
apparatus. Fiduciary media tap a lucrative source of revenue for
their issuer; they enrich both the person that issues them and the
community that employs them. In the early days of the modern
banking system they played a further part still by strengthening the
credit-negotiating activities of the banks (which in those times could
hardly have proved profitable if carried on for their own sake alone)
and so brought the system safely past those obstacles which ob-
structed its beginnings.

Prohibition of the issue of all notes except those with a full backing
and of the lending of the deposits which serve as the basis of the
check-and-clearing business would mean almost completely suppressing the note issue and almost strangling the check-and-clear-

---

[2] See for example, Tellkampf, *Die Prinzipien des Geld- und Bankwesens* (Berlin, 1867),
pp. 181 ff.; *Erfordernis voller Metalldeckung der Banknoten* (Berlin, 1873), pp. 23 ff.;
Geyer, *Theorie und Praxis des Zettelbankwesens*, 2d ed. (Munich, 1874), p. 227.

ing system. If notes are still to be issued and accounts opened in spite of such a prohibition, then somebody must be found who is prepared to bear unrecompensed the costs involved. Only very rarely will this be the issuer, although occasionally such a thing happens. The United States created silver certificates in order to relieve the business world of the inconveniences of the clumsy silver coinage and to remove one of the obstacles in the way of an extended use of the silver dollar, which it was thought desirable to encourage for reasons of currency policy. Similarly for reasons of currency policy, gold certificates were created, so as to bring gold money into use despite the public preference for paper.[3]

Sometimes the public may be willing to use notes, checks, or giro transfers for technical reasons, even if it has to make a certain payment to the bank for the facility. There are sometimes objections to the physical use of coins, which are not involved in the transfer of claims to deposited sums of money. The storage of considerable sums of money and their insurance against risk from fire and flood and from robbery and theft are not always a small matter even for the individual merchant, and still less so for the private person. Warrants payable to order and checkbooks whose folios have no significance until they have been signed by an authorized person are less liable to dishonest handling than are coins, whose smooth faces tell no tales of the methods by which they have been acquired. But even banknotes, which retain no relationships to individuals, are yet easier to preserve against destruction and to secure against depredation than are bulky pieces of metal. It is true that the large accumulations of money deposited in the banks constitute all the more profitable and therefore attractive an objective for criminal enterprise; but in their case it is possible to take such precautionary measures as will afford almost complete safety, and it is similarly easier to safeguard such large deposits against the risk of accidental damage by the elements. It has proved a more difficult matter to withdraw the coffers of the banks from the grasp of those in political power; but even this has eventually been achieved, and such *coups de main* as those of the Stuarts or Davousts have not been repeated in modern times.

---

[3] See Hepburn, *History of Coinage and Currency in the United States* (New York, 1903), p. 418.

A further motive for the introduction of payment through the mediation of the banks has been provided by the difficulty of determining the weight and fineness of coins in the ordinary course of daily business. In this way debasement of the coinage led to the establishment of the famous banks of Amsterdam and Hamburg. The commission of one-fortieth percent which the customers of the Bank of Amsterdam had to pay on each deposit or withdrawal[4] was far outweighed by the advantages offered by the trustworthiness of the bank currency. Finally, the saving of costs of transport and the greater handiness are other advantages of banking methods of payment that have similarly entered into consideration, especially in countries with a silver, or even a copper, standard. Thus in Japan as early as the middle of the fourteenth century, certain notes issued by rich merchants were in great demand because they offered a means of avoiding the costs and inconveniences involved in the transport of the heavy copper coinage.[5] The premium at which banknotes sometimes stood as against metallic currency before the development of the interlocal check-and-clearing business and the post-office-order service can most easily be explained along these lines.[6]

It is clear that prohibition of fiduciary media would by no means imply a death sentence for the banking system, as is sometimes asserted. The banks would still retain the business of negotiating credit, of borrowing for the purpose of lending. Not consideration for the banks, but appreciation of the influence of fiduciary media on the objective exchange value of money, is the reason why they have not been suppressed.

4

The Redemption Fund

A person who holds money substitutes and wishes to transact business with persons to whom these money substitutes are unfamiliar and therefore unacceptable in lieu of money is obliged to

---

[4] See Dunbar, *Chapters on the Theory and History of Banking*, 2d ed. (New York, 1907), p. 99.
[5] See Kiga, *Das Bankwesen Japans*, Leipziger Inaug. Diss., p. 9.
[6] See Oppenheim, *Die Natur des Geldes* (Mainz, 1855), pp. 241 f.

change the money substitutes into money. He goes to the body that is responsible for maintaining equivalence between the money substitutes and money and proceeds to enforce the claim that the money substitutes embody. He presents the notes (or token coins or similar form of currency) for conversion or withdraws his deposits. It follows from this that whoever issues money substitutes is never able to put more of them into circulation than will meet the needs of his customers for business among themselves. All issues in excess of this will return to the issuer, who will have to accept them in exchange for money if he does not wish to destroy the confidence on which his whole business is built up. (In view of what has been said in the preceding chapter and remains to be said in the following chapter, it should not be necessary to state expressly in this place also that this is true only when several coexisting banks issue money substitutes which have a limited capacity of circulation. If there is only a single bank issuing money substitutes, and if these money substitutes have an unlimited capacity of circulation, then there are no limits to the extension of the issue of fiduciary media. The case would be the same if all the banks had a common understanding as to the issue of their money substitutes and extended the circulation of them according to uniform principles.)

Thus, in the circumstances assumed, it is not possible for a bank to issue more money substitutes than its customers can use; everything in excess of this must flow back to it. There is no danger in this so long as the excess issue is one of money certificates; but an excess issue of fiduciary media is catastrophic.

Consequently the chief rule to be observed in the business of a credit-issuing bank is quite clear and simple: it must never issue more fiduciary media than will meet the requirements of its customers for their business with each other. But it must be admitted that there are unusually big difficulties in the practical application of this maxim for there is no way of determining the extent of these requirements on the part of customers. In the absence of any exact knowledge on this point the bank has to rely upon an uncertain empirical procedure which may easily lead to mistakes. Nevertheless, prudent and experienced bank directors—and most bank directors are prudent and experienced—usually manage pretty well with it.

It is only exceptionally that the clienteles of the credit-issuing banks as such extend beyond political boundaries. Even those banks that have branches in different countries give complete independence to their individual branches in the issue of money substitutes. Under present political conditions, uniform administration of banking firms domiciled in different countries would hardly be possible; and difficulties of banking technique and legislation, and finally difficulties of currency technique, stand in the way also. Furthermore, within individual countries it is usually possible to distinguish two categories of credit banks. On the one hand there is a privileged bank, which possesses a monopoly or almost a monopoly of the note issue, and whose antiquity and financial resources, and still more its extraordinary reputation throughout the whole country, give it a unique position. And on the other hand there is a series of rival banks, which have not the right of issue and which, however great their reputation and the confidence in their solvency, are unable to compete in the capacity for circulation of their money substitutes with the privileged bank, behind which stands the state with all its authority. Different principles apply to the policies of the two kinds of bank. For the banks of the second group, it is sufficient if they keep in readiness for the redemption of those money substitutes which are returned to them a certain sum of such assets as will enable them to command on demand the credit of the central bank. They extend the circulation of their fiduciary media as far as possible. If in so doing they exceed the issue that their customers can absorb, so that some of their fiduciary media are presented for redemption, then they procure from the central bank the necessary resources for this by rediscounting bills from their portfolio, or by pledging securities. Thus the essence of the policy that they must pursue to maintain their position as credit-issuing banks consists in always maintaining a sufficiently large quantity of such assets as the central bank regards as an adequate basis for granting credit.

The central banks have no such support from a more powerful and distinguished institution. They are thrown entirely upon their own resources, and must shape their policy accordingly. If they have put too many money substitutes into circulation so that holders apply for their redemption, then they have no other way out than that provided by their redemption fund. Consequently, it is necessary for them to see that there are never more of their fiduciary media in circulation than will meet the requirements of their customers. As has already been said, it is not possible to make a direct evaluation of these requirements. Only an indirect evaluation is practicable. The proportion of the total demand for money in the broader sense that cannot be satisfied by fiduciary media must be determined. This will be the quantity of money that is necessary for doing business with the persons who are not customers of the central bank; that is, the quantity required for purposes of foreign trade.

The demand for money for international trade is composed of two different elements. It consists, first, of the demand for those sums of money which, as a result of variations in the relative extent and intensity of the demand for money in different countries, are transported from one country to another until that position of equilibrium is reestablished in which the objective exchange value of money has the same level everywhere. It is impossible to avoid the transfers of money that are necessary on this account. It is true that we might imagine the establishment of an international deposit bank in which large sums of money were deposited, perhaps even all the money in the world, and made the basis of an issue of money certificates, that is, of notes or balances completely backed by money. This well might put a stop to the physical use of coins, and might in certain circumstances tend to a considerable reduction of costs; instead of coins being used, notes would be sent or transfers made in the books of the bank. But such external differences would not affect the nature of the process.

The other motive for international transfers of money is provided by those balances that arise in the international exchange of commodities and services. These have to be settled by transfers in opposite directions, and it is therefore theoretically possible to eliminate them completely by developing the clearing process.

In foreign-exchange dealings and the related transactions that in recent times have been united with them, there is a fine mechanism which cancels out nearly all such transfers of money. It is only exceptionally nowadays that two ships meet at sea, one of them taking gold from London to New York and the other bringing gold from New York to London. International transfers of money are controlled as a rule merely by variations in the ratio between the demand for money and the stock of money. Among these variations, those with the greatest practical importance are those which distribute the newly mined precious metals throughout the world, a process in which London often plays the part of a middleman. Apart from this, and provided that no extraordinary cause suddenly alters the relative demand for money in different countries, the transference of money from country to country cannot be particularly extensive. It may be assumed that, as a rule, the variations that occur in this way are not so great as those variations in stocks of money that are due to new production, or at least that they do not exceed them by very much. If this is true—and it is supported only by rough estimates—then the movements which are necessary for bringing the purchasing power of money to a common level will consist largely or entirely of variations in the distribution of the *additional* quantity of money only.

It is possible to estimate on empirical grounds that the relative demand for money in a country, that is, the extent and intensity of its demand for money in relation to the extent and intensity of the demand for money in other countries (this phrase being interpreted throughout in the broader sense), will not decrease within a relatively short period to such an extent as to cause the quantity of money and fiduciary media together in circulation to sink below such and such a fraction of its present amount. Of course, such estimates are necessarily based upon more or less arbitrary combinations of factors and it is obviously never out of the question that they will be subsequently upset by unforeseen events. But if the amount is estimated very conservatively, and if due account is also taken of the fact that the state of international trade may necessitate transfers of money from country to country if only temporarily, then, so long as the quantity of fiduciary media circulating within the country is not increased beyond the estimated amount and no money certificates are issued either, the accumulation of a redemption fund might prove altogether unnecessary. For so long as the issue of fiduciary media does not exceed this limit, and assuming of course the correctness of the estimate on which it is based, there can arise no demand for redemption of the fiduciary media. If, for example, the quantity of the banknotes, treasury notes, token coins, and deposits at present in circulation in Germany were reduced by the sum deposited as cover for it in the vaults of the banks, the money and credit system would not be changed in any way. Germany's power to transact business through the medium of money with foreign countries would not be affected.[7] It is only the notes, deposits, and so forth, that are not covered by money that have the character of fiduciary media; it is these only and not those covered by money that have the effects on the determination of prices which it is the task of this part of our book to describe.

If the amount of fiduciary media in circulation were kept at a level below the limit set by the presumable maximum requirements of foreign trade, then it would be possible to do without a redemption reserve altogether, if it were not for a further circumstance that enters into the question. This circumstance is the following: if persons who needed a sum of money for foreign payments and were obliged to obtain it by the exchange of money substitutes could do this only through numerous money-changing transactions, perhaps involving an expenditure of time and trouble so that the procedure cost them something, this would militate against the complete equivalence of money substitutes and money, causing the former to circulate at a discount. Hence, if only on this account, a redemption fund of a certain amount would have to be maintained, even though the quantity of money actually in circulation was enough for trade with foreign countries. It follows from this that the fully backed note and the fully covered deposit, originally necessary in order to accustom the public to the use of these forms of money substitute, have still to be retained nowadays along with the superficially similar but essentially different fiduciary medium. A note or deposit currency with no money backing at all, that is, one which consists entirely of fiduciary media, still remains a practical impossibility.

If we look at the redemption funds of the self-sufficing banks, we shall observe in them an apparently quite irregular multifariousness. We shall observe that the kind and amount of cover of the money substitutes, especially those issued in note form, are regulated by a series of rules, constructed on quite different lines, partly by mercantile usage and partly by legislation. It is hardly correct to speak of different *systems* in this connection; that ambitious desig-

---

[7] This example assumes the circumstances that existed before 1914.

nation is little suited to empirical rules that have for the most part been founded on erroneous views of the nature of money and fiduciary media. There is, however, one idea that is expressed in all of them; the idea that the issue of fiduciary media needs to be limited by some kind of artificial restriction since it has no natural limits. Thus the question underlying all monetary policy, whether an unlimited increase of fiduciary media with its ineluctable consequence of a diminution in the objective exchange value of money is a thing to be encouraged, is implicitly answered in the negative.

Recognition of the need for an artificial limitation of the circulation of fiduciary media is, both on strictly scientific grounds and also on grounds of practical expediency, a product of economic inquiry during the first half of the nineteenth century. Its triumph over other views ended decades of such lively discussion as our science has seldom known, and at the same time concluded a period of uncertain experiment in the issuing of fiduciary media. During the years that have since elapsed, the grounds on which it was based have been subjected to criticism, sometimes ill founded, sometimes founded upon real objections. But the principle of limiting the issue of uncovered notes has not been abandoned in banking legislation. Nowadays it still constitutes an essential element in the banking policy of civilized nations, even if the circumstance that the limitation only applies to the issue of fiduciary media in the form of notes and not to the constantly growing issue in the form of deposits may make its practical importance less than it was some decades ago.

Limitation of fiduciary media also forms part of the money and credit system in India, the Philippines, and those countries that have imitated them, although in a different garb. No direct numerical proportion has been set up between the redemption fund administered by the government and the quantity of fiduciary media in circulation; any attempt to do this would have met with technical difficulties if only because it was impossible to calculate exactly what the quantity of fiduciary media was at the time of the transition to the new standard. But the further issue of fiduciary media in the form of legal-tender coinage is reserved to the state (it mostly requires special legislation) in a similar fashion to that in which the issue of token coinage and the like is regulated elsewhere.

5

The So-called Banking Type of Cover for Fiduciary Media

The expressions *solvency* and *liquidity* are not always used correctly when they are applied to the circumstances of a bank. They are sometimes regarded as synonymous; but orthodox opinion understands them to refer to two different states. (It must be admitted that a clear definition and distinction of the two concepts is usually not attempted.)

A bank may be said to be solvent when its assets are so constituted that a liquidation would necessarily result at least in complete satisfaction of all of its creditors. Liquidity is that condition of the bank's assets which will enable it to meet all its liabilities, not merely in full, but also in time, that is, without being obliged to ask for anything in the nature of a moratorium from its creditors. Liquidity is a particular sort of solvency. Every enterprise—for the same is true of any body that participates in credit transactions—that is liquid is also solvent; but on the other hand not every undertaking that is solvent is also liquid. A person who cannot settle a debt on the day when it falls due has not a liquid status, even if there is no doubt that he will be able in three or six months' time to pay the debt together with interest and the other costs in which the delay is meanwhile involving the creditor.

Since ancient times commercial law has imposed on everybody the obligation to have regard to liquidity throughout the whole conduct of his business. This requirement is characteristically expressed in mercantile life. Anyone who has to approach his creditor for permission to defer the payment of a debt, anyone who allows matters to reach the point of having his bills protested, has imperiled his business reputation, even if he is afterward able to meet all his outstanding obligations in full. All undertakings are subject to the rule that we have already encountered as the business principle of the credit-negotiating banks, that steps must be taken to permit the full and punctual settlement of every claim as it falls due.[8]

---

[8] See pp. 296 ff. But the fact is often ignored that this "principle of the banking adequate cover" is valid not only for banks but similarly for all other undertakings. See, for example, Schulze-Gaevernitz, "Die deutsche Kreditbank," *Grundriss der Sozialökonomik,* Part V, section 2, pp. 240 ff.

For credit-issuing banks, regard to this fundamental rule of prudent conduct is an impossibility. It lies in their nature to build upon the fact that a proportion—the larger proportion—of the fiduciary media remains in circulation and that the claims arising from this part of the issue will not be enforced, or at least will not be enforced simultaneously. They are bound to collapse as soon as confidence in their conduct is destroyed and the creditors storm their counters. They, therefore, are unable to aim at liquidity of investment like all other banks and undertakings in general; they have to be content with solvency as the goal of their policy.

This is customarily overlooked when the covering of the issue of fiduciary media by means of short-term loans is referred to as a method that is peculiarly suited to their nature and function, and when the appellation "characteristically banking type of cover" is applied to it,[9] because it is supposed that consistent application of the general rule about liquidity to the special circumstances of the credit-issuing banks shows it to be the system of investment that is proper to such banks. Whether the assets of a credit-issuing bank consist of short-term bills or of hypothecary loans remains a matter of indifference in the case of a general run. If the bank is in immediate need of large sums of money it can procure them only by disposing of its assets; when the panic-stricken public is clamoring at its counters for the redemption of notes or the repayment of deposits, a bill that has still thirty days to run is of no more use to it than a mortgage which is irredeemable for just as many years. At such moments the most that can matter is the greater or lesser negotiability of the assets. But in certain circumstances, long-term or even irredeemable claims may be easier to realize than short-term;

---

[9] See Wagner, *System der Zettelbankpolitik* (Freiburg, 1873), pp. 240 ff.—The "golden rule" found its classical expression with regard to the business of credit banks in the famous "Note expédiée du Havre le 29 Mai 1810, à la Banque de France, par ordre de S. M. l'Empereur, et par l'entremise de M. le comte Mollien, ministre du Trésor" (I quote from the reprint in Wolowski, *La Question des Banques* [Paris, 1864], pp. 83–87): "Il faut qu'une banque se maintienne en état de se liquider à tout moment, d'abord, vis-à-vis des porteurs de ses billets, par la réalisation de son portefeuille, et, apres les porteurs de ses billets, viv-à-vis de ses actionnaires, par la distribution à faire entre eux de la portion du capital fourni par chacun d'eux. *Pour ne jamais finir, une banque doit etre toujours prête à finir*" (p. 87). All the same, Mollien had no doubt on the point that a bank that does not issue its notes otherwise "qu'en échange de bonnes et valable lettres de change, *à deux et trois mois de terme* au plus" can only call in its notes from circulation "dans un espace de *trois mois*" (*ibid.*, p. 84).

in times of crisis, government annuities and mortgages may perhaps find buyers more readily than commercial bills.

It has already been mentioned that in most states two categories of banks exist, as far as the public confidence they enjoy is concerned. The central bank-of-issue, which is usually the only bank with the right to issue notes, occupies an exceptional position, owing to its partial or entire administration by the state and the strict control to which all its activities are subjected.[10] It enjoys a greater reputation than the other credit-issuing banks, which have not such a simple type of business to carry on, which often risk more for the sake of profit than they can be responsible for, and which, at least in some states, carry on a series of additional enterprises, the business of company formation for example, besides their banking activities proper, the negotiation of credit and the granting of credit through the issue of fiduciary media. These banks of the second order may under certain circumstances lose the confidence of the public without the position of the central bank being shaken. In this case they are able to maintain themselves in a state of liquidity by securing credit from the central bank on their own behalf (as indeed they also do in other cases when their resources are exhausted) and so being enabled to meet their obligations punctually and in full. It is therefore possible to say that these banks are in a state of liquidity so long as their liabilities as they fall due from day to day are balanced by such assets as the central bank considers a sufficient security for advances. It is well known that some banks are not liquid even in this sense. The central banks of individual countries could similarly attain a state of liquidity if they only carried such assets against their issues of fiduciary media as would be regarded as possible investments by their sister institutions abroad. But even then it would remain true that it is theoretically impossible to maintain the credit bank system in a state of liquidity. A simultaneous destruction of confidence in all banks would necessarily lead to a general collapse.

It is true that the investment of its assets in short-term loans does make it possible for a bank to satisfy its creditors within a certain

---

[10] In the United States, before the reorganization of the banking system under the Federal Reserve Act, the lack of a central bank in times of crises was made up for by *ad hoc* organizations of the banks that were members of the clearinghouses.

comparatively short period. But this would prove adequate in the face of a loss of confidence only if the holders of notes and deposits did not apply simultaneously to the bank for immediate payment of the sums of money owing to them. Such a supposition is not very probable. Either there is no lack of confidence at all or it is general. There is only one way in which liquidity of status might be at least formally secured with regard to the special circumstances of credit-issuing banks. If such banks made loans only on the condition that they had the right to demand repayment at any time, then the problem of liquidity would of course be solved for them in a simple manner. But from the point of view of the community as a whole, this is of course no solution, but only a shelving, of the problem. The status of the bank could only apparently be kept liquid at the expense of the status of those who borrowed from it, for these would be faced with precisely the same insurmountable difficulty. The banks' debtors would not have kept the borrowed sums in their safes, but would have put them into productive investments from which they certainly could not withdraw them without delay. The problem is thus in no way altered; it remains insoluble.

6

The Significance of Short-Term Cover

Credit-issuing banks as a rule give preference to short-term loans as investments. Often the law compels them to do this, but in any case they would be forced to do it by public opinion. But the significance of this preference has nothing to do with the greater ease with which it is generally, but erroneously, supposed to allow the fiduciary media to be redeemed. It is true that it is a policy that has preserved the bank-credit system in the past from severe shocks; it is true that its neglect has always avenged itself; and it is true that it still is important for the present and future; but the reasons for this are entirely different from those which the champions of short-term cover are in the habit of putting forward.

One of its reasons, and the less weighty, is that it is easier to judge the soundness of investments made in the form of short-term loans than that of long-term investments. It is true that there are numerous long-term investments that are sounder than very many short-term investments; nevertheless, the soundness of an investment can as a rule be judged with greater certainty when all that has to be done is to survey the circumstances of the market in general and of the borrower in particular for the next few weeks or months, than when it is a matter of years or decades.

The second and decisive reason has already been mentioned.[11] If the granting of credit through the issue of fiduciary media is restricted to loans that are to be paid back after a short space of time, then there is a certain limitation of the amount of the issue of fiduciary media. The rule that it is desirable for credit-issuing banks to grant only short-term loans is the outcome of centuries of experience. It has been its fate always to be misunderstood; but even so, obedience to it has had the important effect of helping to limit the issue of fiduciary media.

7

The Security of the Investments of the Credit-issuing Banks

The solution of the problem of soundness is no more difficult for the credit-issuing banks than for the credit-negotiating banks. If the fiduciary media are issued only on good security and if a guarantee fund is created out of the bank's share capital for the purpose of covering losses, for even under prudent management losses cannot always be avoided, then the bank can put itself in a position to redeem in full the fiduciary media that it issues, although not within the term specified in its promises to pay.

Nevertheless, the soundness of the cover is only of subordinate importance as far as fiduciary media are concerned. It may disappear entirely, at least in a certain sense, without prejudicing their capacity of circulation. Fiduciary media can even be issued without any cover at all. This occurs, for example, when the state issues token coins and does not devote the seigniorage to a particular fund for their redemption. (Under certain circumstances, the metal value of the coins themselves may be regarded as partial security. And of course the state as a whole has assets that provide far greater se-

---

[11] See above, pp. 346 f.

curity than any sort of special fund could offer.) On the other hand, even if the fiduciary media are completely covered by the assets of the issuer, so that only the time of their redemption and not its ultimate occurrence is open to question, this cannot have any sort of influence whatever in support of their capacity for circulation; for this depends exclusively upon the expectation that the issuer will redeem them *promptly*.

To have overlooked this is the error underlying all those proposals and experiments which have aimed at guaranteeing the issue of fiduciary media by means of funds consisting of nonliquid assets, such as mortgages. If those money substitutes that are presented for redemption are immediately and fully redeemed in money, then, beyond the cash reserve necessary for this redemption, no stock of goods is needed for maintaining equivalence between the fiduciary media and money. If, however, the money substitutes are *not* fully and immediately redeemed for money, then they will not be reckoned as equivalent to money just because there are some goods somewhere that will at some time be used to satisfy the demands that the holders of the money substitutes are entitled to make on the ground of the claims that the money substitutes embody. They will be valued at *less* than the sums of money to which they refer, because their redemption is in doubt and at the best will not occur until after the passage of a period of time. And so they will cease to be money substitutes; if they continue to be used as media of exchange, it will be at an independent valuation; they will be no longer money substitutes, but credit money.

For credit money also, that is for unmatured claims which serve as common media of exchange, "cover" by a special fund is superfluous. So long as the claims are tendered and accepted as money, and thus have obtained an exchange value in excess of that which is attributed to them as mere claims, such a fund has no bearing on the matter. The significance of the regulations as to cover and the funds for that purpose lies here, as with fiduciary media, in the fact that they indirectly set a limit to the quantity that can be issued.[12]

---

[12] See Nicholson, *A Treatise on Money and Essays on Present Monetary Problems* (Edinburgh, 1888), pp. 67 f.

8

Foreign Bills of Exchange as a Component of the Redemption Fund

Since it is not the object of a redemption fund to provide for the redemption of such money substitutes as are returned to the bank because of lack of confidence in their goodness, but only to provide the bank's customers with the media of exchange necessary for dealing with persons who are not among its customers, it is obvious that such a fund might be composed at least in part of such things as, without being money, can be used like money for dealings with outsiders. These things comprise not only foreign money substitutes but also all such claims as form the basis of the international clearing business, primarily, that is to say, foreign bills, that is, bills on foreign places. The issue of money substitutes cannot be increased beyond the quantity given by the demand for money (in the broader sense) of the customers of the bank for intercourse within the clientele of the bank. Only an extension of the clientele could prepare the way for an extension of the circulation; for the national central bank-of-issue, whose influence is limited by political boundaries, such an extension remains impossible. Nevertheless, if part of the redemption fund is invested in foreign banknotes, or in foreign bills, foreign checks, and deposits at short notice with foreign banks, then a larger proportion of the money substitutes issued by the banks can be transformed into fiduciary media than if the bank held nothing but money in readiness for the foreign dealings of its customers. In this way a credit-issuing bank may even transform into fiduciary media almost all the money substitutes that it issues. The private banks of many countries are now no longer far removed from this state of affairs; they are in the habit of providing for the prompt redemption of the money substitutes issued by them by holding a reserve itself consisting of money substitutes; only so far as these covering money substitutes are money certificates do the issued money substitutes not bear the character of fiduciary media. It is only fairly recently that the central banks-of-issue also have begun to adopt the practice of admitting money substitutes and foreign bills into their conversion funds.

Just as the goldsmiths once began to lend out part of the moneys entrusted to them for safekeeping, so the central banks have taken the step of investing their stock of metal partly in foreign bills and other foreign credits. An example was set by the Hamburg Giro Bank, which was accustomed to hold part of its reserve in bills on London; it was followed during the last quarter of the nineteenth century by a series of banks-of-issue. It was with regard to their profits that the banks accepted this system of cover. The investment of a part of the redemption fund in foreign bills and other foreign balances that could be easily and quickly realized was intended to reduce the costs of maintaining the reserve. In certain countries the central banks-of-issue acquired a portfolio of foreign bills because the domestic discount business was not sufficiently remunerative.[13] Generally speaking, it was the central banks-of-issue and the governmental redemption funds of the smaller and financially weaker countries that tried to save expense in this way. Since the war, which has made the whole world poorer, their procedure has been widely imitated. It is clear that the policy of investing the whole redemption fund in foreign claims to gold cannot become universal. If all the countries of the world were to go over to the gold-exchange standard and hold their redemption funds not in gold but in foreign claims to gold, gold would no longer be required for monetary purposes at all. That part of its value which is founded upon its employment as money would entirely disappear. The maintenance of a gold-exchange standard with the redemption fund invested in foreign bills undermines the whole gold-standard system. We shall have to return to this point in chapter 20.

---

[13] See Kalkmann, "Holland's Geldwesen im 19. Jahrhundert," in *Schmoller's Jahrbuch*, vol. 25, pp. 1249 ff.; Witten, "Die Devisenpolitik der Nationalbank von Belgien," in *ibid.*, vol. 42, pp. 625 ff.

CHAPTER 19

Money, Credit, and Interest

1

On the Nature of the Problem

It is the object of this chapter to investigate the connection between the amount of money in circulation and the level of the rate of interest. It has already been shown that variations in the proportion between the quantity of money and the demand for money influence the level of the exchange ratio between money and other economic goods. It now remains for us to investigate whether the variations thus evoked in the prices of commodities affect goods of the first order and goods of higher orders to the same extent. Until now we have considered variations in the exchange ratio between money and consumption goods only and left out of account the exchange ratio between money and production goods. This procedure would seem to be justifiable, for the determination of the value of consumption goods is the primary process and that of the value of production goods is derived from it. Capital goods or production goods derive their value from the value of their prospective products; nevertheless, their value never reaches the full value of these prospective products, but as a rule remains somewhat below it. The margin by which the value of capital goods falls short of that of their expected products constitutes interest; its origin lies in the natural difference of value between present goods and future goods.[1] If price variations due to monetary determinants happened to affect production goods and consumption goods in different degrees—and the possibility cannot be dismissed offhand—then they would lead to a change in the rate of interest. The problem suggested by this is identical with a second, although they are usually dealt with separately: Can the rate of interest be affected by the credit policy of the banks that issue fiduciary media? Are banks able to depress the rate of interest charged by them, for those loans that their power to issue fiduciary media enables them to make, until it reaches the limit set by the technical working costs of their lending business? The question that confronts us here is the much discussed question of the gratuitous nature of bank credit.

In lay circles this problem is regarded as long since solved. Money performs its function as a common medium of exchange in facilitating not only the sale of present goods but also the exchange of present goods for future goods and of future goods for present goods. An entrepreneur who wishes to acquire command over capital goods and labor in order to begin a process of production must first of all have money with which to purchase them. For a long time now it has not been usual to transfer capital goods by way of direct exchange. The capitalists advance money to the producers, who then use it for buying means of production and for paying wages. Those entrepreneurs who have not enough of their own capital at their disposal do not demand production goods, but money. The demand for capital takes on the form of a demand for money. But this must not deceive us as to the nature of the phenomenon. What is usually called plentifulness of money and scarcity of money is really plen-

---

[1] The fact that I have followed the terminology and method of attack of Böhm-Bawerk's theory of interest throughout this chapter does not imply that I am an adherent of that theory or am able to regard it as a satisfactory solution of the problem. But the present work does not afford scope for the exposition of my own views on the problem of interest; that must be reserved for a special study, which I hope will appear in the not too distant future. In such circumstances I have had no alternative but to develop my argument on the basis of Böhm-Bawerk's theory. Böhm-Bawerk's great achievement is the foundation of the work of all those who until now have dealt with the problem of interest since his time, and may well be the foundation of the work of those who will do so in the future. He was the first to clear the way that leads to understanding of the problem; he was the first to make it possible systematically to relate the problem of interest to that of the value of money.

tifulness of capital and scarcity of capital. A real scarcity or plentifulness of money can never be directly perceptible in the community, that is, it can never make itself felt except through its influence on the objective exchange value of money and the consequences of the variations so induced. For since the utility of money depends exclusively upon its purchasing power, which must always be such that total demand and total supply coincide, the community is always in enjoyment of the maximum satisfaction that the use of money can yield.

This was not recognized for a long time and to a large extent it is not recognized even nowadays. The entrepreneur who would like to extend his business beyond the bounds set by the state of the market is prone to complain of the scarcity of money. Every increase in the rate of discount gives rise to fresh complaints about the illiberality of the banks' methods or about the unreasonableness of the legislators who make the rules that limit their powers of granting credit. The augmentation of fiduciary media is recommended as a universal remedy for all the ills of economic life. Much of the popularity of inflationary tendencies is based on similar ways of thinking. And it is not only laymen who subscribe to such views. Even if experts have been unanimous on this point since the famous arguments of David Hume and Adam Smith,[2] almost every year new writers come forward with attempts to show that the size and composition of the stock of capital has no influence on the level of interest, that the rate of interest is determined by the supply of and the demand for credit, and that, without having to raise the rate of interest, the banks would be able to satisfy even the greatest demands for credit that are made upon them, if their hands were not tied by legislative provisions.[3]

The superficial observer whose insight is not very penetrating will discover many symptoms which seem to confirm the above views and others like them. When the banks-of-issue proceed to raise the rate of discount because their note circulation threatens to increase beyond the legally permissible quantity, then the most immediate

---

[2] See Hume, *Essays*, ed. Frowde (London), pp. 303 ff.; Smith, *The Wealth of Nations*, Cannan's ed. (London, 1930), vol. 2, pp. 243 ff.; see also J. S. Mill, *Principles of Political Economy* (London, 1867), pp. 296 f.

[3] See, for example, Georg Schmidt, *Kredit und Zins* (Leipzig, 1910), pp. 38 ff.

cause of their procedure lies in the provisions that have been made
by the legislators for the regulation of their right of issue. The general
stiffening of the rate of interest in the so-called money market, the
market for short-term capital investments, which occurs, or at least
should occur, as a consequence of the rise of the discount rate, is
therefore, and with a certain appearance of justification, laid to the
charge of national banking policy. Still more striking is the procedure
of the central banks when they think it beyond their power to bring
about the desired general dearness in the money market by merely
increasing the bank rate: they take steps which have the immediate
object of forcing up the rate of interest demanded by the other national credit-issuing banks in their short-term-loan business. The
Bank of England is in the habit in such circumstances of forcing
consols on the open market,[4] the German Reichsbank of offering
Treasury bonds for discount. If these methods are considered by
themselves, without account being taken of their function in the
market, then it seems reasonable to conclude that legislation and
the self-seeking policy of the banks are responsible for the rise in the
rate of interest. Inadequate understanding of the complicated relationships of economic life makes all such legislative provisions appear to be measures in favor of capitalism and against the interest
of the producing classes.[5]

But the defenders of orthodox banking policy have been no hap-
pier in their arguments. They evidence no very considerable insight
into the problems lying behind such slogans as "protection of the
standard" and "control of excessive speculation." Their prolix discussions are generously garnished with statistical data that are incapable of proving anything, and they devote scrupulous attention
to the avoidance of the big questions of theory that constitute the
bulk of their subject. It is undeniable that there are some excellent
works of a descriptive nature to be found among the huge piles of

---

[4] The transaction is conducted by the bank selling part of its consols "for money"
and buying them back immediately "on account." The on-account price is higher,
because it contains a large part of the interest that is almost due; the margin between
the two prices represents the compensation that the bank pays for the loan. The cost
that this entails is made up for by the fact that the bank now gets a larger proportion
of the lending business. See Jaffé, *Das englische Bankwesen*, 2d ed. (Leipzig, 1910), p.
250.
[5] See, for example, Arendt, *Geld—Bank—Börse* (Berlin, 1907), p. 19.

valueless publications on banking policy of recent years, but it is equally undeniable that with a few honorable exceptions their contribution to theory cannot compare with the literary memorials left by the great controversy of the Currency and Banking Schools.

The older English writers on the theory of the banking system made a determined attempt to apprehend the essence of the problem. The question around which their investigations centered is whether there is a limit to the granting of credit by the banks; it is identical with the question of the gratuitous nature of credit; it is most intimately connected with the problem of interest. During the first four decades of the nineteenth century the Bank of England was able to regulate only to a limited degree the amount of credit granted by varying the rate of discount. Because of the legislative restriction of the rate of interest which was not removed until 1837 it could not raise its rate of discount above five percent; and it never allowed it to fall below four percent.[6] At that time the best means it had of adjusting its portfolio to the state of the capital market was the expansion and contraction of its discounting activities. That explains why the old writers on banking theory mostly speak only of increases and diminutions of the note circulation, a mode of expression that was still retained long after the circumstances of the time would have justified reference to rises and falls in the rate of discount. But this does not affect the essence of the matter; in both problems, the only point at issue is whether the banks can grant credit beyond the available amount of capital or not.[7]

Both parties were agreed in answering this question in the negative. This is not surprising. These English writers had an extraordinarily deep understanding of the nature of economic activities; they combined thorough knowledge of the theoretical literature of their time with an insight into economic life that was based upon their own observations. Their strictly logical training permitted them rapidly and easily to separate essentials from nonessentials and guarded them from mistaking the outer husk of truth for the

---

[6] See Gilbart, *The History, Principles and Practice of Banking*, rev. ed. (London, 1904), vol. 1, p. 98.

[7] See Wicksell, *Geldzins und Güterpreise* (Jena, 1898), p. 74. Indeed, even the writers of that period do frequently deal with the problem of a change in the rate of interest; see, for example, Tooke, *An Inquiry into the Currency Principle* (London, 1844), p. 124.

kernel that it encloses. Their views on the nature of interest might diverge considerably—many of them, in fact, had but the vaguest ideas on this important problem, whose significance was not made explicit until a later stage in the development of the science—but they harbored no doubts that the level of the rate of interest as determined by general economic conditions could certainly not be influenced by an increase or diminution in the quantity of money or other media of payment in circulation, apart from considerations of the increase in the stock of goods available for productive purposes that might be brought about by the diminution of the demand for money.

But beyond this the paths of the two schools diverged. Tooke, Fullarton, and their disciples flatly denied that the banks had any power to increase the amount of their note issue beyond the requirements of business. In their view, the media of payment issued by the banks at any particular time adjust themselves to the requirements of business in such a way that with their assistance the payments that have to be made at that time at a given level of prices can all be settled by the use of the existing quantity of money. As soon as the circulation is saturated, no bank, whether it has the right to issue notes or not, can continue to grant credit except from its own capital or from that of its depositors.[8] These views were directly opposed to those of Lord Overstone, Torrens, and others, who started by assuming the possibility of the banks having the power of arbitrarily extending their note issue, and who attempted to determine the way in which the disturbed equilibrium of the market would reestablish itself after such a proceeding.[9] The Currency School propounded a theory, complete in itself, of the value of money and the influence of the granting of credit on the prices of commodities and on the rate of interest. Its doctrines were based upon an untenable fundamental view of the nature of economic value; its version of the quantity theory was a purely mechanical

---

[8] See Tooke, *An Inquiry into the Currency Principle* (London, 1844), pp. 121 ff.; Fullarton, *On the Regulation of Currencies,* 2d ed. (London, 1845), pp. 82 ff.; Wilson, *Capital, Currency and Banking* (London, 1847), pp. 67 ff. Wagner follows the train of thought of these writers in his *Die Geld- und Kredittheorie der Peelschen Bankakte,* pp. 135 ff.
[9] See Torrens, *The Principles and Practical Operation of Sir Robert Peel's Act of 1844 Explained and Defended,* 2d ed. (London, 1857), pp. 57 ff.; Overstone, *Tracts and Other Publications on Metallic and Paper Currency* (London, 1858), *passim.*

one. But the school should certainly not be blamed for this: its members had neither the desire nor the power to rise above the economic doctrine of their time. Within the Currency School's own sphere of investigation, it was extremely successful. This fact deserves grateful recognition from those who, coming after it, build upon the foundations it laid. This needs particular emphasis in the face of the belittlements of its influence which now appear to be part of the stock contents of all writings on banking theory. The shortcomings exhibited by the system of the Currency School have offered an easy target to the critical shafts of their opponents, and doubtless the adherents of the banking principle deserve much credit for making use of this opportunity. If this had been all that they did, if they had merely announced themselves as critics of the currency principle, no objection could be raised against them on that account. The disastrous thing about their influence lay in their claiming to have created a comprehensive theory of the monetary and banking systems and in their imagining that their *obiter dicta* on the subject constituted such a theory. For the classical theory, whose shortcomings should not be extenuated but whose logical acuteness and deep insight into the complications of the problem are undeniable, they substituted a series of assertions that were not always formulated with precision and often contradicted one another. In so doing they paved the way for that method of dealing with monetary problems that was customary in our science before the labors of Menger began to bear their fruit.[10]

The fatal error of Fullarton and his disciples was to have overlooked the fact that even convertible banknotes remain permanently in circulation and can then bring about a glut of fiduciary media the consequences of which resemble those of an increase in the quantity of money in circulation. Even if it is true, as Fullarton insists, that banknotes issued as loans automatically flow back to the bank after the term of the loan has passed, still this does not tell us anything about the question whether the bank is able to maintain them in circulation by repeated prolongation of the loan. The assertion that lies at the heart of the position taken up by the Banking School, namely, that it is impossible to set and permanently maintain in

---

[10] See Wicksell, *op. cit.*, pp. 1 ff.

circulation more notes than will meet the public demand, is untenable; for the demand for credit is not a fixed quantity; it expands as the rate of interest falls, and contracts as the rate of interest rises. But since the rate of interest that is charged for loans made in fiduciary media created expressly for that purpose can be reduced by the banks in the first instance down to the limit set by the marginal utility of the capital used in the banking business, that is, practically to zero, the whole edifice built up by Tooke's school collapses.

It is not our task to give a historical exposition of the controversy between the two famous English schools, however tempting an enterprise that may be. We must content ourselves with reiterating that the works of the much abused Currency School contain far more in the way of useful ideas and fruitful thoughts than is usually assumed, especially in Germany, where as a rule the school is known merely through the writings of its opponents, such as Tooke and Newmarch's *History of Prices,* J. S. Mill's *Principles,* and German versions of the banking principle which are deficient in comprehension of the nature of the problems they deal with.

Before proceeding to investigate the influence of the creation of fiduciary media on the determination of the objective exchange value of money and on the level of the rate of interest, we must devote a few pages to the problem of the relationship between variations in the quantity of money and variations in the rate of interest.

2

The Connection Between Variations in the Ratio Between the Stock of Money and the Demand for Money and Fluctuations in the Rate of Interest

Variations in the ratio between the stock of money and the demand for money must ultimately exert an influence on the rate of interest also; but this occurs in a different way from that popularly imagined. There is no direct connection between the rate of interest and the amount of money held by the individuals who participate in the transactions of the market; there is only an indirect connection operating in a roundabout way through the displacements in the social distribution of income and wealth which occur as a consequence of variations in the objective exchange value of money.

A change in the ratio between the stock of money and the demand for money, and the consequent variations in the exchange ratio between money and other economic goods, can exert a *direct* influence on the rate of interest only when metallic money is employed and variations arise in the quantity of metal available for industrial purposes. The augmentation or diminution of the quantity of metal available for nonmonetary uses signifies an augmentation or diminution of the national subsistence fund and thus it influences the level of the rate of interest. It is hardly necessary to state that the practical significance of this phenomenon is quite trifling. We may, for example, imagine how small in comparison with the daily accumulation of capital was the increase in the subsistence fund caused by the discoveries of gold in South Africa, or even the increase in the subsistence fund that would have occurred if the whole of the newly mined precious metal had been used exclusively for industrial purposes. But however that may be, all that is important for us is to show that this is a phenomenon that is only connected with *nonmonetary* avenues of employment of the metal.

Now as far as the monetary function is concerned, a long discussion is not necessary to show that everything here depends on whether or not the additional quantity of money is employed *uniformly* for procuring production goods and consumption goods. If an additional quantity of money were to increase the demand both for consumption goods and for the corresponding goods of higher orders in exactly the same proportion, or if the withdrawal from circulation of a quantity of money were to diminish these demands in exactly the same proportion, then there could be no question of such variations having a permanent effect on the level of the rate of interest.

We have seen that displacements in the distribution of income and property constitute an essential consequence of fluctuations in the objective exchange value of money. But every variation in the distribution of income and property entails variations in the rate of interest also. It is not a matter of indifference whether a total income of a million kronen is distributed among a thousand persons in such a way that a hundred persons get 2,800 kronen each and nine hundred persons 800 kronen each or in such a way that each of the thousand persons gets 1,000 kronen. Generally speaking, individuals with large incomes make better provision for the future than individuals with small incomes. The smaller an individual's income is, the greater is the premium which he sets on present goods in comparison with future goods. Conversely, increased prosperity means increased provision for the future and higher valuation of future goods.[11]

Variations in the ratio between the stock of money and the demand for money can *permanently* influence the rate of interest only through the displacements in the distribution of property and income that they evoke. If the distribution of income and property is modified in such a way as to increase capacity for saving, then eventually the ratio between the value of present goods and future goods must be modified in favor of the latter. In fact, one of the elements that help to determine the rate of interest, the level of the national subsistence fund, is necessarily altered by the increase of savings. The greater the fund of means of subsistence in a community, the lower the rate of interest.[12] It follows immediately from this that particular variations in the ratio between the stock of money and the demand for money cannot be always accredited with the same effects on the level of the rate of interest; for example, it cannot be asserted that an increase in the stock of money causes the rate of interest to fall and a diminution of the stock of money causes it to rise. Whether the one or the other consequence occurs always depends on whether the new distribution of property is more or less favorable to the accumulation of capital. But this circumstance may be different in each individual case, according to the relative quantitative weight of the particular factors composing it. Without knowledge of the actual data it is impossible to say anything definite about it.

These are the long-run effects on the rate of interest caused by variations in the ratio between the total demand for money and the total stock of it. They come about in consequence of displacements in the distribution of income and property evoked by fluctuations in the objective exchange value of money, and are as permanent as

[11] See Fisher, *The Rate of Interest* (New York, 1907), pp. 94 f.
[12] See Böhm-Bawerk, *Kapital und Kapitalzins*, p. 622.

these fluctuations. But during the period of transition there occur other variations in the rate of interest that are only of a transitory nature. Reference has already been made to the fact that the general economic consequences of variations in the exchange value of money arise in part from the fact that the variations do not appear everywhere simultaneously and uniformly, but start from a particular point and only spread gradually throughout the market. So long as this process is going on, differential profits or differential losses occur, which are in fact the source from which the variations in the distribution of income and property arise. As a rule, it is the entrepreneurs who are first affected. If the objective exchange value of money falls, the entrepreneur gains; for he will still be able to meet part of his expenses of production at prices that do not correspond to the higher price level, while, on the other hand, he will be able to dispose of his product at a price that is in accordance with the variation that has meanwhile occurred. If the objective exchange value of money rises, the entrepreneur loses; for he will only be able to secure for his products a price in accordance with the fall in the price level, while his expenses of production must still be met at the higher prices. In the first case, the incomes of entrepreneurs will rise during the transition period; in the second case, they will fall. This cannot fail to have an influence on the rate of interest. An entrepreneur who is making bigger profits will be prepared if necessary to pay a higher rate of interest, and the competition of other would-be borrowers, who are attracted by the same prospect of increased profits, will make payment of the higher rate necessary. The entrepreneur with whom business is bad will only be able to pay a lower rate of interest and the pressure of competition will oblige lenders to be content with the lower rate. Thus a falling value of money goes hand in hand with a rising rate of interest, and a rising value of money with a falling rate of interest. This lasts as long as the movement of the objective exchange value of money continues. When this ceases, then the rate of interest is reestablished at the level dictated by the general economic situation.[13]

Thus, variations in the rate of interest do not occur as immediate consequences of variations in the ratio between the demand for

---

[13] See Fisher and Brown, *The Purchasing Power of Money* (New York, 1911), pp. 58 ff.

money and the stock of it; they are only produced by the displacements in the social distribution of property that accompany the fluctuations in the objective exchange value of money that the variations in the ratio between the stock of money and the demand for it evoke. Moreover, the oft-repeated question of the precise connection between variations in the objective exchange value of money and variations in the rate of interest betrays an unfortunate confusion of ideas. The variations in the relative valuations of present goods and future goods are not different phenomena from the variations in the objective exchange value of money. Both are part of a single transformation of existing economic conditions, determined in the last resort by the same factors. In now devoting to it the consideration it deserves, we atone for a negligence and fill a gap in the argument contained in our second part.

3

The Connection Between the Equilibrium Rate
and the Money Rate of Interest

An increase in the stock of money in the broader sense caused by an issue of fiduciary media means a displacement of the social distribution of property in favor of the issuer. If the fiduciary media are issued by the banks, then this displacement is particularly favorable to the accumulation of capital, for in such a case the issuing body employs the additional wealth that it receives solely for productive purposes, whether directly by initiating and carrying through a process of production or indirectly by lending to producers. Thus, as a rule, the fall in the rate of interest in the loan market, which occurs as the most immediate consequence of the increase in the supply of present goods that is due to an issue of fiduciary media, must be in part permanent; that is, it will not be wiped out by the reaction that is afterward caused by the diminution of the property of other persons. There is a high degree of probability that extensive issues of fiduciary media by the banks represent a strong impulse toward the accumulation of capital and have consequently contributed to the fall in the rate of interest.

One thing must be clearly stated at this point: there is no direct

arithmetical relationship between an increase or decrease in the issue of fiduciary media on the one hand and the reduction or increase
in the rate of interest which this indirectly brings about through its
effects on the social distribution of property on the other hand. This
would follow merely from the circumstance that there is no direct
relationship between the redistribution of property and the differences in the way in which the existing stock of goods in the community is employed. The redistribution of property causes
individual economic agents to take different decisions from those
they would otherwise have taken. They deal with the goods at their
disposal in a different way; they allocate them differently between
present (consumptive) employment and future (productive) employment. This may give rise to an alteration in the size of the national subsistence fund if the alterations in the uses to which the
goods are put by the individual economic agents do not offset one
another but leave a surplus in the one direction or the other. This
alteration in the size of the national subsistence fund is the most
immediate cause of the variation which occurs in the rate of interest;
and since, as has been shown, it is by no means unequivocally determined by the extent and direction of the fluctuation in the stock
of money in the broader sense, but depends upon the whole social
distributive structure, no direct relationship can be established between the variations in the stock of money in the broader sense and
the variations in the rate of interest. In fact it is obvious that however
great the increase in the stock of money in the broader sense might
be, whether it occurred by way of an increase in fiduciary media or
by way of an increase in the stock of money in the narrower sense,
the rate of interest could never be reduced to zero. That could take
place only if the displacements that occurred increased the national
subsistence fund to such an extent that all possibilities of increasing
production by engaging in more productive "roundabout" methods
of production were exhausted. This would mean that in all branches
of production the time that elapsed between the commencement of
production and the enjoyment of the product was not taken into
consideration, and production was carried so far that the prices of
the products were only just sufficient to pay an equal return to the
primary factors in each employment. In particular, as far as very
durable goods are concerned, this would mean that their quantity

and durability would be tremendously increased, until the prices of their services fell so low that they would only just provide for the amortization of the investments. It is impossible to conceive of the extent to which, for example, the supply of houses would have to be increased for their annual rental value to fall to a sum which would only just give a total return equal to their original cost by the time when their lengthened lives came to an end. Where the lifetime of a good can be almost indefinitely increased under conditions of decreasing cost, the result is that its services will become practically free goods. It seems hardly likely that a rigid proof could be given to show that the increase in the size of the national subsistence fund that may follow a redistribution of property could never go so far as this. But we have sufficient capacity for estimating the quantities involved without this unobtainable precise proof. As regards the displacements in the distribution of property that are evoked by an increase in the circulation of fiduciary media, it seems that we might go still further and safely assert that it can in no circumstances be very considerable. Although we cannot prove this in any way, whether deductively or inductively, it nevertheless appears a reasonable assertion to make. And we may content ourselves with that; for we do not intend to base any kind of further argument on such an undemonstrable proposition.

The question to which we now turn is the following: It is indisputable that the banks are able to reduce the rate of interest on the credit they grant down to any level above their working expenses (for example, the cost of manufacturing the notes, the salaries of their staffs, etc.). If they do this, the force of competition obliges other lenders to follow their example. Accordingly, it would be entirely within the power of the banks to reduce the rate of interest down to this limit, provided that in so doing they did not set other forces in motion which would automatically reestablish the rate of interest at the level determined by the circumstances of the capital market, that is, the market in which present goods and future goods are exchanged for one another. The problem that is before us is usually referred to by the catch-phrase "gratuitous nature of credit." It is the chief problem in the theory of banking.

It is a problem whose great theoretical and practical importance has often been overlooked. The chief responsibility for this belongs to the not altogether fortunate manner in which it has been formulated. At the present time, the problem of the gratuitous nature of bank credit does not appear to be a very practical issue, and since the inclination toward questions of pure theory is hardly prominent among the economists of our day, it is a problem that has been much neglected. Yet, if the way in which the problem is stated is modified only a little the unjustifiability of neglecting it becomes obvious, even from the point of view of those who are only concerned with the needs of everyday life. A new issue of fiduciary media, as we have seen, indirectly gives rise to a variation in the rate of interest by causing displacements in the social distribution of income and property. But the new fiduciary media coming on to the loan market have also a *direct* effect on the rate of interest. They are an additional supply of present goods and consequently they tend to cause the rate of interest to fall. The connection between these two effects on the rate of interest is not obvious. Is there a force that brings both into harmony or not? It is probable in the highest degree that the increase in the supply of fiduciary media in the market in which present goods are exchanged for future goods at first exerts a stronger influence than the displacement of the social distribution which occurs as a consequence of it. Does the matter remain at that stage? Is the immediate reduction of interest which indubitably follows the increase of fiduciary media definitive or not?

Until now, the treatment that this problem has met with at the hands of economists has fallen a long way short of its importance. Its real nature has for the most part been misunderstood; and where the problem was incorrectly stated to start with, it was natural that the subsequent attempts at its solution should not have been successful. But even the few theories in which the essence of the problem has been correctly apprehended have fallen into error in their efforts to solve it.

To one group of writers, the problem appeared to offer little difficulty. From the circumstance that it is possible for the banks to reduce the rate of interest in their bank-credit business down to the limit set by their working costs, these writers thought it permissible to deduce that credit can be granted gratuitously or, more correctly, almost gratuitously. In drawing this conclusion, their doctrine implicitly denies the existence of interest. It regards interest as compensation for the temporary relinquishing of money in the broader sense—a view, indeed, of insurpassable naivety. Scientific critics have been perfectly justified in treating it with contempt; it is scarcely worth even cursory mention. But it is impossible to refrain from pointing out that these very views on the nature of interest hold an important place in popular opinion, and that they are continually being propounded afresh and recommended as a basis for measures of banking policy.[14]

No less untenable is the attitude of orthodox scientific opinion toward the problem. Orthodox scientific opinion, following in this the example set by the adherents of the banking principle, is content to question the problem's existence. In fact, it cannot do otherwise. If the opinion is held that the quantity of fiduciary media in circulation can never exceed the demand—in the sense defined above—the conclusion necessarily follows that the banks have not the ability to grant credit gratuitously. Of course, they might not exact any reimbursement or compensation beyond the prime costs of the loans granted by them. But doing this would not fundamentally change the matter, except that the profits from the issue of fiduciary media that the banks would otherwise receive themselves would now go to the benefit of the borrowers. And since, according to this view, it does not lie in the power of the banks arbitrarily to increase the quantity of fiduciary media in circulation, the limitation of the issue of these would leave only small scope for the influence of their discount policy on the general rate of interest. It follows that only insignificant differences could arise between the rate of interest charged by credit-issuing banks and that determined by the general economic situation for other credit transactions.

We have already had an opportunity of finding out where the error in this argument lies. The quantity of fiduciary media flowing from the banks into circulation is admittedly limited by the number and extent of the requests for discounting that the banks receive. But the number and extent of these requests are not independent of the credit policy of the banks; by reducing the rate of interest

---

[14] See, for instance, the most recent literature on the German banking reform; for example, the above-cited work by Schmidt (see p. 379 n. 3). An historical study would have to examine the extent to which Law, Cieszkowski, Proudhon, Macleod, and others, are to be regarded as inventors and adherents of this doctrine.

charged on loans, it is possible for the banks indefinitely to increase the public demand for credit. And since the banks—as even the most orthodox disciples of Tooke and Fullarton cannot deny—can meet all these demands for credit, they can extend their issue of fiduciary media arbitrarily. For obvious reasons an individual bank is not in a position to do this so long as its competitors act otherwise; but there seems to be no reason why all the credit-issuing banks in an isolated community, or in the whole world, taken together could not do this by uniform procedure. If we imagine an isolated community in which there is only a single credit-issuing bank in business, and if we further assume (what indeed is obvious) that the fiduciary media issued by it enjoy general confidence and are freely employed in business as money substitutes, then the weakness of the assertions of the orthodox theory of banking is most clear. In such a situation there are no other limits to the bank's issue of fiduciary media than those which it sets itself.

But even the Currency School has not treated the problem in a satisfactory manner. It would appear—exhaustive historical investigation might perhaps lead to another conclusion—that the Currency School was merely concerned to examine the consequences of an inflation of fiduciary media in the case of the coexistence of several independent groups of banks in the world, starting from the assumption that these groups of banks did not all follow a uniform and parallel credit policy. The case of a general increase of fiduciary media, which for the first half of the nineteenth century had scarcely any immediate practical importance, was not included within the scope of its investigations. Thus it did not even have occasion to consider the most important aspect of the problem. What is necessary for clearing up this important problem still remains to be done; for even Wicksell's most noteworthy attempt cannot be said to have achieved its object. But at least it has the merit of having stated the problem clearly.

Wicksell distinguishes between the natural rate of interest (*natürliche Kapitalzins*), or the rate of interest that would be determined by supply and demand if actual capital goods were lent without the mediation of money, and the money rate of interest (*Geldzins*), or the rate of interest that is demanded and paid for loans in money or money substitutes. The money rate of interest and the natural

rate of interest need not necessarily coincide, since it is possible for
the banks to extend the amount of their issues of fiduciary media
as they wish and thus to exert a pressure on the money rate of
interest that might bring it down to the minimum set by their costs.
Nevertheless, it is certain that the money rate of interest must
sooner or later come to the level of the natural rate of interest, and
the problem is to say in what way this ultimate coincidence is
brought about.[15] Up to this point Wicksell commands assent; but
his further argument provokes contradiction.

According to Wicksell, at every time and under all possible economic conditions there is a level of the average money rate of interest at which the general level of commodity prices no longer has
any tendency to move either upward or downward. He calls it the
normal rate of interest; its level is determined by the prevailing
natural rate of interest, although, for certain reasons which do not
concern our present problem, the two rates need not coincide exactly. When, he says, from any cause whatever, the average rate of
interest is below this normal rate, by any amount, however small,
and remains at this level, a progressive and eventually enormous
rise of prices must occur "which would naturally cause the banks
sooner or later to raise their rates of interest."[16] Now, so far as the
rise of prices is concerned, this may be provisionally conceded. But
it still remains inconceivable why a general rise in commodity prices
should induce the banks to raise their rates of interest. It is clear
that there may be a motive for this in the regulations, whether
legislative or established by mercantile custom, that limit the circulation of fiduciary media; or necessary consideration of the procedure of other banks might have the same sort of effect. But if we
start with the assumption, as Wicksell does, that only fiduciary
media are in circulation and that the quantity of them is not legis-
latively restricted, so that the banks are entirely free to extend their
issues of them, then it is impossible to see why rising prices and an
increasing demand for loans should induce them to raise the rate
of interest they charge for loans. Even Wicksell can think of no other
reason for this than that since the requirements of business for gold

---

[15] See Wicksell, *op. cit.*, pp. v ff.
[16] See *ibid.*, pp. v ff., III; also "The Influence of the Rate of Interest on Prices,"
Economic Journal 18 (1907): 213 ff.

coins and banknotes becomes greater as the price level rises, the banks do not receive back the whole of the sums they have lent, part of them remaining in the hands of the public; and that the bank reserves are consequently depleted while the total liabilities of the banks increase; and that this must naturally induce them to raise their rate of interest.[17] But in this argument Wicksell contradicts the assumption that he takes as the starting point of his investigation. Consideration of the level of its cash reserves and their relation to the liabilities arising from the issue of fiduciary media cannot concern the hypothetical bank that he describes. He seems suddenly to have forgotten his original assumption of a circulation consisting exclusively of fiduciary media, on which assumption, at first, he rightly laid great weight.

Wicksell incidentally makes cursory mention of a second limit to the circulation of fiduciary media. He thinks that the banks that charge a lower rate of interest than that which corresponds to the average level of the natural rate of interest encounter a limit which is set by the employment of the precious metals for industrial purposes. If the purchasing power of money is too low it discourages the production of gold but increases, *ceteris paribus*, the industrial consumption of gold, and the deficiency which would arise as soon as consumption began to exceed production has to be made up from the bank reserves.[18] This is perfectly true when metallic money is employed; an increase of fiduciary media must be stopped before the reduction of the objective exchange value of money that it brings about absorbs the value arising from the monetary employment of the metal. As soon as the objective exchange value of money had sunk below the value of the metal in industrial uses, every further loss in value (which, of course, would also affect the purchasing power of the money substitutes in the same degree), would send all those who needed the metal for industrial purposes to the counters of the banks as their cheapest source of supply. The banks would not be able to extend their issue any further since it would be possible for their customers to make a profit simply by the ex-

---

[17] See Wicksell, "The Influence of the Rate of Interest," p. 215.
[18] See Wicksell, *Geldzins und Güterpreise*, pp. 104 f.

change of fiduciary media for money; all fiduciary media issued beyond the given limit would return immediately to the banks.[19]

But demonstrating this does not bring us a step nearer to the solution of our problem. The mechanism, by which a further issue of fiduciary media is restricted as soon as the falling objective exchange value of the material from which the money is made has reached the level set by its industrial employment, is, of course, effective only in the case of commodity money; in the case of credit money, it is effective only when the embodied claim refers to commodity money. And it is never effective in the case of fiat money. Of greater importance is a second factor: this limit is a distant one, so that even when it is eventually effective it still leaves considerable scope for an increase in the issue of fiduciary media. But it by no means follows from this that it remains possible for the banks to reduce the rate of interest on loans as much as they like within these wide limits; as the following argument will attempt to prove.

4

The Influence of the Interest Policy of the Credit-issuing Banks on Production

Assuming uniformity of procedure, the credit-issuing banks are able to extend their issues indefinitely. It is within their power to stimulate the demand for capital by reducing the rate of interest on loans, and, except for the limits mentioned above, to go so far in this as the cost of granting the loans permits. In doing this they force their competitors in the loan market, that is all those who do not lend fiduciary media which they have created themselves, to make a corresponding reduction in the rate of interest also. Thus the rate of interest on loans may at first be reduced by the credit-issuing banks almost to zero. This, of course, is true only under the assumption that the fiduciary media enjoy the confidence of the public so that if any requests are made to the banks for liquidation of the promise of prompt cash redemption which constitutes the nature of fiduciary media, it is not because the holders have any doubts as to their soundness. Assuming this, the only possible rea-

---

[19] See Walras, *Études d'économie politique appliquée* (Lausanne, 1898), pp. 345 f.

son for the withdrawal of deposits or the presentation of notes for redemption is the existence of a demand for money for making payments to persons who do not belong to the circle of customers of the individual banks. The banks need not necessarily meet such demands by paying out money; the fiduciary media of those banks among whose customers are those persons to whom the banks' own customers wish to make payments are equally serviceable in this case. Thus there ceases to be any necessity for the banks to hold a redemption fund consisting of money; its place may be taken by a reserve fund consisting of the fiduciary media of other banks. If we imagine the whole credit system of the world concentrated in a single bank, it will follow that there is no longer any presentation of notes or withdrawal of deposits; in fact, the whole demand for money in the narrower sense may disappear. These suppositions are not at all arbitrary. It has already been shown that the circulation of fiduciary media is possible only on the assumption that the issuing bodies enjoy the full confidence of the public, since even the dawning of mistrust would immediately lead to a collapse of the house of cards that comprises the credit circulation. We know, furthermore, that all credit-issuing banks endeavor to extend their curculation of fiduciary media as much as possible, and that the only obstacles in their way nowadays are legal prescriptions and business customs concerning the covering of notes and deposits, not any resistance on the part of the public. If there were no artificial restriction of the credit system at all, and if the individual credit-issuing banks could agree to parallel procedure, then the complete cessation of the use of money would only be a question of time. It is, therefore, entirely justifiable to base our discussion on the above assumption.

Now, if this assumption holds good, and if we disregard the limit that has already been mentioned as applying to the case of metallic money, then there is no longer any limit, practically speaking, to the issue of fiduciary media; the rate of interest on loans and the level of the objective exchange value of money is then limited only by the banks' running costs—a minimum, incidentally, which is extraordinarily low. By making easier the conditions on which they will grant credit, the banks can extend their issue of fiduciary media almost indefinitely. Their doing so must be accompanied by a fall in the objective exchange value of money. The course taken by the depreciation that is a consequence of the issue of fiduciary media by the banks may diverge in some degree from that which it takes in the case of an increase of the stock of money in the narrower sense, or from that which it takes when the fiduciary media are issued otherwise than by banks; but the essence of the process remains the same. For it is a matter of indifference whether the diminution in the objective exchange value of money begins with the mine owners, with the government which issues fiat money, credit money, or token coins, or with the undertakings that have the newly issued fiduciary media placed at their disposal by way of loans.

Painful consideration of the question whether fiduciary media really could be indefinitely augmented without awakening the mistrust of the public would be not only supererogatory, but otiose. For the problems of theory that we are dealing with, it is a question that has scarcely any significance. We are not conducting our investigation in order to show that the objective exchange value of money and the rate of interest on loans could be reduced almost to zero; but in order to disclose the consequences that arise from the divergence (which we have shown to be possible) between the money rate and the natural rate of interest. For this reason, it is also a matter of indifference to us, as we have just shown, that under a system of commodity money the fiduciary media cannot continue to be augmented after the objective exchange value of the money is reduced to the level determined by the industrial employment of the metal.

If it is possible for the credit-issuing banks to reduce the rate of interest on loans below the rate determined at the time by the whole economic situation (Wicksell's *natürliche Kapitalzins* or natural rate of interest), then the question arises of the particular consequences of a situation of this kind. Does the matter rest there, or is some force automatically set in motion which eliminates this divergence between the two rates of interest? It is a striking thing that this problem, which even at a first glance cannot fail to appear extremely interesting, and which moreover under more detailed examination proves to be one of the greatest importance for comprehension of many of the processes of modern economic life, has until now hardly been dealt with seriously at all.

We shall not say anything further here of the effects of an increased issue of fiduciary media on the determination of the objective exchange value of money; they have already been dealt with exhaustively. Our task now is merely to discover the general economic consequences of any conceivable divergence between the natural and money rates of interest, given uniform procedure on the part of the credit-issuing banks. We obviously need only consider the case in which the banks reduce the rate of interest below the natural rate. The opposite case, in which the rate of interest charged by the banks is raised above the natural rate, need not be considered; if the banks acted in this way, they would simply withdraw from the competition of the loan market, without occasioning any other noteworthy consequences.

The level of the natural rate of interest is limited by the productivity of that lengthening of the period of production which is just justifiable economically and of that additional lengthening of the period of production which is just not justifiable; for the interest on the unit of capital upon whose aid the lengthening depends must always amount to less than the marginal return of the justifiable lengthening and to more than the marginal return of the unjustifiable lengthening. The period of production which is thus defined must be of such a length that exactly the whole available subsistence fund is necessary on the one hand and sufficient on the other for paying the wages of the laborers throughout the duration of the productive process. For if it were shorter, all the workers could no longer be provided for throughout its whole course, and the consequence would be an urgent offer of the unemployment economic factors which could not fail to bring about a transformation of the existing arrangement.[20] Now if the rate of interest on loans is artificially reduced below the natural rate as established by the free play of the forces operating in the market, then entrepreneurs are enabled and obliged to enter upon longer processes of production. It is true that longer roundabout processes of production may yield an *absolutely* greater return than shorter processes; but the return from them is *relatively* smaller, since although continual lengthening of the capitalistic process of production does lead to continually in-

[20] See Böhm-Bawerk, *op. cit.*, pp. 611 ff.

creasing returns, after a certain point is reached the increments themselves are of decreasing amount.[21] Thus it is possible to enter upon a longer roundabout process of production only if this smaller additional productivity will still pay the entrepreneur. So long as the rate of interest on loans coincides with the natural rate, it will not pay him; to enter upon a longer period of production would involve a loss. On the other hand, a reduction of the rate of interest on loans must necessarily lead to a lengthening of the average period of production. It is true that fresh capital can be employed in production only if *new* roundabout processes are started. But every new roundabout process of production that is started must be more roundabout than those already started; new roundabout processes that are shorter than those already started are not available, for capital is of course always invested in the shortest available roundabout processes of production, because they yield the greatest returns. It is only when all the short roundabout processes of production have been appropriated that capital is employed in the longer ones.

A lengthening of the period of production is only practicable, however, either when the means of subsistence have increased sufficiently to support the laborers and entrepreneurs during the longer period or when the wants of producers have decreased sufficiently to enable them to make the same means of subsistence do for the longer period. Now it is true that an increase of fiduciary media brings about a redistribution of wealth in the course of its effects on the objective exchange value of money which may well lead to increased saving and a reduction of the standard of living. A depreciation of money, when metallic money is employed, may also lead directly to an increase in the stock of goods in that it entails a diversion of some metal from monetary to industrial uses. So far as these factors enter into consideration, an increase of fiduciary media does cause a diminution of even the natural rate of interest, as we could show if it were necessary. But the case that we have to investigate is a different one. We are not concerned with a reduction in the natural rate of interest brought about by an increase in the issue of fiduciary media, but with a reduction *below* this rate in the money rate charged by the banks, inaugurated by the credit-issuing banks

---

[21] *Ibid.*, pp. 151 ff.

and necessarily followed by the rest of the loan market. The power of the banks to do such a thing has already been demonstrated.

The situation is as follows: despite the fact that there has been no increase of intermediate products and there is no possibility of lengthening the average period of production, a rate of interest is established in the loan market which corresponds to a longer period of production; and so, although it is in the last resort inadmissible and impracticable, a lengthening of the period of production promises for the time to be profitable. But there cannot be the slightest doubt as to where this will lead. A time must necessarily come when the means of subsistence available for consumption are all used up although the capital goods employed in production have not yet been transformed into consumption goods. This time must come all the more quickly inasmuch as the fall in the rate of interest weakens the motive for saving and so slows up the rate of accumulation of capital. The means of subsistence will prove insufficient to maintain the laborers during the whole period of the process of production that has been entered upon. Since production and consumption are continuous, so that every day new processes of production are started upon and others completed, this situation does not imperil human existence by suddenly manifesting itself as a complete lack of consumption goods; it is merely expressed in a reduction of the quantity of goods available for consumption and a consequent restriction of consumption. The market prices of consumption goods rise and those of production goods fall.

This is one of the ways in which the equilibrium of the loan market is reestablished after it has been disturbed by the intervention of the banks. The increased productive activity that sets in when the banks start the policy of granting loans at less than the natural rate of interest at first causes the prices of production goods to rise while the prices of consumption goods, although they rise also, do so only in a moderate degree, namely, only insofar as they are raised by the rise in wages. Thus the tendency toward a fall in the rate of interest on loans that originates in the policy of the banks is at first strengthened. But soon a countermovement sets in: the prices of consumption goods rise, those of production goods fall. That is, the rate of interest on loans rises again, it again approaches the natural rate.

This countermovement is now strengthened by the fact that the increase of the stock of money in the broader sense that is involved in the increase in the quantity of fiduciary media reduces the objective exchange value of money. Now, as has been shown, so long as this depreciation of money is going on, the rate of interest on loans must rise above the level that would be demanded and paid if the objective exchange value of money remained unaltered.[22]

At first the banks may try to oppose these two tendencies that counteract their interest policy by continually reducing the rate of interest charged for loans and forcing fresh quantities of fiduciary media into circulation. But the more they thus increase the stock of money in the broader sense, the more quickly does the value of money fall, and the stronger is its countereffect on the rate of interest. However much the banks may endeavor to extend their credit circulation, they cannot stop the rise in the rate of interest. Even if they were prepared to go on increasing the quantity of fiduciary media until further increase was no longer possible (whether because the money in use was metallic money and the limit had been reached below which the purchasing power of the money-and-credit unit could not sink without the banks being forced to suspend cash redemption, or whether because the reduction of the interest charged on loans had reached the limit set by the running costs of the banks), they would still be unable to secure the intended result. For such an avalanche of fiduciary media, when its cessation cannot be foreseen, must lead to a fall in the objective exchange value of the money-and-credit unit to the paniclike course of which there can be no bounds.[23] Then the rate of interest on loans must also rise in a similar degree and fashion.

Thus the banks will ultimately be forced to cease their endeavors to underbid the natural rate of interest. That ratio between the prices of goods of the first order and of goods of higher orders which is determined by the state of the capital market and has been disturbed merely by the intervention of the banks will be approximately re-

---

[22] The fact that the two movements occur in opposite directions, so that they cancel one another, had been emphasized by Mill (*Principles*, pp. 391 ff.) in order to show that the increase in the rate of interest caused by inflation would be counteracted by the circumstance that the additional quantity of notes, if issued by the banks (and the additional quantity of gold so far as it was used productively), have a reducing effect on the bank rate of interest.

[23] See p. 259-60 above.

established, and the only remaining trace of the disturbance will be a general increase in the objective exchange value of money due to factors emanating from the monetary side. A precise reestablishment of the old price ratios between production goods and consumption goods is not possible, on the one hand because the intervention of the banks has brought about a redistribution of property, and on the other hand because the automatic recovery of the loan market involves certain of the phenomena of a crisis, which are signs of the loss of some of the capital invested in the excessively lengthened roundabout processes of production. It is not practicable to transfer all the production goods from those uses that have proved unprofitable to other avenues of employment; a part of them cannot be withdrawn and must therefore either be left entirely unused or at least be used less economically. In either case there is a loss of value. Let us, for example, suppose that an artificial extension of bank credit is responsible for the establishment of an enterprise which only yields a net profit of four percent. So long as the rate of interest on loans was four and one-half percent, the establishment of such a business could not be thought of; we may suppose that it has been made possible by a fall to a rate of three and one-half percent which has followed an extension of the issue of fiduciary media. Now let us assume the reaction to begin, in the way described above. The rate of interest on loans rises to four and one-half percent again. It will no longer be profitable to conduct this enterprise. Whatever may now occur, whether the business is stopped entirely or whether it is carried on after the entrepreneur has decided to make do with the smaller profits, in either case—not merely from the individual point of view, but also from that of the community—there has been a loss of value. Economic goods which could have satisfied more important wants have been employed for the satisfaction of less important; only insofar as the mistake that has been made can be rectified by diversion into another channel can loss be prevented.

5

Credit and Economic Crises

Our theory of banking, like that of the currency principle, leads ultimately to a theory of business cycles. It is true that the Currency

School did not inquire thoroughly into even this problem. It did not ask what consequences follow from the unrestricted extension of credit on the part of the credit-issuing banks; it did not even inquire whether it was possible for them permanently to depress the natural rate of interest. It set itself more modest aims and was content to ask what would happen if the banks in one country extended the issue of fiduciary media more than those of other countries. Thus it arrived at its doctrine of the "external drain" and at its explanation of the English crises that had occurred up to the middle of the nineteenth century.

If our doctrine of crises is to be applied to more recent history, then it must be observed that the banks have never gone as far as they might in extending credit and expanding the issue of fiduciary media. They have always left off long before reaching this limit, whether because of growing uneasiness on their own part and on the part of all those who had not forgotten the earlier crises, or whether because they had to defer to legislative regulations concerning the maximum circulation of fiduciary media. And so the crises broke out before they need have broken out. It is only in this sense that we can interpret the statement that it is apparently true after all to say that restriction of loans is the cause of economic crises, or at least their immediate impulse; that if the banks would only go on reducing the rate of interest on loans they could continue to postpone the collapse of the market. If the stress is laid upon the word *postpone,* then this line of argument can be assented to without more ado. Certainly, the banks would be able to postpone the collapse; but nevertheless, as has been shown, the moment must eventually come when no further extension of the circulation of fiduciary media is possible. Then the catastrophe occurs, and its consequences are the worse and the reaction against the bull tendency of the market the stronger, the longer the period during which the rate of interest on loans has been below the natural rate of interest and the greater the extent to which roundabout processes of production that are not justified by the state of the capital market have been adopted

CHAPTER 20

Problems of Credit Policy

(I)
Prefatory Remark

1

The Conflict of Credit Policies

Since the time of the Currency School, the policy adopted by the governments of Europe and America with regard to the issue of fiduciary media has been guided, on the whole, by the idea that it is necessary to impose some sort of restriction upon the banks in order to prevent them from extending the issue of fiduciary media in such a way as to cause a rise of prices that eventually culminates in an economic crisis. But the course of this policy has been continually broken by contrary aims. Endeavors have been made by means of credit policy to keep the rate of interest low; "cheap money" (that is, low interest) and "reasonable" (that is, high) prices have been aimed at. Since the beginning of the twentieth century these endeavors have noticeably gained in strength; during the war and for some time after it they were the prevailing aims.

The strange vicissitudes of credit policy cannot be described except by passing in review the actual tasks that it has had to solve and will have to solve in the future. Although the problems themselves may always be the same, the form they assume changes.

And, for the very reason that our task is to strip them of their disguises, we must first study them in their contemporary garb. In what follows, separate consideration will be given to such problems, first, as they exhibited themselves before the war, and then, as they have exhibited themselves in the period immediately after the war.[1]

(II)

Problems of Credit Policy Before the War[2]

2

Peel's Act

Peel's Bank Act, and the ideas on which it was based, still sets the standard by which credit policy is ultimately governed nowadays; even those countries that do not follow the example of the English bank legislation, or do not follow it so faithfully as others, have yet not been able to withstand its influence altogether. Here we are confronted with a strange phenomenon. While the economic literature of all countries was directing the most violent and passionate attacks against the system of having a fixed quota of the note issue not backed by metal; while people were untiring in calling Peel's Act the unfortunate legislative product of a mistaken theory; while the currency principle continued to be represented as a system of erroneous hypotheses that had long been confuted; yet one legislature after another took steps to limit the issue of uncovered banknotes. And, remarkably enough, this procedure on the part of governments evoked but little censure, if any at all, from those whose views on banking theory should logically have led them most severely to condemn it. To start from the banking principle, which denies the possibility of an overissue of banknotes and regards "elasticity" as their essential characteristic, is necessarily to arrive at the conclusion that any limitation of the circulation of notes, whether they are backed by money or not, must prove injurious, since it prevents the exercise of the chief function of the note issue, the contrivance of an adjustment between the stock of money and the demand for money with-

---

[1] [Some of the problems that have arisen since are referred to on pp. 23–31. H.E.B.]
[2] [See editor's Introduction, pp. 21–22, above. H.E.B.]

out changing the objective exchange value of money. It might easily have appeared desirable to Tooke's followers that provision should be made for backing that part of the note circulation that was not backed by metal; but logically they should have condemned the prescription that a certain proportion was to be maintained between the stock of metal and the note circulation. There is an irreconcilable contradiction, however, between the theoretical arguments of these writers and the practical conclusions that they draw from them. Scarcely any writer that need be taken seriously ventures to put forward proposals that might fundamentally disturb the various systems for restricting the unbacked note issue; not a single one definitely demands their complete abolition. Nothing could show the inherent uncertainty and lack of independence of modern banking theory better than this inconsistency. That the note issue must somehow be restricted in order to guard against serious evils is still accepted today as the essence of government wisdom in matters of banking policy, and the science which claims to have produced proof to the contrary always ends up by deferring to this dogma, which nobody is nowadays able to prove and everybody thinks himself able to refute. The conversatism of the English hinders them from meddling with a law which stands as a monument to an intellectual contest which went on for many years and in which the best men of the time participated; and the example of the world's chief bank influences all the other banks. The conclusions of two generations of economists have not been able to shake the opinions which are supposed to be the result of practical banking experience.

Many serious errors are involved in the currency principle. The most serious lies in its failure to recognize the essential similarity of banknotes and bank deposits.[3] Its opponents have skillfully discovered these weak spots in the system and directed their sharpest attacks accordingly.[4] But the doctrine of the Currency School does not stand or fall by its views on the nature of checks and deposits. It is enough to correct it on this one point—to take its propositions concerning the issue of notes and apply them also to the opening of deposit accounts—to silence the censures of those who adhere

[3] See Torrens, *The Principles and Practical Operation of Sir Robert Peel's Act of 1844 Explained and Defended*, 2d ed. (London, 1857), pp. 8 ff.
[4] See Tooke, *An Inquiry into the Currency Principle* (London, 1844), pp. 23 ff.

to the banking principle. That its mistake on this point is of small significance in comparison with that made by the banking principle can hardly need further discussion. And in any case, it does not seem an inexcusable mistake to have made if we take into account the relatively backward development of even the English deposit system at the time when the foundations of the classical theory of banking were being laid, and if we further consider the ease with which the legal differences between payment by note and payment by check might give rise to error.

As far as Peel's Act was concerned, however, this very shortcoming of the theory that had created it turned out to be an advantage; it caused the incorporation in it of the safety valve without which it would not have been able to cope with the subsequent increase in the requirements of business. The fundamental mistake of Peel's system, which it shares with all other systems which proceed by restricting the note circulation, lies in its failure to foresee the extension of the quota of notes not backed by metal that went with the increase in the demand for money in the broader sense. As far as the past was concerned, the act sanctioned the creation of a certain amount of fiduciary media and the influence that this had on the determination of the objective exchange value of money; it did not do anything to counteract the effects of this issue of fiduciary media. But at the same time, in order to guard the capital market from shocks, it removed all future possibility of partly or wholly satisfying the increasing demand for money by the issuing of fiduciary media and so of mitigating or entirely preventing a rise in the objective exchange value of money. This amounts to the same thing as suppressing the creation of fiduciary media altogether and so renouncing all the attendant advantages for the stabilization of the objective exchange value of money. It is an heroic remedy with a vengeance, in essence hardly differing at all from the proposals of the downright opponents of all fiduciary media.

Nevertheless, something was overlooked in the calculations of the currency theorists. They did not realize that unbacked deposits were substantially the same as unbacked notes, and so they omitted to legislate for them in the same way as for the notes. So far as the development of fiduciary media depended on the issue of notes, Peel's Act completely restricted it; so far as it depended on the opening of deposit accounts, it was not interfered with at all. This forced the technique of the English banking system in a direction in which it had already been urged in some degree by the circumstance that the right of note issue in London and its environs was an exclusive privilege of the Bank of England. The deposit system developed at the expense of the note system. From the point of view of the community this was a matter of indifference because notes and deposits both fulfill the same functions. Thus Peel's Act did not achieve its aim, or at least not in the degree and manner that its authors had intended; fiduciary media, suppressed as banknotes, developed in the form of deposits.

It is true that German writers on banking held that it was possible to discover a fundamental difference between notes and deposits. But they did not succeed in demonstrating their contention; in fact they did not really attempt to do so. Nowhere is the inherent weakness of German banking theory more obvious than in connection with this particular question of the note *versus* the check, which for years has been the central issue of all discussion. Anybody who, like them, had learned from the English Banking School that there is no fundamental difference between notes and checks, and was in the constant habit of stressing this,[5] should at least be prepared to supply a detailed proof in support of an assertion that the banknote system represents "an earlier and lower stage of development of the credit economy" than the deposit bank and the check, with the connected system of the account current, book credit, and clearinghouse.[6] Certainly reference to England and the United States cannot be accepted as proof of the correctness of this assertion, least of all in the mouth of a decided opponent of Peel's Act and of the restriction of the note issue in general; for it is undeniable that the great importance of the deposit system and the decreasing relative importance of the banknote in Anglo-Saxon countries are the result of that act. The consequence is that the German literature on banking theory is full of almost unbelievable contradictions.[7]

The repression of the banknote, as it has occurred in England and

[5] See Wagner, "Banknote," in Rentzsch, *Handwörterbuch der Volkswirtschaftslehre* (Leipzig, 1866), p. 91.
[6] See Wagner, "Kredit," *ibid.*, p. 201.
[7] See Schumacher's criticism of this contradiction, *Weltwirtschaftliche Studien* (Leipzig, 1911), pp. 62 ff.

in the United States—in different ways and for different reasons, but as a result of the same fundamental ideas—and the corresponding growth in importance of the deposit, and the additional circumstance that the organization of the deposit banks has not attained that soundness that would have enabled it to retain the public confidence during dangerous crises, have led to serious disturbances. In England, as also in the United States, it has repeatedly happened in times of crisis that confidence has been destroyed in those banks that circulate fiduciary media in the form of deposits, while confidence in banknotes has been maintained. The measures by which the consequences which such a collapse of a part of the national business organization would infallibly have involved were avoided are well known. In England an attempt was made to fill the gap in the circulation which was due to the lack of large quantities of fiduciary media by the Bank of England being ready to increase the issue of its own notes. In the United States, where the law made this solution impossible, the clearinghouse certificates served the same purpose.[8] In both countries, attempts to give this device a legislative basis were made. But Lowe's bill was not passed, and even the Aldrich-Vreeland Act in the United States had only a partial success.[9]

None of the many systems of limiting the note circulation has proved ultimately capable of interposing an insurmountable obstacle in the way of further creation of fiduciary media. This is equally true of Peel's Act, which completely forbids the new issue of fiduciary media in the shape of notes, and of such bank-of-issue legislation in other states as does leave a certain scope for the augmentation of notes not backed by money. Between the English act of 1844 and, say, the German act of 1875, there seems to be a fundamental difference: while the one rigidly fixes, for all time, the quota of the note circulation not backed by metal, the other, inasmuch as it only requires that a certain proportion of the note circulation shall be backed by metal and puts a tax upon the rest, does make provision within certain limits for its future extension. But

---

[8] See Cannon, *Clearinghouses: Their History, Methods and Administration* (New York, 1900), pp. 79 ff.
[9] The Federal Reserve Act has since provided the United States with a basis for issuing notes in order to allay a panic.

everything depends upon the scope that is thus provided for extending the issue of fiduciary media. If it had been wide enough to give free play to the development of the unbacked note circulation, then the German law —and the same is true, not only of other laws based on the same principle (for example, the Austrian), but also of those that attempt to limit the circulation of notes in other ways, as for example, the French—would have had fundamentally different results from the English. Since in fact it proved to be too narrow for this, the difference between the two laws is merely one of degree, not one of kind. All these laws have limited the issue of fiduciary media in the form of notes, but have set no limits to their issue in the form of deposits. Making the issue of notes more difficult was bound to promote an increased employment of deposits; in place of the note, the deposit account came into prominence. For the development of the credit system, this change was not altogether a matter of indifference. The note is technically superior to the deposit in medium and small transactions; in many cases for which it might have been used as a money substitute, checks or clearing transfers could not be used, and in such cases restriction of the issue of fiduciary media in the form of notes was bound to have the effect of restriction of the issue of fiduciary media in general. Under the law of the United States of America, the issue of fiduciary media in the shape of deposits is also restricted; but since this only applies to some of the banks, namely, the national banks, it is not enough to make a big difference between the deposit business of the United States and that of the other countries in which no similar regulations have been established.

The real obstacle in the way of an unlimited extension of the issue of fiduciary media is not constituted by legislative restriction of the note issue, which, after all, only affects a certain kind of fiduciary medium, but the lack of a centralized world bank or of uniform procedure on the part of all credit-issuing banks. So long as the banks do not come to an agreement among themselves concerning the extension of credit, the circulation of fiduciary media can indeed be increased slowly, but it cannot be increased in a sweeping fashion. Each individual bank can only make a small step forward and must then wait until the others have followed its example. Every bank is obliged to regulate its interest policy in accordance with that of the others.

3

The Nature of Discount Policy

The most obscure and incorrect concepts are current concerning the nature of the discount policy of the central banks-of-issue. Often the principal task of the banks is said to be the protection of their cash reserves, as if it would pay them to make sacrifices for such an aim as that. No less widespread, however, is the view that the banks' obligation to follow a discount policy that takes account of the circumstances of other banks is imposed upon them merely by a perverse legislation and that the ideal of cheap money—in a double sense, namely, a low purchasing power of money and a low rate of interest—could be realized by the abandonment of certain out-of-date legal provisions.

It is unnecessary to devote very much time to the refutation of such views as these. After all that has been said on the nature of money and fiduciary media, there can hardly be very much doubt as to the aim of the discount policy of the banks. Every credit-issuing bank is obliged to fix the rate of interest it charges for loans in a certain conformity with that of the other credit-issuing banks. The rate cannot be allowed to sink below this level, for if it did, the sums of money needed by the bank's rapidly extending clientele for making payments to customers of other banks would increase in such a fashion that the bank's solvency would be imperiled. It is by raising the rate of discount that the bank safeguards its own capacity to pay. This end is certainly not attained by protecting the redemption fund, the small insignificance of which for maintaining the value of the fiduciary media has already been demonstrated, but by avoiding the artificial extension of the circulation of fiduciary media that would result from asking less interest than the other banks, and so also avoiding an increase in the demands for the redemption of the fiduciary media. The banks would still have to have a discount policy even if there were no legislative regulation of the note cover.

In Germany there has been a controversy as to whether certain measures of the Reichsbank are dictated by regard to the circumstances of the domestic money market or to those of the international. In the form in which it is usually put, the question is meaningless. The mobility of capital goods, which nowadays is but little restricted by legislative provisions such as customs duties, or by other obstacles, has led to the formation of a homogeneous world capital market. In the loan markets of the countries that take part in international trade, the net rate of interest is no longer determined according to national, but according to international, considerations. Its level is settled, not by the natural rate of interest in the country, but by the natural rate of interest *anywhere*. Just as the exchange ratio between money and other economic goods is the same in all places, so also the ratio between the prices of goods of the first order and those of goods of higher orders is the same everywhere. The whole system of modern international trade would be completely changed if the mobility of capital goods were to be restricted. In Germany there are many who demand such a prohibition or at least a considerable restriction of the investment of capital abroad. It is not our task to demonstrate what a small prospect of success a policy like this would have, or to show that the time is now past for a nation to decide whether or not it will take part in international trade. So long and insofar, however, as a nation participates in international trade, its market is only a part of the world market; prices are determined not nationally but internationally. The fact that the rate of interest in Germany may rise, not because any change has occurred in its determinants within the Reich but because there have been changes, say, in the United States, should not seem any more remarkable than, say, a rise in the price of corn that is due to the state of foreign harvests.

It has not been easy to reconcile policy with the extension and combination of national markets into a world market. Stronger than the resistance encountered centuries ago by the development of the town economy into the national economy is that which the nineteenth and twentieth centuries have opposed to the further stage of development into a world economy. Nowadays there is nothing like the feeling of homogeneity which previously overcame regional interests; the pronounced emphasis upon national antagonisms which sets the keynote of modern policy would perhaps stand in the way of attempts at economic unification even if there were no interests to which these attempts might prove injurious. From the point of view of the producer, low prices seem to be the greatest of all evils,

and in every state those producers who are unable to meet competition strive with all the means at their disposal to keep the cheap
commodities of the world market out of the national market. But
whether they succeed in this in each individual case or not depends
to a large extent on the strength of the political influence of the
opposing interests. For in the case of every individual commodity,
the producers' interest in high prices is opposed by the interest of
consumers in the opening of the market to the cheapening effect of
foreign competition. The matter is only decided by the conflict of the
two groups. The distribution of forces is otherwise when the problem of freedom of capital transactions is under discussion. We have
already seen that creditor interests always get the worst of it when
they clash with debtor interests. The interests of the capitalists are
scarcely ever represented in monetary policy. Nobody ever objects
to the importation of capital from abroad on the ground that it leads
to a depression of the rate of interest in the home market and a
reduction of the income of the capitalists; quite the reverse. The
universally prevailing view is that it is in the interest of the community that the rate of interest should be as low as possible. In those
European states with large capital resources, which so far as international dealings in capital are concerned need be considered only
as creditors and not as debtors, this policy is expressed in the endeavor to put obstacles in the way of foreign investment. Undoubtedly, this is not the *only* point of view from which modern states
judge the export of capital. Other considerations enter into the matter as well, some in favor of exportation, some against it. There is,
for instance, the fact that it is frequently impossible to export commodities except by allowing the payment for them to be postponed,
so that future goods are acquired in exchange for the present goods
surrendered; and that for this reason alone it is consequently necessary to promote the export of capital or at least not to hinder it. [10]
Nevertheless, it must be insisted that the policy adopted by these
states with regard to the export of capital is guided by the endeavor,
among others, to keep the domestic rate of interest low. On the
other hand, the same motive leads these states which because they

---

[10] See Sartorious von Waltershausen, *Das volkswirtschaftliche System der Kapitalanlage
im Auslande* (Berlin, 1907), pp. 126 ff.

are poor in capital have to play the part of international borrowers to encourage its importation.

The attempt to depress the domestic rate of interest by influencing the international movement of capital is particularly pronounced in the so-called money market, that is, in the market for short-term capital investments. In the so-called capital market, that is, the market for long-term capital investments, there is less possibility of effecting anything by intervention; in any case, any steps that may be taken become effective much more quickly in the former than in the latter. Consequently there is a greater propensity toward exerting an influence on the rate of interest on loans in the money market than in the long-term capital market. But the most important cause of the persistence of demands for the exertion of influence upon the money market lies in the universally prevalent errors concerning the nature of fiduciary media and of bank credit. When a relatively small efflux of gold induces the powerful central bank-of-issue of a rich country to raise the discount rate there is a tendency to think that there must be some other way than this, by which the efflux of gold could be prevented without involving the community in what is regarded as the injurious effect of a rise in the rate of interest. It is not seen that what is happening is the automatic adjustment of the national to the world rate of interest owing to the way in which the country is involved in international trade. That the country cannot be cut off from participation in international capital dealings simply and solely by measures of banking and currency policy, is completely overlooked. This alone can explain how it can come about in large exporting countries that the very persons who demand measures for "cheapening" credit are those who benefit most from the export trade. If those manufacturers, for whom every increase in the rate of discount that can be traced to events abroad is an inducement to plead for a modification of the banking system in the direction of releasing the central bank-of-issue from its obligation to provide gold for export on demand, would realize that the increase in the rate of interest could be effectively stopped only by a suppression of the export of capital and complete exclusion of the country from international trade, then they would soon change their minds. And it seems that these implications have already won some degree of general recognition, even if the literary treatment

of the problem may still leave something to be desired. In Germany
and Austria it was only the groups that demanded the seclusion of
the national market that also demanded the "isolation" of the currency.

Further explanation is unnecessary. Nevertheless, it may not be
supererogatory to examine one by one the measures that are recommended by those who favor a low rate of interest and to show
how incapable they would prove of leading to the expected result.

4

The Gold-Premium Policy[11]

Let us first review the systems which are supposed to be able to
maintain the level of the rate of discount in the national money
market by making it more difficult or more expensive to procure
gold at a rate below that determined by the circumstances of the
international market. The most important and most well known of
these is the gold-premium policy, as it was carried out by the Bank
of France.

In view of the circumstances that nowadays the silver five-franc
piece is still legally current coin, the Bank of France is authorized
to redeem its notes at its own choice either in gold or in these pieces.
It sometimes used to make use of this authority for the purpose of
increasing the difficulty of procuring gold for export purposes. As
a rule it made no difficulty about surrendering gold in exchange for
notes. And it exchanged five-franc pieces in the same way for gold
coins, although it was not obliged to do so, and by so doing it
endowed the latter with the property of being money substitutes.
Naturally, these facilities were not requisitioned to a great extent for
purposes of domestic business. Notes and five-franc pieces enjoyed
unlimited public confidence so that their employability as money
substitutes was not in the least in question. But if the bank was
asked to surrender gold for export, it did not necessarily do so. It
is true that it used to hand over gold unhesitatingly for the requirements of what was called "legitimate" trade, that is, when it was
needed to pay for imported commodities, especially corn and cot-

---

[11] [See pp. 21–22 above. H.E.B.]

ton. But if gold was demanded for the purpose of speculating on the difference between home and foreign interest rates, it was not handed over as a matter of course. For this purpose, the bank did not issue Napoleons, the French gold coins, at all; and it issued ingots and foreign gold coins only at an additional charge, varying from four to eight percent of the 3,437 francs at which it was legally bound to purchase a kilogram of fine gold. It is impossible to state the exact amount of this "gold premium," because the rate has never been published officially.[12]

The purpose of the gold-premium policy was to postpone as long as ever possible the moment when the condition of the international money market would force the bank to raise the discount rate in order to prevent an efflux of gold. The lowness of the rate of discount is of extraordinary importance in French financial policy. In the interest of those classes of the community by which it is supported, the government of the Third Republic is obliged to avoid anything that might injure the high standing of the *rentes* which constitute the chief investment of those classes. Even a merely temporary high rate of discount is always dangerous to the *rentes* market, for it might induce some holders of *rentes* to dispose of their bonds in order to reinvest their capital more fruitfully, and the disturbance of the market that might result from this would have a disproportionately adverse effect on the quotation of the *rentes*. It is undeniable that the result aimed at was to a certain extent attained, even though the premium policy by no means possessed the significance that was erroneously ascribed to it.

It is above all mistaken to ascribe the lowness of the rate of discount in France to the procedure that has been described. If the rate of discount has been lower in France than in other countries, this is due to altogether different causes. France is of all the countries in the whole world that which is richest in capital; but its people are not greatly endowed with the spirit of initiative and enterprise.[13] Consequently its capital has to emigrate. Now in a country which exports capital, even disregarding the premium for risk-bearing that

---

[12] See Rosendorff, "Die Goldprämienpolitik der Banque de France und ihre deutschen Lobredner," *Jahrbücher für Nationalökonomie und Statistik* 21 (1901): 632 ff.; Dunbar, *Chapters on the Theory and History of Banking*, 2d ed. (New York, 1907), pp. 147 ff.
[13] See Kaufmann, *Das französische Bankwesen* (Tübingen, 1911), pp. 35 ff.

is contained in the gross rate of interest, the rate of interest on loans must be lower than in a country which imports capital. Capitalists, when comparing the yields of home and foreign investment, are led by a series of psychological factors to prefer the former to the latter when other circumstances are equal. This is enough to explain why long-term and short-term investments bear lower interest in France than in other countries, such as Germany. The cause is a general economic cause; it is a matter in which measures of banking or currency policy can have no influence. The ratio between the rate of interest in France and that abroad could not for long be forced away by the premium policy of the Bank of France from that determined by the general economic situation. The Bank of France was not above the laws that govern the course of economic affairs. In fixing the level of its discount rate, it was not exempt from the necessity for paying due attention to the level of the natural rate of interest. Like every other credit-issuing bank that has an influence on the domestic market, it had to endeavor to keep the rate of interest on domestic short-term investments at such a level that foreign investment did not appear so attractive to home capitalists as to endanger the bank's own solvency. Like the others, the Bank of France could effectively prevent an outflow of gold in one way only—by raising its discount rate.[14] Employing the premium policy could do no more than postpone for a short time a rise in the rate of discount that the state of the international money market had made necessary. The premium made it more expensive to export gold and so reduced the profitability of interest arbitrage transactions. When it was widely believed that the difference between the French and the foreign rates of interest was about to be altered in France's favor through a fall in the foreign rate, then arbitrage dealers would not export gold at all, since the small profit of the transaction would be too greatly reduced by the premium. In this way the Bank of France may sometimes have avoided raising the discount rate when it would otherwise have been necessary to do so for a short time. But whenever the difference between the rates of

---

[14] On this, see Rosendorff, *op. cit.*, pp. 640 ff., and passages cited in the essay "Die neue Richtung in der Goldpolitik der Bank von Frankreich," *Bank-Archiv.* 7 (1907): 72 ff., taken from the statements of account of the Bank of France, in which the raising of the discount rate is spoken of as the "seul moyen connu de défendre l'encaisse."

interest was significant enough to make short-term foreign investment still promise to be profitable in spite of the increased cost of
procuring gold due to the premium, and whenever the result of
arbitrage dealings was not jeopardized by the prospect of an imminent reduction of the foreign rate, then even the Bank of France
could not avoid raising the rate of interest.

It has been asserted that it is possible for a central bank to use
successive increases of the premium so as entirely to prevent the
export of gold if it continually forces back the gold point or export
limit as the fall in the rate of exchange requires.[15] This is undoubtedly correct. The procedure, as is well known, has been employed
repeatedly; it is known as cessation of cash payments. The bank
that adopts it deprives its fiduciary media of their character of
money substitutes. If they continue to function as general media of
exchange, it is in the role of credit money. Their value will have
become subject to independent variation. In such a case, it is admittedly possible for the bank to follow a completely independent
discount policy; it may now reduce to any desired extent the rate
of interest it charges without running the risk of insolvency. But this
brings to light the consequences that must follow a banking policy
that endeavors by extending the issue of fiduciary media to depress
the rate of interest on loans below the natural rate of interest. This
point has already been discussed in detail; in the present connection
there is a second point that is of importance. If the intervention of
the bank leads to the artificial retention of the rate of interest on
loans at a level below that of the rate given by international conditions, then the capitalists will be all the more anxious to invest
their capital abroad as the gap between the domestic and foreign
rates of interest increases. The demand for foreign common media
of exchange will increase, because foreign capital goods will be desired more and home capital goods less. And there is no way in
which the fall in the rate of exchange could automatically set forces
in motion to reestablish between the bank money and gold, the
world money, that exchange ratio which had previously existed
when the notes and deposits of the bank were not credit money but
still money substitutes. The mechanism of the monetary system

---

15 See Landesberger, *Währungssystem und Relation* (Vienna, 1891), p. 104.

tends to bring the exchange value of the two kinds of money to that "natural" level determined by the exchange ratio between each of them and the remaining goods. But in the present case it is the natural exchange ratio itself which has moved against the country that refuses to pay out gold. An "autonomous" interest policy must necessarily lead to progressive depreciation.

There are many advocates of the gold-premium policy who make no attempt to deny that its employment in the way in which they intend must infallibly lead to a credit-money or fiat-money standard with a rapidly falling objective exchange value of the unit. In fact, they are inclined to regard this very fact as a special advantage; for they are, more or less, inflationists.[16]

Nevertheless, this was by no means the way in which the Bank of France carried out its premium policy. It observed a fixed limit, above which it never allowed the premium to rise in any circumstances whatever. Eight per mill is probably the highest premium that it has ever demanded. And this was certainly not an error on the part of the bank; it was founded on the nature of the case. In the eyes of the French government and of the administration of the bank controlled by it, the amount of depreciation consequent upon a gold premium of eight percent was not intolerable; but, in view of the unpredictable reactions throughout the whole community, it was thought better to avoid further depreciation. Thus the French gold-premium policy was not able to prevent the export of gold altogether, but could only postpone it for a short time. Now this fact alone, and not only when the difference between the rates of interest was so inconsiderable and transient that the rate of discount did not need to be raised at all, meant a cheapening of the rate of interest on loans. But this was offset by the increase in the rate of interest during those periods when the rate of interest abroad was relatively low. Whenever the loan rate abroad sank so low that it might have seemed advantageous to capitalists to transfer capital to France for investment, they nevertheless refrained from doing so if a long continuance of the situation could not be reckoned with or if the difference between the rates was not very great, because they had reason to fear that a subsequent repatriation of the capital when the

---

[16] *Ibid.*, p. 105, and *Über die Goldprämienpolitik der Zettelbanken* (Vienna, 1892), p. 28.

situation was reversed would be possible only at an increased cost. Thus the gold-premium policy did not merely constitute a hindrance to the efflux of gold from France; it also hindered an influx. It reduced the rate of interest on loans at certain times, but raised it at other times. It is true that it did not altogether exclude the country from international dealings in capital; it only made participation in them harder; but it did this in both directions. Its effect, the intensity of which should not be overestimated, was principally expressed in the fact that the rate of interest for short-term investments has been more stable in France than in other countries. It has never sunk so low as in England, for example; but neither has it ever risen so high. This is shown quite clearly by a comparison of movements in the London and Paris loan rates.

It has become more and more clearly recognized that the gold-premium policy could not have these effects ascribed to it. Those who once regarded it as the remedy for all ills are gradually becoming silent.

5

Systems Similar to the Gold-Premium Policy

The legal provisions which have permitted the Bank of France to follow the gold-premium policy were absent in those countries which until recently were on a pure gold standard. Where the gold coins have not been supplemented by any money substitutes, fiat money, or credit money, with unlimited legal tender by any payer including the central credit-issuing bank, the fiduciary media have had to be redeemed at their full face value in money without a premium being charged in addition.[17] But in actual fact these banks also were tending to adopt a policy different in degree but certainly not in kind from the described procedure of the Bank of France.

---

[17] Even at the time when the thaler was still unlimited legal tender and so occupied a position analogous to that of the French five-franc piece, the German Reichsbank never followed a gold-premium policy on the French pattern, although it was often advised to do so. This is probably to be ascribed not so much to the circumstance that the number of thalers was relatively small as to the influence of Bamberger's ideas throughout the Reich. An open break with the principles of the banking and currency reform of the period after 1870–71 was, in view of the prevailing opinion, out of the question.

In most countries, the central bank-of-issue was only obliged to redeem its notes in legal tender gold coins of its own country, after the pattern of English banking law. It is in accordance with the spirit of the modern monetary system and with the ultimate aims of monetary policy that this obligation has been understood also to refer to the surrender of gold ingots to exporters at the legal ratio or at least at a price that made it more profitable to procure bullion than coins. Thus until 1889 the Bank of England voluntarily extended its obligation to redeem its notes by paying out on demand in ingots the value of the notes in full-weight gold coins. It did this by fixing its selling price for gold bullion once for all at 77s. 10½d. per ounce of standard gold.[18] For a time the Continental banks-of-issue followed this example. But they soon determined upon a different procedure, and eventually the Bank of England too relinquished its old policy and adopted the practice of the Continental banks.

The Bank of England and the German Reichsbank, apart from the Bank of France the two most important credit-issuing banks in the world, were in the habit of issuing for export purposes worn gold coins only of inferior value. Sovereigns, as issued by the Bank of England for export, were usually from two to three percent worse than newly minted sovereigns. The weight of the twenty-mark pieces received by a person who withdrew gold coins from the German Reichsbank for purposes of exportation was, according to the calculations of experts, 7.943 grams on an average as against a standard average of 7.965 grams; that is, something over a quarter of one percent less than their mint value.[19] The Bank of England sometimes refused altogether to issue gold ingots, and sometimes would only issue them at a price in excess of the 77s. 10½d. which alone was usual until 1889. It sometimes raised the selling price of ingots to as much as 77s. 11d.[20]

As regards the range and the effect of these measures, nothing need be added to what has already been said about the French gold-premium policy. The difference—as has been said—is only quantitative, not qualitative.[21]

---

[18] See Koch, *Der Londoner Goldverkehr* (Stuttgart, 1905), p. 708.

[19] *Ibid.*, pp. 81 f.

[20] See Clare, *A Money Market Primer and Key to the Exchanges*, 2d ed. (London, 1893), p. 22.

[21] Rosendorff ("Die Goldprämienpolitik der Banque de France," p. 636) would ap-

The other "little devices" which have also been employed for making the export of gold more difficult have their effect in precisely the same fashion. As, for example, when the German Reichsbank sometimes prohibited the issue of gold for export purposes except in Berlin by invoking the letter of section 18 of the Bank Act, which had the effect of making the export of gold more costly by burdening the gold exporters with the risk and cost of transporting the gold from Berlin to the place of export.

6

The Nonsatisfaction of the So-called Illegitimate Demand for Money

In the returns of the Bank of France it has been repeatedly asserted that the gold-premium policy was directed only against those who wished to withdraw gold from the bank for speculative purposes. The bank, it was said, never put difficulties in the way of procuring gold for satisfying the legitimate demands of French trade.[22] No explanation was given of the idea of "legitimate" demand and its contrary "illegitimate" demand.

The idea on which this distinction is obviously based is that trade in commodities and dealings in capital are two perfectly distinct and

---

pear to be mistaken in thinking it possible to detect a difference of principle between the procedure of the Bank of England and the Reichsbank in paying out gold and the gold-premium policy of the Bank of France. He bases his view on the argument that, whereas the latter refuses altogether to pay out French gold coins and is thus theoretically able to raise the amount of the premium indefinitely, the Bank of England and the Reichsbank, which in contrast to the Bank of France always redeem their notes at their full value in current gold coin and have never attempted to refuse to pay out gold, are able to raise the selling price of bullion only by the amount of the cost of minting and an allowance for wear and tear. Rosendorff, in arguing from the statement that the Bank of France is "theoretically" able to raise the amount of the gold-premium indefinitely, flatly contradicts what he says in the rest of his book. *In fact* it does *not* do it, quite apart from the consideration that the law forbids it also. But if it did it, then it would completely alter the character of the French monetary system. It could not be expected that the French government and the Chambers would sanction the transaction to a credit-money standard which would be involved in such a procedure.

[22] Thus, in the *Compte rendu* for 1898 (pp. 12 f.): "Si nous nous efforçons de conserver de grandes disponibilités métalliques et de les ménager le mieux possible, nous ne devons pas non plus perdre de vue les intérêts du commerce et lui refuser les moyens de payement qu'il réclame pour les besoins les plus légitimes, c'est-à-dire pour l'approvisionnement du marché français."

independent branches of economic activity and that it would be possible to restrict the one without affecting the other; that refusal to surrender gold for arbitrage dealing could not increase the expense of procuring commodities from abroad so long as no difficulty was made about placing at the disposal of the importer the sums needed by him to pay for his purchases.

On closer examination this argument can hardly be accepted as valid. Even if we completely ignore the fact that dealings in capital only constitute one form of the general process of exchange of goods and consider nothing beyond the technical problem of the withdrawal of gold, it is clear that the bank cannot achieve its aim by discriminatory treatment of different requests for gold. If exportation of gold did not seem profitable because of the difference between the rates of interest, imported raw materials would actually be paid for, partly or wholly, by the commodities exported. The importer would not try to obtain gold from the bank; he would go into the market and buy bills originating in the French export business. If gold were delivered to him by the bank without a premium while the rate of exchange rose roughly by the amount of and on account of the premium that was charged to arbitrage dealers, this might well mean a favoring of the import business, and might possibly in some circumstances benefit the consumer as well, although that depends entirely upon the state of competition among importers. But all the same, the rate of exchange would experience the variation that the bank wished to avoid. The upper gold point would be fixed too high by an amount equal to the amount of the premium.

Finally, it must be pointed out that the distinction between a legitimate and an illegitimate demand for gold for export cannot be applied in practice. The demand for gold with which to pay for imported goods may be called legitimate, the demand for gold with which to buy foreign bills as a temporary investment with a view to exploiting a difference in interest rates may be called illegitimate. But there are many remaining intermediate cases, which cannot be placed in either one or the other category. Would it have been possible, say, for the Bank of France to put obstacles in the way of the withdrawal of deposits held by foreign states, municipalities, and companies, perhaps as the balances of loans? Or for the Austro-Hungarian Bank, which has repeatedly been accused of refusing to issue bills to persons who intend to carry out arbitrage dealings, to increase the difficulty of speculative repurchase of home securities from abroad?[23]

7

Other Measures for Strengthening the Stock of Metal Held by the Central Banks-of-Issue

The endeavors of the central banks-of-issue to build up as large gold reserves as possible have led to the employment of devices which have just the opposite appearance to that of the premium policy and the systems similar to it. By raising the price they paid for gold imports the banks used to try to diminish the cost to the importer of importing gold and so to reduce the lower gold point.

Among these devices was the practice of granting interest-free or low-interest-bearing advances to importers of gold, a practice which was not unknown in England, France, and Germany.[24] There was also the practice of buying gold not only at the chief office, but also at branches situated near the national boundary.[25] Perhaps the most interesting of these devices was that of buying certain kinds of gold

---

[23] See my article *Das Problem gesetzlicher Aufnahme der Barzahlungen in Österreich-Ungarn*, p. 1017. If the Austro-Hungarian Bank were to follow the example of the Bank of France in this or some other way it would achieve an exactly opposite result to that achieved by the French institution. Like that of the Bank of France, its action would restrict not merely the efflux but also the influx of gold. In France, the creditor nation, this means something very different from what it means in Austria, the debtor nation. In France, restriction of the importation of capital (which would only exceptionally occur) is unobjectionable; in Austria, the country that is dependent on constant importation of capital from abroad, it would have quite a different effect. The fact that there was a possibility of difficulties in subsequently repatriating the capital would mean that a greater gap than otherwise would have to occur between the Viennese and the foreign rates of interest before capital would be sent to Austria, and this would mean that the rate of interest in Austria would always be higher. The fact, on the other hand, that the export of Austrian short-term capital would also not be profitable except when there was a greater gap than otherwise between the home and foreign rates would not counteract the above disadvantage, because the question of capital exportation from Austria-Hungary to western countries very seldom arises.

[24] See Koch, *op. cit.*, p. 79; *Die Reichsbank 1876–1900* (Berlin, 1901), p. 146.

[25] See Obst, *Banken und Bankpolitik* (Leipzig, 1909), pp. 90 f.; Hertz, "Die Diskont und Devisenpolitik der österreichisch-ungarischen Bank," *Zeitschrift für Volkswirtschaft, Sozialpolitik und Verwaltung* 12 (1903): 496.

coin at a price in excess of their bullion value. If the bank issued to a gold exporter, instead of ingots or coins of the country, coins of the country to which he intended to send the gold, it could get a higher price for them than that corresponding to their gold content. For the exporter would save the expense of melting and recoinage and avoid the loss in which he would be involved by the fact that the domestic coins would be worn down to some extent. So the bank would be able to agree to pay a higher price than that corresponding to their metal content for the current gold coins of the states into which a future export of gold was probable.[26]

All of these measures can best be described as weapons against the premium policies and related devices employed by foreign banks. If the central bank in a country A endeavored to raise the upper gold point for export from A to country B, then the bank in B took steps to lower it. If only used coins were issued for export purposes in A, this procedure was rendered nugatory when a price in excess of the gold content was paid in B for coins of country A. It is very probable that the devices and counterdevices were largely compensatory, so that the extension of the gap between the gold points, which otherwise would necessarily have resulted from the intervention of the banks, did not in fact occur.

8

The Promotion of Check and Clearing Transactions as a Means of Reducing the Rate of Discount

In Germany, where before the war relatively very much gold was in circulation, there was a constantly growing endeavor to withdraw it from circulation by an extension of check and clearing transactions and to divert it into the vaults of the Reichsbank. The aim of this propaganda is set forth in a circular of the elders of the Kaufmannschaft of Berlin, s.d. May 2, 1907, to the following effect: "The causes to which the high rate of interest in Germany are to be traced are rooted to a large extent in the circumstance that the German people make greater use than those in other countries of cash media of

---

[26] See Koch, *op. cit.*, pp. 79 ff.; Hertz, *op. cit.*, p. 521; Spitzmüller, "Valutareform und Währungsgesetzgebung," in *Oesterreichischen Staatswörterbuch*, 2d ed., vol. 2, p. 300.

circulation (gold and silver) for payments arising in and out of the course of business, but have not yet sufficiently accustomed themselves to the procedure which might replace the use of gold and silver, and also of banknotes and Treasury notes, as media of circulation, namely, the use of checks and the clearing system. If a considerable proportion of payments could be settled by means of transfers from one account to another or by checks, then this would save large sums of currency, in gold and silver as well as in banknotes, and this saved currency would then accumulate in the reserves of the banks-of-issue, especially of the central bank-of-issue, the Reichsbank. The more this happened, the smaller would be the demand for currency that had to be satisfied by the Reichsbank, and the stronger would be the cash reserve of the Reichsbank, which circumstances would contribute considerably toward a reduction of the rate of interest at the Reichsbank and in the whole country."[27]

In this is a very clear demonstration of the weakness of the theoretical views that underlie modern banking policy. The level of the rate of interest is said to depend on the demand for currency. A strengthening of the cash reserve of the central bank-of-issue is credited with the effect of reducing the rate of interest in the whole country, and of reducing it appreciably. And this is not just the opinion of some private person or other, but that of the highly respected corporation of the Berlin Kaufmannschaft, and also, as everybody knows, that of the leaders of German economic policy in general. On this one point, all parties seem to be agreed, however much their views on the nature of economic phenomena may otherwise diverge. But even if this fundamental error is for a moment disregarded it is impossible to overlook the weakness of the doctrines expounded, and, above all, their contradictoriness. The proportion of cover for the Reichsbank notes provided for in the banking legislation of the seventies is treated as sacrosanct. The possibility of changing these provisions by substituting, say, a cover of one-quarter or one-fifth for that of one-third is never contemplated. The letter of the law has to be preserved while the assumptions on which it was based are being altered. When money substitutes in the form of deposits

---

[27] See also Proebst, *Die Grundlagen unseres Depositen- und Scheckwesens* (Jena, 1908), pp. 1 ff.

are augmented without provision being made for a monetary cover, the quantity of fiduciary media is increased. This is further demonstrative of the fact that even that part of the argument of the banking principle which was theoretically correct was unable to exert any influence on practical politics. Tooke and Fullarton repeatedly point out that there is no fundamental difference between notes and deposits (which they speak of as checks). Their modern successors do not dare to draw the logical conclusion from this incontrovertible fact; they stand for the differential treatment of fiduciary media according to whether they are notes or deposits.[28]

If part of the gold in circulation in Germany and part of the banknotes had been replaced by fiduciary media in the shape of deposits, this might have led to a diminution of the rate of interest only insofar as the gold that had become superfluous was employed for obtaining capital goods from abroad. The replacement of notes without a metal backing by deposits without a metal backing is of no consequence in this connection. Only so far as notes covered by metal were replaced by deposits not covered by metal would there be any increase of the circulation of fiduciary media at the expense of that of money certificates, by which gold would be released for export to other countries. But the same result could have been attained by a diminution of the ratio between cover and banknotes; nevertheless this simpler device was generally held to be impracticable, in spite of the fact that it was precisely as safe or precisely as dangerous as the other. If the gold dispensed with in this way had been exported, then the stock of other economic goods at the disposal of the German nation would have increased correspondingly. This might have led to a fall, if only a trifling one, in the rate of interest, assuming that the quantity of gold expelled from Germany was absorbed abroad with a general fall in the objective exchange value of money. But the German champions of an extension of the checks and clearing system did not think of that when making proposals of this sort. They recommended the extension of the circulation of fiduciary media in the form of deposits because they believed that this would reduce the number and extent of those applications that made demands upon the credit that the Reichsbank granted in the form of notes; and they hoped that this would lead to a reduction

---

[28] It is only in very recent years that views on this point in dominant circles have begun slowly to change.

in the rate of interest on loans. There is a serious error in all this. The level of the rate of interest on loans depends not on the amount of the national stock of money in the wider sense, nor, of course, on the amount of fiduciary media in circulation. It was not the legal regulations concerning cover that forced the Reichsbank to aim at a discount policy that would prevent any tension from arising between the natural rate of interest and the discount rate, but its inevitable concern for its own solvency.

In all those countries whose credit system is organized on the so-called single-reserve basis so that the stock of money needed for the redemption on demand of money substitutes is administered by a central bank on which in times of emergency all the credit-issuing banks must ultimately fall back, it is the directors of this bank who are the first to notice the outward flow of gold; and it is they who must be the first to take steps to stop it, since its first effects are directed against the institution for which they are responsible. Therefore, the raising of the discount rate by the central bank usually precedes the increased severity of lending terms in the open market and in the dealings between the private banks and their clients. And so superficial critics jump to the conclusion *post hoc ergo propter hoc.* Nothing could be more mistaken. Even quite apart from the proceedings of the central bank-of-issue, the private banks and others who issue money have to adjust their interest policy to the rate of interest ruling in the world market. Sums could be withdrawn from them for the purposes of interest arbitrage, just as from the central bank. In fact, so long as the mobility of capital is not restricted it remains impossible for the credit-issuing banks of any single country to follow an independent credit policy.

(III)
Problems of Credit Policy in the Period
Immediately After the War

9

The Gold-Exchange Standard[29]

Wherever inflation has thrown the monetary system into confusion, the primary aim of currency policy has been to bring the print-

---

[29] [The reader will remember that this was written in 1924. H.E.B.]

ing presses to a standstill. Once that is done, once it has at last been learned that even the policy of raising the objective exchange value of money has undesirable consequences, and once it is seen that the chief thing is to stabilize the value of money, then attempts are made to establish a gold-exchange standard as quickly as possible. This, for example, is what occurred in Austria at the end of 1922 and since then, at least for the time being, the dollar rate in that country has been fixed. But in existing circumstances, invariability of the dollar rate means invariability of the price of gold also. Thus Austria has a dollar-exchange standard and so, indirectly, a gold-exchange standard. That is the currency system that seems to be the immediate aim in Germany, Poland, Hungary, and many other European countries. Nowadays, European aspirations in the sphere of currency policy are limited to a return to the gold standard. This is quite understandable, for the gold standard previously functioned on the whole satisfactorily; it is true that it did not secure the unattainable ideal of a money with an invariable objective exchange value, but it did preserve the monetary system from the influence of governments and changing policies.

Yet the gold-standard system was already undermined before the war. The first step was the abolition of the physical use of gold in individual payments and the accumulation of the stocks of gold in the vaults of the great banks-of-issue. The next step was the adoption of the practice by a series of states of holding the gold reserves of the central banks-of-issue (or the redemption funds that took their place), not in actual gold, but in various sorts of foreign claims to gold. Thus it came about that the greater part of the stock of gold that was used for monetary purposes was gradually accumulated in a few large banks-of-issue; and so these banks became the central reserve banks of the world, as previously the central banks-of-issue had become central reserve banks for individual countries. The war did not create this development; it merely hastened it a little. Neither has the development yet reached the stage when all the newly produced gold that is not absorbed into industrial use flows to a single center. The Bank of England and the central banks-of-issue of some other states still control large stocks of gold; there are still several of them that take up part of the annual output of gold. Yet fluctuations in the price of gold are nowadays essentially dependent on the policy followed by the Federal Reserve Board. If the United States did not absorb gold to the extent to which it does, the price of gold would fall and the gold prices of commodities would rise. Since, so long as the dollar represents a fixed quantity of gold, the United States admits the surplus gold and surrenders commodities for gold to an unlimited extent, a rapid fall in the value of gold has hitherto been avoided. But this policy of the United States, which involves considerable sacrifices, might one day be changed. Variations in the price of gold would then occur and this would be bound to give rise in other gold countries to the question whether it would not be better in order to avoid further rises in prices to dissociate the currency standard from gold. Just as Sweden attempted for a time to raise the krone above its old gold parity by closing the mint to gold, so other countries that are now still on the gold standard or intend to return to it might act similarly. This would mean a further drop in the price of gold and a further reduction of the usefulness of gold for monetary purposes. If we disregard the Asiatic demand for money, we might even now without undue exaggeration say that gold has ceased to be a commodity the fluctuations in the price of which are independent of government influence. Fluctuations in the price of gold are nowadays substantially dependent on the behavior of *one* government, namely, that of the United States.[30]

All that could not have been foreseen in this result of a long process of development is the circumstance that the fluctuations in the price of gold should have become dependent upon the policy of one government only. That the United States should have achieved such an economic predominance over other countries as it now has, and that it alone of all the countries of great economic importance should have retained the gold standard while the others (England, France, Germany, Russia, and the rest) have at least temporarily abandoned it—that is a consequence of what took place during the war. Yet the matter would not be essentially different if the price of gold was dependent not on the policy of the United States alone, but on those of four or five other governments as well. Those protagonists of the gold-exchange standard who have rec-

---

[30] See Keynes, *A Tract on Monetary Reform* (London, 1923), pp. 163 ff.

ommended it as a general monetary system and not merely as an expedient for poor countries, have overlooked this fact. They have not observed that the gold-exchange standard must at last mean depriving gold of that characteristic which is the most important from the point of view of monetary policy—its independence of government influence upon fluctuations in its value. The gold-exchange standard has not been recommended or adopted with the object of dethroning gold. All that Ricardo wanted was to reduce the cost of the monetary system. In many countries which from the last decade of the nineteenth century onward have wished to abandon the silver or credit-money standard, the gold-exchange standard rather than a gold standard with an actual gold currency has been adopted in order to prevent the growth of a new demand for gold from causing a rise in its price and a fall in the gold prices of commodities. But whatever the motives may have been by which the protagonists of the gold-exchange standard have been led, there can be no doubt concerning the results of its increasing popularity.

If the gold-exchange standard is retained, the question must sooner or later arise as to whether it would not be better to substitute for it a credit-money standard whose fluctuations were more susceptible to control than those of gold. For if fluctuations in the price of gold are substantially dependent on political intervention, it is inconceivable why government policy should still be restricted at all and not given a free hand altogether, since the amount of this restriction is not enough to confine arbitrariness in price policy within narrow limits. The cost of additional gold for monetary purposes that is borne by the whole world might well be saved, for it no longer secures the result of making the monetary system independent of government intervention.

If this complete government control is not desired, there remains one alternative only: an attempt must be made to get back from the gold-exchange standard to the actual use of gold again.

10

A Return to a Gold Currency

A return to the actual use of gold would be certain to have effects that would scarcely be welcomed. It would lead to a rise in the price of gold, or, what is the same thing, to a fall in the prices of commodities. The fact that this is not generally desired, and the reason why it is not, have already been dealt with. We may confidently suppose that such a fall in prices would cause just as much dissatisfaction as was caused by the process of expelling gold from circulation. And it hardly demands an excessive amount of insight to be able to predict that in such circumstances it would not be long before the gold standard was again accused of responsibility for the bad state of business. Once again the gold standard would be reproached with depressing prices and forcing up the rate of interest. And once again proposals would be made for some sort of "modification" of the gold standard. In spite of all these objections, the question of the advisability of a return to an actual gold standard demands serious consideration.

One thing alone would recommend the abandonment of the gold-exchange standard and the reintroduction of the actual use of gold; this is the necessity for making a recurrence of inflationary policies if not impossible at least substantially more difficult. From the end of the last century onward it was the aim of etatism in monetary policy to restrict the actual circulation of gold for three reasons: first, because it wished to inflate, without repealing the existing banking laws, by concentrating gold reserves in the central bank-of-issue; second, because it wished to accumulate a war chest; and third, because it wished to wean the people from the use of gold coins so as to pave the way for the inflationary policy of the coming Great War.

Admittedly it will not be possible to prevent either war or inflation by opposing such endeavors as these. Kant's proposal to prohibit the raising of loans for war purposes is extremely naive;[31] and it would be still more naive to bring within the scope of such a prohibition the issue of fiduciary media too. Only one thing can conquer war—that liberal attitude of mind which can see nothing in war but destruction and annihilation, and which can never wish to bring about a war, because it regards war as injurious even to the victors. Where liberalism prevails, there will never be war. But where there are other opinions concerning the profitability and in-

---

[31] See Kant, *Werke,* vol. 5, *Zum ewigen Frieden* (Insel-Ausgabe), pp. 661 f.

juriousness of war, no rules and regulations, however cunningly devised, can make war impossible. If war is regarded as advantageous, then laws regulating the monetary systems will not be allowed to stand in the way of going to war. On the first day of any war, all the laws opposing obstacles to it will be swept aside, just as in 1914 the monetary legislation of all the belligerent states was turned upside down without one word of protest being ventured. To try to oppose future war policies through currency legislation would be foolish. But it may nevertheless be conceded that the argument in favor of making war more difficult cannot be neglected when the question is being debated whether the actual domestic circulation of gold should be done away with in the future or not. If the people are accustomed to the actual use of gold in their daily affairs they will resist an inflationary policy more strongly than did the peoples of Europe in 1914. It will not be so easy for governments to disavow the reactions of war on the monetary system; they will be obliged to justify their policy. The maintenance of an actual gold currency would impose considerable costs on individual nations and would at first lead to a general fall of prices; there can hardly be any doubt about that. But all its disadvantages must be accepted as part of the bargain if other services are demanded of the monetary system than that of preparing for war, revolution, and destruction.

It is from this point of view that we should approach the question of the denominations of notes. If the issue of notes which do not make up a multiple of at least the smallest gold coins is prohibited, then in the business of everyday life gold coins will have to be used. This could best be brought about by an international currency agreement. It would be easy to force countries into such an agreement by means of penal customs duties.

11

The Problem of the Freedom of the Banks

The events of recent years reopen questions that have long been regarded as closed. The question of the freedom of the banks is one of these. It is no longer possible to consider it completely settled as it must have been considered for decades now. Unfortunate experiences with banknotes that had become valueless because they were no longer actually redeemable led once to the restriction of the right of note issue to a few privileged institutions. Yet experience of state regulation of banks-of-issue has been incomparably more unfavorable than experience of uncontrolled private enterprise. What do all the failures of banks-of-issue and clearing banks known to history matter in comparison with the complete collapse of the banking system in Germany? Everything that has been said in favor of control of the banking system pales into insignificance beside the objections that can nowadays be advanced against state regulation of the issue of notes. The etatistic arguments, that were once brought forward against the freedom of the note issue, no longer carry conviction; in the sphere of banking, as everywhere else, etatism has been a failure.

The safeguards erected by the liberal legislation of the nineteenth century to protect the bank-of-issue system against abuse by the state have proved inadequate. Nothing has been easier than to treat with contempt all the legislative provisions for the protection of the monetary standard. All governments, even the weakest and most incapable, have managed it without difficulty. Their banking policies have enabled them to bring about the state of affairs that the gold standard was designed to prevent: subjection of the value of money to the influence of political forces. And, having arrogated this power to themselves, the governments have put it to the worst conceivable use. But, so long as the other political and ideological factors were what they were, we cannot conclude that the mere freedom of the banks would or could have made things different.

Let us suppose that freedom of banking had prevailed throughout Europe during the last two generations before the outbreak of the Great War; that banknotes had not become legal tender; that notes were always examined, not only with respect to their genuineness, but also with respect to their soundness, whenever they were tendered, and those issued by unknown banks rejected; but that the notes of large and well-known banking firms nevertheless were just as freely current as the notes of the great central banks-of-issue in the period when *they* were not legal tender. Let us further suppose that since there was no danger of a world banking cartel, the banks had been prevented, by the mere necessity for redeeming their notes in cash, from making immoderate endeavors to extend their

issue by charging a low rate of interest; or at least, that the risk of
this was no greater than under legislative regulation of the note
system. Let us suppose, in short, that up to the outbreak of the war,
the system had worked no better and no worse than that which
actually existed. But the question at issue is whether it would have
held its own any better after July 28, 1914. The answer to this question seems to be that it would not have done so. The governments
of the belligerent—and neutral—states overthrew the whole system
of bank legislation with a stroke of the pen, and they could have
done just the same if the banks had been uncontrolled. There would
have been no necessity at all for them to proceed to issue Treasury
notes. They could simply have imposed on the banks the obligation
to grant loans to the state and enabled them to fulfill this obligation
by suspending their obligation to redeem their notes and making
the notes legal tender. The solution of a few minor technical problems would have been different, but the effect would have been the
same. For what enabled the governments to destroy the banking
system was not any technical, juristic, or economic shortcoming of
the banking organization, but the power conferred on them by the
general sentiment in favor of etatism and war. They were able to
dominate the monetary system because public opinion gave them
the moral right to do so. "Necessity knows no law" was the principle
which served as an excuse for all the actions of all governments
alike, and not only that of Germany, which was much blamed because of the candor with which it confessed its adherence to the
maxim.

At the most, as has been explained, an effective if limited protection against future etatistic abuse of the banking system might be
secured by prohibiting the issue of notes of small denominations.
That is to say, not by uncontrolled private enterprise in banking,
but on the contrary by interference with the freedom of the note
issue. Apart from this single prohibition, it would be quite possible
to leave the note issue without any legislative restrictions and, of
course, without any legislative privileges either, such as the granting of legal tender to the notes. Nevertheless, it is clear that banking
freedom *per se* cannot be said to make a return to gross inflationary
policy impossible.

Apart from the question of financial preparation for war, the arguments urged in favor of the centralization, monopolization, and state control of banks-of-issue in general and of credit-issuing banks in particular are thoroughly unsound. During the past twenty or thirty years, the literature of banking has got so thoroughly lost among the details of commercial technique, has so entirely abandoned the economic point of view and so completely surrendered itself to the influence of the most undisguised kinds of etatistic argument, that in order to discover what the considerations are that are supposed to militate against the freedom of the banks it is necessary to go back to the ideas that dominated the banking literature and policy of two or three generations ago. The bank-of-issue system was then supposed to be regulated in the interests of the poor and ignorant man in the street, so that bank failures might not inflict loss upon those who were unskilled and unpracticed in business matters—the laborer, the salaried employee, the civil servant, the farmer. The argument was that such private persons should not be obliged to accept notes whose value they were unable to test, an argument which only needs to be stated for its utter invalidity to be apparent. No banking policy could have been more injurious to the small man than recent etatism has been.

The argument, however, that was then supposed to be the decisive one was provided by the currency principle. From the point of view of this doctrine, any note issue that is not covered by gold is dangerous, and so, in order to obviate the recurrence of economic crises, such issues must be restricted. On the question of the theoretical importance of the currency principle, and on the question of whether the means proposed by the Currency School were effective, or could have been effective, or might still be effective, there is nothing that need be added to what has been said already. We have already shown that the dangers envisaged by the currency principle exist only when there is uniform procedure on the part of all the credit-issuing banks, not merely within a given country, but throughout the world. Now the monopolization of the banks-of-issue in each separate country does not merely fail to oppose any hindrance to this uniformity of procedure; it materially facilitates it.

What was supposed to be the decisive argument against freedom of banking in the last generation before the war is just the opposite to that which was held by the Currency School. Before the war, state control of banking was desired with the very object of artificially depressing the domestic rate of interest below the level that considerations of the possibility of redemption would have dictated if the banks had been completely free. The attempt was made to render as nugatory as possible the obligations of cash redemption, which constitutes the foundation stone of all credit-issuing bank systems. This was the intention of all the little expedients, individually unimportant but cumulatively of definite if temporary effect, which it was then customary to call banking policy. Their one intent may be summed up in the sentence: By hook or by crook to keep the rate of discount down. They have achieved the circumvention of all the natural and legal obstacles that hinder the reduction of the bank rate below the natural rate of interest. In fact, the object of all banking policy has been to escape the necessity for discount policy, an object, it is true, which it was unable to achieve until the outbreak of the war left the way free for inflation.

If the arguments for and against state regulation of the bank-of-issue system and of the whole system of fiduciary media are examined without the etatistic prejudice in favor of rules and prohibitions, they can lead to no other conclusion than that of one of the last of the defenders of banking freedom: "There is only one danger that is peculiar to the issue of notes; that of its being released from the common-law obligation under which everybody who enters into a commitment is strictly required to fulfill it at all times and in all places. This danger is infinitely greater and more threatening under a system of monopoly."[32]

12

Fisher's Proposal for a Commodity Standard

The more the view regains ground that general business fluctuations are to be explained by reference to the credit policy of the banks, the more eagerly are ways sought for by which to eliminate the alternation of boom and depression in economic life. It was the aim of the Currency School to prevent the periodical recurrence of general economic crises by setting a maximum limit to the issue of

---

[32] See Horn, *Bankfreiheit* (Stuttgart, 1867), pp. 376 f.

uncovered banknotes. An obvious further step is to close the gap that was not reckoned with in their theory and consequently not provided for in their policy by limiting the issue of fiduciary media in whatever form, not merely that of banknotes. If this were done, it would no longer be possible for the credit-issuing banks to underbid the equilibrium rate of interest and introduce into circulation new quantities of fiduciary media with the immediate consequence of an artificial stimulus to business and the inevitable final consequence of the dreaded economic crisis.

Whether a decisive step such as this will actually be taken apparently depends upon the kind of credit policy that is followed in the immediate future by the banks in general and by the big central banks-of-issue in particular. It has already been shown that it is impossible for a single bank by itself, and even for all banks in a given country or for all the banks in several countries, to increase the issue of fiduciary media, if the other banks do not do the same. The fact that tacit agreement to this effect among all the credit-issuing banks of the world has been achieved only with difficulty, and, even at that, has only effected what is after all but a small increase of credit, has constituted the most effective protection in recent times against excesses of credit policy. In this respect, we cannot yet[33] know how circumstances will shape. If it should prove easier now for the credit-issuing banks to extend their circulation, then failure to adopt measures for limiting the issue of fiduciary media will involve the greatest danger to the stability of economic life.

During the years immediately preceding the Great War, the objective exchange value of gold fell continuously. From 1896 onward, the commodity price level rose continuously. This movement, which is to be explained on the one hand by the increased production of gold and on the other hand by the extended employment of fiduciary media, became still more pronounced after the outbreak of the war. Gold disappeared from circulation in a series of populous countries and flowed into the diminishing region within which it continued to perform a monetary function as before. Of course, this resulted in a decrease in the purchasing power of gold. Prices rose, not only

---

[33] [It should be remembered that this was written in 1924. H.E.B.]

in the countries with an inflated currency, but also in the countries that had remained on the gold standard. If the countries that nowadays have a paper currency should return to gold, the objective exchange value of gold would rise; the gold prices of commodities and services would fall. This effect might be modified if the gold-exchange variety of standard were adopted instead of a gold currency; but if the area within which gold is employed as money is to be extended again, it is a consequence that can hardly be eliminated altogether. It would only come to stop when all countries had again adopted the gold standard. Then perhaps the fall in the value of gold which lasted for nearly thirty years might set in again.

The prospect is not a particularly pleasant one. It is hardly surprising in the circumstances that the attention of theorists and politicians should have been directed with special interest to a proposal that aims at nothing less than the creation of a money with the most stable purchasing power possible.

The fundamental idea of Fisher's scheme for stabilizing the purchasing power of money is the replacement of the gold standard by a "commodity" standard. Previous proposals concerning the commodity standard have conceived it as supplementing the precious-metal standard. Their intention has been that monetary obligations which did not fall due until after a certain period of time should be dischargeable, by virtue either of general compulsory legislation or of special contractual agreements between the parties, not in the nominal sum of money to which they referred, but by payment of that sum of money whose purchasing power at the time when the liability was discharged was equal to the purchasing power of the borrowed sum of money at the time when the liability was incurred. Otherwise they have intended that the precious metal should still fulfill its monetary office; the tabular standard was to have effect only as a standard of deferred payments. But Fisher has more ambitious designs. His commodity standard is not intended merely to supplement the gold standard, but to replace it altogether. This end is to be attained by means of an ingenious combination of the fundamental concept of the gold-exchange standard with that of the tabular standard.

The money substitutes that are current under a gold-exchange standard are redeemable either in gold or in bills on countries that are on the gold standard. Fisher wishes to retain redemption in gold, but in such a way that the currency units are no longer to be converted into a fixed weight of gold, but into the quantity of gold that corresponds to the purchasing power of the monetary unit at the time of the inauguration of the scheme. The dollar—according to the model bill worked out by Fisher for the United States—ceases to be a fixed quantity of gold of variable purchasing power and becomes a variable quantity of gold of invariable purchasing power. Calculations based on price statistics are used month by month for the construction of an index number which indicates by how much the purchasing power of the dollar has risen or fallen in comparison with the preceding month. Then, in accordance with this change in the value of money, the quantity of gold that represents one dollar is increased or diminished. This is the quantity of gold for which the dollar is to be redeemed at the banks entrusted with this function, and this is the quantity of gold for which they have to pay out one dollar to anybody who demands it.

Fisher's plan is ambitious and yet simple. Perhaps it is unnecessary to state that it is in no way dependent upon Fisher's particular theory of money, whose inadequacy as regards certain crucial matter has already been indicated.[34]

There is no need to criticize Fisher's scheme again with reference to the considerable dubiety attaching to the scientific correctness of index numbers and to the possibility of turning them to practical account in eliminating those unintended modifications of long-term contracts that arise from variations in the value of money.[35] In Fisher's scheme, the function of the index number is to serve as an indicator of variations in the purchasing power of the monetary unit from month to month. We may suppose that for determining changes in the value of money over very short periods—and in the present connection the month may certainly be regarded as a very short period—index numbers could be employed with at least sufficient exactitude for practical purposes. Yet even if we assume this,

---

[34] See pp. 166 f. above. Fisher particularly refers to this independence (*Stabilizing the Dollar* [New York, 1920], p. 90) and Anderson similarly affirms it, although in his book *The Value of Money* he has most severely criticized Fisher's version of the quantity theory of money. See Anderson, *The Fallacy of "The Stabilized Dollar"* (New York, 1920), pp. 6 f.

[35] See pp. 215 ff. and 232 ff. above.

we shall still be forced to conclude that the execution of Fisher's scheme could not in any way ameliorate the social consequences of variations in the value of money.

But before we enter upon this discussion, it is pertinent to inquire what demands the proposal makes concerning business practice.

If it is believed that the effects of variations in the value of money on long-term credit transactions are compensated by variations in the rate of interest, then the adoption of a commodity standard based on the use of index numbers as a supplement to the gold standard must be regarded as superfluous. But, in any case, this is certainly not true of gradual variations in the value of money of which neither the extent nor even the direction can be foreseen; the depreciation of gold which has gone on since toward the end of the nineteenth century has hardly found any expression at all in variations in the rate of interest. Thus, if it were possible to find a satisfactory solution of the problem of measuring variations in the value of money, the adoption of a tabular for long-term credit transactions (the decision as to the employment of the index being left to the parties to each particular contract) could by no means be regarded as superfluous. But the technical difficulties in the way are so great as to be insurmountable. The scientific inadequacy of all methods of calculating index numbers means that there can be no "correct" one and therefore none that could command general recognition. The choice among the many possible methods which are all equally inadequate from the purely theoretical point of view is an arbitrary one. Now since each method will yield a different result, the opinions of debtors and creditors concerning them will differ also. The different solutions adopted, in the law or by the administrative authority responsible for calculating the index numbers, as the various problems arise will constitute a new source of uncertainty in long-term credit transactions—an uncertainty that might affect the foundations of credit transactions more than variations in the value of gold would.

All this would be true of Fisher's proposals also insofar as they concern long-term credit transactions. Insofar as they concern short-term credit transactions, it must be pointed out that even under the present organization of the monetary system future fluctuations of the value of money are not ignored. The difficulty about taking account of future variations in the value of money in long-term credit transactions lies in the impossibility of foreknowing the direction and extent of long-period variations even with only relative certainty. But for shorter periods, over weeks and even over periods of a few months, it is possible to a certain extent to foretell the movement of the commodity-price level; and this movement consequently is allowed for in all transactions involving short-term credit. The money-market rate of interest, as the rate of interest in the market for short-term investments is called, expresses among other things the opinion of the business world as to imminent variations in commodity prices. It rises with the expectation of a rise in prices and falls with the expectation of a fall in prices. In those commercial agreements in which interest is explicitly allowed for there would be no particular difficulty under Fisher's scheme in making the necessary adjustment of business technique; the only adjustment that would be necessary in the new circumstances would be to leave out of account all considerations of variations in the commodity-price level in future calculations of the rate of interest. But the matter is somewhat more complicated in those transactions in which an explicit rate of interest does not appear, but is allowed for implicitly in some other terms of the agreement.

An example of a case of purchase on credit will assist the discussion of this point. Let us assume that in such a case the index number over a period of five successive months rises each month in arithmetical progression by one percent of the index number proper to the first month, as shown in the following table:

Month	Index No.	Quantity of fine gold for which a dollar may be redeemed, in hundredths of a gram
1	100	160.0
2	101	161.6
3	102	163.2
4	103	164.8
5	104	166.4

A person who had bought commodities in February on three months' credit would have to pay back in May .048 of a gram of fine gold for every dollar over and above the gold content of the dollars in which he had made the bargain. Now according to present practice, the terms of the transaction entered into in February would make allowance for the expected general rise of prices; in the purchase then determined the views held by the buyer and the seller as to immediate probabilities concerning future prices would already be expressed. Now since under Fisher's plan the purchase price would still have to be settled by payment of the agreed *number* of dollars, this rise of prices would be allowed for a second time. Clearly this will not do. In other words, the present ordinary practice concerning purchases on credit and other credit transactions must be modified.

All that a person will have to do after the introduction of the commodity standard, who would have bought a commodity in January on three months' credit at $105 under a simple gold standard, is to take account of the expected fluctuations in the value of gold *in a different way* in order not to buy dearer than he would have bought in gold dollars. If he correctly foresees these fluctuations as amounting to three dollars, then he would have to agree to pay a purchase price of only $\frac{160 \times 105}{164.8}$ dollars = 101.94 dollars. Fisher's project makes a different technique necessary in business; it cannot be claimed that this technique would be any simpler than that used under the pure gold standard. Both with and without Fisher's plan it is necessary for buyers and sellers to allow for variations in the general level of prices as well as for the particular variations in the prices of the commodities in which they deal; the only difference is in the method by which they evaluate the result of their speculative opinion.

We can thus see what value Fisher's scheme has as far as the consequences of variations in the value of money arising in connection with credit transactions are concerned. For long-term credit transactions, in which Fisher's scheme is no advance on the old and oft-discussed tabular standard which has never been put into execution because of its disadvantages, the use of the commodity standard as a supplement to the gold standard is impracticable because of the fundamental inadequacy of all methods of calculating index numbers. For short-term credit transactions, in which variations in the value of money are already taken account of in a different way, it is superfluous.

But variations in the objective exchange value of money have another kind of social consequence, arising from the fact that they are not expressed simultaneously and uniformly with regard to all commodities and services. Fisher's scheme promises no relief at all from consequences of this sort; Fisher, indeed, never refers to this kind of consequence of variations in the value of money and seems to be aware only of such effects as arise from their reactions on debt relationships contracted in terms of money.

However it may be calculated, an index number expresses nothing but an average of price variations. There will be prices that change more and prices that change less than the calculated average amount; and there will even be prices that change in the opposite direction. All who deal in those commodities whose prices change differently from the average will be affected by variations in the objective exchange-value of gold in the way already referred to (part 2, chap. 12, secs. 3 and 4), and the adjustment of the value of the dollar to the *average* movement of commodity prices as expressed in the chosen index number will be quite unable to affect this. When the value of gold falls, there will be persons who are favored by the fact that the rise in prices begins earlier for the commodities that they sell than for the commodities that they have to buy; and on the other hand there will be persons whose interests suffer because of the fact that they must continue to sell the commodities in which they deal at the lower prices corresponding to earlier circumstances although they already have to buy at the higher prices. Even the execution of Fisher's proposal could not cause the variations in the value of money to occur simultaneously and uniformly in relation to all other economic goods.

Thus, the social consequences of variations in the value of money could not be done away with even with the help of Fisher's commodity standard.

13

The Basic Questions of Future Currency Policy

Irving Fisher's scheme is symptomatic of a tendency in contemporary currency policy which is antipathetic to gold. There is an inclination in the United States and in Anglo-Saxon countries generally to overestimate in a quite extraordinary manner the significance of index methods. In these countries, it is entirely overlooked that the scientific exactness of these methods leaves much to be desired, that they can never yield anything more than a rough result at best, and that the question whether one or other method of calculation is preferable can never be solved by scientific means. The question of which method is preferred is always a matter for political judgment. It is a serious error to fall into to imagine that the methods suggested by monetary theorists and currency statisticians can yield unequivocal results that will render the determination of the value of money independent of the political decisions of the governing parties. A monetary system in which variations in the value of money and commodity prices are controlled by the figure calculated from price statistics is not in the slightest degree less dependent upon government influences than any other sort of monetary system in which the government is able to exert an influence on values.

There can be no doubt that the present state of the market for gold makes a decision between two possibilities imperative: a return to the actual use of gold after the fashion of the English gold standard of the nineteenth century, or a transition to a fiat-money standard with purchasing power regulated according to index numbers. The gold-exchange standard might be considered as a possible basis for future currency systems only if an international agreement could impose upon each state the obligation to maintain a stock of gold of a size corresponding to its capacity. A gold-exchange standard with a redemption fund chiefly invested in foreign bills in gold currencies is in the long run not a practicable general solution of the problem.

The first German edition of this work, published in 1912, concluded with an attempt at a glimpse into the future history of money and credit. The important parts of its argument ran as follows:

"It has gradually become recognized as a fundamental principle of monetary policy that intervention must be avoided as far as possible. Fiduciary media are scarcely different in nature from money; a supply of them affects the market in the same way as a supply of money proper; variations in their quantity influence the objective exchange value of money in just the same way as do variations in the quantity of money proper. Hence, they should logically be subjected to the same principles that have been established with regard to money proper; the same attempts should be made in their case as well to eliminate as far as possible human influence on the exchange ratio between money and other economic goods. The possibility of causing temporary fluctuations in the exchange ratios between goods of higher and of lower orders by the issue of fiduciary media, and the pernicious consequences connected with a divergence between the natural and money rates of interest, are circumstances leading to the same conclusion. Now it is obvious that the only way of eliminating human influence on the credit system is to suppress all further issue of fiduciary media. The basic conception of Peel's Act ought to be restated and more completely implemented than it was in the England of his time by including the issue of credit in the form of bank balances within the legislative prohibition.

"At first it might appear as if the execution of such radical measures would be bound to lead to a rise in the objective exchange-value of money. But this is not necessarily the case. It is not improbable that the production of gold and the increase in the issue of bank credit are at present increasing considerably faster than the demand for money and are consequently leading to a steady diminution of the objective exchange value of money. And there can be no doubt that a similar result follows from the apparently one-sided fixing of prices by sellers, the effect of which in diminishing the value of money has already been examined in detail. The complaints about the general increase in the cost of living, which will continue for a long time yet, may serve as a confirmation of the correctness of this assumption, which can be neither confirmed nor refuted statistically. Thus, a restriction of the growth of the stock of money in the broader sense need not unconditionally lead to a rise in the purchasing power of the monetary unit; it is possible that it might have the effect of completely or partly counteracting the fall in the value of money which might otherwise have occurred.

"It is not entirely out of the question that the monetary and credit policy of the future will attempt to check any further fall in the objective exchange value of money. Large classes of the population—wage and salary earners—feel that the continuous fall in the value of money is unjust. It is most certain that any proposals that promise them any relief in this direction will receive their warmest support. What these proposals will be like, and how far they will go, are matters that it is difficult to foresee. In any case, economists are not called upon to act as prophets."

Elsewhere in the course of the argument it was claimed that it would be useless to try and improve the monetary system at all in the way envisaged by the tabular standard. "We must abandon all attempts to render the organization of the market even more perfect than it is and content ourselves with what has been attained already; or rather, we must strive to retain what has been attained already; and that is not such an easy matter as it seems to appear to those who have been more concerned to improve the apparatus of exchange than to note the dangers that implied its maintenance at its present level of perfection.

"It would be a mistake to assume that the modern organization of exchange is bound to continue to exist. It carries within itself the germ of its own destruction; the development of the fiduciary medium must necessarily lead to its breakdown. Once common principles for their circulation-credit policy are agreed to by the different credit-issuing banks, or once the multiplicity of credit-issuing banks is replaced by a single world bank, there will no longer be any limit to the issue of fiduciary media. At first, it will be possible to increase the issue of fiduciary media only until the objective exchange value of money is depressed to the level determined by the other possible uses of the monetary metal. But in the case of fiat money and credit money there is no such limit, and even in the case of commodity money it cannot prove impassable. For once the employment of money substitutes has superseded the employment of money for actual employment in exchange transactions mediated by money, and we are by no means very far from this state of affairs, the moment the limit was passed the obligation to redeem the money substitutes would be removed and so the transition to bank-credit money would easily be completed. Then the only limit to the issue would be constituted by the technical costs of the banking business. In any case, long before these limits are reached, the consequences of the increase in the issue of fiduciary media will make themselves felt acutely."

Since then we have experienced the collapse, sudden enough, of the monetary systems in a whole series of European states. The inflation of the war and postwar periods, exceeding everything that could have been foreseen, has created an unexampled chaos. Now we are on the way to mastering this chaos and to returning to a new organization of the monetary system which will be all the better the less it differs from the system in force before the war.

The organization of exchange that will thus be achieved again will exhibit all the shortcomings that have continually been referred to with emphasis throughout the present book. It will be a task for the future to erect safeguards against the inflationary misuse of the monetary system by the government and against the extension of the circulation of fiduciary media by the banks.

Yet such safeguards alone will not suffice to avert the dangers that menace the peaceful development of the function of money and fiduciary media in facilitating exchange. Money is part of the mechanism of the free market in a social order based on private property in the means of production. Only where political forces are not antagonistic to private property in the means of production is it possible to work out a policy aiming at the greatest possible stability of the objective exchange value of money.

PART FOUR

MONETARY RECONSTRUCTION

(This part was written in 1952 and
first appeared in the 1953 American
edition of Yale University Press)

CHAPTER 21

The Principle of Sound Money

1

The Classical Idea of Sound Money

The principle of sound money that guided nineteenth-century monetary doctrines and policies was a product of classical political economy. It was an essential part of the liberal program as developed by eighteenth-century social philosophy and propagated in the following century by the most influential political parties of Europe and America.

The liberal doctrine sees in the market economy the best, even the only possible, system of economic organization of society. Private ownership of the means of production tends to shift control of production to the hands of those best fitted for this job and thus to secure for all members of society the fullest possible satisfaction of their needs. It assigns to the consumers the power to choose those purveyors who supply them in the cheapest way with the articles they are most urgently asking for and thus subjects the entrepreneurs and the owners of the means of production, namely, the capitalists and the landowners, to the sovereignty of the buying public. It makes nations and their citizens free and provides ample sustenance for a steadily increasing population.

453

As a system of peaceful cooperation under the division of labor, the market economy could not work without an institution warranting to its members protection against domestic gangsters and external foes. Violent aggression can be thwarted only by armed resistance and repression. Society needs an apparatus of defense, a state, a government, a police power. Its undisturbed functioning must be safeguarded by continuous preparedness to repel aggressors. But then a new danger springs up. How keep under control the men entrusted with the handling of the government apparatus lest they turn their weapons against those whom they were expected to serve? The main political problem is how to prevent the rulers from becoming despots and enslaving the citizenry. Defense of the individual's liberty against the encroachment of tyrannical governments is the essential theme of the history of Western civilization. The characteristic feature of the Occident is its peoples' pursuit of liberty, a concern unknown to Orientals. All the marvelous achievements of Western civilization are fruits grown on the tree of liberty.

It is impossible to grasp the meaning of the idea of sound money if one does not realize that it was devised as an instrument for the protection of civil liberties against despotic inroads on the part of governments. Ideologically it belongs in the same class with political constitutions and bills of rights. The demand for constitutional guarantees and for bills of rights was a reaction against arbitrary rule and the nonobservance of old customs by kings. The postulate of sound money was first brought up as a response to the princely practice of debasing the coinage. It was later carefully elaborated and perfected in the age which—through the experience of the American continental currency, the paper money of the French Revolution and the British restriction period—had learned what a government can do to a nation's currency system.

Modern cryptodespotism, which arrogates to itself the name of liberalism, finds fault with the negativity of the concept of freedom. The censure is spurious as it refers merely to the grammatical form of the idea and does not comprehend that all civil rights can be as well defined in affirmative as in negative terms. They are negative as they are designed to obviate an evil, namely omnipotence of the police power, and to prevent the state from becoming totalitarian.

They are affirmative as they are designed to preserve the smooth operation of the system of private property, the only social system that has brought about what is called civilization.

Thus the sound-money principle has two aspects. It is affirmative in approving the market's choice of a commonly used medium of exchange. It is negative in obstructing the government's propensity to meddle with the currency system.

The sound-money principle was derived not so much from the Classical economists' analysis of the market phenomena as from their interpretation of historical experience. It was an experience that could be perceived by a much larger public than the narrow circles of those conversant with economic theory. Hence the sound-money idea became one of the most popular points of the liberal program. Friends and foes of liberalism considered it one of the essential postulates of a liberal policy.

Sound money meant a metallic standard. Standard coins should be in fact a definite quantity of the standard metal as precisely determined by the law of the country. Only standard coins should have unlimited legal-tender quality. Token coins and all kinds of moneylike paper should be, on presentation and without delay, redeemed in lawful standard money.

So far there was unanimity among the supporters of sound money. But then the battle of the standards arose. The defeat of those favoring silver and the unfeasibility of bimetallism eventually made the sound-money principle mean the gold standard. At the end of the nineteenth century there was all over the world unanimity among businessmen and statesmen with regard to the indispensability of the gold standard. Countries which were under a fiat-money system or under the silver standard considered adoption of the gold standard the foremost goal of their economic policy. Those who disputed the eminence of the gold standard were dismissed as cranks by the representatives of the official doctrine—professors, bankers, statesmen, editors of the great newspapers and magazines.

It was a serious blunder of the supporters of sound money to adopt such tactics. There is no use in dealing in a summary way with any ideology however foolish and contradictory it may appear. Even a manifestly erroneous doctrine should be refuted by careful analysis and the unmasking of the fallacies implied. A sound doctrine can win only by exploding the delusions of its adversaries.

The essential principles of the sound-money doctrine were and are impregnable. But their scientific support in the last decades of the nineteenth century was rather shaky. The attempts to demonstrate their reasonableness from the point of view of the Classical value theory were not very convincing and made no sense at all when this value concept had to be discarded. But the champions of the new value theory for almost half a century restricted their studies to the problems of direct exchange and left the treatment of money and banking to routinists unfamiliar with economics. There were treatises on catallactics which dealt only incidentally and cursorily with monetary matters, and there were books on currency and banking which did not even attempt to integrate their subject into the structure of a catallactic system.[1] Finally the idea evolved that the modern doctrine of value, the subjectivist or marginal utility doctrine, is unable to explain the problems of money's purchasing power.[2]

It is easy to comprehend how under such circumstances even the least tenable objections raised by the advocates of inflationism remained unanswered. The gold standard lost popularity because for a very long time no serious attempts were made to demonstrate its merits and to explode the tenets of its adversaries.

2

The Virtues and Alleged Shortcomings of the Gold Standard

The excellence of the gold standard is to be seen in the fact that it renders the determination of the monetary unit's purchasing power independent of the policies of governments and political parties. Furthermore, it prevents rulers from eluding the financial and budgetary prerogatives of the representative assemblies. Parliamentary control of finances works only if the government is not in a position to provide for unauthorized expenditures by increasing the circulating amount of fiat money. Viewed in this light, the gold

---

[1] See Mises, *Human Action* (New Haven: Yale University Press, 1949), pp. 204–6.
[2] See pp. 139–44 above.

standard appears as an indispensable implement of the body of constitutional guarantees that make the system of representative government function.

When in the 1850s gold production increased considerably in California and Australia, people attacked the gold standard as inflationary. In those days Michel Chevalier, in his book *Probable Depreciation of Gold*, recommended the abandonment of the gold standard, and Béranger dealt with the same subject in one of his poems. But later these criticisms subsided. The gold standard was no longer denounced as inflationary but on the contrary as deflationary. Even the most fanatical champions of inflation like to disguise their true intentions by declaring that they merely want to offset the contractionist pressure which the allegedly insufficient supply of gold tends to produce.

Yet it is clear that over the last generations there has prevailed a tendency of all commodity prices and wage rates to rise. We may neglect dealing with the economic effects of a general tendency of money prices and money wages to drop.[3] For there is no doubt that what we have experienced over the last hundred years was just the opposite, namely, a secular tendency toward a drop in the monetary unit's purchasing power, which was only temporarily interrupted by the aftermath of the breakdown of a boom intentionally created by credit expansion. Gold became cheaper in terms of commodities, not dearer. What the foes of the gold standard are asking for is not to reverse a prevailing tendency in the determination of prices, but to intensify very considerably the already prevailing upward trend of prices and wages. They simply want to lower the monetary unit's purchasing power at an accelerated pace.

Such a policy of radical inflationism is, of course, extremely popular. But its popularity is to a great extent due to a misapprehension of its effects. What people are really asking for is a rise in the prices of those commodities and services they are selling while the prices of those commodities and services which they are buying remain unchanged. The potato grower aims at higher prices for potatoes. He does not long for a rise in other prices. He is injured if these other prices rise sooner or in greater proportion than the price of potatoes. If a politician addressing a meeting declares that the gov-

---

[3] About this problem, see *Human Action*, pp. 463–68.

ernment should adopt a policy which makes prices rise, his hearers are likely to applaud. Yet each of them is thinking of a different price rise.

From time immemorial inflation has been recommended as a means to alleviate the burdens of poor worthy debtors at the expense of rich harsh creditors. However, under capitalism the typical debtors are not the poor but the well-to-do owners of real estate, of firms, and of common stock, people who have borrowed from banks, savings banks, insurance companies, and bondholders. The typical creditors are not the rich but people of modest means who own bonds and savings accounts or have taken out insurance policies. If the common man supports anticreditor measures, he does it because he ignores the fact that he himself is a creditor. The idea that millionaires are the victims of an easy-money policy is an atavistic remnant.

For the naive mind there is something miraculous in the issuance of fiat money. A magic word spoken by the government creates out of nothing a thing which can be exchanged against any merchandise a man would like to get. How pale is the art of sorcerers, witches, and conjurors when compared with that of the government's Treasury Department! The government, professors tell us, "can raise all the money it needs by printing it."[4] Taxes for revenue, announced a chairman of the Federal Reserve Bank of New York, are "obsolete."[5] How wonderful! And how malicious and misanthropic are those stubborn supporters of outdated economic orthodoxy who ask governments to balance their budgets by covering all expenditures out of tax revenue!

These enthusiasts do not see that the working of inflation is conditioned by the ignorance of the public and that inflation ceases to work as soon as the many become aware of its effects upon the monetary unit's purchasing power. In normal times, that is in periods in which the government does not tamper with the monetary standard, people do not bother about monetary problems. Quite naively they take it for granted that the monetary unit's purchasing power is "stable." They pay attention to changes occurring in the money prices of the various commodities. They know very well that

[4] See A. B. Lerner, *The Economics of Control* (New York, 1944), pp. 307–8.
[5] See B. Ruml, "Taxes for Revenue Are Obsolete," *American Affairs* 8 (1946): 35–36.

the exchange ratios between different commodities vary. But they are not conscious of the fact that the exchange ratio between money on the one side and all commodities and services on the other side is variable too. When the inevitable consequences of inflation appear and prices soar, they think that commodities are becoming dearer and fail to see that money is getting cheaper. In the early stages of an inflation only a few people discern what is going on, manage their business affairs in accordance with this insight, and deliberately aim at reaping inflation gains. The overwhelming majority are too dull to grasp a correct interpretation of the situation. They go on in the routine they acquired in noninflationary periods. Filled with indignation, they attack those who are quicker to apprehend the real causes of the agitation of the market as "profiteers" and lay the blame for their own plight on them. This ignorance of the public is the indispensable basis of the inflationary policy. Inflation works as long as the housewife thinks: "I need a new frying pan badly. But prices are too high today; I shall wait until they drop again." It comes to an abrupt end when people discover that the inflation will continue, that it causes the rise in prices, and that therefore prices will skyrocket infinitely. The critical stage begins when the housewife thinks: "I don't need a new frying pan today; I may need one in a year or two. But I'll buy it today because it will be much more expensive later." Then the catastrophic end of the inflation is close. In its last stage the housewife thinks: "I don't need another table; I shall never need one. But it's wiser to buy a table than keep these scraps of paper that the government calls money, one minute longer."

Let us leave the problem of whether or not it is advisable to base a system of government finance upon the intentional deception of the immense majority of the citizenry. It is enough to stress the point that such a policy of deceit is self-defeating. Here the famous dictum of Lincoln holds true: You can't fool all of the people all of the time. Eventually the masses come to understand the schemes of their rulers. Then the cleverly concocted plans of inflation collapse. Whatever compliant government economists may have said, inflationism is not a monetary policy that can be considered as an alternative to a sound-money policy. It is at best a temporary expedient. The main problem of an inflationary policy is how to stop it before the masses have seen through their rulers' artifices. It is a display of considerable naivety to recommend openly a monetary system that can work only if its essential features are ignored by the public.

The index-number method is a very crude and imperfect means of "measuring" changes occurring in the monetary unit's purchasing power. As there are in the field of social affairs no constant relations between magnitudes, no measurement is possible and economics can never become quantitative.[6] But the index-number method, notwithstanding its inadequacy, plays an important role in the process which in the course of an inflationary movement makes the people inflation-conscious. Once the use of index numbers becomes common, the government is forced to slow down the pace of the inflation and to make the people believe that the inflationary policy is merely a temporary expedient for the duration of a passing emergency, one that will be stopped before long. While government economists still praise the superiority of inflation as a lasting scheme of monetary management, governments are compelled to exercise restraint in its application.

It is permissible to call a policy of intentional inflation dishonest as the effects sought by its application can be attained only if the government succeeds in deceiving the greater part of the people about the consequences of its policy. Many of the champions of interventionist policies will not scruple greatly about such cheating; in their eyes what the government does can never be wrong. But their lofty moral indifference is at a loss to oppose an objection to the economist's argument against inflation. In the economist's eyes the main issue is not that inflation is morally reprehensible but that it cannot work except when resorted to with great restraint and even then only for a limited period. Hence resort to inflation cannot be considered seriously as an alternative to a permanent standard such as the gold standard is.

The proinflationist propaganda emphasizes nowadays the alleged fact that the gold standard collapsed and that it will never be tried again: nations are no longer willing to comply with the rules of the gold-standard game and to bear all the costs which the preservation of the gold standard requires.

---

[6] See chap. 11 above; *Human Action,* pp. 55–57, 347–49.

First of all there is need to remember that the gold standard did not collapse. Governments abolished it in order to pave the way for inflation. The whole grim apparatus of oppression and coercion—policemen, customs guards, penal courts, prisons, in some countries even executioners—had to be put into action in order to destroy the gold standard. Solemn pledges were broken, retroactive laws were promulgated, provisions of constitutions and bills of rights were openly defied. And hosts of servile writers praised what the governments had done and hailed the dawn of the fiat-money millennium.

The most remarkable thing about this allegedly new monetary policy, however, is its complete failure. True, it substituted fiat money in the domestic markets for sound money and favored the material interests of some individuals and groups of individuals at the expense of others. It furthermore contributed considerably to the disintegration of the international division of labor. But it did not succeed in eliminating gold from its position as the international or world standard. If you glance at the financial page of any newspaper you discover at once that gold is still the world's money, and not the variegated products of the divers government printing offices. These scraps of paper are the more appreciated the more stable their price is in terms of an ounce of gold. Whoever today dares to hint at the possibility that nations may return to a domestic gold standard is cried down as a lunatic. This terrorism may still go on for some time. But the position of gold as the world's standard is impregnable. The policy of "going off the gold standard" did not relieve a country's monetary authorities from the necessity of taking into account the monetary unit's price in terms of gold.

What those authors who speak about the rules of the gold-standard game have in mind is not clear. Of course, it is obvious that the gold standard cannot function satisfactorily if to buy or to sell or to hold gold is illegal, and hosts of judges, constables, and informers are busily enforcing the law. But the gold standard is not a game; it is a market phenomenon and as such a social institution. Its preservation does not depend on the observation of some specific rules. It requires nothing else than that the government abstain from deliberately sabotaging it. To refer to this condition as a rule of an alleged game is no more reasonable than to declare that the preservation of Paul's life depends on compliance with the rules of the Paul's-life game because Paul must die if somebody stabs him to death.

What all the enemies of the gold standard spurn as its main vice is precisely the same thing that in the eyes of the advocates of the gold standard is its main virtue, namely, its incompatibility with a policy of credit expansion. The nucleus of all the effusions of the antigold authors and politicians is the expansionist fallacy.

The expansionist doctrine does not realize that interest, that is, the discount of future goods as against present goods, is an originary category of human valuation, actual in any kind of human action and independent of any social institutions. The expansionists do not grasp the fact that there never were and there never can be human beings who attach to an apple available in a year or in a hundred years the same value they attach to an apple available now. In their opinion interest is an impediment to the expansion of production and consequently to human welfare that unjustified institutions have created in order to favor the selfish concerns of money lenders. Interest, they say, is the price people must pay for borrowing. Its height therefore depends on the magnitude of the supply of money. If laws did not artificially restrict the creation of additional money, the rate of interest would drop, ultimately even to zero. The "contractionist" pressure would disappear, there would no longer be a shortage of capital, and it would become possible to execute many business projects which the "restrictionism" of the gold standard obstructs. What is needed to make everyone prosperous is simply to defy "the rules of the gold-standard game," the observance of which is the main source of all our economic ills.

These absurd doctrines greatly impressed ignorant politicians and demagogues when they were blended with nationalist slogans. What prevents our country from fully enjoying the advantages of a low-interest-rate policy, says the economic isolationist, is its adherence to the gold standard. Our central bank is forced to keep its rate of discount at a height that corresponds to conditions on the international money market and to the discount rates of foreign central banks. Otherwise "speculators" would withdraw funds from our country for short-term investment abroad and the resulting outflow of gold would make the gold reserves of our central bank drop below the legal ratio. If our central bank were not obliged to redeem its banknotes in gold, no such withdrawal of gold could occur and there would be no necessity for it to adjust the height of the money rate to the situation of the international money market, dominated by the world-embracing gold monopoly.

The most amazing fact about this argument is that it was raised precisely in debtor countries for which the operation of the international money and capital market meant an inflow of foreign funds and consequently the appearance of a tendency toward a drop in interest rates. It was popular in Germany and still more in Austria in the 1870s and 80s, but it was hardly ever seriously mentioned in those years in England or in the Netherlands, whose banks and bankers lent amply to Germany and Austria. It was advanced in England only after World War I, when Great Britain's position as the world's banking center had been lost.

Of course, the argument itself is untenable. The inevitable eventual failure of any attempt at credit expansion is not caused by the international intertwinement of the lending business. It is the outcome of the fact that it is impossible to substitute fiat money and a bank's circulation credit for nonexisting capital goods. Credit expansion initially can produce a boom. But such a boom is bound to end in a slump, in a depression. What bring about the recurrence of periods of economic crises are precisely the reiterated attempts of governments and banks supervised by them to expand credit in order to make business good by cheap interest rates.[7]

3

The Full-Employment Doctrine

The inflationist or expansionist doctrine is presented in several varieties. But its essential content remains always the same.

The oldest and most naive version is that of the allegedly insufficient supply of money. Business is bad, says the grocer, because my customers or prospective customers do not have enough money

---

[7] Part 3 of this book is entirely devoted to the exposition of the trade-cycle theory, the doctrine that is called the monetary- or circulation-credit theory, sometimes also the Austrian theory. See also *Human Action*, pp. 535–83, 787–94.

to expand their purchases. So far he is right. But when he adds that what is needed to render his business more prosperous is to increase the quantity of money in circulation, he is mistaken. What he really has in mind is an increase of the amount of money in the pockets of his customers and prospective customers while the amount of money in the hands of other people remains unchanged. He asks for a specific kind of inflation; namely, an inflation in which the additional new money first flows into the cash holdings of a definite group of people, his customers, and thus permits him to reap inflation gains. Of course, everybody who advocates inflation does it because he infers that he will belong to those who are favored by the fact that the prices of the commodities and services they sell will rise at an earlier date and to a higher point than the prices of those commodities and services they buy. Nobody advocates an inflation in which he would be on the losing side.

This spurious grocer philosophy was once and for all exploded by Adam Smith and Jean-Baptiste Say. In our day it has been revived by Lord Keynes, and under the name of full-employment policy is one of the basic policies of all governments which are not entirely subject to the Soviets. Yet Keynes was at a loss to advance a tenable argument against Say's law. Nor have his disciples or the hosts of economists, pseudo and other, in the offices of the various governments, the United Nations, and divers other national or international bureaus done any better. The fallacies implied in the Keynesian full-employment doctrine are, in a new attire, essentially the same errors which Smith and Say long since demolished.

Wage rates are a market phenomenon, are the prices paid for a definite quantity of labor of a definite quality. If a man cannot sell his labor at the price he would like to get for it, he must lower the price he is asking for it or else he remains unemployed. If the government or labor unions fix wage rates at a higher point than the potential rate of the unhampered labor market and if they enforce their minimum-price decree by compulsion and coercion, a part of those who want to find jobs remain unemployed. Such institutional unemployment is the inevitable result of the methods applied by present-day self-styled progressive governments. It is the real outcome of measures falsely labeled prolabor. There is only one efficacious way toward a rise in real wage rates and an improvement of the standard of living of the wage earners: to increase the per-head quota of capital invested. This is what laissez-faire capitalism brings about to the extent that its operation is not sabotaged by government and labor unions.

We do not need to investigate whether the politicians of our age are aware of these facts. In most universities it is not good form to mention them to the students. Books that are skeptical with regard to the official doctrines are not widely bought by the libraries or used in courses, and consequently publishers are afraid to publish them. Newspapers seldom criticize the popular creed because they fear a boycott on the part of the unions. Thus politicians may be utterly sincere in believing that they have won "social gains" for the "people" and that the spread of unemployment is one of the evils inherent in capitalism and is in no way caused by the policies of which they are boasting. However this may be, it is obvious that the reputation and the prestige of the men who are now ruling the countries outside the Soviet bloc and of their professorial and journalistic allies are so inseparably tied up with the "progressive" doctrine that they must cling to it. If they do not want to forsake their political ambitions, they must stubbornly deny that their own policy tends to make mass unemployment a permanent phenomenon and must try to put on capitalism the blame for the undesired effects of their procedures.

The most characteristic feature of the full-employment doctrine is that it does not provide information about the way in which wage rates are determined on the market. To discuss the height of wage rates is taboo for the "progressives." When they deal with unemployment, they do not refer to wage rates. As they see it, the height of wage rates has nothing to do with unemployment and must never be mentioned in connection with it.

If there are unemployed, says the progressive doctrine, the government must increase the amount of money in circulation until full employment is reached. It is, they say, a serious mistake to call inflation an increase in the quantity of money in circulation effected under these conditions. It is just "full-employment policy."

We may refrain from frowning upon this terminological oddity of the doctrine. The main point is that every increase in the quantity of money in circulation brings about a tendency of prices and wages to rise. If, in spite of the rise of commodity prices, wage rates do not rise at all or if their rise lags sufficiently behind the rise in commodity prices, the number of people unemployed on account of the height of wage rates will drop. But it will drop merely because such a configuration of commodity prices and wage rates means a drop in real wage rates. In order to attain this result it would not have been necessary to embark upon increasing the amount of money in circulation. A reduction in the height of the minimum-wage rates enforced by the government or union pressure would have achieved the same effect without at the same time starting all the other consequences of an inflation.

It is a fact that in some countries in the 1930s, recourse to inflation was not immediately followed by a rise in the height of money wage rates as fixed by the governments or unions, that this was tantamount to a drop in real wage rates, and that consequently the number of unemployed decreased. But this was merely a passing phenomenon. When in 1936 Lord Keynes declared that a movement of employers to revise money-wage bargains downward would be much more strongly resisted than a gradual and "automatic" lowering of real wage rates as a result of rising prices,[8] he had already been outdated and refuted by the march of events. The masses had already begun to see through the artifices of inflation. Problems of purchasing power and index numbers became an important issue in the unions' dealings with wage rates. The full-employment argument in favor of inflation was already behind the times at the very moment when Keynes and his followers proclaimed it as the fundamental principle of progressive economic policies.

4

The Emergency Argument in Favor of Inflation

All the economic arguments in favor of inflation are untenable. The fallacies have long since been exploded in an irrefutable way.

There is, however, a political argument in favor of inflation that requires special analysis. This political argument is only rarely resorted to in books, articles, and political speeches. It does not lend

---

[8] See Keynes, *The General Theory of Employment, Interest and Money* (London, 1936), p. 264.

itself to such public treatment. But the underlying idea plays an important role in the thinking of statesmen and historians.

Its supporters fully accept all the teachings of the sound-money doctrine. They do not share the errors of the inflationist quacks. They realize that inflationism is a self-defeating policy which must inevitably lead to an economic cataclysm and that all its allegedly beneficial effects are, even from the point of view of the authors of the inflationary policy, more undesirable than the evils which were to be cured by inflation. In full awareness of all this, however, they still believe that there are emergencies which peremptorily require or at least justify recourse to inflation. A nation, they say, can be menaced by evils which are incomparably more disastrous than the effects of inflation. If it is possible to avoid the total annihilation of a nation's freedom and culture by a temporary abandonment of sound money, no reasonable objection can be raised against such a procedure. It would simply mean preferring a smaller evil to a greater one.

In order to appraise correctly the weight of this emergency argument in favor of inflation, there is need to realize that inflation does not add anything to a nation's power of resistance, either to its material resources or to its spiritual and moral strength. Whether there is inflation or not, the material equipment required by the armed forces must be provided out of the available means by restricting consumption for nonvital purposes, by intensifying production in order to increase output, and by consuming a part of the capital previously accumulated. All these things can be done if the majority of citizens are firmly resolved to offer resistance to the best of their abilities and are prepared to make such sacrifices for the sake of preserving their independence and culture. Then the legislature will adopt fiscal methods which warrant the achievement of these goals. They will attain what is called economic mobilization or a defense economy without tampering with the monetary system. The great emergency can be dealt with without recourse to inflation.

But the situation those advocating emergency inflation have in mind is of a quite different character. Its characteristic feature is an irreconcilable antagonism between the opinions of the government and those of the majority of the people. The government, in this regard supported by only a minority of the people, believes that there exists an emergency that necessitates a considerable increase in public expenditure and a corresponding austerity in private households. But the majority of the people disagree. They do not believe that conditions are so bad as the government depicts them or they think that the preservation of the values endangered is not worth the sacrifices they would have to make. There is no need to raise the question whether the government's or the majority's opinion is right. Perhaps the government is right. However, we deal not with the substance of the conflict but with the methods chosen by the rulers for its solution. They reject the democratic way of persuading the majority. They arrogate to themselves the power and the moral right to circumvent the will of the people. They are eager to win its cooperation by deceiving the public about the costs involved in the measures suggested. While seemingly complying with the constitutional procedures of representative government, their conduct is in effect not that of elected officeholders but that of guardians of the people. The elected executive no longer deems himself the people's mandatory; he turns into a führer.

The emergency that brings about inflation is this: the people or the majority of the people are not prepared to defray the costs incurred by their rulers' policies. They support these policies only to the extent that they believe their conduct does not burden themselves. They vote, for instance, only for such taxes as are to be paid by other people, namely, the rich, because they think that these taxes do not impair their own material well-being. The reaction of the government to this attitude of the nation is, at least sometimes, directed by the sincere wish to serve what it believes to be the true interests of the people in the best possible way. But if the government resorts for this purpose to inflation, it is employing methods which are contrary to the principles of representative government, although formally it may have fully complied with the letter of the constitution. It is taking advantage of the masses' ignorance, it is cheating the voters instead of trying to convince them.

It is not just an accident that in our age inflation has become the accepted method of monetary management. Inflation is the fiscal complement of statism and arbitrary government. It is a cog in the complex of policies and institutions which gradually lead toward totalitarianism.

Western liberty cannot hold its ground against the onslaughts of Oriental slavery if the peoples do not realize what is at stake and are not ready to make the greatest sacrifices for the ideals of their civilization. Recourse to inflation may provide the government with the funds which it could neither collect by taxation nor borrow from the savings of the public because the people and its parliamentary representatives objected. Spending the newly created fiat money, the government can buy the equipment the armed forces need. But a nation reluctant to make the material sacrifices necessary for victory will never display the requisite mental energy. What warrants success in a fight for freedom and civilization is not merely material equipment but first of all the spirit that animates those handling the weapons. This heroic spirit cannot be bought by inflation.

CHAPTER 22

Contemporary Currency Systems

1

The Inflexible Gold Standard

The mark of all the varieties of the gold standard and the gold-exchange standard as they existed on the eve of World War I was the gold parity of the country's monetary unit, precisely determined by a duly promulgated law. It was understood that this parity would never be changed. In virtue of the parity law the unit of the national currency system was practically a definite quantity of the metal gold. It was of no consequence whether or not banknotes had been endowed with legal-tender power. They were redeemable in gold, and the central banks really did redeem them fully on demand.

The difference between the standard that was later called the orthodox or the classical gold standard and the gold-exchange standard was a difference of degree. Under the former there were gold coins in the cash holdings of the individual citizens and firms and they were—together with banknotes, checks, and fractional coins—employed in business transactions. Under the gold-exchange standard no gold was used in transacting domestic business. But the central bank sold gold bullion and foreign exchange against domestic currency at rates that did not exceed the legal parity by more than the gold margin would be under the classical gold standard.

Thus the countries under the gold-exchange standard were no less integrated into the system of the international gold standard than those under the classical gold standard.

2

The Flexible Standard

The flexible standard, a development of the period between World War I and World War II, originated from the gold-exchange standard. Its characteristic features are:

1. The domestic standard's parity as against gold and foreign exchange is not fixed by a law but simply by the government agency entrusted with the conduct of monetary affairs.

2. This parity is subject to sudden changes without previous notice to the public. It is flexible. But this flexibility is practically always employed for lowering the domestic currency's exchange value as against gold and those foreign currencies which did not drop against gold. If the downward jump of parity was rather conspicuous, it was called a devaluation. If it was slight only, it was usual to speak of a newly manifested weakness of the currency concerned.

3. The only method available for preventing a currency's exchange value from dropping below the parity chosen is unconditional redemption of any amount offered. But the term *redemption* has in the ears of the self-styled unorthodox statesman an unpleasant connotation. It reminds him of the past when the holder of a banknote had a legally warranted right to redemption at par. The modern bureaucrat prefers the term *pegging*. In fact, in this connection pegging and redeeming mean exactly the same thing. They mean that the currency concerned is prevented from dropping below a certain point by the fact that any amount offered for sale is bought at this price by the redeeming or pegging agency.

Of course, this point—the parity—is not fixed by a law under the flexible standard, and the agency is free to decline to buy an amount offered at this rate. Then the price of foreign exchange begins to rise as against this parity. If the government does not intend to adopt the freely vacillating standard, the pegging is soon resumed at a lower level, that is, the price of foreign exchange is now higher in terms of the domestic currency. Such an event is sometimes referred to as raising the price of gold.

4. In some countries the conduct of pegging operations is entrusted to the central bank, in others to a special agency called foreign-exchange equalization account or a similar name.[1]

3

The Freely Vacillating Currency

If the government practices restraint in the issuance of additional amounts of its credit or fiat money and if public opinion assumes that the inflationary policy will be stopped altogether in a not too distant future, an inflationary currency system can prevail for a series of years. The country experiences all the effects resulting from a currency the unit of which vacillates in exchange value as against the international gold standard. With regard to these effects the freely vacillating currency may be called a bad currency. But it can last and is not inevitably headed for a breakdown.

The characteristic mark of this freely vacillating currency is that the owner of any amount of it has no claim whatever against the Treasury, a bank, or any other agency. There is no redemption either *de jure* or *de facto*. The pieces are not money substitutes but money proper in themselves.

It sometimes happened, especially in the European inflations of the 1920s, that the government, frightened by a speedy decline in its currency's price in terms of gold or foreign exchange, tried to counteract the decline by selling on the market a certain amount of gold and foreign exchange against domestic currency. It was a rather nonsensical operation. It would have been much simpler and much more effective if the government had never issued those amounts which it later bought back on the market. Such ventures did not affect the course of events. The only reason they must be mentioned is that governments and their agents sometimes falsely referred to them as pegging.

The outstanding instance of a freely vacillating currency today is

---

[1]For the reasons that led to the establishment of such foreign-exchange equalization accounts, see *Human Action*, pp. 458–59.

the United States dollar, the New Deal dollar. It is not redeemable in gold or any foreign exchange. The administration is committed to an inflationary policy, increasing more and more the amount of notes in circulation and of bank deposits subject to check. If the Treasury had been permitted to act according to the designs of its advisers, the dollar would have long since gone the way of the German mark of 1923. But lively protests on the part of a few economists alarmed the nation and enjoined restraint on the Treasury. The speed of the inflation was slowed down. Yet the future of the dollar is precarious, dependent on the vicissitudes of the continuing struggle between a small minority of economists on the one hand and hosts of ignorant demagogues and their "unorthodox" allies on the other hand.

4

The Illusive Standard

The illusive standard is based on a falsehood. The government decrees that there exists a parity between the domestic currency and gold or foreign exchange. It is fully aware of the fact that on the market there prevail exchange ratios lower than the illusory parity it is pleased to ordain. It knows that nothing is done to make the illusory parity an effective parity. It knows that there is no convertibility. But it clings to its pretense and forbids transactions at a ratio deviating from its fictitious exchange rate. He who sells or buys at any other ratio is guilty of a crime and severely punished.

Strict enforcement of such a decree would make all monetary transactions with foreign countries cease. Therefore the government goes a step further. It expropriates all foreign exchange owned by its subjects and indemnifies the expropriated by paying them the amount of domestic currency which according to the official decree is the equivalent of the confiscated foreign-exchange holdings. These confiscations convey to the government the national monopoly of dealing with foreign exchange. It is now the only seller of foreign exchange in the country. In compliance with its own decree it should sell foreign exchange at the official rate.

On the market not hampered by government interference there

prevails a tendency to establish and to maintain such an exchange ratio between the domestic currency (A) and foreign exchange (B) that it does not make any difference whether one buys or sells merchandise against A or against B. As long as it is possible to make a profit buying a definite commodity against B and selling it against A, there will be a specific demand for amounts of B originating from merchants selling amounts of A. This specific demand will cease only when no further profits can be reaped on account of price discrepancies between prices expressed in terms of each of these two currencies. The market rate is maintained by the fact that there is no longer an advantage for anybody in paying a higher price for foreign exchange. Buying either of A against B or of B against A at a higher price (expressed in the first case in terms of B and in the second in terms of A) than the market price would not bring specific profits. Arbitrage operations tend to cease at this price. This is the process that the purchasing-power-parity theory of foreign exchange describes.

The policy pretentiously called foreign-exchange control tries to counteract the operation of the purchasing-power-parity principle and fails lamentably. Confiscating foreign exchange against an indemnity below its market price is tantamount to an export duty. It tends to lower exports and thus the amount of foreign exchange that the government can seize. On the other hand, selling foreign exchange below its market price is tantamount to subsidizing imports and thereby to increasing the demand for foreign exchange. The illusive standard and its main tool, foreign-exchange control, result in a state of affairs which is—rather inappropriately—called shortage of foreign exchange.

Scarcity is the essential feature of an economic good. Goods which are not scarce in relation to the demand for them are not economic goods but free goods. Human action is not concerned with them, and economics does not deal with them. No prices are paid for such free goods and nothing can be obtained in exchange for them. To establish the fact that gold or dollars are in short supply is to pronounce a truism.

The state of affairs which those talking of a scarcity of dollars want to describe is this: At the fictitious parity, arbitrarily fixed by the government and enforced by the whole governmental apparatus of oppression and compulsion, demand for dollars exceeds the supply of dollars offered for sale. This is the inescapable consequence of every attempt on the part of a government or other agency to enforce a maximum price below the height at which the unhampered market would have determined the market price.

The Ruritanians would like to consume more foreign goods than they can buy by exporting Ruritanian products. It is a rather clumsy way of describing this situation to declare that the Ruritanians suffer from a shortage of foreign exchange. Their plight is brought about by the fact that they are not producing more and better things either for domestic or for foreign consumption. If the dollar buys at the free market 100 Ruritanian rurs and the government fixes a fictitious parity of 50 rurs and tries to enforce it by foreign-exchange control, things become worse. Ruritanian exports drop and the demand for foreign goods increases.

Of course, the Ruritanian government will then resort to various measures allegedly devised to "improve" the balance of payments. But no matter what is tried, the "scarcity" of dollars does not disappear.

Foreign-exchange control is today primarily a device for the virtual expropriation of foreign investments. It has destroyed the international capital and money market. It is the main instrument of policies aiming at the elimination of imports and thereby at the economic isolation of the various countries. It is thus one of the most important factors in the decline of Western civilization. Future historians will have to deal with it circumstantially. In referring to the actual monetary problems of our day it is enough to stress the point that it is an abortive policy.

CHAPTER 23

The Return to Sound Money

1

Monetary Policy and the Present Trend Toward All-round Planning

The people of all countries agree that the present state of monetary affairs is unsatisfactory and that a change is highly desirable. However, ideas about the kind of reform needed and about the goal to be aimed at differ widely. There is some confused talk about stability and about a standard which is neither inflationary nor deflationary. The vagueness of the terms employed obscures the fact that people are still committed to the spurious and self-contradictory doctrines whose very application has created the present monetary chaos.

The destruction of the monetary order was the result of deliberate actions on the part of various governments. The government-controlled central banks and, in the United States, the government-controlled Federal Reserve System were the instruments applied in this process of disorganization and demolition. Yet without exception all drafts for an improvement of currency systems assign to the governments unrestricted supremacy in matters of currency and design fantastic images of superprivileged superbanks. Even the manifest futility of the International Monetary Fund does not deter authors from indulging in dreams about a world bank fertilizing mankind with floods of cheap credit.

The inanity of all these plans is not accidental. It is the logical outcome of the social philosophy of their authors.

Money is the commonly used medium of exchange. It is a market phenomenon. Its sphere is that of business transacted by individuals or groups of individuals within a society based on private ownership of the means of production and the division of labor. This mode of economic organization—the market economy or capitalism—is at present unanimously condemned by governments and political parties. Educational institutions, from universities down to kindergartens, the press, the radio, the legitimate theater as well as the screen, and publishing firms are almost completely dominated by people in whose opinion capitalism appears as the most ghastly of all evils. The goal of their policies is to substitute "planning" for the alleged planlessness of the market economy. The term *planning* as they use it means, of course, central planning by the authorities, enforced by the police power. It implies the nullification of each citizen's right to plan his own life. It converts the individual citizens into mere pawns in the schemes of the planning board, whether it is called Politburo, Reichswirtschaftsministerium, or some other name. Planning does not differ from the social system that Marx advocated under the names of socialism and communism. It transfers control of all production activities to the government and thus eliminates the market altogether. Where there is no market, there is no money either.

Although the present trend of economic policies leads toward socialism, the United States and some other countries have still preserved the characteristic features of the market economy. Up to now the champions of government control of business have not yet succeeded in attaining their ultimate goal.

The Fair Deal party has maintained that it is the duty of the government to determine what prices, wage rates, and profits are fair and what not, and then to enforce its rulings by the police power and the courts. It further maintains that it is a function of the government to keep the rate of interest at a fair level by means of credit expansion. Finally, it urges a system of taxation that aims at the equalization of incomes and wealth. Full application of either the first or the last of these principles would by itself consummate the establishment of socialism. But things have not yet moved so far in this country. The resistance of the advocates of economic freedom has not yet been broken entirely. There is still an opposition that has prevented the permanent establishment of direct control of all prices and wages and the total confiscation of all incomes above a height deemed fair by those whose income is lower. In the countries on this side of the Iron Curtain the battle between the friends and the foes of totalitarian all-round planning is still undecided.

In this great conflict the advocates of public control cannot do without inflation. They need it in order to finance their policy of reckless spending and of lavishly subsidizing and bribing the voters. The undesirable but inevitable consequence of inflation, the rise in prices, provides them with a welcome pretext to establish price control and thus step by step to realize their scheme of all-round planning. The illusory profits which the inflationary falsification of economic calculation makes appear are dealt with as if they were real profits; in taxing them away under the misleading label of excess profits, parts of the capital invested are confiscated. In spreading discontent and social unrest, inflation generates favorable conditions for the subversive propaganda of the self-styled champions of welfare and progress. The spectacle that the political scene of the last two decades has offered has been really amazing. Governments without any hesitation have embarked upon vast inflation and government economists have proclaimed deficit spending and "expansionist" monetary and credit management as the surest way toward prosperity, steady progress, and economic improvement. But the same governments and their henchmen have indicted business for the inevitable consequences of inflation. While advocating high prices and wage rates as a panacea and praising the administration for having raised the "national income" (of course, expressed in terms of a depreciating currency) to an unprecedented height, they blamed private enterprise for charging outrageous prices and profiteering. While deliberately restricting the output of agricultural products in order to raise prices, statesmen have had the audacity to contend that capitalism creates scarcity and that but for the sinister machinations of big business there would be plenty of everything. And millions of voters have swallowed all this.

There is need to realize that the economic policies of self-styled progressives cannot do without inflation. They cannot and never will accept a policy of sound money. They can abandon neither their policies of deficit spending nor the help their anticapitalist propaganda receives from the inevitable consequences of inflation. It is true they talk about the necessity of doing away with inflation. But what they mean is not to end the policy of increasing the quantity of money in circulation but to establish price control, that is, futile schemes to escape the emergency arising inevitably from their policies.

Monetary reconstruction, including the abandonment of inflation and the return to sound money, is not merely a problem of financial technique that can be solved without change in the structure of general economic policies. There cannot be stable money within an environment dominated by ideologies hostile to the preservation of economic freedom. Bent on disintegrating the market economy, the ruling parties will certainly not consent to reforms that would deprive them of their most formidable weapon, inflation. Monetary reconstruction presupposes first of all total and unconditional rejection of those allegedly progressive policies which in the United States are designated by the slogans New Deal and Fair Deal.

2

The Integral Gold Standard

Sound money still means today what it meant in the nineteenth century: the gold standard.

The eminence of the gold standard consists in the fact that it makes the determination of the monetary unit's purchasing power independent of the measures of governments. It wrests from the hands of the "economic tsars" their most redoubtable instrument. It makes it impossible for them to inflate. This is why the gold standard is furiously attacked by all those who expect that they will be benefited by bounties from the seemingly inexhaustible government purse.

What is needed first of all is to force the rulers to spend only what, by virtue of duly promulgated laws, they have collected as taxes. Whether governments should borrow from the public at all and, if so, to what extent are questions that are irrelevant to the treatment of monetary problems. The main thing is that the government should no longer be in a position to increase the quantity of money in circulation and the amount of checkbook money not fully—that is, 100 percent—covered by deposits paid in by the public. No back-door must be left open where inflation can slip in. No emergency can justify a return to inflation. Inflation can provide neither the weapons a nation needs to defend its independence nor the capital goods required for any project. It does not cure unsatisfactory conditions. It merely helps the rulers whose policies brought about the catastrophe to exculpate themselves.

One of the goals of the reform suggested is to explode and to kill forever the superstitious belief that governments and banks have the power to make the nation or individual citizens richer, out of nothing and without making anybody poorer. The shortsighted observer sees only the things the government has accomplished by spending the newly created money. He does not see the things the nonperformance of which provided the means for the government's success. He fails to realize that inflation does not create additional goods but merely shifts wealth and income from some groups of people to others. He neglects, moreover, to take notice of the secondary effects of inflation: malinvestment and decumulation of capital.

Notwithstanding the passionate propaganda of the inflationists of all shades, the number of people who comprehend the necessity of entirely stopping inflation for the benefit of the public treasury is increasing. Keynesianism is losing face even at the universities. A few years ago governments proudly boasted of the "unorthodox" methods of deficit spending, pump-priming, and raising the "national income." They have not discarded these methods but they no longer brag about them. They even occasionally admit that it would not be such a bad thing to have balanced budgets and monetary stability. The political chances for a return to sound money are still slim, but they are certainly better than they have been in any other period since 1914.

Yet most of the supporters of sound money do not want to go beyond the elimination of inflation for fiscal purposes. They want to prevent any kind of government borrowing from banks issuing banknotes or crediting the borrower on an account subject to check. But they do not want to prevent in the same way credit expansion for the sake of lending to business. The reform they have in mind is by and large bringing back the state of affairs prevailing before the inflations of World War I. Their idea of sound money is that of the nineteenth-century economists with all the errors of the British Banking School that disfigured it. They still cling to the schemes whose application brought about the collapse of the European banking systems and currencies and discredited the market economy by generating the almost regular recurrence of periods of economic depression.

There is no need to add anything to the treatment of these problems as provided in part three of this volume and also in my book *Human Action.* If one wants to avoid the recurrence of economic crises, one must avoid the expansion of credit that creates the boom and inevitably leads into the slump.

Even if for the sake of argument we neglect to refer to these issues, one must realize that conditions are no longer such as the nineteenth-century champions of bank-credit expansion had in mind.

These statesmen and authors regarded the government's financial needs as the main and practically the only threat to the privileged bank's or banks' solvency. Ample historical experience had proved that the government could and did force the banks to lend to them. Suspension of the banknotes' convertibility and legal-tender provisions had transformed the "hard" currencies of many countries into questionable paper money. The logical conclusion to be drawn from these facts would have been to do away with privileged banks altogether and to subject all banks to the rule of common law and the commercial codes that oblige everybody to perform contracts in full faithfulness to the pledged word. Free banking would have spared the world many crises and catastrophes. But the tragic error of nineteenth-century bank doctrine was the belief that lowering the rate of interest below the height it would have on an unhampered market is a blessing for a nation and that credit expansion is the right means for the attainment of this end. Thus arose the characteristic duplicity of the bank policy. The central bank or banks must not lend to the government but should be free, within certain limits, to expand credit to business. The idea was that in this way one could make the central banking function independent of the government.

Such an arrangement presupposes that government and business are two distinct realms of the conduct of affairs. The government levies taxes but it does not interfere with the way the various enterprises operate. If the government meddles with central-bank affairs, its objective is to borrow for the treasury and not to induce the banks to lend more to business. In making bank loans to the government illegal, the bank's management is enabled to gauge its credit transactions in accordance with the needs of business only.

Whatever the merits or demerits of this point of view may have been in older days,[1] it is obvious that it is no longer of any consequence. The main inflationary motive of our day is the so-called full-employment policy, not the treasury's incapacity to fill its empty vaults from sources other than bank loans. Monetary policy is regarded—wrongly, of course—as an instrument for keeping wage rates above the height they would have reached on an unhampered labor market. Credit expansion is subservient to the unions. If a hundred or seventy years ago the government of a Western nation had ventured to extort a loan from the central bank, the public would unanimously have sided with the bank and thwarted the plot. But for many years there has been little opposition to credit expansion for the sake of "creating jobs," that is, for providing business with the money needed for the payment of the wage rates which the unions, strongly aided by the government, force business to grant. Nobody took notice of warning voices when England in 1931 and the United States in 1933 entered upon the policy for which Lord Keynes, a few years later in his *General Theory*, tried to concoct a justification, and when in 1936 Blum, in imposing upon the French employers the so-called Matignon agreements, ordered the Bank of

---

[1] About the fundamental error of this point of view, see chap. 19 above.

France to lend freely the sums business needed for complying with the dictates of the unions.

Inflation and credit expansion are the means to obfuscate the fact that there prevails a nature-given scarcity of the material things on which the satisfaction of human wants depends. The main concern of capitalist private enterprise is to remove this scarcity as much as possible and to provide a continuously improving standard of living for an increasing population. The historian cannot help noting that laissez-faire and rugged individualism have to an unprecedented extent succeeded in their endeavors to supply the common man more and more amply with food, shelter, and many other amenities. But however remarkable these improvements may be, there will always be a strict limit to the amount that can be consumed without reducing the capital available for the continuation and, even more, the expansion of production.

In older ages social reformers believed that all that was needed to improve the material conditions of the poorer strata of society was to confiscate the surplus of the rich and to distribute it among those having less. The falsehood of this formula, despite the fact that it is still the ideological principle guiding present-day taxation, is no longer contested by any reasonable man. One may neglect stressing the point that such a distribution can add only a negligible amount to the income of the immense majority. The main thing is that the total amount produced in a nation or in the whole world over a definite period of time is not a magnitude independent of the mode of society's economic organization. The threat of being deprived by confiscation of a considerable or even the greater part of the yield of one's own activities slackens the individual's pursuit of wealth and thus results in a diminution of the national product. The Marxian socialists once indulged in reveries concerning a fabulous increase in riches to be expected from the socialist mode of production. The truth is that every infringement of property rights and every restriction of free enterprise impairs the productivity of labor. One of the foremost concerns of all parties hostile to economic freedom is to withhold this knowledge from the voters. The various brands of socialism and interventionism could not retain their popularity if people were to discover that the measures whose adoption is hailed as social progress curtail production and tend to bring about capital decumulation. To conceal these facts from the public is one of the services inflation renders to the so-called progressive policies. Inflation is the true opium of the people and it is administered to them by anticapitalist governments and parties.

3

Currency Reform in Ruritania

When compared with conditions in the United States or in Switzerland, Ruritania appears a poor country. The average income of a Ruritanian is below the average income of an American or a Swiss.

Once, in the past, Ruritania was on the gold standard. But the government issued little sheets of printed paper to which it assigned legal-tender power in the ratio of one paper rur to one gold rur. All residents of Ruritania were made to accept any amount of paper rurs as the equivalent of the same nominal amount of gold rurs. The government alone did not comply with the rule it had decreed. It did not convert paper rurs into gold rurs in accordance with the ratio 1 : 1. As it went on increasing the quantity of paper rurs, the effects resulted which Gresham's law describes. The gold rurs disappeared from the market. They were either hoarded by Ruritanians or sold abroad.

Almost all the nations of the earth have behaved in the way the Ruritanian government did. But the rates of the inflationary increase of the quantities of their national fiat money have been different. Some nations were more moderate in issuing additional quantities, some less. The result is that the exchange ratios between the various nations' local fiat-money currencies are no longer the same ratios that prevailed between their currencies in the period before they went off the gold standard. In those old days five gold rurs were equal to one gold dollar. Although today's dollar is no longer the equivalent of the weight of gold it represented under the gold standard, that is, before 1933, 100 paper rurs are needed to buy one of these depreciated dollars. A short time ago eighty paper rurs could buy one dollar. If the present rates of inflation both in the United States and in Ruritania do not change, the paper rur will drop more and more in terms of dollars.

The Ruritanian government knows very well that all it has to do in order to prevent a further depreciation of the paper rur as against the dollar is to slow down the deficit spending it finances by continued inflation. In fact, in order to maintain a stable exchange rate against the dollar, it would not be forced to abandon inflation altogether. It would only have to reduce it to a rate in due proportion to the extent of American inflation. But, government officials say, it is impossible for Ruritania, being a poor country, to balance its budget with a smaller amount of inflation than the present one. For such a reduction would enjoin upon it the necessity of undoing some of the results of social progress and of relapsing into the conditions of "social backwardness" of the United States. The government has nationalized railroads, telegraphs, and telephones and operates various plants, mines, and branches of industry as national enterprises. Every year the conduct of affairs of almost all the public undertakings produces a deficit that must be covered by taxes collected from the shrinking group of nonnationalized and nonmunicipalized businesses. Private business is a source of the treasury's revenue. Nationalized industry is a drain upon the government's funds. But these funds would be insufficient in Ruritania if not swelled by more and more inflation.

From the point of view of monetary technique the stabilization of a national currency's exchange ratio as against foreign, less-inflated currencies or against gold is a simple matter. The preliminary step is to abstain from any further increase in the quantity of domestic currency. This will at the outset stop the further rise in foreign-exchange rates and the price of gold. After some oscillations a somewhat stable exchange rate will appear, the height of which depends on the purchasing-power parity. At this rate it no longer makes any difference whether one buys or sells against currency A or currency B.

But this stability cannot last indefinitely. While an increase in the production of gold or an increase in the issuance of dollars continues abroad, Ruritania now has a currency the quantity of which is rigidly limited. Under these conditions there can no longer prevail full correspondence between the movements of commodity prices on the Ruritanian markets and those on foreign markets. If prices in terms of gold or dollars are rising, those in terms of rurs will lag behind them or even drop. This means that the purchasing-power parity is changing. A tendency will emerge toward an enhancement of the price of the rur as expressed in gold or dollars. When this trend becomes manifest, the propitious moment for the completion of the monetary reform has arrived. The exchange rate that prevails on the market at this juncture is to be promulgated as the new legal parity between the rur and either gold or the dollar. Unconditional convertibility at this legal rate of every paper rur against gold or dollars and vice versa is henceforward to be the fundamental principle.

The reform thus consists of two measures. The first is to end inflation by setting an insurmountable barrier to any further increase in the supply of domestic money. The second is to prevent the relative deflation that the first measure will, after a certain time, bring about in terms of other currencies the supply of which is not rigidly limited in the same way. As soon as the second step has been taken, any amount of rurs can be converted into gold or dollars without any delay and any amount of gold or dollars into rurs. The agency, whatever its appellation may be, that the reform law entrusts with the performance of these exchange operations needs for technical reasons a certain small reserve of gold or dollars. But its main concern is, at least in the initial stage of its functioning, how to provide the rurs necessary for the exchange of gold or foreign currency against rurs. To enable the agency to perform this task, it has to be entitled to issue additional rurs against a full—100 percent—coverage by gold or foreign exchange bought from the public.

It is politically expedient not to charge this agency with any responsibilities and duties other than those of buying and selling gold or foreign exchange according to the legal parity. Its task is to make this legal parity an effective real market rate, preventing, by unconditional redemption of rurs, a drop of their market price against legal parity, and, by unconditional buying of gold or foreign exchange, an enhancement of the price of rurs as against legal parity.

At the very start of its operations the agency needs, as has been mentioned, a certain reserve of gold or foreign exchange. This reserve has to be lent to it either by the government or by the central bank, free of interest and never to be recalled. No business other than this preliminary loan must be negotiated between the government and any bank or institution dependent on the government on the one hand and the agency on the other hand.[2] The total amount of rurs issued before the start of the new monetary regime must not be increased by any operations on the part of the government; only the agency is free to issue additional new rurs, rigidly complying in such issuance with the rule that each of these new rurs must be fully covered by gold or foreign exchange paid in by the public in exchange for them.

The government's mint may go on to coin and to issue as many fractional or subsidiary coins as seem to be needed by the public. In order to prevent the government from misusing its monopoly of mintage for inflationary ventures and flooding the market, under the pretext of catering to peoples' demand for "change," with huge quantities of such tokens, two provisons are imperative. To these fractional coins only a strictly limited legal-tender power should be given for payments to any payee but the government. Against the government alone they should have unlimited legal-tender power, and the government, moreover, must be obliged to redeem in rurs, without any delay and without any cost to the bearer, any amount presented, either by any private individual, firm, or corporation or by the agency. Unlimited legal-tender power must be reserved to the various denominations of banknotes of one rur and upward, issued either before the reform or, if after the reform, against full coverage in gold or foreign exchange.

Apart from this exchange of fractional coins against legal-tender rurs the agency deals exclusively with the public and not with the government or any of the institutions dependent on it, especially not with the central bank. The agency serves the public and deals exclusively with that part of the public that wants to avail itself, of its own free accord, of the agency's services. But no privileges are accorded to the agency. It does not get a monopoly for dealing in gold or foreign exchange. The market is perfectly free from any restriction. Everybody is free to buy or sell gold or foreign exchange. There is no centralization of such transactions. Nobody is forced to sell gold or foreign exchange to the agency or to buy gold or foreign exchange from it.

---

[2] For the only exception to this rule, see next paragraph below.

When these measures are once achieved, Ruritania is either on the gold-exchange standard or on the dollar-exchange standard. It has stabilized its currency as against gold or the dollar. This is enough for the beginning. There is no need for the moment to go further. No longer threatened by a breakdown of its currency, the nation can calmly wait to see how monetary affairs in other countries will develop.

The reform suggested would deprive the government of Ruritania of the power to spend any rur above the sums collected by taxing the citizens or by borrowing from the public, whether domestic or foreign. Once this is achieved, the specter of an unfavorable balance of payment fades away. If Ruritanians want to buy foreign products, they must export domestic products. If they do not export, they cannot import.

But, says the inflationist, what about the flight of capital? Will not unpatriotic citizens of Ruritania and foreigners who have invested capital within the country try to transfer their capital to other countries offering better prospects for business?

John Badman, a Ruritanian, and Paul Yank, an American, have invested in Ruritania in the past. Badman owns a mine, Yank a factory. Now they realize that their investments are unsafe. The Ruritanian government is committed to a policy that confiscates not only all the yields of their investments but step by step the substance too. Badman and Yank want to salvage what still can be salvaged; they want to sell against rurs and to transfer the proceeds by buying dollars and exporting them. But their problem is to find a buyer. If all those who have the funds needed for such a purchase think like them, it will be absolutely impossible to sell even at the lowest price. Badman and Yank have missed the right moment. Now it is too late.

But perhaps there are buyers. Bill Sucker, an American, and Peter Simple, a Ruritanian, believe that the prospects of the investments concerned are more propitious than Badman and Yank assume. Sucker has dollars ready; he buys rurs and against these rurs Yank's factory. Yank buys the dollars Sucker has sold to the agency. Simple has saved rurs and invests his savings in purchasing Badman's mine. It would have been possible for him to employ his savings in a different way, to buy producers' or consumers' goods in Ruritania. The fact that he does not buy these goods brings about a drop in their prices or prevents a rise which would have occurred if he had bought them. It disarranges the price structure on the domestic market in such a way as to make exports possible that could not be effected before or to prevent imports which were effected before. Thus it produces the amount of dollars which Badman buys and sends abroad.

A specter that worries many advocates of foreign-exchange control is the assumption that the Ruritanians engaged in export trade could leave the foreign-exchange proceeds of their business abroad and thus deprive their country of a part of its foreign exchange.

Miller is such an exporter. He buys commodity A in Ruritania and sells it abroad. Now he chooses to go out of business and to transfer all his assets to a foreign country. But this does not stop Ruritania's exporting A. As according to our assumption there can be profits earned by buying A in Ruritania and selling it abroad, the trade will go on. If no Ruritanian has the funds needed for engaging in it, foreigners will fill the gap. For there are always people in markets not entirely destroyed by government sabotage who are eager to take advantage of any opportunity to earn profits.

Let us emphasize this point again: If people want to consume what other people have produced, they must pay for it by giving the sellers something they themselves have produced or by rendering them some services. This is true in the relation between the people of the state of New York and those of Iowa no less than in the relation between the people of Ruritania and those of Laputania. The balance of payments always balances. For if the Ruritanians (or New Yorkers) do not pay, the Laputanians (or Iowans) will not sell.

4

The United States' Return to a Sound Currency

With Washington politicians and Wall Street pundits the problem of a return to the gold standard is taboo. Only imbecile or ignorant people, say the professorial and journalistic apologists of inflation, can nurture such an absurd idea.

These gentlemen would be perfectly right if they were merely to assert that the gold standard is incompatible with the methods of deficit spending. One of the main aims of a return to gold is precisely to do away with this system of waste, corruption, and arbitrary government. But they are mistaken if they would have us believe that the reestablishment and preservation of the gold standard is economically and technically impossible.

The first step must be a radical and unconditional abandonment of any further inflation. The total amount of dollar bills, whatever their name or legal characteristic may be, must not be increased by further issuance. No bank must be permitted to expand the total amount of its deposits subject to check or the balance of such deposits of any individual customer, be he a private citizen or the U.S. Treasury, otherwise than by receiving cash deposits in legal-tender banknotes from the public or by receiving a check payable by another domestic bank subject to the same limitations. This means a rigid 100 percent reserve for all future deposits; that is, all deposits not already in existence on the first day of the reform.

At the same time all restrictions on trading and holding gold must be repealed. The free market for gold is to be reestablished. Everybody, whether a resident of the United States or of any foreign country, will be free to buy and to sell, to lend and to borrow, to import and to export, and, of course, to hold any amount of gold, whether minted or not minted, in any part of the nation's territory as well as in foreign countries.

It is to be expected that this freedom of the gold market will result in the inflow of a considerable quantity of gold from abroad. Private citizens will probably invest a part of their cash holdings in gold. In some foreign countries the sellers of this gold exported to the United States may hoard the dollar bills received and leave the balances with American banks untouched. But many or most of these sellers of gold will probably buy American products.

In this first period of the reform it is imperative that the American government and all institutions dependent upon it, including the Federal Reserve System, keep entirely out of the gold market. A free gold market could not come into existence if the administration were to try to manipulate the price by underselling. The new monetary regime must be protected against malicious acts by officials of the Treasury and the Federal Reserve System. There cannot be any doubt that officialdom will be eager to sabotage a reform whose main purpose is to curb the power of the bureaucracy in monetary matters.

The unconditional prohibition of the further issuance of any piece of paper to which legal-tender power is granted refers also to the issuance of the type of bills called silver certificates. The constitutional prerogative of Congress to decree that the United States is bound to buy definite quantities of a definite commodity, whether silver or potatoes or something else, at a definite price exceeding the market price and to store or to dump the quantities purchased must not be infringed. But such purchases are henceforth to be paid out of funds collected by taxing the people or by borrowing from the public.

It is probable that the price of gold established after some oscillations on the American market will be higher than $35 per ounce, the rate of the Gold Reserve Act of 1934. It may be somewhere between $36 and $38, perhaps even somewhat higher. Once the market price has attained some stability, the time will have come to decree this market rate as the new legal parity of the dollar and to secure its unconditional convertibility at this parity.

A new agency is to be established, the Conversion Agency. The United States government lends to it a certain amount, let us say one billion dollars, in gold bullion (computed at the new parity), free of interest and never to be recalled. The Conversion Agency has two functions only: First, to sell gold bullion at the parity price to the public against dollars without any restriction. After a short time, when the mint will have coined a sufficient quantity of new American gold coins, the Conversion Agency will be obliged to hand out such gold pieces against paper dollars and checks drawn upon a solvent American bank. Second, to buy, against dollar bills at the legal parity, any amount of gold offered to it. To enable the Conversion Agency to execute this second task it is to be entitled to issue dollar bills against a 100 percent reserve in gold.

The Treasury is bound to sell gold—bullion or new American coins—to the Conversion Agency at legal parity against any kind of American legal-tender bills issued before the start of the reform, against American token coins, or against checks drawn upon a member bank. To the extent that such sales reduce the government's gold holdings, the total amount of all varieties of legal-tender paper sheets, issued before the start of the reform, and of member-bank deposits subject to check is to be reduced. How this reduction is to be distributed among the various classes of these types of currency can be left, apart from the problem of the banknotes of small denominations, to be dealt with later,[3] to the discretion of the Treasury and the Federal Reserve Board.

It is essential for the reform suggested that the Federal Reserve System should be kept out of its way. Whatever one may think about the merits or demerits of the Federal Reserve legislation of 1913, the fact remains that the system has been abused by the most reckless inflationary policy. No institution and no man connected in any way with the blunders and sins of the past decades must be permitted to influence future monetary conditions.

The Federal Reserve System is saddled with an awkward problem, namely, the huge amount of government bonds held by the member banks. Whatever solution may be adopted for this question, it must not affect the purchasing power of the dollar. Government finance and the nation's medium of exchange have in the future to be two entirely separate things.

The banknotes issued by the Federal Reserve System as well as the silver certificates may remain in circulation. Unconditional convertibility and the strict prohibition of any further increase of their amount will have radically changed their catallactic character. It is this alone that counts.

However, a very important change concerning the denomination of these notes is indispensable. What the United States needs is not the gold-exchange standard but the classical old gold standard, decried by the inflationists as orthodox. Gold must be in the cash holdings of everybody. Everybody must see gold coins changing hands, must be used to having gold coins in his pockets, to receiving gold coins when he cashes his paycheck, and to spending gold coins when he buys in a store.

This state of affairs can be easily achieved by withdrawing all bills of the denominations of five, ten, and perhaps also twenty dollars from circulation. There will be under the suggested new monetary regime two classes of legal-tender paper bills: the old stock and the

---

[3] See pp. 493–94 below.

new stock. The old stock consists of all those paper sheets that at the start of the reform were in circulation as legal-tender paper, without regard to their appellation and legal quality other than legal-tender power. It is strictly forbidden to increase this stock by the further issuance of any additional notes of this class. On the other hand, it will decrease to the extent that the Treasury and the Federal Reserve Board decree that the reduction in the total amount of legal-tender notes of this old stock plus bank deposits subject to check, existing at the start of the reform, has to be effected by the final withdrawal and destruction of definite quantities of such old-stock legal-tender notes. Moreover, the Treasury is bound to withdraw from circulation, against the new gold coins, and to destroy, within a period of one year after the promulgation of the new legal gold parity of the dollar, all notes of five, ten, and perhaps also twenty dollars.

It does not require any special mention that the new-stock legal-tender notes to be issued by the Conversion Agency must be issued only in denominations of one dollar or fifty dollars and upward.

Old British banking doctrine banned small banknotes (in their opinion, notes smaller than £5) because it wanted to protect the poorer strata of the population, supposed to be less familiar with the conditions of the banking business and therefore more liable to be cheated by wicked bankers. Today the main concern is to protect the nation against a repetition of the inflationary practices of governments. The gold-exchange standard, whatever argument may be advanced in its favor, is vitiated by an incurable defect. It offers to governments an easy opportunity to embark upon inflation unbeknown to the nation. With the exception of a few specialists, nobody becomes aware in time of the fact that a radical change in monetary matters has occurred. Laymen, that is 9,999 out of 10,000 citizens, do not realize that it is not commodities that are becoming dearer but their tender that is becoming cheaper.

What is needed is to alarm the masses in time. The workingman in cashing his paycheck should learn that some foul trick has been played upon him. The President, Congress, and the Supreme Court have clearly proved their inability or unwillingness to protect the common man, the voter, from being victimized by inflationary machinations. The function of securing a sound currency must pass into new hands, into those of the whole nation. As soon as Gresham's law begins to come into play and bad paper drives good gold out of the pockets of the common man, there should be a stir. Perpetual vigilance on the part of the citizens can achieve what a thousand laws and dozens of alphabetical bureaus with hordes of employees never have and never will achieve: the preservation of a sound currency.

The classical or orthodox gold standard alone is a truly effective check on the power of the government to inflate the currency. Without such a check all other constitutional safeguards can be rendered vain.

5

The Controversy Concerning the Choice of the New Gold Parity

Some advocates of a return to the gold standard disagree on an important point with the scheme designed in the preceding section. In the opinion of these dissenters there is no reason to deviate from the gold price of $35 per ounce as decreed in 1934. This rate, they assert, is the legal parity, and it would be iniquitous to devalue the dollar in relation to it.

The controversy between the two groups, those advocating the return to gold at the previous parity (whom we may call the restorers) and those recommending the adoption of a new parity consonant with the present market value of the currency that is to be put upon a gold basis (we may call them the stabilizers), is not new. It has flared up whenever a currency depreciated by inflation has had to be returned to a sound basis.

The restorers look upon money primarily as the standard of deferred payments. A consistent restorer would have to argue in this way: People have in the past, that is, before 1933, made contracts in virtue of which they promised to pay a definite amount of dollars which at that time meant standard dollars, containing 25.8 grains of gold, nine-tenths fine. It would be manifestly unfair to the creditors to give the debtors the right to fulfill such contracts by the payment of the same nominal number of dollars containing a smaller weight of gold.

However, the reasoning of such consistent restorers would be correct only if all existing claims to deferred payments had been contracted before 1933 and if the present creditors of such contracts were the same people (or their heirs) who had originally made the contracts. Both these assumptions are contrary to fact. Most of the pre-1933 contracts have already been settled in the two decades that have elapsed. There are, of course, also government bonds, corporate bonds, and mortgages of pre-1933 origin. But in many or even in most cases these claims are no longer held by the same people who held them before 1933. Why should a man who in 1951 bought a corporate bond issued in 1928 be indemnified for losses which not he himself but one of the preceding owners of this bond suffered? And why should a municipality or a corporation that borrowed depreciated dollars in 1945 be liable to pay back dollars of greater gold weight and purchasing power?

In fact there are in present-day America hardly any consistent restorers who would recommend a return to the old pre-Roosevelt dollar. There are only inconsistent restorers who advocate a return to the Roosevelt dollar of 1934, the dollar of 15 5/21 grains of gold, nine-tenths fine. But this gold content of the dollar, fixed by the President in virtue of the Gold Reserve Act of January 30, 1934, was never a legal parity. It was, as far as the domestic affairs of the United States are concerned, merely of academic value. It was without any legal-tender validity. Legal tender under the Roosevelt legislation was only various sheets of printed paper. These sheets of paper could not be converted into gold. There was no longer any gold parity of the dollar. To hold gold was a criminal offense for the residents of the United States. The Roosevelt gold price of $35 per ounce (instead of the old price of $20.67 per ounce) had validity only for the government's purchases of gold and for certain transactions between the American Federal Reserve and foreign governments and central banks. Those juridical considerations that the consistent restorers could possibly advance in favor of a return to the pre-Roosevelt dollar parity are of no avail when advanced in favor of the rate of 1934 that was not a parity.

It is paradoxical indeed that the inconsistent restorers try to justify their proposal by referring to honesty. For the role the gold content of the dollar they want to restore played in American monetary history was certainly not honest in the sense in which they employ this term. It was a makeshift in a scheme which these very restorers themselves condemn as dishonest.

However, the main deficiency of any form of the restorers' arguments, whether they consistently advocate the McKinley dollar or inconsistently the Roosevelt dollar, is to be seen in the fact that they look upon money exclusively from the point of view of its function as the standard of deferred payments. As they see it, the main fault or even the only fault of an inflationary policy is that it favors the debtors at the expense of the creditors. They neglect the other more general and more serious effects of inflation.

Inflation does not affect the prices of the various commodities and services at the same time and to the same extent. Some prices rise sooner, some lag behind. While inflation takes its course and has not yet exhausted all its price-affecting potentialities, there are in the nation winners and losers. Winners—popularly called profiteers if they are entrepreneurs—are people who are in the fortunate position of selling commodities and services the prices of which are already adjusted to the changed relation of the supply of and the demand for money while the prices of commodities and services they are buying still correspond to a previous state of this relation. Losers are those who are forced to pay the new higher prices for the things they buy while the things they are selling have not yet risen at all or not sufficiently. The serious social conflicts which inflation kindles, all the grievances of consumers, wage earners, and salaried people it originates, are caused by the fact that its effects appear neither synchronously nor to the same extent. If an increase in the quantity of money in circulation were to produce at one blow proportionally the same rise in the prices of every kind of commodities and services, changes in the monetary unit's purchasing power would, apart from affecting deferred payments, be of no social consequence; they would neither benefit nor hurt anybody and would not arouse political unrest. But such an evenness in the effects of inflation—or, for that matter, of deflation—can never happen.

The great Roosevelt-Truman inflation has, apart from depriving all creditors of a considerable part of principal and interest, gravely hurt the material concerns of a great number of Americans. But one cannot repair the evil done by bringing about a deflation. Those favored by the uneven course of the deflation will only in rare cases be the same people who were hurt by the uneven course of the inflation. Those losing on account of the uneven course of the deflation will only in rare cases be the same people whom the inflation has benefited. The effects of a deflation produced by the choice of the new gold parity at $35 per ounce would not heal the wounds inflicted by the inflation of the two last decades. They would merely open new sores.

Today people complain about inflation. If the schemes of the restorers are executed, they will complain about deflation. As for psychological reasons, the effects of deflation are much more unpopular than those of inflation; a powerful proinflation movement would spring up under the disguise of an antideflation program and would seriously jeopardize all attempts to reestablish a sound-money policy.

Those questioning the conclusiveness of these statements should study the monetary history of the United States. There they will find ample corroborating material. Still more instructive is the monetary history of Great Britain.

When, after the Napoleonic wars, the United Kingdom had to face the problem of reforming its currency, it chose the return to the prewar gold parity of the pound and gave no thought to the idea of stabilizing the exchange ratio between the paper pound and gold as it had developed on the market under the impact of the inflation. It preferred deflation to stabilization and to the adoption of a new parity consonant with the state of the market. Calamitous economic hardships resulted from this deflation; they stirred social unrest and begot the rise of an inflationist movement as well as the anticapitalistic agitation from which after a while Engels and Marx drew their inspiration.

After the end of World War I England repeated the error committed after Waterloo. It did not stabilize the actual gold value of the pound. It returned in 1925 to the old prewar and preinflation parity of the pound. As the labor unions would not tolerate an adjustment of wage rates to the increased gold value and purchasing power of the pound, a crisis of British foreign trade resulted. The government and the journalists, both terrorized by the union leaders, timidly refrained from making any allusion to the height of wage rates and the disastrous effects of the union tactics. They blamed a mysterious overvaluation of the pound for the decline in British exports and the resulting spread of unemployment. They knew only one remedy, inflation. In 1931 the British government adopted it.

There cannot be any doubt that British inflationism got its strength from the conditions that had developed out of the deflationary currency reform of 1925. It is true that but for the stubborn policy of the unions the effects of the deflation would have been absorbed long before 1931. Yet the fact remains that in the opinion of the masses, conditions gave an apparent justification to the Keynesian fallacies. There is a close connection between the 1925 reform and the popularity that inflationism enjoyed in Great Britain in the thirties and forties.

The inconsistent restorers advance in favor of their plans the fact that the deflation they would bring about would be small, since the difference between a gold price of $35 and a gold price of $37 or $38 is rather slight. Now whether this difference is to be regarded as slight or not is a matter of an arbitrary judgment. Let us for the sake of argument accept its qualification as slight. It is certainly true that a smaller deflation has less undesirable effects than a bigger one. But this truism is no valid argument in favor of a deflationary policy the inexpediency of which is undeniable.

6

Concluding Remarks

The present unsatisfactory state of monetary affairs is an outcome of the social ideology to which our contemporaries are committed and of the economic policies which this ideology begets. People lament over inflation, but they enthusiastically support policies that could not go on without inflation. While they grumble about the inevitable consequences of inflation, they stubbornly oppose any attempt to stop or to restrict deficit spending.

The suggested reform of the currency system and the return to sound monetary conditions presuppose a radical change in economic philosophies. There cannot be any question of the gold standard as long as waste, capital decumulation, and corruption are the foremost characteristics of the conduct of public affairs.

Cynics dispose of the advocacy of a restitution of the gold standard by calling it utopian. Yet we have only the choice between two utopias: the utopia of a market economy, not paralyzed by government sabotage on the one hand, and the utopia of totalitarian all-round planning on the other hand. The choice of the first alternative implies the decision in favor of the gold standard.

APPENDICES

APPENDIX A

On the Classification of Monetary Theories

(This Appendix was first published as a journal article in 1917–1918, it was later used as a chapter in the 2nd German edition of 1924, but was then relegated to the Appendix in the Batson translation of 1934.)

1

Catallactic and Acatallactic Monetary Doctrine

The phenomenon of money occupies so prominent a position among the other phenomena of economic life, that it has been speculated upon even by persons who have devoted no further attention to the problems of economic theory, and even at a time when thorough investigation into the processes of exchange was still unknown. The results of such speculations were various. The merchants and, following them, the jurists who were closely connected with mercantile affairs, ascribed the use of money to the properties of the precious metals, and said that the value of money depended on the value of the precious metals. Canonist jurisprudence, ignorant of the ways of the world, saw the origin of the employment of money in the command of the state; it taught that the value of money was a *valor impositus*. Others, again, sought to explain the problem by means of analogy. From a biological point of view, they compared money with the blood; as the circulation of the blood animates the body, so the circulation of money animates the economic organism. Or they compared it with speech, which likewise had the function of facilitating human *Verkehr* (interchange,

503

trade). Or they made use of juristic terminology and defined money as a draft by everybody on everybody else.

All these points of view have this in common: they cannot be built into any system that deals realistically with the processes of economic activity. It is utterly impossible to employ them as foundations for a theory of exchange. And the attempt has hardly been made; for it is clear that any endeavor to bring, say, the doctrine of money as a draft into harmony with any explanation of prices must lead to disappointing results. If it is desired to have a general name for these attempts to solve the problem of money, they may be called *acatallactic*, because no place can be found for them in catallactics.

The catallactic theories of money, on the other hand, do fit into a theory of exchange ratios. They look for what is essential in money in the negotiation of exchanges; they explain its value by the laws of exchange. It should be possible for every general theory of value to provide a theory of the value of money also, and for every theory of the value of money to be included in a general theory of value. The fact that a general theory of value or a theory of the value of money fulfills these conditions is by no means a proof of its correctness. But no theory can prove satisfactory if it does *not* fulfill these conditions.

It may seem strange that acatallactic views on money were not completely suppressed by the growth of the catallactic doctrine. There were many reasons for this.

It is not possible to master the problems of theoretical economics unless questions of the determination of prices (commodity prices, wages, rent, interest, etc.) are at first dealt with under the supposition of direct exchange, indirect exchange being temporarily left out of account. This necessity gives rise to a division of the theory of catallactics into two parts—the doctrine of direct, and that of indirect, exchange. Now so abundant and difficult are the problems of pure theory, that the opportunity of putting part of them on one side, at least for the time being, has been very welcome. So it has come about that most recent investigators have devoted either no attention at all or very little to the theory of indirect exchange; any way, it has been the most neglected section of our science. The consequences of this omission have been most unfortunate. They have been expressed not only in the sphere of the theory of indirect exchange, the theory of money and banking, but also in the sphere of the theory of direct exchange. There are problems of theory full comprehension of which can be attained only with the aid of the theory of indirect exchange. To seek a solution of these problems, among which, for example, is the problem of crises, with no instruments but those of the theory of direct exchange, is inevitably to go astray.

Thus the theory of money was meanwhile surrendered to the acatallactists. Even in the writings of many catallactic theorists, odd relics of acatallactic views are to be found. Now and then statements are met with which are not in harmony with their authors' other statements on the subject of money and exchange and which obviously have been accepted merely because they were traditional and because the author had not noticed that they clashed with the rest of his system.

On the other hand, the currency controversy had aroused greater interest than ever in questions of monetary theory just at the time when the coming modern theory was devoting very little attention to them. Many "practical men" ventured into this sphere. Now the practical man without general economic training who begins to meditate upon monetary problems at first sees nothing else and limits his investigation to their immediate restricted sphere without taking account of their connections with other things; it is therefore easy for his monetary theory to become acatallactic. That the "practical man," so proudly looked down upon by the professional "theorist," can proceed from investigations of monetary problems to the most penetrating comprehension of economic theory, is best shown by the development of Ricardo. The period of which we speak saw no such development. But it produced writers on monetary theory who did all that was necessary for the monetary policy of the time. From among a large number it is only necessary to mention two names—Bamberger and Soetbeer. A considerable portion of their activity was devoted to fighting the doctrines of contemporary acatallactists.

At present, acatallactic doctrines of money find ready acceptance among those economists who have no use for "theory." Those who, openly or implicitly, deny the necessity of theoretical investigation are not in a position to demand of a monetary doctrine that it should be possible to fit it into a theoretical system.

2

The "State" Theory of Money

The common characteristic of all acatallactic monetary doctrines is a negative one; they cannot be fitted into any theory of catallactics. This does not mean that they involve a complete absence of views as to the value of money. Without any such views, they would not be monetary doctrines at all. But their theories of the value of money are constructed subconsciously; they are not made explicit; they are not completely thought out. For if they were consistently thought out to their logical conclusions, it would become obvious that they were self-contradictory. A consistently developed theory of money must be merged into a theory of exchange, and so cease to be acatallactic.

According to the naivest and most primitive of the acatallactic doctrines, the value of money coincides with the value of the monetary material. But to attempt to go farther and begin to inquire into the grounds of the value of the precious metals, is already to have arrived at the construction of a catallactic system. The explanation of the value of goods is sought either in their utility or in the difficulty of obtaining them. In either case, the starting point has been discovered for a theory of the value of money also. Thus this naive approach, logically developed, conducts us automatically to the real problems. It is acatallactic, but it leads to catallactics.

Another acatallactic doctrine seeks to explain the value of money by the command of the state. According to this theory, the value of money rests on the authority of the highest civil power, not on the estimation of commerce.[1] The law commands, the subject obeys. This doctrine can in no way be fitted into a theory of exchange; for apparently it would have a meaning only if the state fixed the actual level of the money prices of all economic goods and services as by

---

[1] See Endemann, *Studien in der romanisch-kanonistischen Wirtschafts- und Rechtslehre bis gegen Ende des 17. Jahrhunderts* (Berlin, 1874–1883), vol. 2, p. 199.

means of general price regulation. Since this cannot be asserted to be the case, the state theory of money is obliged to limit itself to the thesis that the state command establishes only the *Geltung* or validity of the money in nominal units, but not the validity of these nominal units in commerce. But this limitation amounts to abandonment of the attempt to explain the problem of money. By stressing the contrast between *valor impositus* and *bonitas intrinseca*, the canonists did indeed make it possible for scholastic sophistry to reconcile the Roman-canonist legal system with the facts of economic life. But at the same time they revealed the intrinsic futility of the doctrine of *valor impositus;* they demonstrated the impossibility of explaining the processes of the market with its assistance.

Nevertheless the nominalistic doctrine did not disappear from monetary literature. The princes of the time, who saw in the debasement of money an important means of improving their financial position, needed the justification of this theory. If, in its endeavors to construct a complete theory of the human economy, the struggling science of economics kept itself free from nominalism, there were nevertheless always enough nominalists for fiscal needs. At the beginning of the nineteenth century, nominalism still had representatives in Gentz and Adam Müller, writing in support of the Austrian monetary policy of the *Bankozettel* period. And nominalism was used as a foundation for the demands of the inflationists. But it was to experience its full renascence in the German "realistic" economics of the twentieth century.

An acatallactic monetary theory is a logical necessity for the empirico-realistic trend in economics. Since this school, unfavorable to all "theory," refrains from propounding any system of catallactics, it is bound to oppose any monetary doctrine that leads to such a system. So at first it avoided any treatment of the problem of money whatever; so far as it did touch upon this problem (in its often admirable work on the history of coinage and in its attitude toward political questions), it retained the traditional Classical theory of value. But gradually its views on the problem of money glided unconsciously into the primitive acatallactic ideas described above, which regard money made of precious metal as a good that is valuable "in itself." Now this was inconsistent. To a school that has inscribed the device of etatism on its banner, and to which all economic problems appear as questions of administration, the state theory of nominalism is more suitable.[2] Knapp completed this connection. Hence the success of his book in Germany.

The fact that Knapp has nothing to say about the catallactic monetary problem, the problem of purchasing power, cannot be regarded as an objection from the point of view of a doctrine which repudiates catallactics and has abandoned in advance any attempt at a causal explanation of the determination of prices. The difficulty over which the older nominalistic theories had come to grief did not exist for Knapp, whose public consisted solely of the disciples of the realistic economics. He was able—in fact, considering his public, he was bound—to abandon all attempt at an explanation of the validity of money in commerce. If important questions of monetary policy had arisen in Germany in the years immediately succeeding the appearance of Knapp's work, then the inadequacy of a doctrine that was unable to say anything about the value of money would naturally have soon become evident.

That the new state theory did compromise itself immediately it was put forward, was due to its unlucky attempt to deal with currency history from an acatallactic point of view. Knapp himself, in the fourth chapter of his work, had briefly related the monetary history of England, France, Germany, and Austria. Works on other countries followed, by members of his seminar. All of these accounts are purely formal. They endeavor to apply Knapp's scheme to the individual circumstances of different states. They provide a history of money in Knappian terminology.

There could be no doubt of the results that were bound to follow from these attempts. They expose the weaknesses of the state theory. Currency policy is concerned with the value of money, and a doctrine that cannot tell us anything about the purchasing power of money is not suitable for dealing with questions of currency policy. Knapp and his disciples enumerate laws and decrees, but are unable to say anything about their motives and effects. They do not mention that there have been parties supporting different currency policies. They know nothing, or nothing of great importance, about bimetallists, inflationists, or restrictionists; for them, the supporters

---

[2] See Voigt, "Die staatliche Theorie des Geldes," *Zeitschrift für die gesamte Staatswissenschaft* 62: 318 f.

of the gold standard were led by "metallistic superstition," the opponents of the gold standard were those who were free from "prejudices." They studiously avoid all reference to commodity prices and wages and to the effects of the monetary system on production and exchange. Beyond making a few remarks about the "fixed rate of exchange," they never touch upon the connections between the monetary standard and foreign trade, the problem which has played so great a part in currency policy. Never has there been a more miserable and empty representation of monetary history.

As a result of the World War, questions of currency policy have again become very important, and the state theory feels itself obliged to produce something on topical questions of currency policy. That it has nothing more to say about these than about the currency problems of the past is shown by Knapp's article "Die Währungsfrage bei einem deutsch-österreichischen Zollbündnis" in the first part of the work published by the Verein für Sozialpolitik: *Die wirtschaftliche Annäherung zwischen dem deutschen Reiche und seinen Verbündeten.* There can hardly be two opinions about this essay.

The absurdity of the results at which the nominalistic doctrine of money is bound to arrive as soon as it begins to concern itself with the problems of monetary policy is shown by what has been written by Bendixen, one of Knapp's disciples. Bendixen regards the circumstance that the German currency had a low value abroad during the war as "even in some ways desirable, because it enabled us to sell foreign securities at a favourable rate."[3] From the nominalistic point of view this monstrous assertion is merely logical.

Bendixen, incidentally, is not merely a disciple of the state theory of money; he is at the same time a representative of that doctrine also which regards money as a *claim*. In fact, acatallactic views can be blended according to taste. Thus Dühring, who in general regards metallic money as "an institution of Nature," holds the claim theory but at the same time rejects nominalism.[4]

The assertion that the state theory of money has been disproved by the events of currency history since 1914 must not be understood to mean that it has been disproved by "facts." Facts *per se* can neither

---

[3] Bendixen, *Währungspolitik und Geldtheorie im Lichte des Weltkriegs* (Munich and Leipzig, 1916), p. 37 (2d ed., 1919, p. 44).
[4] Dühring, *Cursus der National-und Sozialökonomie,* 3d ed. (Leipzig, 1892), pp. 42 ff., 401.

prove nor disprove; everything depends upon the significance that can be given to the facts. So long as a theory is not thought out and worked up in an absolutely inadequate manner, then it is not a matter of supreme difficulty to expound it so as to explain the "facts"—even if only superficially and in a way that can by no means satisfy truly intelligent criticism. It is not true, as the naive scientific doctrine of the empirico-realistic school has it, that one can save oneself the trouble of thinking if one will only allow the facts to speak. Facts do not speak; they need to be spoken *about* by a theory.

The state theory of money—and all acatallactic theories of money in general—breaks down not so much because of the facts as because of its inability even to attempt to explain them. On all the important questions of monetary policy that have arisen since 1914, the followers of the state theory of money have maintained silence. It is true that even in this period their industry and zeal have been demonstrated in the publication of ample works; but they have not been able to say anything on the problems that occupy us nowadays. What could they, who deliberately reject the problem of the value of money, have to say about those problems of value and price which alone constitute all that is important in the monetary system? Their peculiar terminology does not bring us a step nearer to a decision about the questions that are agitating the world at present.[5] Knapp is of the opinion that these questions do not need to be solved except by the "economists," and concedes that his doctrine has nothing to say about them.[6] But if the state theory does not help to elucidate the questions that seem important to us, what is its use? The state theory is not a *bad* monetary theory; it is not a monetary theory at all.[7]

To ascribe to the state theory a large share of the blame for the collapse of the German monetary system, does not imply that Knapp directly provoked the inflationary policy that led to it. He did not do that. Nevertheless, a doctrine that does not mention the

---

[5] See also Palyi, *Der Streit um die staatliche Theorie des Geldes* (Munich and Leipzig, 1922), pp. 88 ff.

[6] Knapp, *Staatliche Theorie des Geldes*, 3d ed. (1921), pp. 445 ff.

[7] To imagine that the state theory is a juristic theory, is to be ignorant of the purpose that a juristic theory of money has to fulfill. Anybody who holds this opinion should refer to any work on the law of contract and note what questions are there dealt with in the chapter on money.

quantity of money at all, that does not speak of the connection between money and prices, and that asserts that the only thing that is essential in money is the authentication of the state, directly encourages fiscal exploitation of the "right" of creating money. What is to prevent a government from pouring more and more notes into circulation if it knows that this will not affect prices, because all rises in prices can be explained by "disturbed trade conditions" or "disturbances in the home market," but on no account whatever by anything to do with money? Knapp is not so incautious as to speak of the *valor impositus* of money as did the canonists and jurists of past generations. All the same, his doctrine and theirs lead indifferently to the same conclusions.

Knapp, unlike some of his enthusiastic disciples, was certainly not a government hireling. When he said anything, he said it from genuine personal conviction. That speaks well for his own trustworthiness, but it has no bearing on that of his doctrine.

It is quite incorrect to say that the monetary doctrine of etatism springs from Knapp. The monetary doctrine of etatism is the balance-of-payments theory, which Knapp only refers to casually in speaking of the "pantopolic origin of the exchange rates."[8] The balance-of-payments theory, if an untenable, is at least a catallactic, theory of money. But it was invented long before Knapp's time. It had already been propounded, with its distinction between the internal value (*Binnenwert*) and the external value (*Aussenwert*) of money, by the etatists, by Lexis, for example.[9] Knapp and his school added nothing to it.

But the etatist school is responsible for the facility and rapidity with which the state theory of money succeeded in becoming the accepted doctrine in Germany, Austria, and Russia. This school had struck out catallactics, the theory of exchange and prices, as superfluous from the series of problems with which economics was concerned; it undertook the attempt to represent all the phenomena of social life merely as emanations of the exercise of power by princes and others in authority. It is only a logical extension of its doctrine to endeavor eventually to represent money also as being created

---

[8] Knapp, *op. cit.*, pp. 206, 214.
[9] Lexis, "Papiergeld," in *Handwörterbuch der Staatswissenschaften*, 3d. ed., vol. 6, pp. 987 ff.

merely by force. The younger generation of etatists had so little notion even of what economics really was concerned with, that it was able to accept Knapp's paltry discussion as a theory of money.

3

Schumpeter's Attempt to Formulate a Catallactic Claim Theory

To call money a claim is to suggest an analogy to which there is no real objection. Although this comparison, like all others, falls short at certain points, it may nevertheless make it easier for many to form a conception of the nature of money. Admittedly, analogies are not explanations, and it would be a gross exaggeration to speak of a claim theory of money, for mere construction of an analogy does not take us even halfway to any sort of monetary theory that can be expressed in intelligible arguments. The only possible way of building a monetary theory upon the claim analogy would be to regard the claim, say, as a ticket of admission to a room of limited size, so that an increase in the number of tickets issued would mean a corresponding diminution of the amount of room at the disposal of each ticketholder. But the danger in this way of thinking is that taking this illustration as a starting point could lead only to the drawing of a contrast between the total amount of money and the total amount of commodities; but this amounts to nothing but one of the oldest and most primitive versions of the quantity theory, the untenability of which needs no further discussion.

Thus until recently the claim analogy led a precarious existence in the expositions of monetary doctrine, without having any greater significance—as was imagined—than that of a means of expression that could easily be understood by all. Even in the writings of Bendixen, who would have been glad to see his obscure arguments designated a claim theory, the claim concept has no greater significance ascribed to it. But very recently an ingenious attempt has been made by Schumpeter to arrive at a real theory of the value of money starting from the claim analogy, that is, an attempt to construct a catallactic claim theory.

The fundamental difficulty that has to be reckoned with in every attempt to construct a theory of the value of money starting from the claim concept is the necessity for comparing the quantity of money with some other total, just as in the ticket illustration the total number of tickets is compared with the total amount of room available. Such a comparison is a necessity for a doctrine which regards money as "claims" whose peculiarity consists in the fact that they do not refer to definite objects but to shares in a mass of goods. Schumpeter seeks to avoid this difficulty by starting, in elaboration of a line of argument first developed by Wieser, not from the quantity of money, but from the sum of money incomes, which he compares with the total prices of all consumption goods.[10] There might be some justification for such a comparison if money had no other use than to purchase consumption goods. But such an assumption is obviously quite unjustifiable. Money bears a relationship, not only to consumption goods, but also to production goods; and—the point is a particularly important one—it does not serve only for the exchange of production goods against consumption goods but very much oftener for the exchange of production goods against other production goods. So Schumpeter is only able to maintain his theory by simply putting out of consideration a large part of that which circulates as money. He says that commodities are actually related only to the *circulating* portion of the total quantity of money, that only this portion has an immediate connection with the sum of all incomes, that it alone fulfills the essential function of money. Thus "to obtain the quantity of money in circulation, which is what we are concerned with," the following items, among others, have to be eliminated:

1 Hoards
2 "Sums that are unemployed but awaiting employment"
3 Reserves by which we are to understand those sums of money "below which the economic agents never let their holdings fall; in order to be prepared for unexpected demands"

But even the elimination of these sums is not enough; we must go still farther. For the total incomes theory is "not concerned even with the total quantity of money in circulation." In addition we must exclude "all those sums that circulate in the 'income-distributing' markets, in the real estate, mortgage, security and similar markets."[11]

---

[10] Schumpeter, "Das Sozialprodukt und die Rechenpfennige," *Archiv für Sozialwissenschaft und Sozialpolitik* 44: 635, 647 ff.
[11] *Ibid.*, pp. 665 f.

These limitations do not merely serve, as Schumpeter thinks, to demonstrate the impossibility of dealing statistically with the notion of money in effective circulation; they also cut away the ground from beneath his own theory. All that needs to be said about the separation of hoards, unemployment sums, and reserves, from the remaining amount of money has already been mentioned above.[12] It is inadmissible to speak of "sums that are unemployed but awaiting employment." In a strict and exact sense—and theory must take everything in a strict and exact sense—all money that is not changing owners at the very moment under consideration is awaiting employment. Nevertheless, it would be incorrect to call such money "unemployed"; as part of a reserve it satisfies a demand for money, and consequently fulfills the characteristic function of money. And when Schumpeter further proposes to eliminate the sums in circulation in the income-distributing markets, we can only ask, What then remains?

Schumpeter has to do violence to his own theory in order to make it appear even fairly tenable. It cannot be compared with the point of view which opposes the total stock of money to the total demand for it (that is, to the total demand of economic agents for reserves), because it does not really attempt to solve more than a small part of the problem. To be of any use, a theory must try to explain the whole of the problem that is before us. Schumpeter's theory arbitrarily splits up the stock of money and the demand for money in order to institute a comparison that would otherwise be impossible. If Schumpeter starts from the statement that the total quantity of money is distributed between three spheres, the sphere of circulation, that of hoards and reserves, and that of capital, then, if he wishes to provide a complete theory of money, the comparison which he makes for the sphere of circulation between total incomes and total amount of consumption goods should be repeated for the two other spheres also; for these also are not without significance in the determination of the value of money. Variations in the amount of money demanded or available for hoards and reserves—to retain this vague distinction—or for the sphere of capital, influence the value of money just as much as variations in the sphere of circula-

---

[12] See above, pp. 168 ff.

tion. No theory of the value of money with pretensions to completeness dare omit an explanation of the influence on the value of money exerted by processes in the sphere of hoards and reserves and in that of capital.

We see, then, that even Schumpeter has not been able to make a complete catallactic theory of money out of the claim theory. The fact that his attempt to make the claim theory into a catallactic theory of money obliged him to set such extraordinary limits to the problem is the best proof that a comprehensive catallactic theory of money cannot be constructed on the basis of the claim analogy. His having arrived in the course of his admirable discussion at conclusions for the rest which do not differ essentially from those which have been discovered in other ways and with other instruments by the catallactic doctrine of money is merely to be ascribed to his having found them in the theory of money already and having therefore been able to adopt them. They by no means follow from the fragmentary theory of money that he himself has put forward.

4

"*Metallism*"

It is no longer necessary to continue to argue against the nominalistic theory of money. For theoretical economics it has long been finished with. Nevertheless, the nominalist controversy has propagated errors in the history of doctrine that need to be weeded out.

First of all, there is the use of the term *metallism*. The expression comes from Knapp. "Those writers who start from weight and fineness and see in the stamp nothing but an attestation of these properties," Knapp christens metallists. "The metallist defines the unit of value as a certain quantity of metal."[13]

This definition of metallism given by Knapp is by no means a clear one. It should be pretty well known that there can hardly have been a single writer worth mentioning who has thought of the unit of value as consisting of a quantity of metal. But it must be remem-

---

[13] Knapp, *op. cit.*, p. 281; "Die Beziehungen Oesterreichs zur staatlichen Theorie des Geldes," *Zeitschrift für Volkswirtschaft*, etc. 17: 440.

bered that, with the exception of the nominalists, there has never been a school so easily satisfied in the interpretation of the concept of value as that of Knapp, for whom the unit of value "is nothing but the unit in which the amount of payments is expressed."[14]

But it is easy to see what Knapp means by metallism even if he does not explicitly say it. For Knapp metallism is all the theories of money that are not nominalistic;[15] and since he formulates the nominalistic doctrine with precision, it is clear what he understands by metallism. That those theories of money which are not nominalistic have no uniform characteristic, that there are catallactic and acatallactic theories among them, that each of these two groups is again divided into various opposed doctrines, is either unknown to Knapp, or willfully overlooked by him. For him, all nonnominalistic theories of money are but one. Nowhere in his writing is there anything to suggest that he knows of the existence of other monetary doctrines than that which regards metallic money as material valuable "in itself." He even completely ignores the existence of economic theories of value—not merely the existence of any particular theory, but the existence of all of them. He invariably polemizes against the only theory of money known to him, which he believes to be the only theory opposed to nominalism, and which he calls metallism. His arguments are useless because they apply only to this one acatallactic doctrine which, with all other acatallactic theories, including nominalism, was long ago overthrown by economic science.

All controversial writers have to set themselves limits. In any field that has been much worked over it is impossible to confute all opposing views. The most important opposing opinions, the typical ones, those which seem to threaten most one's own point of view, must be selected, and the rest passed over in silence. Knapp writes for the German public of the present day, which, under the influence of the etatistic version of political economy, acquainted only with acatallactic theories of money, and even among these only with those which he calls metallistic. The success that he has met with here shows that he was right in directing his criticism only against

---

[14] Knapp, *Staatliche Theorie,* pp. 6 f.

[15] "Alle unsere Nationalökonomen sind Metallisten," Knapp, "Über die Theorien des Geldwesens," *Jahrbuch für Gesetzgebung,* etc. 33: 432.

this version, which is hardly represented in literature, and on the other hand in ignoring Bodin, Law, Hume, Senior, Jevons, Menger, Walras, and everybody else.

Knapp makes no attempt at all to determine what economics says about money. He only asks, "What does the educated man think of when he is asked about the nature of money?"[16] He then criticizes the views of the "educated man," that is, apparently, the layman. Nobody will deny him the right to do this. But it is not permissible, having done it, to set up these views of the educated man as those of scientific economics. Nevertheless, this is what Knapp does when he describes the monetary theory of Adam Smith and David Ricardo as "entirely metallistic" and adds: "This theory teaches that the unit of value (the pound sterling) is definable as a certain weight of metal."[17] The mildest thing that can be said about this assertion of Knapp's is that it is entirely unfounded. It most bluntly contradicts the views of Smith and Ricardo on the theory of value, and it does not find the least support in any of their writings. It will be obvious to all who have even only a superficial acquaintance with the value theory of the Classicals and their theory of money that Knapp has here committed an incomprehensible error.

But neither were the Classicals "metallists" in the sense that their only contribution to the problems of paper money was "indignation."[18] Adam Smith expounded the social advantages arising from the "substitution of paper in the room of gold and silver money" in a manner that has hardly been equaled by any writer before or after him.[19] But it was Ricardo, in his pamphlet "Proposals for an Economical and Secure Currency," published in 1816, who elaborated this point of view and recommended a monetary system under which precious-metal money should be entirely eliminated from actual domestic circulation. This suggestion of Ricardo's was the basis of that monetary system, first established at the end of the last century in India, then in the Straits Settlements, then in the Philippines, and finally in Austria-Hungary, that is usually known nowadays as

---

[16] Knapp, "Die Währungsfrage vom Staat aus betrachtet," *Jahrbuch für Gesetzgebung,* etc. 41: 1528.
[17] Knapp, "Über die Theorien des Geldwesens," p. 430.
[18] *Ibid.,* p. 432.
[19] See also pp. 332 f. above.

the gold-exchange standard. Knapp and his fellow enthusiasts for "modern monetary theory" could easily have avoided the mistakes they made in explaining the policy followed by the Austro-Hungarian Bank between 1900 and 1911, if they had taken note of what Smith and Ricardo had said in these passages.[20]

5

The Concept of "Metallism" in Wieser and Philippovich

Knapp's mistakes in the history of theory have unfortunately already been accepted by other writers. This started with the attempt to expound Knapp's theory in the most kindly manner possible, that is, to judge its weaknesses gently and if possible to credit it with some sort of usefulness. But this was not possible without reading into the state theory things that simply cannot be found in it, things in fact which definitely contradict both its spirit and its letter, or without taking over Knapp's mistakes in the history of theory.

First, Wieser must be mentioned. Wieser draws a contrast between two monetary theories. "For the metallists, money has an independent value, arising from itself, from its substance; for modern theory, its value is derived from that of the objects of exchange, the commodities."[21] Again, in another place, Wieser says: "The value of the monetary material is a conflux from two different sources. It is constituted from the use value which the monetary material obtains by reason of its various industrial employments—for jewelry, for utensils, for technical uses of all kinds—and from the exchange value which the money obtains by reason of being a

---

[20] From the pamphlet of Ricardo's referred to above it may suffice to quote the following passage only: "A well-regulated paper currency is so great an improvement in commerce that I should greatly regret if prejudice should induce us to return to a system of less utility. The introduction of the precious metals for the purposes of money may with truth be considered as one of the most important steps toward the improvement of commerce and the arts of civilized life; but it is no less true, that, with the advancement of knowledge and science, we discover that it would be another improvement to banish them again from the employment to which, during a less enlightened period, they had been so advantageously applied" (*Works*, 2d ed. [London, 1852], p. 404). Thus the real appearance of Ricardo's "metallistic indignation."

[21] Wieser, *Über die Messung der Veränderungen des Geldwerts*, p. 542.

means of payment . . . The service performed by the coins as a medium of exchange and that performed by the money in its industrial uses, lead in combination to a common estimate of its value . . . We may . . . assert, that each of the two services is independent enough to be able to go on existing even if the other ceased. Just as the industrial functions of gold would not cease if gold were no longer coined, so its monetary functions would not come to an end if the state decided to forbid its use in industry and requisitioned it all for minting . . . The dominant metallistic opinion is different. From this point of view, the metal value of the money means the same thing as the use value of the metal; it has only the one source—industrial employment—and if the exchange value of the money coincides with its metal value, then it is nothing but a reflection of the use value of the metal. According to the prevailing metallistic opinion, money made from valueless material is inconceivable; for, it is said, money could not measure the value of commodities if it was not valuable itself, by virtue of the material from which it is made."[22]

Here Wieser contrasts two theories of the value of money: the modern and the metallistic. The theory which he calls the modern is the monetary theory that logically follows from that theory of value which traces value to utility. Now since the utility theory has only recently received scientific exposition (to have contributed to which is one of Wieser's great merits), and since it undoubtedly may nowadays be regarded as the prevailing doctrine (*pace* Wieser himself, who calls metallism the prevailing doctrine), it may well be admissible to call that monetary theory which is based upon it the modern theory κατ' ἐξοχήν. But in so doing we must not forget that, just as the subjective theory of value can look back over a long history, so also the theory of money corresponding to it is already more than two hundred years old. For example, as early as the year 1705 John Law had expressed it in classical form in his *Money and Trade*. A comparison of Law's arguments with those of Wieser will demonstrate the fundamental agreement between their views.[23]

But this theory, which Wieser calls the modern, is certainly not the doctrine of Knapp; in Knapp, not the slightest suggestion of it

---

[22] Wieser, "Theorie der gesellschaftlichen Wirtschaft," *Grundriss der Sozialökonomik* (Tübingen, 1914), p. 316.

[23] See the passages quoted on pp. 125 f. above.

can be discovered. All that it has in common with his nominalism, which ignores the problem of the value of money, is the fact that neither is "metallistic."

Wieser himself sees quite clearly that his theory has nothing to do with that of Knapp. Unfortunately, however, he takes over from Knapp the opinion that according to the "prevailing metallistic opinion," the "metal value of the money means the same as the use value of the metal." Several serious mistakes in the history of theory are here all mixed up together.

The first thing to observe is that by metallism Wieser means something different from Knapp. Wieser contrasts the "modern" theory of the value of money with the "metallistic," and describes exactly what he understands by the terms. According to this, the two views are opposed to each other; the one excludes the other. But, for Knapp, the theory that Wieser calls the modern theory is just as metallistic as the others. The truth of this can easily be demonstrated.

In his principal book, Knapp never mentions the names of any writers who themselves have dealt with the problem of money; neither does he quote any work on the subject. He nowhere argues against any of the trains of thought that are usually met with in the abundant literature of money. His quarrel is always only with the metallism that he sets up as the general opinion on money. In his preface, it is true, he refers expressly to two writers as metallists: Hermann and Knies.[24] But both Hermann and Knies expounded theories very similar to the "modern" theory expounded by Wieser. This should not appear strange, for both of these writers take their stand on the subjective theory of value,[25] from which the "modern" doctrine of the value of money logically follows, so that both regard the foundation of the use-value of the precious metals as lying both in their monetary uses and their "other" uses.[26] Between Wieser and Knies there is a difference, it is true, concerning the effect on the monetary function of the possibility of cessation of the "other" functions. Yet Knapp could not have regarded this as the decisive

---

[24] See Knapp, *Staatliche Theorie*, 1st ed., pp. 5, 7.
[25] See Zuckerkandl, *Zur Theorie des Preises mit besonderer Berücksichtigung der geschichtlichen Entwicklung der Lehre* (Leipzig, 1899), pp. 98, 115 f.
[26] See Hermann, *Staatswirtschaftliche Untersuchungen*, 2d ed. (Munich, 1870), p. 444; Knies, *Das Geld*, 2d ed. (Berlin, 1885), p. 324.

characteristic, or he would have been sure to mention it somewhere, and in fact he has nothing more to say about it than about any other problem of the value of money.

It is, indeed, not among the economists that we must seek the metallists, as they are portrayed by Knapp and his school. Knapp knows very well why he always argues only against this arbitrary caricature of a metallist, and prudently refrains from quoting chapter and verse for the opinions that he puts in the mouth of this metallist. In fact the metallist that Knapp has in mind is none other than Knapp himself; not the Knapp that wrote the *State Theory of Money,* but the Knapp that, "disregarding all theory," as he himself testifies, used to lecture on the "pragmatic" of the monetary system;[27] the Knapp that, as one of the standard-bearers of historicism in political economy, had thought that a substitute for thinking about economic problems could be found in the publication of old documents. If Knapp had not looked down so arrogantly on the work of the much abused "theorists," if he had not disdained to have anything to do with it, he would have discovered that he had been entertaining an entirely false opinion of its content. The same is true of Knapp's disciples. Indeed, their leader Bendixen openly admits that he was once a "metallist."[28]

It is by no means desirable to follow Wieser's example in giving the title of prevailing doctrine to the view that the value of the monetary material arises solely from its industrial employment. Surely a view concerning money that has been rejected by Knies cannot be regarded as the prevailing doctrine.[29] There can be no question that the whole literature of money, so far as it is based on the conclusions of modern theory, is not metallistic in Wieser's sense; but neither, for that matter, is any other catallactic theory of money.

In fact Wieser's opinion of the monetary theories of his precursors has been distorted by his acceptance of the expression *metallism.* He himself did not fail to notice this; for he supplements the remarks quoted above with the following words: "The dominant doctrine does not remain true to itself, for it . . . develops a special theory to explain the exchange value of money. If the value of money was

---

[27] Knapp, *Staatliche Theorie,* p. 5.
[28] Bendixen, *op. cit.,* p. 134.
[29] See Wieser, "Theorie der gesellschaftlichen Wirtschaft," p. 317.

always limited by the use value of the metal, what influence would remain to be exerted by the demand for money, the velocity of circulation, or the amount of credit substitutes?" The solution of this apparent contradiction must be sought in the fact that what Wieser calls the prevailing metallistic doctrine is in the very sharpest contrast to those catallactic theories which "develop a special theory to explain the exchange value of money."

Like Wieser, Philippovich also draws a contrast between two theories of the value of money; the nominalistic (represented by Adam Müller, Knapp, and others; Philippovich also includes Adolf Wagner in this group); and those which reject the nominalistic attitude. As representing this second group, he names only my *Theorie des Geldes und der Umlaufsmittel*.[30] He adds the remark that, in discussing the value of money, I had been forced to admit that the value of commodity money only bears upon the theory of the value of money insofar as it depends upon its function as a common medium of exchange.[31] In this, through following the historical views of Knapp, Philippovich falls into the same errors as Wieser.

While Wieser rejects the chartal and nominal theory of money, Philippovich confesses his allegiance to it, but at the same time interprets it in a way that entirely effaces the difference between the catallactic and the nominalistic conception. On the one hand, he declares that "the essential thing about the monetary unit is its nominal *Geltung* or validity as a unit of value." And on the other hand, he says that "the monetary unit is not really this technically defined quantity of precious metal, but its power of purchase or payment."[32] These are two theses that cannot be reconciled. We have already met the former, as Knapp's definition; the latter is the starting point of all catallactic theories of money. A sharper contrast could hardly be imagined.

That the identification of the monetary unit with purchasing power, so far from expressing Knapp's views, completely contradicts them, may be clearly deduced from several passages in his writings.[33] The very thing that characterizes nominalism—like all aca-

---

[30] [Of which the present work is a translation. H.E.B.]

[31] Philippovich, *Grundriss* (Tübingen, 1916), p. 275.

[32] *Ibid.*

[33] See esp. Knapp, *Schriften des Vereins für Sozialpolitik*, vol. 132, pp. 560 ff.

tallactic theory in general—is the fact that it does not speak of the value, the purchasing power, of money. It is easy to show how irreconcilable are the two theses that Philippovich propounds. Within the limits of his own theory, Knapp is formally correct when he defines the mark as "the third part of the preceding unit of value, the thaler."[34] However uninformative this definition may be, it contains nothing contradictory in itself. It is otherwise when Philippovich declares that "the silver mark, as the third part of the thaler, was previously the unit of money for reckoning purposes, which, in the experience of economic agents, represented a certain purchasing power. This purchasing power had to be retained in the unit of coinage of the new metal; that is, the mark as a gold coin had to represent the same quantity of value as had previously been represented by the silver mark. The technical determination of the unit of coinage therefore has *the aim of maintaining the value of the monetary unit.*"[35] These sentences, in connection with those previously quoted, can apparently only mean that the reform of the German monetary system had aimed to establish the purchasing power of the thaler at its transmitted level. But this can hardly be Philippovich's real opinion.

There is yet another historical error that has been taken over by Philippovich from Knapp, namely, the belief that the catallactic doctrine of money disregards actual experience, "which provides examples enough of the forced circulation of state paper money."[36] Any catallactic writing, including the first edition of the present book, which is the only work referred to by Philippovich in this connection, would prove the contrary. It is possible to assert that the catallactists have not solved the problem of such paper money in a satisfactory manner—that is still an open question; but it will not do to assert that they have disregarded its existence. This is a particularly important point, because many of Knapp's disciples think that catallactic theories of money have been confuted by the paper-money economics of the war period; as if this was not a problem that has been dealt with by all monetary theories since Ricardo.

When Knapp's mistakes about the views on monetary theory of earlier and contemporary economists have been accepted by two

---

[34] Knapp, *Geldtheorie, staatliche* in *H. d . S.,* 3d ed.
[35] Philippovich, *op. cit.*
[36] *Ibid.,* pp. 272 ff.

such eminent experts in the history and literature of political economy as Wieser and Philippovich, it should not surprise us if the majority of those now at work in Germany on monetary problems base their history of theory entirely on Knapp.

6

Note: The Relation of the Controversy About Nominalism to the Problems of the Two English Schools of Banking Theory

A writer identifies the metallistic theory with the currency principle and calls the chartal theory "a variety of the old banking principle."[37] Again, another writer is of the opinion that there is "a certain justification for giving the name of economic nominalism to the doctrine of the Currency School, so far as it is based upon a like treatment of both metallic and paper money."[38] Both would appear to be mistaken. The opposition between the two famous schools of the theory of credit lies in quite another sphere.[39] Knapp and his disciples have never so much as perceived the problems with which they were concerned, much less attempted to solve them.

Bendixen's doctrine of the creation of money, which is connected only accidentally and loosely with Knapp's nominalism, is admittedly nothing but an exaggerated and extremely naive version of the Banking principle. It is a particularly characteristic sign of the low state of German economic theory that for many years Bendixen's doctrine could have been regarded as something new without it being remarked that it was at most only in the way in which it was expounded that it differed from the doctrine that had been predominant in Germany for decades.

---

[37] Lansburgh, *Kriegskostendeckung* (Berlin, 1915), pp. 52 ff.
[38] Bortkiewicz, *Frage der Reform*, A. s. P. G., vol. 6, p. 98.
[39] See pp. 379 ff. above.

Translator's Note on the Translation of Certain Technical Terms

It is never possible to be certain that the full significance of a technical term has been brought out in a translation. A short list of the original German terms for the kinds of money and money substitutes mentioned in the present work, and of the English expressions which have been used to translate them, is therefore appended.

The word *Umlaufsmittel* presented a peculiarly difficult problem. There is no established English equivalent for the sense in which Professor Mises uses the term. "Circulating medium," the literal translation, is clearly inappropriate, for it suggests associations with currency which are quite foreign to Professor Mises' meaning. "Bank money" is inadequate, for *Umlaufsmittel* includes, not merely bank deposits, but also money substitutes issued by the state (such as token money). "Credit instrument," which at first sight might appear satisfactory, is inconsistent with Professor Mises' insistence on the difference between *Umlaufsmitteln* and bills of exchange; and, furthermore, Professor Mises explicitly argues that the issue of *Umlaufsmitteln* is not a credit transaction in the more fundamental sense. For want of a better equivalent, therefore, the expression "fiduciary medium" has been adopted. It accords with Professor Mises' definition of *Umlaufsmitteln* as money substitutes not covered by money,[1]

---

[1] See p. 155 above.

and it evokes associations with the controversies about the Peel Act of 1844 that are in harmony with Professor Mises' attitude. It also draws attention to Professor Mises' emphasis upon the similarity between uncovered bank deposits and uncovered notes.

The following equivalents for other technical terms have also been adopted:[2]

> Money in the broader sense (*Geld im weiteren Sinne*)
> Money in the narrower sense (*Geld im engeren Sinne*)
> Money substitute (*Geldsurrogat*)
> Commodity money (*Sachgeld*)
> Credit money (*Kreditgeld*)
> Fiat money (*Zeichengeld*)
> Token money (*Scheidemünzen*)
> Money certificate (*Geldzertifikat*)
> Commodity credit (*Sachkredit*)
> Circulation credit (*Zirkulationskredit*)

The following diagram shows the relationships between some of these terms in Professor Mises' system:

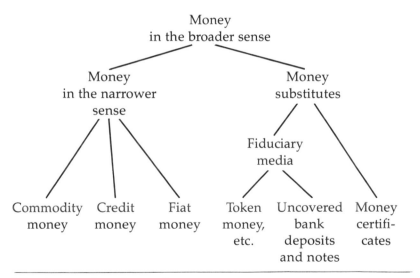

---

[2] See also pp. 146 n and 247 n above.

INDEX

acatallactic theory, 503–12
  common characteristic of, 506
  state monetary policy of, 506–12
accountancy
  money-value variations and, 235–37
  objective exchange value of money
    and, 234–37
  shortcomings in, 234–35
Allen, 15
Altmann, 35
Amsterdam, Bank of, 361
Anderson, B. M., 144 n. 24, 441 n
Aristotle
  Politics, 105
Austria-Hungary, 92, 192
  monetary system of, 72–73
Austrian National Bank, 148
Austrian Post Office Savings Bank, 326
Austrian school of economics, 180
  beginning of, 13–14
  classical economics and, 13
  Mises and, 14
Austro-Hungarian Bank, 72, 73, 148, 424
autarchy, 30

balance of payments, 208, 211, 273
  etatism and theory of, 282–86
  failure of, 284
Bamberger, 69, 505

bank(s)
  categories of, 363, 370
  chief rule for, 362
  fiduciary media issued by, 296–300
  freedom of, 434–38
  interest rate and credit policy of,
    377–404
  investment security of, 372–73
  nonconfidence in, 357–59
  privilege and, 363
  redemption funds of, 361–67, 374–75
  runs on, 358
  world, 327–29, 478
  See also banking
Bank Act, German (1875), 347–48, 410
Bank Act, German (1909), 352
bankers
  capitalists vs., 295
  definition of, 302
banking, 35, 36
  business of, 294–310
  cover for fiduciary media in, 368–73
  credit negotiation of, 293, 295–96
  definition of, 295
  deposits in relation to, 302–4
  German weakness in theory of, 409–10
  money and, 291–449
  prohibition of fiduciary media and,
    359–61

527

banking (*cont.*)
  short-term cover in, 371–72
  state-controlled, 477–78
  theory of, 379–84
  two branches of, 293
  See also bank(s)
banking school, 482, 494
  credit theory and, 381–84
  error of, 341
  nominalism and, 524
banknote(s), 64, 71, 307, 313–14, 318
  current account and, 313
  denominations of, 434–35
  deposits and, 314, 343, 408–9, 428
  money substitutes and, 343–44
  repression of, 409
Bank of France, 416, 483
banks-of-issue, 27, 306, 345–46
  etatism and, 437–39
  See also banking
Barbarossa, 135
Bendixen, 509, 521, 524
Benham, Frederic, 15
Béranger, 457
Bible, 106
bills
  commodity, 342–43, 344, 345
  fiduciary media and, 317–19
  fiduciary media covered by, 347–48
  redemption fund and foreign-exchange, 374–75
bimetallism, 249
  legislated, 90–91
  See also gold; silver
Blum, 483
Bodin, 225, 227, 517
Böhm-Bawerk, Eugen von, 118
  Capital and Interest, 14, 55 n. 3, 100
  capital and money in, 103–4
  interest theory of, 378 n
  Jacoby vs., 100
  law of price in, 129
  money as production good in, 99, 100, 101
  productive capital in, 106–7
  valuation in, 54, 55
Brentano, 191
Brown
  money supply in, 166–67
business
  influence of, on medium of exchange, 93

business cycles
  banking theory and, 403–4
  Mises' theory of, 15

capital
  definition of, 103–4
  development of concept of, 104–6
  fiduciary media and demand for, 349–52. *See also* money, demand for
  money and productive, 106–7
  money as private, 103–7
  private, 104
  productive, 104
  social. *See* capital, productive
Capital and Interest (Böhm-Bawerk), 14, 55 n. 3, 100
capitalism
  critics of, 111–13
  laissez-faire, 465, 484
capitalists
  bankers vs., 295
Carver, 138
Cassel, Gustave, 15, 207 n, 277 n. 3
catallactic theory, 503–6
  metallistic, 515–24
  Schumpeter's, 512–15
checking transactions
  discount rate and, 426–29
Chevalier, Michael
  Probable Depreciation of Gold, 457
church, 105
Cieszkowski, 392 n
circulation credit
  attitude toward, 298–299
  deposits as origin of, 297
  description of, 297
  granting of, 304–8
  peculiarities of, 298
  term, 297–298, 526
  ways of issuing, 305–6
Civil War, 176
claims, 65–67
  definition of, 65
  goods and, 65
  See also money, claims to
Clark, 104 n
classical economics
  Austrian school and, 13
  banking defined by, 295
  fiduciary media and, 332–33
  sound money in, 453–56

clearing system, 337–39, 427, 429
  fiduciary media and, 314–20, 325–27
coinage
  debasement of, 78–80
  free, 81
  regulation of, 78
  state and, 87–88
  value and, 79–81
Coinage Act, German (1873), 68
coinage, token, 68–71
  "concept" of, 70–71
  nature of, 69–70
commodity credit
  description of, 296–97
  term, 297–298, 526
commodity money, 73–81, 124, 132
  definition of, 74, 75
  state's influence on, 88–89
  value of, 125, 136
  word for, 526
commodity standard
  basic idea of, 440
  Fisher's proposal for, 438–45
  gold standard vs., 440–41
consumption, 42, 399
consumption good(s), 41, 106, 399–400
  money not, 95–102
contracts
  objective exchange value of money
    and, 226–29, 232
cost of living, 177–78
  local "differences" in, 200–3
credit, 36, 173
  circulation. *See* circulation credit
  commodity. *See* commodity credit
  conflicting policies of, 405–6
  deflation and, 267
  economic crises and, 403–4
  elasticity of circulation of, 339–47
  expansion of, 30, 462–63, 482–84. *See
    also* inflation
  granting of, 293. *See also* circulation
    credit, granting of
  interest rate in relation to, 377–404
  meaning of, 300
  money as facilitating, 47
  negotiation of, 293
  problems of, 405–49
  variations in requests for bank, 348–52
credit money, 73–76, 124, 132, 251, 283,
    334
  definition of, 74, 75

credit money (*cont.*)
  increase in, 161. *See also* credit, expan-
    sion of
  origin of, 265
  value of, 125–26, 127
  word for, 526
creditors, 229, 230–32
  deflation's effect on, 264, 266–67
  inflation's effect on, 252, 255, 258, 262
Cuhel
  subjective valuation in, 54–55
Cuhel-Mises theory, 15
Currency Inquiry Commission (Vienna,
    1892), 235 n
currency policy, 247 n
  future of, 445–49
  objective exchange value of money
    and, 248–49
  present-day, 471–76
Currency Regulation Law (1892), 149
currency school, 34, 156 n, 210, 405,
    437–38
  credit theory and, 381–84, 393
  economic crises and, 403
  errors of, 407–11
  nominalism and, 524

Davanzati, 137
debtors, 229, 230–32, 252
  deflation's effect on, 264, 266
  inflation's effect on, 252, 255, 258, 262
deflation(ism), 262–68, 286
  concept of, 271–73
  definition of, 262–63
  purpose of, 263
  unpopularity of, 263–64
deposits, 318
  banking and, 302–4
  banknotes and, 314, 343, 408–9, 428
  circulation credit born of, 300–4
  investment, 302–3
  savings, 302–3
depreciation, 236–37, 252–53, 255–56
devaluation, 265
Diehl, 172
Diocletian, 84
discount policy
  France's, 417–18
  nature of, 412–16
distribution
  money, 210–12
  production and, 100–1

Douglass, William, 252 n
Dühring, 509
dynamics
  statics and, 35

economic policy, 27
  liberal, 30
economics
  chief task of, 17–18
  classical. *See* classical economics
  crises of, 31
  revolution in, 137
  task of, 118
economists, 99
  money value and, 124
Edison (inventor), 251 n
employment
  characteristic feature of full, 465
  full, 463–66
  inflation and full, 483
Engels, 498
England, 267
  Bank of, 196, 304, 380, 381, 409, 422,
    431
  currency reform in, 498–99
  Peel's Act in, 348, 406–11
etatism
  balance-of-payments   theory   and,
    282–86
  bank freedom and, 434–38
  exchange rate and, 277–78
  heyday of, 277
  ideal society of, 275
  individual and, 276
  monetary policy of, 275–90
  monetary theory of 275–77, 506–12
  money in, 277–78
  price regulation of, 279–82
  speculation suppressed by, 286–90
  war and, 277
  See also state
exchange
  control of foreign, 475–76
  direct, 42, 44, 45
  fiduciary media and indirect, 308–10,
    315–16
  goods and ratio of, 145–46, 150–51
  goods as media of, 44–46
  indirect, 42–43, 44, 45, 48, 63–65, 102
  law of price and, 130
  money-goods ratio of, 196, 200–3
  money's suitability in, 63–64
  natural ratio of, between different
    kinds of money, 207–13

exchange (*cont.*)
  preexisting prices and ratio of, 133–36
  rate of, 277–78
  ratio of, between different kinds of
    money, 205–13, 243–46
  transport and, 100
  value presupposed in, 51–52
  variations in market ratio of, 238

Fair Deal party, 478–79, 480
Falkner, 219
Federal Reserve Act, 370 n
Federal Reserve Bank of New York, 458
Federal Reserve Board, 431, 493, 494
Federal Reserve System, 477, 491
  problem of, 493
fiat money, 73–76, 124, 132, 251, 283, 334
  definition of, 74
  existence of, 75
  increase in, 161
  naive ideas about, 458–59
  value of, 125–26, 127
  word for, 526
  See also inflation(ism)
fiduciary media, 155, 156, 210, 211, 212
  banks as issuers of, 296–300
  bills and, 317–19, 347–48
  capital demand and, 349–52
  case against issuing, 359–61
  clearing system and, 314–20
  cover for, 368–73
  definition of, 293
  domestic trade and, 320–25
  elasticity of, 339–47
  evolution of, 311–29, 331–32
  fluctuations in money demand and,
    334–36
  foreign trade and, 325–29, 364–66
  indirect exchange and, 308–10, 315–16
  influence of, 331–34
  limitation of circulation of, 367, 410–12
  money certificates and, 314
  money demand and, 331–53
  money supply and, 300
  nature of, 446
  nature of issue of, 341
  necessary condition of, 357–58
  objective exchange value of money
    and, 352–53
  payment elasticity and, 336–39
  redemption funds and, 361–67, 374–75
  redemption of, 355–75
  source of, 302, 312–13

fiduciary media (*cont.*)
  term, 526
  two ways of issuing, 311–14
Fisher, Irving, 230 n
  commodity-standard proposal of, 438–45
  money supply in, 166–67
  value measurement in, 55–58
flexible standard
  features of, 472–73
  origin of, 472
Ford, Henry, 251 n
Franklin, Benjamin, 248 n
French Revolution, 84, 254
  price regulations of, 84
Fullarton, 112, 339, 342, 393
  banking theory of, 382, 383–84, 428
  quantity theory of, criticized, 169–74

General Theory (Keynes), 483
Gentz, 507
gold, 45, 46, 77, 230
  abandonment of, 25–26, 28
  buildup of, 425–26
  fiduciary media and, 332
  gold-exchange standard and, 432–33
  return to, 491–95
  use of, 124–25, 432–35
  value of, 126
  See also gold standard
gold-exchange standard, 429–32
  defect of, 494
  effect of, 432
  gold and, 432–33
  gold standard and, 471–72
gold-premium policy, 416–21
  Bank of France and, 416–19, 420–21
  purpose of, 417
  systems similar to, 421–23
Gold Reserve Act (1934), 492, 496
gold standard, 24, 192, 208, 212, 446–47
  alleged shortcomings of, 456–63
  commodity standard vs., 440–41
  flexible standard and, 472–73
  gold-exchange standard and, 471–72
  inflexible, 471–76
  integral, 480–85
  interest rate and, 462–63
  money value and, 27
  parity controversy regarding, 495–99
  return to, 493–99
  shortcomings of, 29–30
  sound money and, 455, 456–63, 480–85

gold standard (*cont.*)
  undermining of, 430–31
  use of gold and, 433
  virtues of, 456–63
  See also gold; sound money
good(s)
  claims and, 63
  consumption, 41, 95–102
  exchange of, 42–46, 85
  exchange of present for future, 225–34
  exchange ratio between, 145–46, 150–51
  marketability of, 44–45
  money as economic, 95–107
  nature of, 97
  objective exchange value of, 121–22
  production, 41, 95–102
  scarcity of, 475
  situation of, 98
  twofold division of economic, 95–102
Gossen's law, 54–55
government
  high wages and, 25
  See also etatism; state
Great Depression, 16
Great War. *See* World War I
Gresham's law, 90, 93, 283, 485

Haberler, Gottfried von, 16
Hamburg Giro Bank, 375
Hammer, 77
Hansen, Alvin H., 16
Havenstein, 230 n
Hayek, Friedrich A. von
  Mises' business cycle theory and, 15–16
Helfferich, 89, 96
  marginal-utility theory and, 141, 143
Hermann, 135, 520
Hicks, John R., 15
Hilferding, 230 n
historico-empirico-realistic school, 34
History of Prices (Tooke; Newmarch), 384
Human Action (Mises), 482
Hume, David, 163, 167, 209, 379, 517,

illusive standard, 474–76
index numbers, 446
  calculating, 219–23
  significance of, 221–23, 460
  usefulness of, 222–23
  weakness of, 460
  Wieser's method of calculating, 219–23

index, price
  money as, 61–63
India, 321–23
individual
  economic role of, 157
  etatism and, 276
  money supply and demand and, 153, 157–58
  state vs., 454
inflation(ism), 33, 234, 249, 285, 429
  combating, 485–90
  concept of, 271–73
  conditional, 253
  consequences of, 258–61
  definition of, 251
  emergency argument of, 466–69
  full employment and, 463–66, 483
  goals of, 255–56, 261–62
  gold standard and, 460–61, 480–85
  government, 236
  index numbers and, 460
  monetary policy and, 250–62
  naive, 251
  political use of emergency argument
    of, 466–67
  popularity of, 263
  prices affected by, 497
  taxation and, 253–55
  variations of, 251–53
  war and, 252–55
interest, 104–6, 344–45
  attempt to depress rate of, 415–16
  circulating money and rate of, 377–404
  deflation and, 264
  equilibrium rate and money rate of,
    388–96
  gold standard and rate of, 462–63
  money rate of, 105, 398
  money variations and fluctuations in,
    384–88
  "natural" rate of, 105, 345, 398, 399–
    400, 402, 413
  problem of, 377–84
  production as influenced by, 396–403
  role of, 462
  theory of, 34–35
  See also credit, expansion of; fiat
    money
International Monetary Fund, 477
International Postal Union, 190 n

Jacoby
  Böhm-Bawerk vs., 100
Jevons, 138, 517

Kaldor, Nicholas, 15
Kant
  naive proposal of, 433
Kemmerer, 138
Keynes, Lord, 17, 466
  General Theory, 483
  grocer philosophy of, 464
  Treatise on Money, 20
Keynesianism, 481, 499
  disarray of, 16
Keynesian revolution, 16
Kinley, 138
Knapp, 76, 276, 522, 523
  influence of, 518, 524
  metallism in, 515–17, 520, 521
  monetary theory of, 508–9, 510–12
  State Theory of Money, 88, 521
Knies, 96, 520–21
  economic goods in, 99, 102

labor, division of, 30, 41, 43, 123, 454
Ladd (U.S. senator), 251 n
Laughlin
  Mises-Lotz controversy and, 191–92
  money value in, 147–48, 150
law
  Greek, 105
  money and, 84–87
  objective exchange value of money
    and, 226–29, 232–33
  Roman, 105
Law, John, 17, 126 n, 392 n, 517
  Money and Trade, 519–20
League of Nations, 29
Lerner, Abba P., 15
Lexis, 276, 511
liberalism, classical, 433
  modern liberalism vs., 454–55
  sound money in, 453–56
liberty, 469
  sound money and, 454
Lincoln (president), 459
Lindsay, 322, 323
liquidity
  usage of, 368
Lotz, Walter
  methodology of, 191–93
  Mises vs., 191–92

Machlup, Fritz, 16
Macleod, 392 n
macroeconomics
  microeconomics and, 14, 15

marginal-utility theory
  Helfferich and, 141, 143
  objective exchange value of money
    and, 136–44
  Wicksell and, 139–41
marketplace
  function of, 42
  influence of, on objective exchange
    value of money, 135–36, 185–89
  price changes in, 133
  state and, 83–84, 270, 279–82, 475
Marshall (economist), 21
Marx, 478, 498
mathematics
  value measurement by, 55–58
Matigon agreements, 483
Menger, Carl, 13, 62, 104 n, 132, 138,
    146 n, 154, 217 n. 1, 235 n, 383, 517
  law of price in, 129
  Principles of Economics, 14
  secondary functions of money in, 47,
    48
mercantilism, 34, 209, 285
metallism, 515–24
  Knapp's, 515–17, 520, 521
  modern monetary theory vs., 519–20
  nominalism and, 516, 522–23
  Philippovich's, 522–24
  term, 515
  Wieser's, 518–22
Michaelis, 69
microeconomics
  macroeconomics and, 14, 15
Midas theory, 209
Middle Ages, 319
  price regulations in, 84
Mill, J. S., 163, 167, 402
  Principles, 384
Mises, Ludwig von
  acceptance of ideas of, 15
  business cycle theory of, 15–16
  great achievement of, 14
  Human Action, 482
  Lotz vs., 191–92
  neo-Austrian school of, 14–15
  resurgence of economics of, 16
  terminology of, 525–26
Mollien, 369 n
monetary policy, 247–73
  definition of, 247–50
  etatism's, 275–90
  future of, 445–49
  inflationism and, 251–62
  instruments of, 250–51

monetary policy (*cont.*)
  limits of, 270–71
  objective exchange value of money
    and, 268–70
  planning and, 477–80
  purpose of, 268–70
  reconstruction of, 451–500
  state's influence on, 87–94. *See also*
    etatism
  war and, 434
  See also currency policy
monetary standard
  state's influence on, 88–94
  See also gold standard
monetary theory, classification of,
    503–24
  acatallactic, 503–6
  catallactic, 503–6
  metallistic, 515–24
  state, 506–12. *See also* monetary policy,
    etatism's
money
  appreciation of, 243
  banking and, 291–449
  business influence on, 93
  cheap, 78. *See also* fiat money; infla-
    tion(ism)
  claims to, 68, 299, 300, 317, 356
  coexistence of different kinds of, 205–7
  commodity. *See* commodity money
  concept of, 64–67
  credit. *See* credit money
  critics of, 111–13
  definition of, 31, 46, 49, 101
  demand for, 153–68, 174–75, 188, 317,
    378–79. *See also* supply and demand
  depreciation of, 236–37, 252–53, 255–
    56
  distribution of, 210–12
  economic good and, 95–107
  enemies of, 109–13
  equivalence between money substi-
    tutes and, 355–57
  etatism's view of, 277–78. *See also*
    monetary policy, etatism's
  evil and, 111
  exchange ratio between different
    kinds of, 205–13
  fiat. *See* fiat money
  fiduciary media and demand for,
    331–53
  fluctuations in demand for, 334–36
  hoarding of, 169–73
  "idle," 170

money (*cont.*)
"illegitimate" demand for, 423–25
interest fluctuations and variations in, 384–88
interest rate in relation to circulating, 377–404
kinds of, 63–81
legal concept of, 84–87
metallic, 75, 146–47, 269–70, 283, 333
metallistic theory of, 515–24
nature of, 39–113
necessity of, for calculation, 61–62
nominalistic theory of, 77, 78, 80
origin of, 42–46
paper, 75, 147, 228–29, 240–41. *See also* fiat money; inflation(ism)
presupposition of, 41
price index and, 61–62, 122
price of, 130
private capital and, 103–7
production and, 98–99
secondary uses of, 47–49
social capital and, 107
social demand for, 158–59
socialism and, 109–11. *See also* monetary policy, etatism's
sound. *See* sound money
state and, 83–94
state theory of, 506–12
storage of, 360
substitutes for. *See* money substitutes
suitability of, in exchange, 63–64
supply of, 153–68, 188
task of economic theory of, 65, 77
terminology of theory of, 73, 525–26
token, word, 526
transport of, 195
unfruitfulness of, 106
vacillating, 475–74
value of. *See* money, value of
words for, 526
Money and Trade (Law), 519–20
money certificate(s), 155, 156
fiduciary media and, 314
word for, 526
money, function(s) of, 20, 41–49, 378
economic conditions for, 41–42
money variations and, 385
purpose of, 42
secondary, 46–49
money substitutes, 63–73
banknotes and, 343–44
confidence in, 355–56

money substitutes (*cont.*)
description of, 65
equivalence between money and, 355–57
international, 327–29
money supply and demand and, 155–56
peculiarities of, 67–73
two types of, 313–14
word for, 526
money, value of, 34, 115–290
concept of, 117–28
cost-of-production theory of, 136, 152, 199
exchange, 110, 119
foundations of, 125–27
gold standard and, 27
independent criterion for, 131–32
Laughlin and, 147–48, 191–92
objective exchange. *See* objective exchange value of money
objective use- , 128
presupposition of, 144
problems in theory of, 122–28
social consequences of variations in, 225–46, 442–43, 444–45
stability of, 229, 265–66
subjective, 117–20, 128, 152
subjective exchange, 118
subjective use- , 118, 119
task of theory of, 127
Wieser's natural and money economy theory of, 180–85
monometallism, 91
monopolists, 186
More, Thomas, 112
Müller, Adam, 507, 522

Neue Freie Presse, 192
New Deal, 474, 480
Newmarck
History of Prices, 384
nominalism
banking school and, 524
currency school and, 524
metallism and, 516, 522–23
state monetary theory and, 507–8, 509

objective exchange value of money, 117, 118, 119, 120–22, 123–24
accountancy and, 234–37
consequences of variations in, 225–46

objective exchange (*cont.*)
continuity in, 129–46
contracts and, 226–29, 232
determinants of, 129–93
fiduciary media and fluctuations in, 352–53
fluctuations in, 146–77
law and, 226–29, 232–33
local differences and, 195–203
marginal-utility theory and, 136–44
marketplace and, 135–36, 185–89
measuring, 215–23
monetary influences on, 145–46
monetary policy's purpose regarding, 268–70
monetary unit's size and, 189–91
nonmonetary influences on, 145–46
origins of, 142–43
quantity theory and, 146–53, 168–77
special cause of fluctuations in, 177–89
subjective valuation and, 129–31
supply and demand for money and, 153–68
Wagner's supply-demand theory and, 178–80
Wieser on, 120–23, 180–85
Overstone, Lord, 382

Paulus, Pandects of, 43 n. 2
Peel's Act, 348, 406–12, 447, 526
basic error of, 408–9
Philippovich
metallism in, 522–24
Philip VI (king of France), 78
Pirmez, M., 71 n
Politics (Aristotle), 105
price(s), 24, 464
determinants of, 218–19
etatism and regulation of, 279–82
exchange ratio and preexisting, 133–36
"fixed," 186–87
inertia of, 133–34
inflation's effect on, 497
interlocal relations of, 195–97
law of, 129–30
marketplace's influence on, 185–89
money and, 122
money increase and, 161–63
speculation and, 286–87
value and, 77–78
Wagner's supply-demand theory and, 178–80

price(s) (*cont.*)
Wieser's money value theory and, 180–85
Principles (Mill), 384
Principles of Economics (Menger), 14
Probable Depreciation of Gold (Chevalier), 457
Probyn, 322, 323
production, 41–42
influence of interest policy on, 396–403
means of, 41, 281
money and, 98–99
nature of, 97
transport and, 100–1
production good(s), 41, 399–400
money not, 95–102
value of, 102, 377 78
Prohibition, 134
property, private, 455
etatism and, 281–82
"Proposals for an Economical and Secure Currency" (Ricardo), 517
protectionism, 29. *See also* mercantilism
Proudhon, 392 n
purchasing power of money
"creation" of, 279–80
local "differences" in, 197–200, 201–3
money supply and demand and, 153–59
money supply increase and effect on, 160–68
variability of, 229–34
Wagner's supply-demand theory and, 178–80
See also objective exchange value of money

quantity theory, 19, 168–77, 283, 339–40, 382, 465–66
application of, 174–77
criticism of, 151–52
demand for money and, 174–77
diminishing demand for kinds of money and, 175–77
essence of, 152–53
exponents of, 150
failure of, 153
Fullarton's view of, criticized, 169–72
mechanical version of, 162–63, 174–75, 188–89, 382
money value and, 137
objections to, criticized, 168–74

quantity theory (*cont.*)
  objective exchange value of money and, 146–53
  practicality of, 173–74
  Wieser and, 138–39

Rau, 118
Reichsbank, 380, 412, 422, 423
restrictionism. *See* deflation(ism)
Ricardo, 172, 207 n, 209, 295, 322, 324, 505, 523
  fiduciary media in, 332
  gold-exchange standard and, 432, 517–18
  "Proposals for an Economical and Secure Currency." 517
  value theory of, 121
Robbins, Lionel, 15
Robertson, Dennis H., 15
Roosevelt administration, 496–97
Roscher, 95–96, 100
Rosendorff, 422 n. 21
Rückert
  Weisheit des Brahmanen, 215

savings, 302–3
Say, Jean-Baptist
  grocer philosophy refuted by, 464
Schmidt, 392 n
Schmoller, 191
Schumacher, 342
Schumpeter, 43 n. 2
  monetary theory of, 512–15
  total value and, 59
  value measurement in, 58
Senior, 517
silver, 45, 46, 77, 208, 212, 249
  decreased demand for, 175–76
  fiduciary media and, 332
Smith, Adam, 102, 209, 295, 379, 517
  fiduciary media in, 332
  grocer philosophy refuted by, 464
  value theory of, 121
socialism
  etatism and, 275
  inflationism and, 254–55
  monetary policy and, 477–80, 484–85
  money and, 109–11
  See also etatism; state
Soetbeer, 69, 505
Solvay, Ernest, 112, 113

solvency
  usage of, 368
sound money
  classical idea of, 453–56
  gold standard and, 455, 456–63, 480–85
  liberty and, 454
  metallic standard implied by, 455
  principle of, 453–69
  return to, 477–500
  two aspects of, 455
  See also gold; gold standard
speculation, 245, 260, 294
  prices and, 286–87
  suppression of, 286–90
Spinoza, 35
state
  bank freedom and, 434–38
  coinage and, 87–88
  commodity money and, 88–89
  foreign trade and, 288–90
  inflationism and, 251–62
  lawful activity of, 454
  marketplace and, 83–84, 270, 279–82
  mint controlled by, 91
  monetary system influenced by, 87–94, 477–80
  money and, 83–94
  money theory of, 506–12
  price regulation of, 279–82
  See also etatism
State Theory of Money (Knapp), 88, 521
statics
  dynamics and, 35
Stuart, C. A. Verrijn, 61 n
supply and demand
  consequences of imbalance in money, 160–68
  determinant of money, 153–55
  interest fluctuations and variations in money, 384–88
  money, 153–68, 174–75, 188
  Wagner's theory of money, 178–79

Taussig, Theodor von, 235 n
taxation, 25
  inflationism and, 253–55
Token Coinage Act, Belgian (1860), 71–72 n
Tooke, 112, 339, 340, 382, 393, 407, 428
  History of Prices, 384

Torrens, 382
trade, 210–13
  etatism and foreign, 289–90
  fiduciary media and domestic, 320–25
  fiduciary media and foreign, 325–29,
    364–66
transport
  exchange and, 100
  necessity of, 100 1
Treatise on Money (Keynes), 20
Truman, 497

unemployment
  wage stabilization and, 24–25
  See also employment
unions, labor, 25
United Nations, 464
use-value(s), 42
  immeasurability of subjective, 51–58,
    61
  objective, 128
  quantity and, 58–61
  subjective, 62, 118, 119, 122, 123, 182–84

valuation
  acts of, 52, 60–61
  price changes and subjective, 133–34
  process of, 52
  subjective, 52–53, 129–31
  value and, 59–60
value
  acts and, 60–61
  coinage and, 79–81
  general theory of, 19
  measurement of, 51–63
  modern theory of, 60
  money and. *See* money, value of
  money as transmitter of, 47–48
  objective exchange, 61–62
  objective theory of, 51, 136
  prices and, 77–78

value (*cont.*)
  production goods and, 102
  source of, 51
  subjective theory of, 51–55, 121, 136
  total, 58–61
  valuation and, 59–60
Verkehr, 96
Viennese Stock Exchange, 149

wages, 219, 464–65
  minimum, 466
  stabilization of, 24
  See also prices
Wagner, Adolf, 276, 522
  supply-demand theory of, 178–80
Walras, 138, 517
war
  etatism and, 277
  inflation and, 253–55
  monetary policy and, 434
Washington (president), 278
wealth
  national, 278
  See also capital
Weisheit des Brahmanen (Rückert), 215
Wicksell
  marginal-utility theory and, 139–41
  money and interest theory of, 393–95
  natural interest in, 398
Wieser, 98, 199, 513
  index-number calculation of, 219–22
  metallism in, 518–22
  money value theory of, 180–85
  objective exchange value in, 120–21
  quantity theory criticized by, 138–39
  social demand for money in, 158–59
  total value in, 59
Wilson, 339
World War I, 33

Zwiedineck, 134

BIOGRAPHICAL NOTE

Ludwig von Mises (1881–1973) was the acknowledged leader of the Austrian School of economic thought, a prodigious originator in economic theory, and a prolific author. A library of his books would total twenty-one volumes if confined to first editions, forty-eight volumes if all revised editions and translations were included, and still more if the *Festschriften* and other volumes containing contributions by him were added.

Von Mises' writings and lectures encompassed economic theory, history, epistemology, government, and political philosophy. His contributions to economic theory include important clarifications on the quantity theory of money, the theory of the trade cycle, the integration of monetary theory with economic theory in general, and a demonstration that socialism must fail because it cannot solve the problem of economic calculation. Mises was the first scholar to recognize that economics is part of a larger science of human action, a science which Mises called "praxeology."

Ludwig von Mises received doctorates in law and economics from the University of Vienna in 1906. In 1909 he became Economic Advisor to the Austrian Chamber of Commerce (comparable to the U.S. Department of Commerce). After serving in World War I, he became Professor of Economics at the University of Vienna and, in 1934, Professor of International Relations at the Graduate Institute of International Studies in Geneva. In 1945 he became Visiting Professor at New York University where he remained until his retirement in 1969. In a lecturing and teaching career that spanned many continents and more than half a century, Mises numbered among his students one Nobel Laureate, F.A. Hayek, two presidents of the American Economic Association, Gottfried Haberler and Fritz Machlup, and many other economists of international reputation.

His major works are *The Theory of Money and Credit* (1912), *Socialism* (1922), *Human Action* (1949), *Theory and History* (1957), *Epistemological Problems of Economics* (1960), and *The Ultimate Foundations of Economic Science* (1962).

Murray N. Rothbard, who wrote the Introduction, is Professor of Economics at the Polythechnic Institute of New York. He is the author of *Man, Economy, and State*, *America's Great Depression*, and many other books, essays, and articles.

SILVER DEMERETEIA OF SYRACUSE
(480–479 B.C.)

The silver Demereteia, which is used in the jacket design, was struck by Gelon, Lord of Syracuse, celebrating his victory over the Carthaginians in the decisive battle of Himera in Sicily. On one side of the coin is a charioteer, symbolizing Gelon's forces, with the winged goddess of Victory, Nike, crowning the chariot with laurel. The lion in flight below represents the defeated Carthaginians. On the other side is a head, possibly that of the goddess Arethusa, since the dolphins surrounding her stand for the sea around the island of Ortygia on which the goddess was worshipped. Or, the head could be that of Gelon's queen, Demerete, whose name was given to the coin (Demereteia) and all others of the same issue (Demereteion) in honor of her gift of personal jewelry to the treasury of Syracuse in the war with Carthage. Another legend has it that Demerete gained favorable terms for the vanquished Carthaginians and received from them a hundred talents of gold which she contributed to financing the striking of the Demereteia.

The Greeks had learned the art of coinage from the Lydians who had invented it around 700 B.C. The Lydian Empire comprised most of what is now Turkey. The first Lydian coinage was developed by private individuals—goldsmiths, bankers, merchants—not by authority of the Emperor. The need for coinage as a reliable medium of exchange derived from Lydia's position as the industrial power of the ancient world. Prior to the development of coinage, media of exchange were clumsy bars or pieces of metal.

The Greek city states adopted coinage but habitually and shamelessly debased their coins. Said Demosthenes: "the majority of states are quite open in using silver coins diluted with copper and lead." Only Athens, excepting its one major devaluation by Solon, maintained throughout its history the purity of its coinage, a fact which does much to explain the extension of Athenian commercial and political power over all of Greece.

541

The Palatino typeface used in this volume is the work of Hermann Zapf, the noted European type designer and master calligrapher. Palatino is basically an "old style" letterform, yet it is strongly endowed with Zapf's distinctive exquisiteness. With concern not solely for the individual letter but also for the working visual relationship in a page of text, Zapf's edged pen has given this type a brisk, natural motion.

Printed on paper that is acid-free and meets the requirements of the American National Standard for Permanence of Paper for Printed Library Materials, Z39.84, 1984. ⊗

Book design by JMH Corporation, Indianapolis, Indiana
Typography by Weimer Typesetting Co., Inc., Indianapolis, Indiana
Printed and bound by Worzalla Publishing Co., Stevens Point, Wisconsin